How to Read
the Financial Pages

How to Read the Financial Pages

Michael Brett

Fourth Edition

CENTURY
BUSINESS

Published by Century Limited
Random House, 20 Vauxhall Bridge Road, London SW1V 2SA

Random House Australia (Pty) Limited
20 Alfred Street, Milsons Point, Sydney
New South Wales 2061, Australia

Random House New Zealand Limited
18 Poland Road, Glenfield
Auckland 10, New Zealand

Random House South Africa (Pty) Limited
PO Box 337, Bergvlei, South Africa

Random House UK Limited Reg.No. 954009

A CIP catalogue record for this book
is available from the British Library

Papers used by Random House UK Limited are natural, recyclable
products made from wood grown in sustainable forests.
The manufacturing processes conform to the environmental
regulations of the country of origin.

ISBN 0 7126 7560 4

Typeset in Times by SX Composing Ltd, Rayleigh, Essex
Printed and bound in Great Britain by
Mackays of Chatham plc, Chatham, Kent

Cartoon page 355: Nick Newman

Contents

	Preface	1
	Introduction	3
1	First principles	13
2	Money flows and the money men	31
3	Companies and their accounts	39
4	The investment ratios	58
5	Refining the figurework	82
6	Equities and the Stock Exchange	97
7	What moves share prices	
	a: In 'normal' times	115
	b: In the crash of '87	127
8	Stockmarket launches	135
9	Rights, placings and scrip issues	145
10	Bidders, victims and lawmakers	159
11	Venture capital and leveraged buy-outs	174
12	Pay, perks and reverse capitalism	182
13	Government bonds and company bonds	193
14	Banks, borrowers and bad debts	219
15	The money markets	232
16	Foreign exchange	245
17	International money: the euromarkets	261
18	Financial derivatives and commodities	274
19	Insurance and the troubles at Lloyd's	295
20	Commercial property and market crashes	305
21	Savings, pooled investments and tax shelters	317
22	Supervising the City	337
23	The financial pages	349
	Tailpiece: How to read betweeen the lines	354
	Glossary and index	361

Acknowledgements

This book could not have been written without a great deal of help and advice from City institutions as well as from colleagues in the financial press. A full list of those who have assisted would be impossibly long, but I would like to thank first the *Financial Times*, *The Independent* and the *Investors Chronicle* for permission to reproduce material from their respective publications and Datastream International for the use of its charts.

Detailed comments and advice on the text from John Plender and Danny O'Shea were invaluable and I am also very grateful to Liisa Springham for casting a fresh eye over the typescript. I had the benefit of information and advice on individual sections from, among others, Adrienne Gleeson, Andrew Goodrick-Clarke, Helen Fearnley and Peter Wilson-Smith and considerable help from Prudential Assurance, The Takeover Panel and the press offices of The Stock Exchange and the Securities and Investments Board. I am also grateful to Hugh Partridge and Brian Roy for technical help with the second and third editions. Many of those already named have helped again with this expanded fourth edition and I also very much appreciate Susan Bevan's helpful comments on the final draft. The views expressed – and the mistakes – are my own.

Preface

Money is not complicated. The principles behind financial transactions are simple enough. It is usually the detail that confuses by obscuring the principles.

The money world, like many others, develops its own practices and jargon, which are usually incomprehensible to the layman. Even an intelligent watcher of the financial scene is at a disadvantage. Sometimes the financial world likes to keep it that way, because an aura of mystique can enhance the value of its services.

The financial press, at its best, attempts to bridge this comprehension gap, but it is often forced to satisfy two different markets. It is writing both for those in the money business and for the outsiders who like to follow the financial and economic scene and who, in their personal or business lives, have to choose among many financial services and investment products. A first-time reader of the *Financial Times* or the business pages of the national dailies or Sunday papers may still feel he is faced with a foreign language.

This book sets out to explain the language of money. It does so by explaining the principles and practices behind the markets and financial institutions which deal with money and investments. Understand the principles, and the jargon falls quickly into place. The book consists of two main parts. The narrative chapters provide a guide to the workings of the financial system and its main components. This is suitable for the newcomer to the financial scene, though will also serve as an *aide-memoire* for those with existing knowledge. At the end of the book comes a combined glossary and index, which either provides explanations of financial terms or points to where they are explained in the text. Since the financial community often risks taking itself too seriously, an antidote is provided between the two parts in the form of a light-hearted look at some of the more oblique terms and techniques that financial journalists use in putting their message across.

The approach is intended to be practical. The explanations of financial terms are not aimed at the professional economist or banker and should not be taken as legal definitions. They explain the sense in which these terms are most likely to be encountered in the financial press.

The book follows the pattern of financial press coverage. Much of what is written concerns companies and the stockmarket, which therefore require explanation in detail. The sections on company accounts help to explain the background to the main investment yardsticks in use – they can be skipped if you are familiar with the concepts. Other areas such as the euromarket warrant less space. Though far larger than the domestic stockmarket, the euromarket or international market does not frequently involve the general public in Britain and attracts far less coverage in the national press.

One point of detail. Tax rates can change rapidly and examples incorporating tax calculations therefore risk being outdated soon after they are written. Since the book is more concerned with demonstrating principles than detailed practice at a given time, it standardizes on a basic income tax rate of 25 per cent, an upper rate of 40 per cent, and a corporation tax rate of 35 per cent. In practice, the corporation tax rate in 1995 was 33 per cent.

A final word of warning. In times of boom, investment markets become infected by their own enthusiasm. The money men forget the existence of the word 'bust'.

Journalists who write about the City are not immune to this enthusiasm. It sometimes colours their judgement, as it colours that of the City's professionals. The way to read the financial pages during a stockmarket boom is with a modicum of caution. Booms do not go on for ever and some journalists, like brokers, are better at advising when to buy than when to sell.

Introduction

The second half of the last decade of the twentieth century got off to a bad start for London's financial community. Not only did London's oldest merchant bank – Barings – go bust early in 1995 as a result of speculation in Far Eastern financial markets. But the Bank of England declined to bail out London's oldest merchant bank. And, when the remains of Barings were eventually and ignominiously scooped up by a Dutch banking group, did the City of London resound to the cry 'The Barings investors must be saved'? Not a bit of it. The Barings staff, according to press reports, were more concerned with negotiating to retain their bonuses.

Hardly less edifying was the sight of major insurance companies and other financial institutions forced to set aside many millions of pounds in compensation for members of the public. These were the people they had persuaded to opt out from perfectly good occupational pension schemes to buy inappropriate and expensive personal pension products.

To complete a dismal picture, another one-time colossus of the insurance world was in trouble. Lloyd's of London, the international insurance market, had lost over £8 billion for its investors in recent years and its long-term solvency was being increasingly questioned.

These were the disasters. There were successes as well. But in their own ways, the Barings collapse, the personal pensions fiasco and the problems of Lloyd's highlighted several strands in Britain's financial life as the millennium drew to its close. We will come to some of them in a moment. But first, a little history is in order.

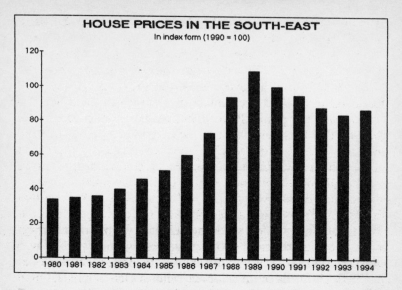

Figure 0.1 Being hit where it hurts. Many who bought homes in 1988 and 1989 shortly found themselves owing more than their house was worth. The over-inflated house price boom of the 1980s paved the way for the 'negative equity' phenomenon of the 1990s. Source: *Building Societies Association.*

For the investing public the early years of the 1990s were relatively sober, if not sombre. The decade kicked off with with the most painful recession in recent memory. It destroyed many long-cherished illusions. House prices could only rise, the post-war generations had been taught to believe. They fell, often by more than 30 per cent, and many buyers of the late 1980s found themselves owing considerably more on their homes than the homes were worth. They learned the miseries of 'negative equity'. Commercial property values slumped and for a time the market almost seized up. Many of the stockmarket's darlings of the 1980s – companies that had expanded rapidy on the back of borrowed money in the boom days – went bust or survived extinction only by the grace of their bankers. The UK banks themselves had to write off many billion pounds worth of loans: much of it representing lending to property companies. And the chill threat of unemployment spread far beyond its traditional bounds to invade professional homes in the once-pampered south-east of

Britain. What later came to be characterized as the 'feel-good factor' was noticeably absent.

The contrast with the 1980s could not have been more marked – which is not surprising, since the early 1990s were forced to pay for the excesses of the previous decade. The feel-good factor had been much in evidence in the 1980s, except among the poor. Share prices on the stockmarket more than trebled between 1982 and 1987 and house prices trebled over the decade. The Thatcher boom had created the illusion of wealth-without-effort as the former state industries were sold to the public at prices below their true value. A generation which had known nothing different came to believe that shares could move only upwards. And there was plenty of encouragement from the booming financial community, which made the fatal mistake of believing its own sales pitch and convinced itself that it had discovered the philosophers' stone.

The euphoria came to an abrupt end in October 1987, when stockmarkets worldwide crashed. Shares in London dropped 20 per cent in two days and continued on down for a fall of more than 36 per cent from their peak. Investors learned the hard way that no boom continues for ever. Though the events of 1987 are now fading into history, we have retained in this edition a chapter on the crash. Investors forget the lessons of crashes at their peril.

In fact, the 1987 crash was largely a stockmarket phenomenon. An excessive boom which had driven share prices far too high was corrected by a stockmarket bust, remarkable only in its speed. At this point inflation, not recession, was the gathering problem. It was more than two years on that recessionary forces began to bite, with interest rates roughly doubled as the government attempted to restrain the inflation that its policies had fuelled. With the exception of over-borrowed businesses and property-related concerns, companies as a whole survived the recession rather better than might have been expected and the stockmarket was far from being a disaster area in the early 1990s. But the feel-good factor had well and truly evaporated.

Much else was to go with it. The publisher Robert Maxwell went over the back of a boat as his business empire crumbled. In one of Britain's biggest ever financial scandals, it emerged that his company pension funds had been ripped off for

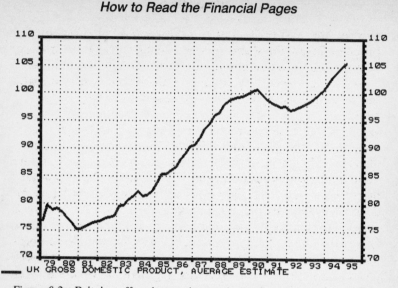

Figure 0.2 Britain suffered recession at the beginning of the 1980s and the beginning of the 1990s, as our chart of gross domestic product shows. But when production of goods and services turned down at the beginning of the 1990s, the fall was accompanied by a collapse in the residential and commercial property markets, which brought the realities of recession into most homes. Source: *Datastream International.*

hundreds of millions of pounds as he had attempted to prop up his crumbling business edifice. Margaret Thatcher went, propelled partly by her adherence to the deeply unpopular poll tax, though a Conservative government survived for the time being. Britain's membership of the Exchange Rate Mechanism of the European Monetary System came and went, and politicians savaged each other in the deep controversy over Britain's place in the European Union. But these domestic preoccupations paled into insignificance on the global scale. Communism had gone. Stock exchanges were springing up in the former Eastern Bloc countries. Every manner of Mafia-style business activity was springing up, too. The inhabitants of the new Wild East were learning the transition pains as well as the joys of a move towards market systems.

Investors in Britain who were active at the beginning of the 1980s have thus experienced two vastly different financial climates. But fundamental changes to Britain's – and the world's – financial systems were taking place throughout, only slightly tempered by the cycle of boom and bust. The process was not over by the mid-1990s, but the most important changes had probably taken place and, indeed, some of the developments of the 1980s were needing review in the light of experience.

In the 1960s and 1970s you could safely have assumed that a life assurance company sold life assurance and pensions, a bank took deposits and lent money and a building society provided mortgages for homebuyers. They still do, but they do a lot of other things as well. The life assurance company may manage unit trusts, provide mortgages for homebuyers and perhaps even own estate agents. The bank probably markets mortgages, unit trusts, pensions and insurance, and may be deeply involved in the stockmarkets. The building society is chasing the banks by offering cheque accounts, credit cards, personal loans and maybe even pensions. It may also be proposing to turn itself into a bank. And a wide range of overseas financial institutions is now competing with the domestic ones on their home patch. The changes mean we have to rethink our definition of traditional financial institutions and learn to accept new words to describe the practices of new markets or the new practices of existing ones.

The changes are part of a **deregulation** process known as the **financial services revolution**. In the course of this revolution the traditional demarcation lines between different types of financial institution have been breaking down. Some of these demarcation lines were the result of legal restraints. Some had grown up over many years following custom and practice. Where the restraints were legal ones the government may have relaxed them, as in the case of the building societies. Where they were merely traditional, the institutions themselves have changed.

Deregulation at its simplest stands for competition in the domestic savings market. The financial community is vying for the privilege – and the profit – that derives from managing the nation's savings.

Another aspect of the deregulation process in Britain is what came to be known as the **Big Bang** on the London Stock Exchange. Traditionally the Stock Exchange had been a club, deciding its own rules, working practices and the very hefty charges clients paid for its services. The government forced a change towards a more competitive trading system and a breakdown of traditional demarcation lines. It became known as the Big Bang because the most important changes took place on one explosive day: 27 October 1986. No longer were banks in Britain prevented from undertaking stockmarket business. Most of the country's traditional stockbrokers and stockjobbers were taken over by UK and overseas banks.

But deregulation means more than a few changes to the domestic financial system. What is happening in Britain is one aspect of changes taking place across the world's financial markets. Changes in the way money is borrowed and lent, changes in the way investments are traded. On the global scale deregulation means the breakdown of restrictions on different types of financial institution in the main financial centres, but also a breakdown of the barriers between the centres themselves. The abandonment of foreign exchange controls – Britain's were suspended in 1979 and later abolished – is one part of the process.

Opening up domestic stock exchanges to foreign members is another. Widening the range of investments that can be traded in each financial centre is a third, opening the way for round-the-clock trading in investments and currencies. The time zones are such that British markets are opening around the time Tokyo markets close and New York opens while London is still going strong. The main **securities houses** which deal in investments are of necessity international, with representation in each of the main financial centres.

Why is the world obsessed with financial markets and the ability to trade round-the-clock? It comes back to another aspect of deregulation – the changing role of traditional banking institutions combined with the need to handle massive cross-frontier flows of money seeking investments.

Traditionally, if someone had spare cash he lent it to the bank and the bank in turn lent it to someone needing to borrow money. Today, the name of the game is often to cut out the middleman: the bank. Would-be lenders seek out would-be borrowers direct – a process known as **disintermediation** – and they need markets to bring them together.

Moreover, the way investors put up the money has changed. Instead of simply making a loan they often prefer to exchange their money for pieces of paper they can later sell if they want their money back. And the markets in which the pieces of paper are bought and sold have blossomed. The banks have had to take on a new role: arranging the issues of these pieces of paper, putting the buyers and sellers together, organizing and participating in the markets where the pieces of paper change hands. It is a different business from simply borrowing and lending money and to an extent has replaced it. The banks have also, sometimes to their cost, become more active dealers in the financial markets on their own account, seeking to replace the lost traditional income with volatile trading profits.

Companies, too, have had to adapt to a new climate. Interest rates can move up and down with frightening speed. Rapid changes in the value of one currency against another take place as the mass of speculative funds washing round the world financial system changes its allegiances. Businesses need to protect themselves against these swings which, in the worst case, could wipe them out. Hence the massive growth in recent years of **derivative** products: financial products that can

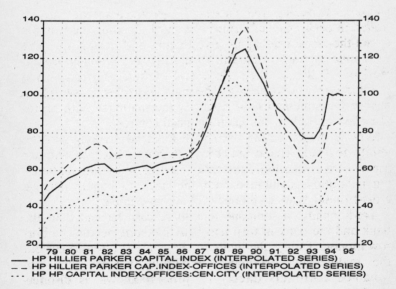

—— HP HILLIER PARKER CAPITAL INDEX (INTERPOLATED SERIES)
— — HP HILLIER PARKER CAP.INDEX-OFFICES (INTERPOLATED SERIES)
... HP HP CAPITAL INDEX-OFFICES:CEN.CITY (INTERPOLATED SERIES)

Figure 0.3 If home-owners thought they were suffering in the early 1990s, they should look at the plight of commercial property owners and of the banks that lent money to them. The solid line shows the rise and subsequent fall in the average value of all commercial property, the broken line gives the picture for office property across the country and the bottom dotted line shows that offices in the City of London suffered worst of all. Sources: *Hillier Parker* and *Datastream International.*

be used to provide protection against interest rate, currency and price movements. But if derivatives can provide protection, on the other side of the coin they also provide limitless opportunity for outright speculation. The merchant bank Barings discovered this to its cost. So did a number of industrial and commercial companies in America, Britain and mainland Europe. If there is a financial nemesis stalking the world's banking system in the second half of the 1990s, it is probably lurking in the derivatives jungle. Some of the derivatives products marketed by the banks and some of the trading techniques used in the futures markets are now of a complexity that may have outrun banking management's ability to impose controls and assess risk.

The 1980s were a period of illusions. Not least among these was the notion that ever more frenetic trading in securities could in itself create lasting value, almost regardless of the product that was traded. Another was that competition in financial products brought nothing but benefits. A third was summed up by the aphorism that 'greed is good'. These ideas have not entirely disappeared in the greyer climate of the 1990s, nor are they necessarily without an element of truth. But they have needed to be re-examined in the light of experience.

The securities houses' dreams of ever-rising volumes of share trades were knocked on the head by the market crash of 1987. The business has seen considerable retrenchment. When merchant bank Warburgs – one time City leader – sought a well-heeled parent in 1995, it questioned whether Britain's investment houses any longer had the financial clout to go it alone. The high-street banks, too, are cutting back their staffing as competition and technical innovation reduce manpower requirements. The outlook for employment in the financial services industry is not entirely good.

Competition has certainly widened the choice among financial products for the consumer. but it may also have brought higher charges for, say, investors in unit trusts. Competition has certainly brought interest on current accounts for bank customers, but it also brought a range of new (and far from transparent) penalties and charges as the banks sought new sources of revenue. And while enlightened self-interest may be no bad principle in financial affairs, greed has also been surfacing in some less constructive forms. The rocketing salaries, bonuses and share-option profits of company directors are by no means always justified by performance. They have begun to feature frequently in general news reports, not solely in the financial pages.

Insufficiently-regulated greed also played a large part in the financial speculation that brought Barings down, in the commission-driven mis-selling of pensions and in the business practices of the 1980s that contributed significantly to the present problems of Lloyd's of London.

The Bank of England's refusal to rescue Barings by signing a bill of unknown size at the taxpayer's expense marked the end of an era in the City. No institution, however august, could automatically count on a bail-out from the authorities. The City contains much that is competent, innovative and of world class. But the events of early 1995 showed that this is not the full picture. If, in future, the public is less ready than it was in the 1980s to take the City at its own estimation, this may be all to the good.

Thus, the transition to a more competitive financial system

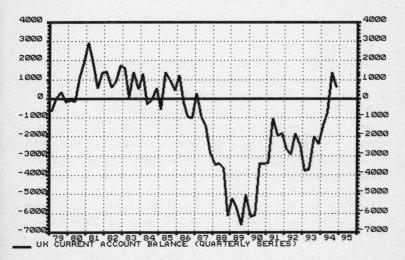

Figure 0.4 The balance of payments problems that helped to bring the Thatcher boom to an end. The chart shows how Britain's current account plummetted into deficit in the latter part of the 1980s as the country's imports vastly exceeded the value of its exports. Source: *Datastream International.*

has not been without its problems. Above all, time-scales have shortened. In the days before deregulation, each financial institution tended to know its place and the extent of its legitimate pickings. Customers may have had to pay too much, but by and large they knew what they must expect to pay. In the cartellized atmosphere of the day there was limited incentive to break long-standing business relationships in search of a better deal.

In contrast, today's business is **transaction-driven**. The industrial company may shop around for the best deal on the loan that it wants to raise, rather than sticking with its traditional banker. The bank that gets the business will be rewarded with the fees for arranging the loan. The bank that advises on a takeover may get a fee only if the deal goes through. The profit on the deal is often more important than the long-term relationship with the client. It does not always lead to the best or the most impartial advice. And the employees of the bank or securities house may be rewarded with a one-off bonus for short-term performance rather than with a stake in the business or a move up the corporate hierarchy. It encourages risk-taking. It does not always foster an equal attention to the long-term health of the employer. The former directors of Barings would probably understand this very well.

Private individuals, too, are inundated with competing financial products and competing salesmen and for them the problem of finding sound, impartial advice grows daily more difficult, as the personal pensions debacle demonstrated. Thrown back on their own resources in the competitive environment, they need more than ever to glean what information they can from the financial pages. And to acquire sufficient knowledge to evaluate what they glean.

1

First principles

Write about money, and you cannot entirely avoid technical terms. The simplest terms and concepts need to be dealt with at the outset. They will crop up time and again.

Fundamental to all financial markets is the idea of earning a **return** on money. Money has to work for its owner. Here – ignoring for the moment some of the tax complications that crop up in practice – are some of the ways it can do so:

- You deposit £1,000 with a bank which pays you, say, 10 per cent a year interest. In other words, your £1,000 of **capital** earns you £100 a year, which is the **return** on your money. When you want your £1,000 back you get £1,000, plus any accumulated interest, not more or less. Provided your bank or building society does not go bust, your £1,000 of **capital** is not at risk, except from **inflation** which may reduce its **purchasing power** each year.
- You buy gold bullion to a value of £1,000 because you think the price of gold will rise. If, say, the price of gold has risen by 20 per cent after a year, you can sell your gold for £1,200. You have made a **profit** or a **capital gain** of £200 on your capital outlay of £1,000. In other words you have a **return** of 20 per cent on your money. If the price of gold fails to move, you've earned nothing because commodities like gold do not pay interest.
- You use your £1,000 to buy **securities** that are traded on a stockmarket. Usually these will be **government bonds** (known as **gilt-edged securities** or **gilts** in the UK) or

ordinary shares in a company. The first almost always provide an **income**; the second normally do. Traditional gilt-edged securities pay a fixed rate of interest. Ordinary shares in companies normally pay a **dividend** from the profits the company earns. If the company's profits rise, the dividend is likely to be increased. But there is no guarantee that there will be a dividend at all. If the company makes losses or runs short of cash, it may have to cease paying a dividend.

But when you buy securities that are traded on a stockmarket, the **return** on your £1,000 is not limited to the interest or dividends you receive. The prices of these securities in the stockmarket will also rise and fall, and your original £1,000 investment accordingly becomes worth more or less. So you are taking the risk of **capital gains** or **capital losses**.

Suppose you buy £1,000 worth of ordinary shares which pay you a gross dividend of £40 a year. You are getting a return or **dividend yield** of 4 per cent a year on your investment (£40 as a percentage of £1,000). If after a year the market value of your £1,000 of shares has risen to £1,100, you can sell them for a **capital gain** of £100 (or a 10 per cent profit on your original outlay). Thus your **overall return** over the year (before tax) consisted of the £40 income and the £100 capital gain: a total of £140, or a 14 per cent overall return on your original £1,000 investment.

Investors are generally prepared to accept much lower initial **yields** on shares than on fixed-interest stocks because they expect the income (and, in consequence, the **capital value** of the shares) to rise in the future. Most investors in ordinary shares are seeking capital gains at least as much as income. Note that if you are buying a security, you are taking the risk that the price may fall whether it is a government bond or a share. But with the government bond the income is at least guaranteed by the government. With the share there is a second layer of risk: the company may not earn sufficient profits or have sufficient cash to pay a dividend.

● Finally, you can put the £1,000 directly to work in a business you run. Since this option does not initially involve the financial markets, we'll ignore it.

To summarize: money can be deposited to produce an income, it can be used to buy commodities or goods which are expected to rise in value but may not (including your own home) or it can be invested in stockmarket securities which normally produce an income but show capital gains or losses as well. There are many variations on each of these themes. But keep the principles in mind and the variations fall into place.

Markets and interest rates

For each type of investment and for many of their derivatives there is a **market**. There is a market in money in London. It is not a physical marketplace: dealings take place over the telephone, and the price a borrower pays for the use of money is the interest rate. There are markets in **commodities**. And there is a market in **government bonds** and company **shares**:

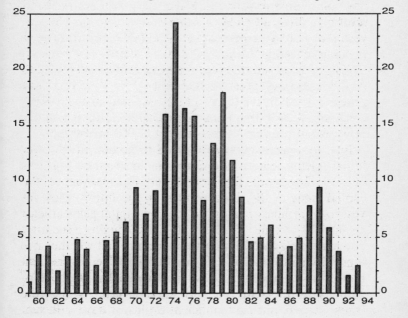

Figure 1.1 The inflation that has dominated investment thinking for much of the past three decades. The chart shows the year-on-year percentage rate of increase in the retail prices index (RPI). Source: *Datastream International.*

the Stock Exchange. Much of what you read in the financial press concerns these markets, their movements and the investments that are dealt on them.

The important point is that no market is entirely independent of the others. The linking factor is the **cost of money** (or the **return** an investor can get on money, which is the other side of the same coin). If interest rates rise or fall there is likely to be a ripple of movement through all the financial markets.

This is the most important single mechanism in the financial sphere and it lies behind a great deal of what is written in the financial press: from discussion of mortgage rates to reasons for movements in the gilt-edged securities market. Money will gravitate to where it earns the best return, commensurate with the risk the investor is prepared to take and the length of time for which he can tie up his money. As a general rule:

● The more money you have to invest, the higher the return you can expect.
● The longer you are prepared to tie your money up, the higher the return you can expect.
● The more risk you are prepared to take, the higher the return you can expect if all goes well.

Note, however, that the main factors influencing short-term interest rates are not always the same as those affecting long-term ones, though the two will interact. Press comment should make it clear what type of interest rate it is primarily referring to.

Different returns on different investments

To match investors' different needs, there is a whole range of different returns available across the financial system. Interest rates can move rapidly, and any real cases we take can be quickly outdated. So we are safer sticking with hypothetical examples. At a particular time an investor might, say, be prepared to accept a return of 7 per cent or less on money he deposited with a bank for a short time and might need in a hurry. The low interest rate is the price of safety and convenience. At the same time he might expect to get 10 per cent if he were prepared to lock up his money by lending it for a year. And if he were prepared to take the chance of capital gain or loss by buying a gilt-edged security in the stockmarket, he might expect a return of, say, 11 per cent.

But these and other returns available to investors would rise and fall with changes in the cost of money in Britain and abroad. What causes these changes is a different matter. Sufficient for the moment to note that there are times when money is cheap (interest rates are low) and times when it is expensive (interest rates are high).

Suppose interest rates rise. The investor who was content with 7 per cent for money he could put his hands on quickly would expect a higher return to match the interest rates being offered elsewhere. So the rate for short-term deposits might rise to 8 per cent. Likewise, the investor who considers tucking his money away for a year would no longer be content with 10 per cent. He'll only be prepared to lend his money for a year if he's offered, say, 11.5 per cent. So anyone wanting to borrow money for a year has to offer the higher rate to lenders.

The precise rates are not important to the argument. The essential fact is that when one interest rate moves significantly, most other rates will move in the same direction. There will still be a differential between the rate the investor gets if he deposits his money for a few weeks and the rate he gets for locking it up for a year, though the size of the differential may change. But both rates will usually move up if interest rates generally are rising.

Opportunity cost of money

There is one other concept we need to introduce at this stage: the **opportunity cost of money**. Look at it like this. Suppose you could invest your money perfectly safely with a bank for a year at a fixed rate of interest of 10 per cent. The £100 you invest will have grown to £110 after a year with the interest added in (again, we are ignoring tax). If you decide to do something different with your money, you are losing the opportunity to earn this perfectly safe 10 per cent. Thus 10 per cent is your opportunity cost of money, and it makes sense to use your money in other ways only if you think you could earn a better return than 10 per cent. If you buy a painting for £100 as an investment with the hope of selling it at a profit after a year, it makes sense only if you reckon you can sell it for more than £110. If you think of investing in a manufacturing process, you would need to be aiming for a return above (and in practice considerably above) 10 per cent. Changes in interest rates alter the opportunity cost of money and have profound effects on a vast range of investment decisions.

An allied concept is the **time value of money**. If you can earn 10 per cent interest, £1 today could be invested to grow to £1.10 in a year with the interest added in. That £1.10 could then be invested for a further year at 10 per cent interest and would grow to £1.21. And so on. Thus we could say that, at a compound interest rate of 10 per cent, £1.21 receivable in two years' time is worth the same as £1 today because £1 today would grow to £1.21 after two years. Another way of putting it is that, again at a 10 per cent interest rate, £1.21 is the **future value** after two years of £1 today. Or, looking at it the other way round, £1 is the **present value** of £1.21 that is receivable in two years.

In other words, even if we forget about inflation, money receivable in the future is worth less than than the same amount of money today. At a 10 per cent rate of interest (or 10 per cent **discount rate**) the present value of £1 that is receivable in one year is £0.909, because £0.909 is the amount in today's money that would grow to £1 in a year's time at 10 per cent interest. At a 15 per cent discount rate, the present value of £1 that is receivable in one year is only 0.870. And so on.

Essentially, most investment is a matter of paying a lump sum today in return for the right to receive a sum or series of sums in the future. So, if somebody says that he will give you £1 in a year's time, what could you afford to pay for that right today? If you expect a 10 per cent return on your money you would discount at 10 per cent and find that you could afford to pay £0.909. If you expect a 15 per cent return, you would discount at 15 per cent and find you could only afford to pay £0.808. Calculations such as these – at a considerably more complex level and applied to a whole series of future receipts – lie at the root of much investment figuring. The important aspect, for our purposes, is that they illustrate the effect of interest rate movements on many types of investment. As interest rates rise and the returns that investors expect also rise, so (all else being equal) the price that they can afford to pay for a given investment will fall.

Interest rates and bond prices

We can see an aspect of this process at work in the bond markets. A change in interest rates has important implications for the stockmarket prices of bonds which pay a fixed rate of interest: **fixed-interest securities**, of which the traditional **gilt-edged securities** issued by the government are the most familiar though companies also issue fixed-interest bonds. It works like this.

Gilt-edged securities are a form of **IOU** (I owe you) or **promissory note** issued by the government when it needs to borrow money. The government undertakes to pay so much a year in interest to the people who put up the money and who get the IOU in exchange. Normally the government agrees to repay (**redeem**) the stock at some date in the future, but to illustrate the interest rate mechanism it is easiest initially to take an **irredeemable** or **undated** stock which does not have to be repaid. The original investors who lend the money to the government do not, however, have to hold on to the IOUs. They can sell them to other investors, who then become entitled to receive the interest from the government.

Suppose the government needs to borrow money at a time when investors would expect an 11 per cent yield on a gilt-edged security. It offers £11 a year interest for every £100 it borrows. The investor is prepared to pay £100 for the right to receive £11 a year interest, because this represents an 11 per cent return on his outlay.

Then suppose that interest rates rise to the point where an investor would expect a 12.5 per cent return if he bought a gilt-edged security. He will no longer pay £100 for the right to £11 a year in income. He will only be prepared to pay a price that gives him a 12.5 per cent return on his outlay. The 'right' price in this case is £88, because if he pays only £88 for the right to receive £11 a year in income, he is getting a 12.5 per cent return on his investment (11 as a percentage of 88). So, in the stockmarket the price of the irredeemable gilt-edged security that pays £11 a year interest would have to fall to £88

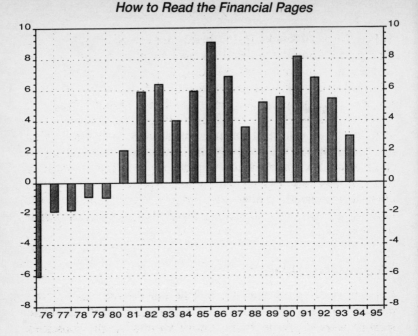

Figure 1.2 For much of the 1970s, rates of interest were below the rate of inflation. In other words, real rates of interest were negative. This was followed in the 1980s by very high real rates of interest. Our chart shows bank base rates minus the rate of inflation. Source: *Datastream International*.

before investors would be prepared to buy it. The original investor who paid £100 thus sees the value of his investment fall because of the rise in interest rates. Conversely, the value of his investment would have risen if interest rates had fallen.

This is one reason why there is so much comment in the financial press on the outlook for interest rates. Higher interest rates mean higher borrowing costs for companies and individuals. They also mean losses for existing investors in fixed-interest bonds.

Markets discount future events

In practice, the movement in stockmarket prices is slightly more complex than this would suggest and there is another vital principle to grasp. Stockmarkets always look ahead and **discount** future events, or what investors expect these events to be. Prices of stocks in the bond markets don't fall or rise simply in response to actual changes in interest rates. If investors think interest rates are going to rise in the near future, they will probably start selling fixed-interest stocks. So there will be more sellers than buyers and the market price will begin to fall before the adjustment in general interest rates actually takes place. Likewise, investors will begin buying fixed-interest stocks if they think interest rates are going to come down, so that they have a profit by the time the interest rate cut has taken place and market prices have adjusted upwards to reflect the new lower interest rates. Making profits in the stockmarkets is all about guessing better (or faster) than the next man.

What is the market?

Reports in the press tend to say 'the market did this' or 'the market expected good news on the economic front', as if the **market** were a single living entity with a single conscious mind. This is not, of course, the case. To understand reports of market behaviour you have to bear in mind the way the market works.

A market is simply a mechanism which allows individuals or organizations to trade with each other. It may be a physical marketplace – a trading floor – where buyers and sellers or their representatives can meet and buy and sell face to face. Or it may simply be a network of buyers and sellers who deal with each other over the telephone or computer screen. The principle is much the same.

In either type of market, the buyers and sellers (or the brokers acting as their agents) may deal direct with each other or they may deal through a middleman known as a **marketmaker**. If they deal direct, each would-be buyer has to find a corrresponding would-be seller. John Smith who wants to sell must locate Tom Jones who wants to buy. If there is a marketmaker, John Smith will sell instead to the marketmaker, who buys on his own account (acts as a **principal**) in the hope that he will later be able to find a Tom Jones to whom he can sell at a profit. Marketmakers **make a book** in shares or bonds. They are prepared to buy shares in the hope of finding somebody to sell to or sell shares (which they may not even have) in the expectation of finding somebody from whom they can buy to **balance their books**. Either way, they make their living on the difference between the prices at which they buy and sell. Marketmakers (in practice there will normally be a number of them competing with each other) lend **liquidity** – fluidity – to a market. A potential buyer can always buy without needing to wait until he can find a potential seller; securities can readily be turned into cash.

The market price of a security (or anything else) reflects a balance between the views of all the possible buyers and sellers in the particular market. This is what commentators really mean when they say 'the market thought . . .' They are describing the dominant view among those operating in the market. An example helps to show how this operates on security prices.

How prices rise or fall

Suppose a security (it could be the government bond we looked at earlier) **stands in the market** at a price of £90. This is the last price at which it changed hands. Suppose there are only ten such securities in existence. But the price has been moving down, and even at £90 there are seven investors who think it is too expensive and would like to sell, and only three who would be prepared to buy. If £90 remained the price, only three sellers could find buyers and there would be an unsatisfied desire to sell.

Suppose the price is £89 instead. At this level one of the previous sellers decides the security is no longer expensive and he may as well hold on, while another investor decides it would be worth buying at this lower price. There are now only six sellers and four buyers. Still no balance.

Now suppose the price is £88. Another potential seller changes his mind if he can only get £88, while another investor reckons it is now attractive and emerges as a potential buyer at this lower price. There are now five sellers and five buyers. Thus at £88 the price has reached an **equilibrium** which holds good until something happens to persuade some of the investors to change their view again.

If there are marketmakers operating in the market, they will probably have moved their quoted price down from £90 to

£88 – the price at which they can balance their books by matching buyers and sellers. Though their operations are in practice more complex (see Chapters 6 and 7a) and they also quote a **spread** between the price at which they are prepared to sell and the one at which they will buy, the principle holds good. Prices will move towards the point where there is equilibrium between buyers and sellers at a given time.

This principle operates in all markets, not just the markets in securities. In the **money markets** banks will need to adjust the interest rates they offer and charge until they have the right balance between those who are prepared to lend to them and those who want to borrow. Building societies need to adjust the rates they pay to savers and charge to borrowers so that they keep a balance between the money coming in and the amount going out as mortgage loans. In the **foreign exchange markets** the value of the pound will need to find a level at which there is a balance between those who want to buy pounds and those who want to sell. Free markets in commodities, in gold bullion and in office accommodation in the City of London are affected by the same interaction of sellers and takers.

Primary and secondary markets

Fixed-interest securities and ordinary shares are the main stock-in-trade of the **securities markets** and the London Stock Exchange is the main domestic securities market. By buying one or the other, investors are helping – directly or indirectly – to provide the finance that government or industry needs. Why do we say 'directly or indirectly'? Because the stockmarket is two markets in one: a **primary market** and a **secondary market**.

A **primary market** is one in which the government, companies or other bodies can sell new securities to investors to raise cash. A **secondary market** is a market in which the investors can buy and sell these securities among themselves, and one market serves both functions. The buying and selling in the secondary market does not directly affect the finances of government or companies. But if investors did not know they could buy and sell securities in the secondary market they might well be reluctant to put up cash for the government or companies by buying securities in the primary market when they were first issued. And the prices established by the buying and selling by investors in the secondary market help to determine the price that government and companies will have to pay next time they need to issue further securities for cash in the primary market. A reasonably **liquid** secondary market is normally considered vital for a healthy primary market.

Interest rates and currencies

Another facet of interest rates: at a time of volatile **exchange rates** between different currencies, the interaction between interest rates and the value of currencies (or **parities**) dominates much financial comment. Investment is increasingly international, and in their search for the best returns investors look not simply at the different options available in their own country but at the relative attractiveness of different countries as a haven for funds.

If Britain offers higher interest rates than, say, the United States or Germany, international investors may be tempted to invest in Britain. This means they will need to exchange whatever currency they hold into pounds sterling in order to make deposits or buy securities in Britain. They will therefore be buying pounds on the foreign exchange market. If the buying of pounds exceeds any selling taking place, the **value of the pound** (the price of the pound in terms of other currencies) is likely to rise.

Interest rates are by no means the only factor affecting the value of a currency. And the **overall return** a foreign investor receives when he invests in Britain depends not only on the yield his money can earn but on the movement in the pound itself. If the pound rises against his own currency he makes a profit on the movement in the pound. If it falls, he makes a loss. So his total return is a combination of the **yield** he can get by investing in Britain and the profit or loss he makes on the currency.

Whatever the level of interest rates in Britain, overseas investors will not invest if they expect the currency itself will fall sharply for other reasons. But interest rates are still an important weapon the government can use in defending the currency by attracting investors to buy pounds to invest in Britain.

Effects of rising interest rates

Now look at some of the effects of a rise in interest rates across the financial system. In describing these effects different papers will highlight different aspects, according to where their readers' interests lie:

Higher interest rates probably mean:

● An increase in **borrowing costs** for industry, meaning that profits for many companies will be lower than they would otherwise have been and that companies may be less keen to borrow money to invest in new projects.

● A rise in the **opportunity cost** of holding non-yielding assets such as gold or commodities (it becomes theoretically more expensive to own them because, at higher interest rates, you lose more by not taking the opportunity of earning interest on your money).

● Higher monthly **mortgage payments** for homebuyers, soaking up more of their available income and leaving them less to spend.

● More expensive **overdrafts** and **personal loans**, and higher **credit card** interest rates, possibly causing consumers to spend less.

● A fall in the value of **gilt-edged securities** on the stockmarket, unless investors think the rise in interest rates is very temporary or unless prices have already fallen in anticipation.

● A possible fall in the value of **ordinary shares** on the stockmarket (though the mechanism here is more complicated than with the gilt-edged market – see below).

● An increase in the returns that **investors** and **savers** can expect to earn on their money.

● A strengthening (all else being equal) in the **value of the pound sterling**, as overseas investors buy pounds to invest in Britain and get the advantage of the higher returns from depositing money in Britain or buying British bonds.

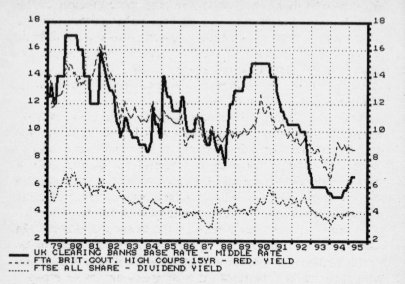

Figure 1.3 How rates of return on different forms of investment influence each other over a long period. The solid line in the graph shows bank base rates, the upper broken line shows the redemption yield on 15-year government bonds and the lower dotted line shows the dividend yield on ordinary shares. Source: *Datastream International*.

In the popular press it is the effects on the individual, and particularly the homebuyer, that are likely to make the headlines: 'Mortgage costs to rocket'. The quality press will probably mention the effect on mortgages, too. In a country where many people used to derive their main sense of economic security from selling their houses to each other at ever-rising prices, nobody is going to ignore the housebuyer. But the more serious papers will also be analysing the effects on sterling, industry, the stockmarket and on the outlook for economic growth. In the *Financial Times*, which regularly covers virtually every financial market, the ripple effects will spread to most corners of the paper.

Debt and equity

Much of the day-to-day comment in the financial press is concerned with the securities markets and the investments that are traded in them. And so far we have talked mainly of the bond market (the market in long-term debt: particularly the gilt-edged market in which the government's own debt is traded). But this leads to another fundamental concept: the difference between **debt** and **equity**.

A company can raise money in a number of different ways. These are the main ones.

First, it can simply borrow money from a bank or elsewhere. Normally the money has to be paid back in due course, and meantime interest has to be paid to the original lender. The interest may be at a **variable** or **floating rate**: it rises or falls with changes in the general level of interest rates in the country. Or it may be at a **fixed rate**, in which case the interest rate remains the same for the life of the loan.

Secondly, it can **issue a loan** in the form of a security. In other words, it creates an IOU and offers it to investors in return for cash, in the same way as the government does in the gilt-edged market. Normally the company agrees to repay – **redeem** – this loan at some future point. But the loan can usually be traded in the stockmarket in the same way as a gilt-edged security. The investor who originally put up the money does not have to hold on to his IOU until it is repaid. If he wants the money sooner, he sells the IOU to somebody else. He may get less for it than he paid, or he may sell it at a profit. The company simply pays interest to whomever owns the IOU when interest is due, and eventually repays the money it originally borrowed to the person who owns the IOU on the **redemption date**.

These loans may pay a fixed rate of interest or a floating rate. If they pay a fixed rate, they are very similar to a fixed-rate government bond. The rate of interest is known as the **coupon** and for convenience it is expressed as a percentage of the **nominal**, **par** or **face** value, which in Britain is taken to be a unit of £100, as with a government stock. The loans issued by companies go under various names such as **loan stock**, **industrial debenture** or **bond**. The value of fixed-interest loans is affected by movements in interest rates, but the health and standing of the company also plays a part. The company has to earn the profits to pay the interest and repay the capital, whereas with a gilt-edged security these payments are guaranteed by the government (see Chapter 13).

Thirdly, a company may raise money by creating new **ordinary shares** and selling them for cash. This is quite different in principle from issuing a loan or borrowing from a bank, because ordinary shares – also known as **equity** – are not a debt of the company. They do not normally have to be repaid. The owner of a share becomes part-owner of the company. In return for putting up his money, he shares in the risks and rewards of the company's operations: hence the term **risk capital**. He is entitled to a share of everything the company owns, after allowing for its debts, and to a share of the profits it earns. If its profits increase he can normally expect higher **dividends** – income payments – on his shares.

A share is also a **security** of the company and can normally be bought and sold in the same way as a loan stock. In the same way, its price in the market depends on the interplay of buyers and sellers, not on the price at which it was originally issued. An investor who wants his money back simply sells the share to somebody else; whether he gets more or less than he paid originally depends on what the market price has done in the interim. If profits of the company rise, it will probably pay higher dividends and – all else being equal – the value of the shares will normally rise. If the company gets into trouble, the owners of the shares or **shareholders** are the last people to get any money back. All of the loans and other debts have to be repaid first.

Interest rate effects on ordinary shares

Investors will generally accept a lower initial **yield** on shares than on fixed-interest securities because they expect their income and the capital value of the shares to rise. Take the earlier example of shares that could be bought at a price that offered a 4 per cent yield but which rose in value by 10 per cent over the year. The overall return to a buyer would have been 14 per cent. This is attractive relative to the 11 per cent return we assumed that he could get at the time on gilt-edged securities. The additional three **percentage points** allow for the risk element in the ordinary shares.

But investors do not know in advance what return they will get from ordinary shares. Even the 4 per cent dividend yield could fall if the company had to cut its dividend. And if it cut its dividend, the value of the shares in the stockmarket would almost certainly fall, too. Hence investing in shares involves a judgement about a company's prospects and its ability to earn the profits out of which the dividends will be paid.

However, share values may be affected by movements in interest rates as well. If yields on gilt-edged stocks rose to 14 per cent, investors would almost certainly want a higher overall return than 14 per cent on ordinary shares to allow for the risk element. In the short run share prices would have to fall in the market to provide the higher return. But the prices of shares in individual companies are also affected by the profits outlook for the company. In the very long run the return from shares will depend on the profits the company earns or is capable of earning. A large proportion of the press's financial coverage concerns the profits companies earn and the profits they are likely to earn in the future.

Don't expect markets to be rational

One final word about markets. We can describe dispassionately how they operate and the main forces at work. This is not always how they present themselves in the short run to those who operate in them or those who comment on their day-to-day behaviour. Markets are moved by tips and rumours, by frenetic temporary enthusiasms and by devastating panics. They are creatures of mood and can sometimes be manipulated. Their enthusiasms and panics are frequently self-feeding, losing all contact with the underlying realities: the **fundamentals**.

Markets are a vital mechanism between investors with money and governments and companies that need money to put to work. But the average dealer in a marketmaking firm may rarely think about his function as a cog in this essential economic process. His business is dealing in shares and he has a gut feeling that share prices are due to rise, so he buys. He will usually find a reason afterwards for what he did. Do not take too seriously all of the reasons for market behaviour you find reported in the financial pages. Market professionals earn their bread from movements one way or another. If no logical reason for movement exists, they are quite capable of inventing one.

The City of London provides the main mechanisms for distributing the flows of money. In the next chapter we look at the sources of money, the markets that distribute the money and the people you will meet in the financial pages who operate in these markets.

2

Money flows and the money men

When a financial journalist describes somebody as 'an eminent City figure', he probably means what he says. The man is perhaps a senior member of the banking establishment. If a journalist describes somebody as 'the controversial City financier', he's probably coming as close as he dares within the libel laws to calling him a financial spiv.

But what exactly is this 'City' which harbours these characters and many more? 'The City' is a convenient blanket term for the commercial institutions at the heart of Britain's financial system. They do not necessarily operate within the square mile of the City of London, though a surprising number of them do. They provide the financial services that oil the wheels of industry and trade. They are not, however, concerned only with serving Britain's domestic economy. Much of the City's activity relates to international finance, trade and securities dealing, and one of the more common criticisms of the City is that it is too remote from Britain's own productive industries.

The City is a major source of **invisible earnings** for Britain's **balance of payments**. The UK financial sector contributed a net £15.6 billion to the current account balance in 1993.

To put into context what we read about the City, we need some idea of the sums of money involved and the relative importance of different institutions. What follows in this chapter is an outline of the main investment flows and the bodies which handle them. Some of these figures (together with other markets not covered here) are described in more detail in the chapters devoted to them.

The savings institutions

The City provides the mechanisms which channel money to where it can be put to work. The main external source of new long-term investment funds for business and government is the **savings** of private individuals, and in Britain these savings are channelled mainly through the large **financial institutions**: primarily the **pension funds** and **life assurance companies**. With some £27 billion a year of new money, they invest funds in companies by buying shares. By buying gilt-edged securities they supply much of the money the government normally needs to borrow (years like 1988–90, when the government was repaying debt, are unfortunately rare). The **London Stock Exchange** allows these institutional funds to find their way into company securities and government and company bonds, and the financial institutions are the London Stock Exchange's largest clients (see Chapter 6).

The financial institutions also invest in **commercial property** and in **overseas securities and property**, and put money to work short term in the **money markets**.

A third type of investment institution is significant in the equity market: the **unit trust**. Unit trusts pool the money of individual investors to provide a spread of risk by investing in a range of shares, mainly via the stockmarket (see Chapter 21).

The **building societies** also act as a funnel for the savings of individuals but the money they take goes primarily into providing **mortgages** for home buyers. However, a proportion of their funds is invested in government securities via the stockmarket, where it can readily be turned into cash if needed.

Banking and money markets

The other major domestic source of external funds for business is the **banking system** and the **money markets** (see Chapter 15). The banks' main sources of funds are shorter-term – the money of individuals and companies deposited with them (**retail deposits**) plus the **wholesale funds** they borrow in the money markets. The banks lend money in one form or another. The high-street banks in Britain do not, as in some other countries, invest in company shares to any significant extent. But increasingly they act as arrangers of finance as well as lenders by organizing and guaranteeing issues of various types of short-term IOU by companies. The banks also invest in government securities via the Stock Exchange. And they are the main participants in the **foreign exchange** or **forex** markets. Some of the banks are directly involved in the Stock Exchange through securities houses they own. The big banks are very active in buying and selling **derivative** financial products. Finally, they often deal quite actively in various financial markets on their own account in an attempt to boost their income.

Euromarkets

A third source of finance for business and governments is the **eurocurrency** market or **euromarket**, also known as the **international market**. Here the sources of funds were originally the deposits of currencies held outside their country of origin, in banks round the world. These days, however, this distinction has become a little unreal and the market is defined more in terms of its trading and issuing techniques, its structure and its international character. The users are borrowers round the world (in spite of the name, this market does not deal solely with deposits held in Europe). London is the main centre of this market, but Britain is neither the main supplier nor the main user of eurocurrency funds (see Chapter 17).

The market mechanisms

The London Stock Exchange, the banking and money markets and the euromarkets are the main markets for investment funds. But the City contains many other markets which provide services for business.

There is a range of markets concerned with the **management of risk**, in which investors or businesses can either **hedge** (protect themselves) against the risks inherent in their operations or opt for high risks and high rewards by betting on movements in prices and interest rates. These are increasingly referred to as the **derivatives** markets. They include the **traded options market** and the **financial futures market** (which are now amalgamated) and a range of **commodities futures markets**. The **foreign exchange** market also comes within this category as a medium for hedging currency risks.

There is another aspect of risk management: a market in **insurance**. This divides into two parts: insurance provided by insurance companies (the **company market**) and the international insurance market operated under the aegis of **Lloyd's of London**.

Savings institutions and intermediaries

Occupational pension schemes – pension schemes provided by companies or industries for their employees – had (at end-1993) investments valued at some £481 billion and invested some £4 billion of new money in 1994. The contributions companies and individuals pay into these schemes are invested in a fund to provide the pensions at the end of the day. Some pension funds manage their own investments – the biggest run into many billions of pounds. Others farm out the investment management, often to merchant banks (see Chapter 6). Others are **insured** schemes where payments are made to an insurance company which contracts to provide the pensions.

Because **life assurance companies** provide pensions as well as life assurance, the distinction between the two types of investment is a little blurred and life assurance funds include a pensions element. The larger life assurance companies are also becoming more diversified investment management groups, offering unit trusts and other financial services. Life assurance is mainly a savings business as opposed to **general insurance** which provides cover against fire, theft and similar risks. The life assurance companies had (in 1993) existing investments of about £434 billion in their long-term funds and invested some £23 billion of new money in 1994.

Both the pension funds and life assurance companies are vehicles for **contractual savings**: money coming in under long-term savings schemes which can safely be invested for the long term because the savers have contracted to make regular payments.

Unit trusts cannot rely on the same regular inflow of funds, though part of the money they receive comes from regular savings plans. Investors tend to pile into unit trusts when the stockmarket is buoyant and may even withdraw funds when it takes a turn for the worse. But, overall, they have still shown strong growth in recent years, particularly as investors can hold unit trust units in a **personal equity plan** or **PEP** (see Chapter 21) and receive tax advantages. In 1990 unit trusts held total funds of £46 billion and by end-1994 this had grown to almost £92 billion. They are often operated by large **investment management groups** which market a range of savings products and services.

The pension funds, life assurance companies and unit trusts between them own close to 60 per cent of all listed shares in British companies and the first two own between a third and a half of the gilt-edged securities in issue.

Life assurance and unit trusts are sold direct by the organizations that provide them, but are also extensively marketed through **financial intermediaries** who operate on commission. These include **insurance brokers** and **independent investment advisers. Accountants, solicitors, bank managers, building societies** and **stockbrokers** may also sell these investment products.

The **building societies** at end-1994 had shares and deposits of some £210 billion, plus other borrowings and their own reserves. They had lent a total of £243 billion to homebuyers and had around £6 billion invested in gilt-edged securities. Under recent legislation their possible range of activities has been widened and some of the larger ones provide a range of services including cheque accounts, personal loans, estate agency services and a variety of financial and savings products. Hitherto they have been **mutual** organizations – owned in theory by the people who deposit money with them and borrow from them – but the larger ones now have the option to become companies owned by shareholders. One of the biggest, the Abbey National, took this course and another, Cheltenham & Gloucester, agreed to a takeover by Lloyds Bank. Other mergers, acquisitions or flotations are in the air.

The banks

At end-1994 **banks** in Britain had sterling domestic deposits of around £364 billion and domestic deposits in other currencies of some £71 billion. Overseas sector deposits were £76 billion in sterling and £601 billion in other currencies. Their sterling lending to the private sector was £432 billion. The bulk of this money is with the major **clearing banks** such as Barclays and Lloyds, whose traditional deposit-taking and lending services are familiar enough. But a major recent change for some of the clearing banks has been their involvement in Stock Exchange business via the acquisition of broking or, in some cases, marketmaking businesses. Their success has not always been unmixed.

The **merchant banks** – the Lazards and the Kleinworts – do not have such large-scale funds of their own. Their expertise lies in arranging finance, not necessarily in providing it. They are very active in the **investment management business** – particularly for pension funds – and their **corporate finance** arms advise companies on capital raising and on takeover attacks and defences. Some of them have also become prime players in the stockmarket by acquiring broking and jobbing firms, though there are doubts as to whether the traditional British merchant banks have the financial substance to compete on a global scale in all aspects of the securities business. Three of the four traditional high street banks have a merchant banking arm.

London is also host to a wide range of **foreign banks** – well over 500 at the last count – many of which were attracted by London's position as centre of the euromarkets though some of the larger ones also do significant domestic banking business in Britain and may be involved in Stock Exchange business.

The Stock Exchange

Britain's domestic **stock exchange** is the third largest stockmarket after those of the United States and Japan. At end 1994 the total market value of listed ordinary shares in UK and Irish companies was £775 billion, while UK government securities listed on the exchange had a value of £222 billion. In 1994 some £25 billion was raised by the first-time sale of shares and domestic bonds in new and existing companies on the stockmarket. London Stock Exchange members are divided between **marketmakers** and **broker-dealers**. The first make a continuous market as principals and the second supply shares from their own stocks or simply act as agents for investors. Marketmaking in gilt-edged securities is undertaken by **primary dealers** known as **gilt-edged marketmakers**.

Most of the major London marketmakers and brokers are now owned by UK or foreign banks or other financial institutions and in some cases several firms have been brought together to form major **securities houses** which undertake all kinds of securities business. A number of major foreign banks and securities houses are now also active in the British market. Many smaller brokers and **country brokers** remain independent, though some have got together into larger groupings. Most of the larger Stock Exchange businesses employ numbers of **investment analysts** who produce research into companies and other investment topics as a service to clients.

The professional back-up

The components of the other markets are described in the chapters devoted to them. But among the City figures encountered in the financial pages there is also a range of professional firms without which the City could not function: notably, accountants, actuaries, lawyers and chartered surveyors.

Accountants are a vital link in the financial chain, if only because they **audit** the accounts of companies (see Chapter 3). Their services are particularly vital in the preparation of a **prospectus** when shares are **marketed** (sold to a range of investors) for the first time. **Audit** and **tax** work is the traditional mainstay of the accountant, with **liquidation** work – **winding up** companies that have gone to the wall – as a specialist sideline for some of them.

But the major international firms which number their employees in tens of thousands worldwide are pushing fast into areas which overlap with other established interests: **corporate finance** and all manner of **management advisory services**.

Consulting actuaries are the firms that advise on the highly complex business of **pension funding** and **pension fund performance** and they crop up with some regularity when pension topics are discussed. This is in addition to the actuary's original function of assessing mortality risks, valuing life assurance assets and liabilities and deciding on bonuses.

Commercial lawyers. Few documents in the investment world can safely be prepared without the advice of a commercial lawyer, and the City boasts a dozen or so major firms specializing in commercial work.

Surveyors and **estate agents** act as intermediaries in the market in investment properties. But they do a great deal besides. **Valuations** of a company's properties may be needed in a new issue or takeover document. They will certainly be needed when finance is to be secured on properties. The chartered surveyor frequently helps to arrange finance for **development of properties**. He manages **property investment portfolios** for numerous institutions and is the main source of information on conditions in both the **property investment market** and the **letting market** (see Chapter 20).

Perhaps the **financial public relations** agencies should also rank as one of the City's back-up services. **Crawford's Directory of City Connections** – the financial journalist's *vade mecum* – lists well over 100 of them and many have a significant client list among stockmarket-listed companies. The reader of the financial press is not necessarily aware of their presence, but much of the routine information from companies – profit announcements and the like – reaches the journalist in the form of a press release on the paper of one of these agencies. They perform a more active role in publicizing the virtues of companies coming to the stockmarket, in helping to present the case for an aggressor or a defendant in a takeover bid and generally in ensuring that information which could be good for the share price of a client company does not remain hidden under a bushel.

Finally, there are the **regulators** whose job is to supervise these diverse bodies and interests and ensure that they remain on the straight and narrow. Since the regulatory system is many-sided and complex, we will deal with this topic where it crops up, and in a distinct chapter towards the end of the book (Chapter 22).

3

Companies and their accounts

Financial journalists write extensively about **companies**. Companies that are growing, companies that are contracting, companies that are taking over other companies, companies that are going bust. They tend to approach company affairs from one of two angles (or, most usefully, from both). Take two examples:

'Mark Hustler, the thirty-year-old accountant who took charge at Interpersonal Video Systems earlier this year, has not let the grass grow under his feet. Following the purchase of Insight Compact Discs in June he plans a further important acquisition in the interpersonal systems field to consolidate the company's lead in this fast growing business. The shares are acquiring a strong institutional following and at 180p – up from 60p earlier this year – look one of the best bets in the high technology sector.'

What do we deduce from this? First, that the writer thinks Interpersonal Video Systems is a good thing, because he is advising you to buy the shares. Secondly, that he is suggesting the investing institutions are buying the shares, which should help the price to rise. Thirdly, that the shares have already risen strongly, presumably since Mark Hustler took charge. Fourthly, that Mark Hustler is expanding his company by buying other companies. Fifthly, that the company is a leader in interpersonal systems and that these are a high-technology area. Finally, we might suspect that the writer probably hasn't the faintest idea what an interpersonal video system is, whether it is a growth business, whether Mark Hustler is paying too much or too little for the companies he is acquiring or who the institutions are that are supposed to be following the company. In other words, the writer has clearly had a **tip**. It's not necessarily to be sneezed at. If enough people follow the tip and buy the shares because they think they are going up, they will go up. For a time at least.

Now take the following:

'Interpersonal Video Systems, the manufacturer of visual sales aids for the toothpaste industry, reports turnover up from £18m to £27m for the year to end-March. Pre-tax profits have risen from £2m to £4.3m, including a first-time contribution of £1.5m from Insight Compact Discs, acquired for shares last June, and earnings per share are up from 10p to 12.5p on the enlarged capital. If the company meets its target of 15 per cent a year internal growth, the 25p shares at 180p are on a prospective PE ratio of only 12.5, which is below the sector average. They look undervalued.'

In fact, the message from the second writer is essentially the same as that from the first: the shares should be bought. Not because Mark Hustler is a great guy, not because another important acquisition is planned, not because institutions are rushing to buy the shares. But because the conventional **investment arithmetic** says that they are cheap. We also learn roughly what Interpersonal Video Systems does and we have an indication that it probably didn't pay too much for Insight Compact Discs.

Neither approach is totally satisfactory on its own. It is useful to know who runs a company. It helps us to get a feel for the operation if we know it plans expansion via take-over. It is useful to know (if, in fact, it is true) that institutions are investing in the company. But it is also useful to know what it does, how much it earns and how it is rated on accepted investment criteria.

Phrases like 'PE ratio' and 'earnings per share' are part of the currency of the investment business. But what do they mean? This requires a gentle incursion into company accounts.

Limited liability

First, what is a company? It is a trading entity that belongs to its shareholders and the **Ltd** or **plc** after the name indicates that it has **limited liability**. The plc also indicates that the company is a **Public Limited Company**: one whose shares or other securities may be held by the investing public and traded on a market. In either case the liability of the owners is limited to the amount of money they have put into the business. Unless they give **personal guarantees** for the debts of the business, the **owners** or **shareholders** (**members**, in the legal jargon) of a limited company cannot be called on to meet the company's debts where these exceed its assets. Only the money put into the company can be lost. Anybody who operates a business as a sole trader or as a partner in a **partnership**, on the other hand, is liable for all the debts of the business.

Voting and control

The owners of the **ordinary shares** in a company normally have the power to **control** the company if they act together, though the directors and managers – who may or may not be shareholders – run the company. Usually each ordinary share carries one **vote**. Owners of more than 50 per cent of the votes will thus – if they all vote the same way – control the company. In practice shareholders can influence the way a company is run primarly by voting on the appointment or dismissal of directors and on certain other major policy matters that have to be presented to shareholders at a formal meeting of the company. Certain major resolutions – to change the aims and objectives of a company, say – will require 75 per cent voting in favour.

Most of the time shareholders vote the way the directors advise them to, especially at the **annual general meeting** or **AGM** of the company, which is normally a non-contentious event where the required resolutions are duly passed. The press will generally pick up the occasions when there is dissent between different groups of shareholders or between shareholders and directors. This is where the question of voting power becomes interesting.

Content of the accounts

Ordinary shareholders are entitled to receive **accounts**. As a rough rule (it's not technically quite correct) companies are required to produce a set of accounts each year. This is a legal requirement. The Stock Exchange further requires that listed companies produce figures showing profits at the **half-year** stage (in America they produce them each **quarter**).

The best way to look on accounts is as a sort of shorthand for what is really going on in a company. The bare figures don't conjure up the smoking chimneys or the salesmen out on the road. But once you are reasonably familiar with the basic figurework you can begin to look at what lies behind it.

The main items in the accounts are a **profit and loss account**, a **cash flow statement** and a **balance sheet**. Under recent accounting rules, the company should also include a **statement of total recognized gains and losses** and a **note of historical cost profits and losses** – but we do not need to bother too much with these for the moment. Various other bits of information required by law, by the accounting standards of the day or by the Stock Exchange in the case of a listed company are usually contained in the **directors' report** or in the detailed **notes to the accounts**. In practice, the report and accounts of Stock Exchange-traded companies normally contain a lot more information in the form of a chairman's statement, a review of the year's trading and statements of compliance with various codes and practices that companies are meant to observe. Lavish colour illustrations may also bulk out the document.

Role of the auditors

With the accounts will come an **auditors' report**. **Auditors** are firms of accountants who hold a watching brief on behalf of the owners of the company (the shareholders). The directors of the company prepare and sign the accounts. It is the auditors' job to certify that these accounts present a **true and fair view** of the company's profits and financial position, or to point out any failings where they do not. The auditors are meant to be independent of the company's management, though obviously need to work quite closely with the managers in agreeing the form of the accounts. The managers appoint them, though the shareholders approve their fees. There is normally a certain amount of give and take when opinions vary on the presentation of different items. An auditors' report which says the accounts do not give a 'true and fair view' or that they do so only with important **qualifications** will normally be picked up by the press as a strong warning bell.

Company reporting

Companies which are quoted on the Stock Exchange need, we have seen, to provide their shareholders with more frequent information than that supplied by the legally required annual accounts. Some weeks after the end of the first half of the company's year it will normally produce an **interim profit statement** (or **interim**) giving unaudited first-half profit figures. The statement also normally gives the size of the **interim dividend** (see below) and includes some comment on trading and prospects from the company.

Some time after the end of the full year a **preliminary announcement** (**prelim**) will usually be published, giving the profits for the year and often a lot of background information. This appears some weeks before the full report and accounts are posted to shareholders. Most daily press comment on the company's figures is based on the interim and preliminary statements which have greater news value – though less depth of information – than the full accounts.

Profit and loss account

A **profit and loss account** shows the results of a company's trading over the last financial period. Usually this means a year, though the year can run to whatever date the company chooses. December 31 and March 31 year-ends are popular, though it could be April 1 or November 5. The profit and loss account thus shows the effect on the company's revenue account of all the transactions over the past year. If a company made profits of £20m in the first ten months of its year and losses of £22m in the last two months, the profit and loss account would show a loss of £2m: the final outcome. It would not by itself reveal that the company had been trading profitably for much of the period.

Cash flow statement

Profits are not necessarily the same as cash flows, and the differences can sometimes be revealing. Take just one example. A company lends £10m to another company for two years at 10 per cent a year interest but agrees that the interest will only be paid when the loan itself is repaid after two years. In its profit and loss account at the end of the first year the lending company will include in its profits the interest of £1m which has **accrued** (built up) by that point. It has earned this interest. On the other hand, it has not yet received any interest in cash, so the £1m will not feature in its cash flow statement for that year.

Companies go bust primarily because they run out of cash. The **cash flow statements** that they have been obliged to publish since the early 1990s make it far easier to see the early warning signs (see also Chapter 4).

Balance sheet

The **balance sheet** is a totally different animal from the profit and loss account and cash flow statement. It gives a snapshot of a company's financial position on one particular date: the last day of its financial year. Everything the company owned on this date and everything it owed on this date will be shown in the balance sheet, grouped under a number of different headings. The balance sheet is usually the best measure an investor has of a company's **financial health**. But it needs interpreting with caution. The position it shows on the last day of the company's year could be very different from what it would have shown if drawn up three months earlier or would show if prepared three months later. Where companies deliberately bring forward some items and delay others, so that the balance sheet gives a picture which is totally untypical of the company's position at any other time during the year, it amounts to excessive **window-dressing**. **Creative accounting** has a similar implication. It usually means that figures have been twisted beyond the bounds of decency to present the picture the company wants.

Note the difference between a balance sheet or **parent company balance sheet** and a **consolidated balance sheet** or **group**

balance sheet. Most companies listed on the Stock Exchange are not, in fact, single companies. Bloggs Engineering Plc may be a group of companies consisting of Bloggs Engineering Plc, Scraggs Scrap Ltd and Muppet Metalbashers Ltd. Bloggs Engineering is the **parent company** and controls the other two by owning all or a majority of their shares. They are therefore **subsidiary companies**. The head company of a group is also sometimes called the **holding company** because it holds the shares of the subsidiaries.

A parent company balance sheet shows the detail for Bloggs Engineering alone; its ownership of the other two companies is represented merely by the **book value** (value for accounting purposes) of its interest in these subsidiaries, which is generally pretty unhelpful. A consolidated balance sheet, on the other hand, treats the three companies as if they were a single entity. The assets and liabilities of all three are grouped together. Thus, if Bloggs owned buildings valued at £2m, Scraggs's buildings were worth £1m and Muppet's worth £1.5m, the figure for buildings (or 'properties') in the consolidated balance sheet of Bloggs Engineering Plc would be £4.5m.

Companies are normally required to present both a balance sheet and a consolidated or group balance sheet, unless there are no subsidiaries, in which case only parent company figures are given. The consolidated balance sheet is the important one and virtually all press comment will be on the consolidated figures. Companies are not required to publish a parent company profit and loss account (unless the business consists of a single company), only a **consolidated** one which shows the aggregate of the profits and losses of all the different companies in the group.

Where the money comes from

In looking at a company's finances as shown by its balance sheet (and when talking of balance sheets from now on we'll be referring to consolidated balance sheets) it is vital to distinguish the different **sources of money** the company uses in its operations. There are three main sources. First, money put up as **permanent capital** by the owners (the shareholders) of the business. This is the company's own money, usually put up in the form of **ordinary share capital** when it is also known as **equity capital**. Then there is the part of the profit the company earns which it **ploughs back** into the business rather than paying out by way of dividend to shareholders. This also becomes part of the equity funds of the business, because it belongs to the shareholders and is shown as **reserves**. Third, there is the money the company borrows and which it will have to repay at some point. The general term for this is **debt** or **borrowings** but it can take a lot of different forms: **overdrafts**, **term loans** (both bank borrowings which are not securities) or **debentures**, **loan stocks** and so on (which are securities of the company).

The main balance sheet items

The easiest way to understand the various accounting terms that crop up in press reports is to take a sample set of accounts. The accounts – for a mythical John Smith & Co Ltd – are slightly simplified to emphasize the main items: some of the complexities that will crop up are examined later in Chapter 5. First, the **balance sheet**. Assume that John Smith is a young company which makes, say, metal paperweights.

In fact, John Smith & Co was set up only a year ago by four friends who decided there was a future in paperweights. Each put £10,000 into the business by subscribing for 10,000 £1 ordinary shares and the company borrowed the rest of the money it required. Let us take the main balance sheet items in order.

Fixed and current assets

First come the **assets** of the business: what it owns. Assets are defined as **fixed assets** or **current assets**. Fixed assets are not necessarily fixed in a physical sense. A company operating oil tankers would show them as a fixed asset. They are 'fixed' because they are not something the company is buying and selling or processing in the course of its normal trade. They represent mainly the buildings and plant in which or with which the company produces its products and services. In this case John Smith's only fixed assets are £27,000 worth of

John Smith & Co Ltd
Balance sheet at 31 December

	£	£
FIXED ASSETS		
Plant and machinery		27,000
CURRENT ASSETS		
Stocks	50,000	
Debtors	35,000	
Cash at bank	5,000	
	90,000	
CURRENT LIABILITIES		
(Creditors: amounts due within one year)		
Trade creditors	20,000	
Tax payable	6,000	
Dividend proposed	4,000	
Bank overdrafts	8,000	
	38,000	
NET CURRENT ASSETS		52,000
TOTAL ASSETS LESS CURRENT LIABILITIES		79,000
CREDITORS		
(Amounts due in more than one year)		
Term loans		30,000
NET ASSETS		49,000
Represented by:		
Share capital		
(£1 ordinary shares)	40,000	
Profit and loss account reserves	9,000	
SHAREHOLDERS' FUNDS		49,000

paperweight-making machinery. Originally John Smith paid
£30,000 for this machinery, but out of its profits it has set
aside £3,000 to allow for a year's **depreciation** or **amortization**
of the equipment and written down the **book value** by this
amount. This recognizes that machinery will eventually wear
out and need to be replaced.

Current assets are the assets which are constantly on the move. Stocks of raw materials that will be turned into products, stocks of products that will be sold to customers, money owing to the company by customers, money temporarily held in the bank that will be withdrawn as it is needed in the business. If there were a company whose business was buying and selling oil tankers, the tankers would be shown under current assets as 'stocks', and not under fixed assets.

John Smith has **stocks** of £50,000. These comprise mainly stocks of raw metal from which the paperweights will be made and stocks of finished paperweights that have not yet been sold.

The **debtors** item shows the money that is owing to John Smith, probably by customers who have bought paperweights they have not yet paid for. In effect, John Smith is making a temporary loan of £35,000 to its customers, on which it receives no interest. **Trade credit** of this kind is a fact of business life, but it poses problems, particularly for younger companies. John Smith has had to bear the costs of producing the paperweights, which soaks up its available cash, and does not get paid by customers till some time later.

Finally, current assets include £5,000 of **cash** sitting in the bank until it has to be spent.

John Smith's total assets are therefore £117,000: the £27,000 of fixed assets and £90,000 of current assets. This figure is known as the **balance sheet total**. It represents everything John Smith & Co owns.

Current liabilities

Next we have to knock off everything the company owes. The short-term debts are shown as **current liabilities** or **creditors: amounts due within one year**. These are the counterpart of current assets and are therefore deducted from current assets in the balance sheet to give **net current assets** (or **net current liabilities** if current liabilities exceed current assets).

The first item under current liabilities is **trade creditors** of £20,000. This is the counterpart of debtors. It represents money the company owes for goods and services it has received but not yet paid for. In other words, it is much like an interest-free loan to the company: **trade credit** from which the company benefits.

Each year a company has to make provision from its profits for the **corporation tax** it must pay on these profits. But corporation tax is payable by instalments and at any time there is likely to be some tax which the company knows it will have to pay but which has not yet been handed over. This therefore appears as a liability of £6,000 under the heading **tax payable**.

Next comes the **dividend** the company plans to pay. A company needs approval from its shareholders for the dividend it intends to pay, and until they have voted to approve the dividend at the **annual general meeting (AGM)** which takes place at least three weeks after they have received the accounts it remains a short-term liability: something that will need to be paid in the near future. A public company normally pays its dividend in two parts: an **interim dividend** in the course of the year and a **final dividend** (which has to be approved by shareholders) when the profits for the full year are known.

Finally, the company owes £8,000 it has borrowed by way of **overdraft**. Since an overdraft is technically repayable on demand, it has to be shown as a current liability.

Deducting the current liabilities of £38,000 from the current assets of £90,000 gives a figure of £52,000 for net current assets.

Longer-term debt

Fixed assets plus net current assets give the figure described as **total assets less current liabilities**. From this figure of £79,000 we still have to knock off any **medium-** or **long-term debts** before arriving at a figure for net assets. In the event, John Smith has borrowed £30,000 in the form of a **term loan**. This is a bank loan, typically for a period of three to seven years, and normally repayable in instalments.

The net asset figure

After knocking off everything the company owes, we find John Smith is 'worth' £49,000: the **net asset** figure. This is the value of the **shareholders' interest** in the company. It equates to the £40,000 the four founder-shareholders provided by subscribing for 40,000 £1 shares at par, plus the £9,000 of profits the company has earned and **retained** in the business rather

than paying out as dividends. The two items together constitute the **shareholders' funds** of £49,000.

After looking at the individual items, translate them into a
picture of the company's financial position. It has assets of
£117,000 (fixed assets plus current assets). Where did the
money come from to acquire these assets? It has effectively
borrowed (partly as trade credit) the £38,000 shown as current
liabilities. It has a longer-term borrowing of £30,000: the term
loan. Knock these two items off the assets figure and you are
left with £49,000. Where did the money come from for this remaining £49,000 of assets? The answer: £40,000 was put up as
share capital by the original shareholders and £9,000 was
'saved' out of the profits of the year's operations.

Gearing

The relationship between **borrowed money (debt)** and **shareholders' money (equity)** in a business is important. Borrowed
money has to be repaid at some point, though it might be a
long way off. More important in the short run, interest has to
be paid on borrowed money, and it has to be paid whether the
company is earning good profits or not. A company that
existed largely on borrowed money could be in bad trouble if
it ran into losses for a year or so. If it was unable to pay the
interest, the lenders could ask for their money back, which
would usually result in the business folding up.

Equity finance does not carry this risk. In the good times
the shareholders reap the rewards of the company's success,
usually in the form of rising dividends. But if the company
should run into trouble and make losses, it does not have to
pay any dividend at all on the ordinary shares. Equity capital
is also called **risk capital** for this reason.

The relationship between borrowed money and equity
money in a business is referred to as **gearing** (or **leverage** in
the United States). It is a term that crops up in other contexts
as well. A **high-geared company** is one which has a large
amount of borrowed money in relation to its equity or its
shareholders' funds. A **low-geared company** has a large equity
and few borrowings. The appropriate mix of borrowings and
equity depends on the type of business (see Chapter 4). If a
journalist points out that a company is high-geared, he is

probably suggesting that this is a good thing for shareholders if the company is doing well. If the company is doing badly, he is probably sounding a warning.

The main profit and loss account items

Next, look at the record of the company's profits for the past year, as shown in the profit and loss (P&L) account.

John Smith & Co Ltd
Profit and loss account for the year ended 31 December

	£
TURNOVER	200,000
OPERATING PROFIT	24,000
Less	
INTEREST PAID	4,000
Leaving	
PROFIT ON ORDINARY ACTIVITIES BEFORE TAX	20,000
Less	
CORPORATION TAX	7,000
Leaving	
PROFIT AFTER TAX ATTRIBUTABLE TO MEMBERS OF JOHN SMITH LTD	13,000
Less	
DIVIDENDS	4,000
Leaving	
RETAINED PROFIT	9,000

Turnover and profit

Most of these terms are pretty much self-explanatory. They don't all have a precise legal or accountancy significance and some can be used in slightly different ways. The **turnover** of £200,000 is the total value of all goods and services sold by the company to third parties in the normal course of trade – it is sometimes called **sales** instead. It does not usually include any taxes (like VAT) charged on these goods or services.

The difference between turnover and the **operating profit** of £24,000 is the costs incurred by the company in its operations during the year: wages, rent, raw materials, distribution costs and so on. These will be broken down to a greater or lesser extent in the notes. The costs also in this case include the **directors' salaries**, the **auditors' fees** and the amount set aside to provide for **depreciation of plant and equipment** (these items will be shown in detail in the **notes to the accounts**). The operating profit is what remains after these costs have been deducted.

The next deduction is the **interest** the company pays on its borrowings of all kinds (for convenience we've ignored the fact that it may also have received a little interest on its temporary bank balances). In the notes this interest should be broken down between interest on **short-term borrowings** and interest on **long-term borrowings**. An overdraft is technically a very short-term borrowing.

After deducting the interest paid we are left with a figure of £20,000 for **profit on ordinary activities before tax**. Mercifully this can be abbreviated to **pre-tax profit** and is the most frequently quoted measure of a company's profit, in the press and elsewhere.

The tax take

Next, the tax man has his cut. Companies pay **corporation tax** on their profits, after all other costs except dividends have been deducted. Tax rates change relatively frequently and examples can be soon outdated. For consistency we have taken a 35 per cent corporation tax rate throughout this book, except where specifically noted. By 1995 the standard corporation tax rate had, in practice, come back to 33 per cent. But the exact rate that companies pay on their profits will depend on a number of factors, including the proportion of profits earned overseas and various allowances that may be available. We have also ignored the fact that there is a lower rate of corporation tax that applies in practice to small companies like John Smith.

There is one further complexity of the **imputation** system of corporation tax that applies in Britain, and it has been additionally complicated by recent changes in the tax rules. The tax the company pays includes **basic rate income tax** paid on behalf of shareholders on the dividends they receive. Again, in our examples we have standardized on a basic income tax rate of 25 per cent and a higher rate of 40 per cent which were – as it happens – the rates applying in 1995, though by that point there was also a lower 20 per cent rate that applied to a small first slice of individuals' incomes.

Shareholders who are not liable for tax – pension funds or pensioners on a very small income, say – can claim back some of the tax paid on their behalf by the company on its dividends. At the other extreme, shareholders who are liable for tax at the higher rate (40 per cent in 1995), have to pay the extra on top. But the dividend cheque the shareholder receives is for an amount from which basic rate tax is deemed to have been deducted. And it includes a **voucher** for part of the tax that has been paid, which the shareholder uses to claim it back if he is not liable.

This income tax paid on behalf of the shareholders is known as **advance corporation tax** (**ACT**) and because it forms part of the company's corporation tax bill, the system means that the total tax paid by the company is not normally affected by the amount of its profits it pays out as dividends. If it pays out nothing, the 35 per cent tax on its profits will all be **mainstream corporation tax**. If it pays dividends, the tax charge on profits will still be 35 per cent, but part of this tax is ACT: basic rate income tax paid on behalf of shareholders and then offset against the company's corporation tax charge.

Equity earnings, dividends and retentions

The **profit after tax attributable to members** or **net profit** is much what it says. Provided there are no further deductions, it belongs to the shareholders or owners of the company and may be referred to as **equity earnings**. But it is up to the company to decide, with the approval of its shareholders, how much of this profit is to be paid out as dividends and how much should be kept in the business to help finance its expansion. Most companies in their early stages need all the money they can get and tend to keep most of the profit in the business. In the case of John Smith & Co the company has decided to pay out just under a third of its profits – £4,000 – as dividends and to 'plough back' the remaining £9,000 which is therefore described as **retained earnings** or **retentions**. The amount of cash a company has available and the amount it needs to retain for the business will affect the dividend decision, which does not depend solely on the level of profits earned. Sometimes shareholders are given the chance of taking their dividend in shares rather than cash (a **scrip dividend** – see Chapter 9). See also **foreign income dividend** in the glossary.

Remember, the £9,000 of retained earnings belongs to the shareholders just as much as the £4,000 they actually receive as dividends, which is why it was shown in the balance sheet as part of shareholders' funds, under the heading of **revenue reserves** or **profit and loss account reserve**.

The £4,000 paid as dividends is divided equally among the 40,000 £1 shares in issue. Normally, the dividend is expressed as an amount (in pence) per share. In this case the dividends are equal to 10p net per ordinary share. However, returns on investments are almost always expressed **gross** (before tax) rather than **net** (after tax) to allow comparisons between them. What the individual tax-payer ends up with in his pocket is another matter, depending on his tax status.

So what sum before tax would be equivalent to 10p after basic rate tax? This is where recent changes to the tax system have complicated matters. These changes may prove to be a temporary stage in the evolution of the tax system, so we need to look at them briefly but not necessarily assume that they will endure.

In the past, the shareholder who was not liable to tax (like a pension fund) could claim back the whole of the tax paid on dividends on his behalf by the company. The company deducted income tax at 25 per cent, the pension fund shareholder could claim back 25 per cent. Thus a 10p net dividend would have been worth 13.3p gross because 13.3p is the figure before tax that would leave you with 10p after 25 per cent tax. The shareholder had a 25 per cent **tax credit** and, if he was not liable to tax, could claim back 3.3p on his 10p dividend. But by 1995 things had changed. Companies still had to deduct income tax on dividends at 25 per cent. But non-tax-paying shareholders could claim a credit of only 20 per cent. Thus, to find the gross equivalent of a net dividend, we have to work out what figure before tax would give 10p after tax at a rate of 20 per cent. The answer is 12.5p, so the pension fund shareholder in 1995 could claim back only 2.5p on his 10p dividend.

Minor complexities

The figures shown for John Smith & Co are obviously simplified. They illustrate the main figures on which the investment ratios explained later are based. But a few technicalities must be mentioned briefly.

If John Smith has **interests in associated companies** or **related companies** (companies which are not subsidiaries, but where it has a significant shareholding – see Chapter 5) it will show as a separate item its proportionate share of the profits of these companies and include them in the pre-tax profit figure.

The profit after tax will not always be the same thing as the **profit attributable to ordinary shareholders** or equity earnings. First, the company may have to make a deduction for **minority interests** or **outside shareholders' interests**. These arise where a parent company controls subsidiary companies but does not own all the shares of all of them. Suppose John Smith had a subsidiary called Super Stampings. Smith holds 70 per cent of the Stampings shares, and the original founders of Stampings have held on to the other 30 per cent. So 30 per cent of the profits of Stampings belongs to these **minority shareholders**. Smith includes the whole of the Stampings profits in its own operating profit figure, but makes a deduction after tax for the amount of the net profit of Stampings belonging to the minority holders.

Secondly, the company may have **preference shares** in issue (see Chapter 5). In this case the dividends on the preference shares must be deducted from the net profits. Both minority interests and preference dividends must be allowed for before arriving at the net profits or earnings that belong to Smith's ordinary shareholders.

Thirdly, the aim of any investment commentator is to assess a company's earning power, present and future. This means he may need to adjust the published profit figures to exclude 'one-off' items that distort the profits in a particular year. Again, a little history helps to explain the position. In the past, these items usually appeared under the heading of **exceptional items** or **extraordinary items**. They could include items such as costs incurred in closing down a subsidiary business or windfall profits on the sale of a surplus factory. Neither item would have been a normal feature of the company's trading.

Exceptional items were added or subtracted in the published accounts **above the line**: before reaching a pre-tax profit figure. Extraordinary items did not affect the published pre-tax profits or published earnings but were deducted **below the line** after striking a **net profits after tax** figure. What was 'exceptional' and what was 'extraordinary' was a matter for some debate. What often happened in practice was that companies treated favourable items such as windfall profits as 'exceptional' and therefore included them in published pre-tax profits. Unpleasant one-off items such as factory closure costs were more likely to be treated as 'extraordinary' and deducted after tax where they would not be so easily spotted.

But this form of **window-dressing** did not escape the accounting authorities and by 1995 a new accounting standard, **FRS 3**, was in force which obliged companies to treat virtually all one-off items as 'exceptional' and add or subtract them before arriving at pre-tax profits and earnings per share. While this remedied the earlier abuses, it also resulted in earnings that were sometimes a lot more volatile and did not necessarily reflect a company's on-going earnings power. So, alongside the volatile **FRS 3 earnings**, investment analysts normally calculate an earnings figure for the company's on-going operations, which excludes the one-off items. Many companies themselves publish an on-going earnings figure – sometimes referred to as **headline earnings** – as well as the obligatory FRS 3 earnings.

The FRS 3 accounting standard also obliged companies to show the division of their profits between continuing operations, profits from new businesses acquired during the year and profits from businesses that were subsequently closed or sold.

Accounting systems and inflation accounting

The accounts we have looked at are prepared according to the **historical cost convention**. This is the traditional way accounts are prepared and is the form required for most taxation and legal purposes. It means that most items – particularly fixed assets and stocks – are normally shown at what they originally cost, less provisions for depreciation or other necessary write-offs. The main exception is that properties are sometimes re-valued, with the new values included in the accounts.

In a period of high inflation, historical cost accounting may be misleading. Plant and equipment will cost more to replace than was paid for it originally. Stocks of raw materials will cost more when they have to be replaced.

To overcome this problem, various forms of **inflation accounting**, including **replacement cost accounting**, have been developed to supplement or replace historical cost accounts. Before reaching a profit figure, deductions will be made for the higher costs of replacing fixed assets and stocks (there are other adjustments, but these are usually the most important). The result for most companies is that profits will be lower than those shown under the historical cost convention. You will see references in the press to inflation accounting. But with the lower rates of inflation prevailing in the 1990s, some of the steam has gone out of the debate on the merits of different accounting systems. The accounting authorities have, however, been examining the possibility of requiring companies to show more items in their accounts at present values and fewer at historical cost.

4

The investment ratios

After a first look at the main accounting items, we can see how they translate into comment on a company's standing and prospects. The figures are used in two main ways to produce the ratios on which investment judgement is often based. Take an example:

'Following the rights issue in July last year, Super Silicon has £4m in cash or near-cash form to see it through the planned expansion programme, and borrowings as a percentage of shareholders' funds are down to 14 per cent.'

This makes it clear that Super Silicon is unlikely to run out of cash (which is a good thing) and that its gearing is low (which is probably also a good thing). What it does not do is to tell you whether the shares look cheap or expensive at their current level. Next take this:

'With the benefit of interest on the proceeds of last year's rights issue, Super Silicon should achieve earnings of 12p per share on the enlarged capital. With the shares at 120p this suggests a prospective price earnings ratio of 10, which is well below the sector average'.

The difference is that the second piece does not merely comment on Super Silicon's prospects. It relates these prospects to the market price of the shares so that readers can form a view on whether the shares are cheap or expensive.

Two types of financial ratio

An investment is only a good investment if you buy it at the right price. Super Silicon may be a superb company. Marks &

Spencer and Sainsbury are both superb companies and have proved it over many years. This does not mean, however, that their shares are always a good buy. As with anything else, there are times when you could pay too much even for the best – though it is obviously better to pay too much for something that is intrinsically good than for a load of rubbish.

So there are two layers of **financial ratios** applied to companies: the ones which tell us something about the operations and health of the company itself and the ones which relate the company's performance to the price you would have to pay for the shares.

Profit margins

First, let's look at the company itself. Look again at the profit & loss account for John Smith & Co. It is making a profit, but how can that profit be quantified in such a way that it could be compared with the profit performances of other companies? One of the more common measures is the **profit margin**. If we take the pre-tax profits of £20,000 and the turnover of £200,000, it is clear that 10 per cent of what the company gets for its products after all costs and overheads have been paid is profit. So the **pre-tax profit margin** is 10 per cent. This figure does not mean a great deal by itself. But if we compared it with other companies in the same field, it could be informative.

Assuming there is another paperweight manufacturer, and that it earns a pre-tax margin of only 6 per cent, we might reckon that John Smith & Co is the more successful company. If the following year's accounts show that John Smith's profit margin has increased to 11.5 per cent, we might deduce that it is strengthening its competitive position still further. If, on the other hand, turnover has doubled to £400,000 but the profit margin is down to 9 per cent, it might seem that John Smith has decided to sacrifice a bit of profitability in order to increase its turnover – possibly by reducing prices or offering bigger bulk discounts. If turnover had dropped to £180,000 and profits were down to £9,000 (a pre-tax margin of only 5 per cent) it would be clear that something had gone wrong: possibly the competitors had hit back with lower prices themselves and made a big dent in John Smith's business.

No ratio on its own will give the full picture, and it can be dangerous to jump to conclusions. But taken together with other indicators from the accounts, and with whatever else we can learn about the company, they can provide valuable clues.

Income gearing

The next ratio to look at is the **gearing** or in this case **income gearing**. How much of the company's operating profit goes to pay interest charges? John Smith produces an operating profit of £24,000, and £4,000 of this goes in interest charges. This is important because the company has to pay the interest whatever profits it makes. Income gearing is normally calculated by expressing the interest charge as a proportion of the profit before interest is deducted: in this case, £4,000 as a proportion of £24,000 or 16.7 per cent. It can be expressed in slightly different ways, but the principle is the same.

At all events, John Smith's income gearing is fairly low, and to see the full significance of gearing we need a more extreme example. Take a company whose profit and loss account looks like this:

	£
OPERATING PROFIT:	100,000
less:	
INTEREST PAID	50,000
leaving:	
PRE-TAX PROFIT	50,000

Assume that the company does not increase or reduce its borrowings and that interest rates remain unchanged. Assume also that the company increases its operating profit by 50 per cent to £150,000. The profit & loss account then looks like this:

	£
OPERATING PROFIT:	150,000
less:	
INTEREST PAID	50,000
leaving:	
PRE-TAX PROFIT	100,000

So for an increase of only 50 per cent in operating profit, pre-tax profits have risen by 100 per cent. Since the profits, after tax has been deducted, will belong to the owners of the company, the gearing is working very much in favour of the shareholders. But do the same sum assuming a 50 per cent fall in operating profits:

	£
OPERATING PROFIT:	50,000
less:	
INTEREST PAID	50,000
leaving:	
PRE-TAX PROFIT	NIL

It has only taken a 50 per cent fall in operating profit to wipe out completely the profits that belong to the shareholders. If operating profits fell by more than 50 per cent, the company would be making losses.

The appropriate level of gearing will vary between companies in different fields. But as a general rule, high gearing might be appropriate for a company whose income is very stable and on a rising trend: a property company deriving its income from rents on good commercial buildings, for example. It would not be appropriate for a company whose profits are liable to shoot up one year and down the next.

Effect of changing interest rates

One final point about income gearing. It is not simply that a company's operating profits can shoot up or down. The interest charge could vary up or down as the general level of **interest rates** changes. This is why you have to look more closely at a company's borrowings. Has it borrrowed its money long-term at a **fixed rate of interest** (in which case the interest charge will not be affected if interest rates rise or fall)? Or are its borrowings at **variable** or **floating** rates of interest, which will change with general movements in interest rates?

In the example we have taken, a doubling of the rate of interest the company has to pay would be just as serious as a

CHEMICALS

	Notes	Price	+ or –	1995 high	1995 low	Mkt Cap£m	Yld Gr's	P/E
AGA SKr	□	£7$\frac{13}{32}$	+$\frac{7}{8}$	£7$\frac{13}{32}$	£5$\frac{3}{4}$	817.0	2.6	Φ
Akzo Fl	□	£74$\frac{21}{32}$	–1$\frac{1}{8}$	£76$\frac{13}{32}$	£65$\frac{13}{32}$	3,452	3.8	Φ
Albright & Wilson	♣Lv□	187	....	188	154	586.2	4.0	Φ
Allied Colloids	✦†h□	132	–$\frac{1}{2}$	135	109	697.5	2.3	18.6
Amber Ind	✦†	783	....	785	780	30.6	3.4	15.5
BASF DM	□	£136$\frac{29}{32}$	–3$\frac{1}{2}$	£143$\frac{25}{32}$	£120$\frac{23}{32}$	8,002	3.3	–
BOC	✦§♣v□	792xd	+$\frac{1}{2}$	798	689	3,793	3.9	16.4
BTP	✦♣F□	276	....	*303	236	440.2	4.9	15.6
Bayer DM	□	£157$\frac{13}{16}$	–1$\frac{1}{32}$	£160$\frac{13}{32}$	£141$\frac{9}{32}$	10,937	3.7	–
Brent	✦♣v□	117	+$\frac{1}{2}$	118	101	79.1	4.5	16.2
British Vita	✦♣□	266	+1	266	210	579.6	3.6	17.8
Cambridge Iso $	✠	41	....	52	30	5.36	–	Φ
Canning (W)	✦♣q□	217xd	+3	217	184	61.6	4.3	–
Cementone	♣v	39	....	46	34	8.58	4.5	17.8
Warrants		12	....	17	11	0.10	–	–
Courtaulds	✦qv□	480	–1$\frac{1}{2}$	489$\frac{1}{2}$	401	1,934	4.1	18.5
Croda	✦qv□	364xd	....	387$\frac{1}{2}$	320	469.8	3.1	17.2
Doeflex	✦♣v	196xa	–4	200	125	20.8	3.4	16.7
Engelhard $		£25$\frac{5}{8}$	–$\frac{19}{32}$	£26$\frac{3}{4}$	£13$\frac{31}{32}$	2,455	1.2	31.6
European Colour	✦♣F□	87	....	*90	58	33.7	2.4	25.2
Gibbon	✦✠	121	....	122	114	11.0	5.7	11.1
Hickson	✦♣v□	129xd	–1	145	120	226.9	4.8	12.3
Hoechst DM	□	£129$\frac{15}{16}$	–7$\frac{17}{32}$	£143$\frac{21}{32}$	£123$\frac{27}{32}$	7,683	4.0	–
Holliday Chemical	✦♣v□	219	....	220	190	227.5	2.9	15.6
ICI	✦v□	790	+3	796$\frac{1}{2}$	660	5,719	4.4	35.3
Inspec	✦qv□	256xa	....	*258	188$\frac{1}{4}$	297.7	2.0	23.2
Kalon	✦♣v□	139#	....	139	97$\frac{1}{2}$	186.1	4.1	13.5
Laporte	✦♣□	755	–3	763	620	1.449	3.7	16.4

Table 4.1 Share price information. Source: *Financial Times.*

halving of its operating profits. So **high income gearing** based on variable-rate loans can be dangerous in a period of sharply rising interest rates. When interest rates do change dramatically, investment analysts and the press tend to comb the gearing statistics for companies that will suffer badly from a rise in interest rates or benefit from a reduction. But nowadays they need to be a little careful. The company might have bought a **cap** which sets a top limit on the interest rate it pays (see Chapter 15).

Earnings per share

The next calculation concerns the **profit after tax** or **net profit**. In the case of John Smith & Co, this is the same thing as **net profit after tax attributable to members** or **available for ordinary shareholders** or **equity earnings**. Again, it is not very useful in isolation, though in subsequent years we can chart its rise or fall. But the key information is the amount of profit the company is making for each share in issue. And to get at this we simply divide the net profit by the number of shares in issue; the result is normally expressed in pence. John Smith has 40,000 shares, for which it earns £13,000 or 1,300,000 pence. This works out at 32.5p for each share.

This 32.5p is the company's **earnings per share** or **eps** and its rise or fall from year to year is an important measure (perhaps the most important measure) of how good a job the company is doing for its shareholders. Why is it more important than the simple profits figure? Again, an example helps.

Suppose John Smith & Co decided to take over another company exactly similar to itself, in exchange for shares. It creates 40,000 new shares and swaps them for shares in the company it is taking over. The enlarged John Smith now has combined net profits of £26,000 (its own £13,000, plus £13,000 from its acquisition). Its net profits have therefore doubled, which looks impressive. But the number of John Smith shares in issue has also doubled to 80,000. Divide the £26,000 net profits by the 80,000 shares and you get earnings per share of 32.5p. In the short run at least, a John Smith shareholder is no better off.

When looking back over a company's profit record it is easy to miss the fact that much of the growth might have come from **acquisitions** or issues of additional shares for cash. But look at the record of earnings per share and you have a far better picture of whether the company is really increasing the amount of profit it earns for shareholders.

Writers tend to talk of **internal growth** or **organic growth** for the profits growth the company generates from its existing activities and **growth by acquisition** or **external growth** for increases in profit resulting from the purchase of other businesses.

Dividends per share

The figure for the cost of dividends – £4,000 in the case of John Smith – is also normally expressed as an amount per share. Divide it by the 40,000 shares in issue and you get a figure of 10p per share. This, remember, is the **net dividend per share**, because income tax at the basic rate of 25p in the pound (at 1995 tax rates) has been paid. As we saw earlier, to find the **gross dividend** you **gross up** the net dividend. In other words, you calculate what figure before tax would give you 10p after tax.

And this, remember, is where recent tax changes have introduced a complication. Though the company has to pay income tax of 25 per cent on dividends on behalf of share-holders, in 1995 shareholders could only claim tax back at a rate of 20 per cent. So at this point, 20 per cent was the appropriate rate for grossing up. Since the net dividend of 10p is eighty hundredths of the figure you are looking for, you multiply the 10p by a hundred and divide the result by 80 (or alternatively you simply divide 10p by 0.80). The result, in any case, is 12.5p. This gross dividend is the one on which yield calculations will be based.

Dividend cover

Remember, too, that it is up to the directors to decide what proportion of profit is paid out as dividend, though shareholders have to approve the decision. In this case £4,000 has been paid out of a net profit of £13,000 available for the ordinary shareholders. **Dividend cover** is thus 3.25 times – this is the result of dividing the £13,000 available profit by the £4,000 paid out. There are other more complex and strictly more accurate ways of calculating it, but this will suffice to illustrate the principle. Dividend cover is an important measure of the safety of the dividend – the more strongly it is covered, the less chance that the company will have to reduce or **pass** (drop altogether) its payment if profits fall. In practice, companies do sometimes continue to pay a dividend even if they are temporarily making losses – it then comes out of **reserves** (see below). But they cannot do so indefinitely. The figure for dividend cover also gives an indication of the maximum dividend a company could have paid if it had distributed all of its profits.

Retained profit and cash flow

The final item is **retained profit** of £9,000. This is money **ploughed back** into the business. But the **depreciation** (£3,000 in the case of John Smith) is also money ploughed back into the business, though it is ploughed back to allow for the gradual wearing-out of plant and equipment. The term **cash flow** is frequently used for the combination of depreciation and retained profits, since both represent money that is retained in the company out of its profits and can be used for any of its various needs. If you know John Smith will need to spend £10,000 on new plant and equipment over the next year, you might look at its cash flow to see if the company can cover this **capital expenditure** from the money it is generating internally. With a cash flow of £12,000, it can – though it will probably need further money for additional **working capital** (to finance higher levels of stocks, and so on).

These sums are a little rough and ready. With the requirement for companies to publish a **cash flow statement** each year in addition to a profit and loss account, it is now possible to look in more detail at their cash-generating ability. A cash flow statement starts with the cash a company generates from its operating activities. There is then a section 'returns on investments and servicing of finance' where the company knocks off the cash paid out in the form of interest charges and dividends to shareholders and adds any cash it receives by way of interest or dividends. Then comes a section for taxation where the company knocks off the cash paid out as corporation tax or overseas tax. If all these deductions do not exceeed the cash generated, you know at least that the company is generating cash rather than bleeding cash on its revenue operations.

Next in the cash flow statement comes a section 'investing activities'. This shows the cash paid out to acquire additional fixed assets, investments and possibly new businesses, and also any cash brought in by the sale of assets or businesses. This enables you to see whether the cash generated by the company was sufficient to cover its new investment as well as its cash operating costs. If it was, there will be a 'net cash inflow before financing'. If not, there will be a 'net cash outflow before financing'. Next, there is a section on 'financing' which shows cash raised during the year from issue of new shares or loans and cash paid out to repay existing loans. To round off the picture, the company shows how the amounts it holds in the form of cash or near-cash have increased or reduced during the year. These detailed cash flow statements – taken together with the picture that the balance sheet gives – have become a very useful tool in analysing the financial health of a company. If they show a big cash outflow, the investment analyst will look closely at the reasons. Investment yardsticks relating to cash flow – such as **cash earnings per share** – are used occasionally, but are less common than yardsticks related to profits.

Stockmarket ratings

The next stage is to take some of the figures we have worked out and relate them to the price of the company's shares in the stockmarket. Assume, for this purpose, that John Smith's shares are quoted on the stockmarket and that the current market price is around 300p. This market price is determined by the balance of buyers and sellers in the stockmarket and has nothing to do with the nominal or par value of the shares, nor with the amount of money subscribed for them originally by the founding shareholders – more of this later.

Yield

An investor who bought a share for 300p would stand to get a dividend equivalent to 12.5p gross or an initial return of about 4.2 per cent on his outlay (12.5 as a percentage of 300). This is the current **yield** on the shares and it will change slightly each time the share price changes on the stockmarket, which will be frequently. It will also change when the other component of the equation – the dividend – changes, though this will obviously not happen so often. The formula to calculate a dividend yield is simply:

$$\frac{\text{Gross dividend per share}}{\text{Share price}} \times 100$$

What is the significance of the yield? Clearly, it gives the investor an indication of the income return he might expect on his shares. An investor mainly concerned with income might select **high-yielding** shares. And it is one of the characteristics on which one company can be compared with another. But as such it is an imperfect instrument.

In theory, a **low yield** should suggest a fast-growing company and a **high yield** would indicate a company that is probably not going to increase its profits very fast or a company that carries an above-average risk. Investors are prepared to accept a low income today if they think the income will rise rapidly in the future as the company earns larger profits and pays higher dividends. If the dividends are not going to rise much, they will want a higher yield today.

The theory holds good up to a point. Unfortunately, it is completely arbitrary how much of its profit a company pays out as dividend. One cynical financial journalist habitually defines a dividend yield as 'five clowns sitting round a boardroom table'. And because the dividend is arbitrary, the dividend yield is an imperfect way of comparing two companies. Look at John Smith again. At 300p the shares yield 4.17 per cent on the 12.5p gross dividend. But out of its profits John Smith might quite easily decide to pay a dividend of twice as much: 25p gross. In this case the yield would be 8.33 per cent if the share price were still 300p. Yet it is the same company, earning the same profits.

Price-earnings ratio

To overcome this problem when comparing one company with another, there is another measure which is not affected by the dividend decision. It is the **price-earnings ratio** or **PE ratio**. Whereas a dividend yield is a fact, though an imperfect comparison tool, a PE ratio is a theoretical concept but much more useful for comparisons. In essence, it is a way of measuring how highly investors value the earnings a company produces. It is derived by dividing the **earnings per share** or **eps** figure into the market price of the shares. If John Smith has earnings per share of 32.5p and the market price is 300p, the shares are on a PE ratio of 9.2 (300 divided by 32.5). Other common ways of saying the same thing are: 'the shares sell at 9.2 **times earnings**' or 'the shares are on a **multiple of** 9.2'.

Why is this relevant? The thinking goes something like this. The amount a company earns determines ultimately what dividend it will be able to pay. If its earnings are growing, there is a good chance that dividends will rise in step. Earnings which are likely to grow fairly fast are therefore more valuable than static earnings, because they point to higher income in the future. Thus, in relation to what a company currently earns, investors will pay more for the shares if they think the earnings will rise rapidly. The investor is buying the right to a future flow of income and what he is prepared to pay today depends on what income he thinks he will get in the future. The way of quantifying this is by relating the earnings per share to the share price.

High and low PE ratios

All else being equal, a **high PE ratio** suggests a growth company and a **low PE ratio** suggests a company with a more static profits outlook or a company in a high risk area. It is not quite as simple as this, because a high PE ratio could indicate a company which had suffered a sharp temporary profits fall (reducing the 'E' element of the PE ratio) whereas the share price (the 'P' element) had not fallen in step because investors expected earnings to recover the following year. But the principle holds good.

Nil and net PE ratios

When we come down to detail, there are several slightly different ways of calculating a PE ratio, though for practical purposes a reader of the financial columns does not have to bother too much with the variations. A **nil PE ratio** calculation ignores how much of its profit a company pays out as dividend. A **net PE ratio** takes account of the dividend distribution. Normally they both give the same answer, but in the case of a company paying large amounts of tax on profits earned overseas there can be a significant difference. It is not worth worrying about: where the difference is material, any comment will normally make this clear.

Share price tables

Most 'serious' papers and magazines which quote share prices will show a yield and PE ratio as well (the *Financial Times* and some other papers give quite a lot of additional information which we will come to in a moment). These figures will not always be worked out in exactly the same way. For example, the dividend used could be the total dividend the company

The investment ratios

paid for its last financial year (the **historical dividend**). It could be the sum of the last two half-yearly payments (perhaps the last year's final and the current year's interim). Or it could be the dividend the company has forecast for its current year (the **forecast** or **prospective dividend**). Hence the terms **historical**

FT - SE Actuaries Share Indices — The UK Series

	May 30	Day's chge%	May 26	May 25	May 24	Year ago	Div. yield%	Net cover	P/E ratio	Xd adj. ytd	Total Return
FT-SE 100	3309.9	......	3311.1	3328.2	3327.3	2970.5	4.16	2.00	14.99	65.78	1290.56
FT-SE Mid 250	3642.6	......	3642.0	3651.6	3623.5	3564.3	3.56	1.83	19.18	52.81	1393.52
FT-SE Mid 250 ex Inv Trusts	3651.0	......	3651.0	3657.7	3626.2	3571.6	3.70	1.89	17.88	54.20	1395.26
FT-SE-A 350	1645.8	......	1646.2	1653.7	1650.5	1506.7	4.03	1.97	15.77	30.72	1311.44
FT-SE-A 350 Higher Yield	1665.6	......	1665.0	1671.7	1666.0	1497.6	4.91	1.75	14.54	37.87	1095.50
FT-SE-A 350 Lower Yield	1624.9	-0.1	1626.5	1635.1	1634.7	1476.9	2.99	2.39	17.51	23.15	1087.28
FT-SE SmallCap	1857.19	......	1857.85	1858.82	1855.63	1877.54	3.29	1.62	23.45	27.62	1474.90
FT-SE SmallCap ex Inv Trusts	1836.28	......	1836.92	1835.69	1832.71	1856.39	3.48	1.69	21.19	28.78	1464.48
FT-SE-A ALL-SHARE	1627.94	......	1628.35	1635.32	1632.16	1501.22	3.97	1.95	16.18	29.90	1318.85

■ FT-SE Actuaries All-Share

	May 30	Day's chge%	May 26	May 25	May 24	Year ago	Div. yield%	Net cover	P/E ratio	Xd adj. ytd	Total Return
10 MINERAL EXTRACTION(24)	2850.31	-0.4	2862.31	2874.24	2899.97	2608.16	3.66	2.07	16.47	61.64	1177.26
12 Extractive Industries(7)	3744.52	-0.8	3775.37	3828.58	3861.63	3792.29	3.76	2.08	15.98	91.94	1060.34
13 Oil, Integrated(3)	2853.53	-0.4	2865.19	2871.72	2898.59	2550.35	3.77	2.16	15.31	61.83	1205.52
16 Oil Exploration & Prod(14)	2063.63	+0.3	2058.12	2063.11	2074.79	1921.10	2.40	0.66	78.61	31.57	1214.11
20 GEN INDUSTRIALS(278)	1957.81	-0.2	1961.13	1963.74	1961.71	1979.72	4.01	1.71	18.24	34.03	1025.81
21 Building & Construction(38)	1000.37	+0.3	997.78	998.07	987.91	1221.84	3.98	1.86	16.90	20.64	807.04
22 Building Matls & Merchs(31)	1825.62	-0.5	1835.58	1843.11	1836.66	1901.13	4.05	1.94	15.89	37.17	887.46
23 Chemicals(22)	2426.72	+0.1	2425.18	2432.95	2417.34	2437.43	3.91	1.53	20.86	44.29	1106.39
24 Diversified Industrials(18)	1863.84	-0.6	1874.47	1870.13	1880.10	1986.14	5.12	1.59	15.33	40.82	987.40
25 Electronic & Elect Equip(36)	2029.64	+0.4	2022.06	2012.68	2030.61	2017.81	3.59	1.94	17.97	14.72	1010.54
26 Engineering(72)	1964.31	+0.3	1958.82	1968.23	1959.32	1830.67	3.17	1.82	21.73	26.94	1149.44
27 Engineering, Vehicles(13)	2287.70	-0.3	2295.06	2285.58	2284.03	2239.99	4.00	0.54	57.33	47.96	1144.97
28 Paper, Pckg & Printing(27)	2971.72	-0.8	2995.96	3021.17	3003.81	2733.50	3.21	2.29	16.98	41.67	1194.41
29 Textiles & Apparel(21)	1669.38	+0.3	1663.81	1668.39	1649.96	1736.87	4.23	1.60	18.48	38.87	979.83
30 CONSUMER GOODS(93)	3083.76	......	3084.51	3092.40	3080.79	2604.24	4.24	1.78	16.56	67.78	1096.85
31 Breweries(18)	2395.21	+0.3	2387.50	2396.63	2377.39	2160.89	4.15	2.03	14.87	30.89	1106.21
32 Spirits, Wines & Ciders(10)	2743.23	......	2743.38	2755.22	2758.13	2895.21	4.32	1.86	15.58	77.07	954.45
33 Food Producers(24)	2464.12	+0.1	2460.90	2463.80	2458.09	2218.91	4.12	1.97	15.38	55.78	1073.17
34 Household Goods(10)	2589.00	-0.3	2597.09	2607.81	2610.57	2474.63	3.55	0.98	35.99	54.80	958.82
36 Health Care(17)	1738.86	-0.2	1742.63	1745.77	1744.51	1660.60	2.82	0.93	47.73	24.09	1030.14
37 Pharmaceuticals(12)	3811.25	-0.2	3817.19	3818.67	3795.43	2670.15	4.07	1.62	18.96	69.31	1244.82
38 Tobacco(2)	4136.76	+0.1	4140.68	4172.79	4153.19	3431.14	5.48	1.90	11.99	131.29	979.08
40 SERVICES(229)	2027.99	+0.2	2024.07	2029.15	2022.45	1923.09	3.29	2.13	17.87	32.12	1022.01
41 Distributors(32)	2577.91	+0.1	2575.33	2580.53	2577.41	2827.96	3.72	1.99	16.93	46.57	918.96
42 Leisure & Hotels(29)	2333.21	+0.2	2329.00	2329.40	2312.98	2073.38	3.35	1.71	21.83	37.23	1177.55
43 Media(43)	2977.50	+0.2	2972.56	2989.52	2989.09	2930.95	2.65	2.34	20.20	51.41	1055.86
44 Retailers, Food(16)	2016.92	+1.4	1989.33	1990.96	1964.54	1549.55	3.44	2.44	14.87	35.45	1240.26
45 Retailers, General(44)	1658.21	-0.2	1660.92	1661.62	1660.76	1654.20	3.40	2.15	17.13	27.38	917.82
48 Support Services(37)	1617.21	+0.8	1604.62	1608.49	1610.55	1588.41	2.72	2.53	18.17	14.71	1000.32
47 Transport(21)	2261.62	-0.8	2279.02	2295.34	2294.47	2299.59	3.86	1.87	17.37	29.32	905.26
51 Other Services & Business(7)	1251.18	-0.3	1254.52	1257.14	1254.05	1194.71	3.63	1.24	27.68	12.40	1096.86
60 UTILITIES(37)	2368.01	-0.1	2369.82	2388.30	2378.90	2175.18	4.66	1.87	14.32	20.45	938.07
62 Electricity(17)	2249.71	......	2249.51	2261.81	2237.60	2099.54	4.58	2.78	9.83	19.89	962.77
64 Gas Distribution(2)	1981.63	+0.3	1975.36	1975.60	1969.21	1857.06	6.05	0.65	31.70	66.79	962.78
66 Telecommunications(5)	2053.67	+0.1	2051.61	2080.41	2094.39	1929.31	4.13	1.47	20.63	0.13	891.35
68 Water(13)	1939.86	-1.2	1963.21	1964.32	1915.62	1682.02	5.11	2.73	8.96	18.85	996.38
69 NON-FINANCIALS(681)	1749.76	-0.1	1750.79	1756.50	1753.74	1626.65	3.95	1.88	16.82	30.11	1272.58
70 FINANCIALS(117)	2390.76	+0.1	2388.29	2408.33	2399.38	2084.36	4.44	2.32	12.11	61.91	982.02
71 Banks, Retail(9)	3180.15	-0.1	3184.02	3223.61	3220.72	2677.16	4.33	2.91	9.91	90.64	988.53
72 Banks, Merchant(8)	3275.72	-0.2	3280.91	3286.71	3267.30	2788.98	3.53	1.90	18.62	56.32	1012.85
73 Insurance(26)	1347.31	+0.9	1335.43	1341.12	1335.69	1195.84	5.27	1.84	12.89	43.40	965.74
74 Life Assurance(6)	2691.89	+0.7	2671.93	2689.22	2674.75	2183.42	5.05	1.36	18.16	91.02	1080.11
77 Other Financial(22)	2022.15	-0.1	2023.79	2032.63	2026.80	1800.84	3.83	2.33	14.01	26.68	1108.00
79 Property(46)	1457.08	......	1457.73	1458.02	1436.26	1540.19	4.17	1.23	24.40	13.91	854.09
80 INVESTMENT TRUSTS(133)	2785.44	+0.1	2781.38	2804.42	2799.61	2737.51	2.34	1.02	52.23	28.32	951.27
89 FT-SE-A ALL-SHARE(911)	1627.94	......	1628.35	1635.32	1632.16	1501.22	3.97	1.95	16.18	29.90	1318.85
FT-SE-A Fledgling	1008.41	+0.1	1007.82	1006.46	1004.30	–	2.96	1.16	36.49	13.55	1022.53
FT-SE-A Fledgling ex Inv Trusts	1002.76	+0.1	1002.05	999.92	997.69	–	3.12	1.19	33.55	13.86	1017.17

Table 4.2 The FT-SE Actuaries UK share indices. Source: *Financial Times*.

dividend yield and **prospective dividend yield**. Be a bit wary of some prospective dividend yields, because they might also be based on the writer's own estimate of what the company is likely to pay, though possibly with a nod and a wink from the company itself; the context normally makes this clear.

You will also come across **historical PE ratios** and **prospective PE ratios**. The principle is the same. The first is based on actual earnings, the second on forecast or estimated earnings for a year for which the figures are not yet available.

Remember that yields and PE ratios move in opposite directions. A low yield and a high PE ratio probably indicate considerable expectations of growth. If the share price rises, the yield will fall further and the PE ratio will rise further. If the share price falls, the yield will rise and the PE ratio will fall. If a share price in a newspaper has **xd** after it, this stands for **ex-dividend**, and means that the buyer does not acquire the right to the recently-announced dividend. **Cum dividend** means the buyer gets the dividend.

The way in which share price information is presented evolves constantly and anything we say on this point is likely to be fairly rapidly outdated. But a glance at the *Financial Times* early in 1995 gives an idea of the range of information available. The *FT*'s Monday coverage differs from its coverage during the rest of the week since there have been no previous day's dealings and the opportunity is taken to give more background information. On Tuesdays to Saturdays the *FT* lists against each share its price at the previous day's market close (this is a **middle price**, remember) and its movement (if any) the previous day. Next comes an historical record of the highest and lowest price reached over the year (or year-and-a bit). The **market capitalisation** of the company comes next. This is the total value of all shares in the company, taken at the market price and is a useful guide to company size. You will see that it varies from less than £1m to many billions of pounds. Next come the basic investment yardsticks: gross yield and price-earnings ratio. Quite a bit of additional information is given in notes, and a hollow box by the company name means that it is one of the more actively traded stocks. Other symbols and accompanying notes give details of how you can get more information on some of the companies – it is worth noting the *FT*'s service for providing company reports.

On Monday the tables give the Friday closing price and the change over the week. This is followed by the amount of the net dividend, the dividend cover, the dates when dividends were last paid and the last date the shares were declared **ex-dividend**. There is also an identification number you can use to get latest price information via a premium-charge telephone service.

Yield and PE ratio yardsticks

Not only are the yields and PE ratios of individual shares constantly changing. Average levels of PE ratio and yield change with the market cycle and investors' outlook. It is worth noting, incidentally, that where share prices in the past have risen to a level where the average PE ratio goes above 20 or so, a heavy fall in the market has often followed before too long. Thus, anything we say about PE ratios will be outdated even more rapidly than our comments on share price presentation, and it is the relative PE ratios rather than the absolute levels that we need to focus on.

For an idea of typical levels of yield and PE ratio, look at the table headed **FT-SE Actuaries Share Indices** in the *Financial Times*. It appears in the 'Companies & Markets' section of the paper. If you had been looking at a point early in 1995 you would have seen that the average PE ratio on the privatized water companies was a low 7.66 per cent and the average yield a fairly high 5.94 per cent. Water is a solid, safe earner, but unlikely in Britain to be one of the great growth industries of the future. Neither are investors looking for great growth from tobacco. The average yield on tobacco companies at this time was 5.69 per cent and the PE ratio 11.31. Compare this with the 20.81 average PE ratio and 2.53 per cent average yield on media companies at the same time. Investors were clearly looking for more growth here. But you have to be a little careful in your interpretation. In early 1995 much of British business was still struggling out of the effects of recession. Building and construction companies at that time were on an average PE ratio of close to 20. It was probably not so much that investors saw this as one of the great long-term growth areas. It was more that construction had suffered very severely in the recession and investors were looking for a recovery in earnings that would have the effect of bringing PE ratios down.

What we have looked at are only averages, and within each sector there will be a wide variation in the ratings of individual companies. Don't be thrown, incidentally, by an occasional rating that looks way outside the normal range. It could be, as we have seen, that profits have suffered a very temporary set-back. It could also be that the market thinks the company might be taken over and has chased the share price up way beyond the levels it could sustain on its own merits.

Share price indices

We have mentioned the **FT-SE Actuaries Indices**, but the question of share price measurement for the stockmarket as a whole needs a little more explanation. In the past the index that newspaper readers would have been most familiar with was the **FT 30-Share Index**, also known as the **Financial Times Ordinary Share Index**. The index, started in 1935 with a base of 100, is compiled from the share prices of 30 leading British companies and calculated as a geometric mean. It is biased towards major industrial and retailing companies – the traditional **blue chips** of the stockmarket – though now includes financial and oil stocks which have assumed greater import-ance. Its ups and downs reflect the mood of the market, but it would not be a good index against which to measure the per-formance of a typical investment **portfolio** ('portfolio' is simply the collective term for the shares an investor or a fund owns).

For this purpose the **FT-SE Actuaries Indices** are a great deal better. First, they reflect the movements of over 900 shares, comprising all companies with a market value above about £40m. Secondly, each company in the index is weighted according to its market value. A movement in the share price of a large company has more effect on the index than move-ment in a small one.

The **FT-SE Actuaries All-Share Index** (the **All-Share**) is the most representative of all, reflecting the full 900-plus com-panies. The **Non-financials Index** includes all except financial and property companies and investment trusts. These indices are in turn further broken down by **industrial sector**, so that there is a yardstick for, say, electronics companies, textiles or property concerns and by broader business groupings such as consumer goods and utilities. Not only do the indices give a measure of price movements but they also show average yields and PE ratios and a measure of the **total return** achieved by the constituent companies (total return combines share price movement with income received as dividend). On Saturdays additional information is published on the **highs** and **lows** for each sector.

But indices are a growth business and new ones are constantly being introduced in response to perceived needs. The **Financial Times-Stock Exchange 100-Share Index (FT-SE** or **Footsie** index) which started with a base of 1,000 at end-December 1983 reflects price movements of the 100 largest companies and because of the smaller number of companies it can be calculated in real time – it changes constantly throughout the day. It was initially introduced mainly as a basis for dealing in equity index options and futures (see Chapter 18) but is now probably the most widely quoted in reports of daily market performance. Then there is the **FT-SE Mid 250 Index**, launched in 1992, which comprises the next range of companies, immediately below the size that would qualify for the Footsie. The **FT-SE Actuaries 350 Index** combines the companies of the Footsie and the FT-SE Mid-250 and is a benchmark for companies in which the market is most liquid. The **FT-SE SmallCap** measures the performance of about 500 smaller companies, with a market value roughly between £40m and £250m. And to reflect the performance of the very small concerns – 700-plus companies with a market value below about £40m – there is the **FT-SE Actuaries Fledgling Index**.

Nor is London's international status forgotten. The *Financial Times* also publishes **FT Actuaries World Indices** of all major (and some minor) stockmarkets, expressed in terms of the local currency, of dollars, yen, deutschmarks and of sterling. There are also two purely European indices: the **FT-SE Eurotrack 100** which covers major continental European companies and the **FT-SE Eurotrack 200** which comprises continental European and British companies.

Journalists frequently refer to shares as cheap or expensive relative to their sector of the FT-SE Actuaries Indices. Movements in an index are frequently referred to in terms of **points**. If the FT 30-share index falls from 2,400 to 2,380 it has dropped 20 points and a point is also sometimes used to mean a 1p price movement in an individual share or a £1 movement for a gilt-edged stock. Why movements are not generally expressed more meaningfully as percentage changes is obscure – at least the *FT* does express movements in its All-Share and World indices in terms of percentages.

Matching the index

Institutional investors attempt to **beat the index** most relevant to their portfolios of shares, but on balance have difficulty in doing so. They control such large volumes of money that they find it difficult to buy adequate numbers of shares in some of the smaller companies represented, which often outperform those of their larger counterparts in certain market conditions.

Some of them do run portfolios which seek merely to match a particular index by buying the stocks which constitute the index in the same proportions as they are represented in the index, or by otherwise trying to mimic the performance of the index. It is more difficult than it sounds. But these **indexed portfolios** mean that when a large company such as British Telecom launches on the stockmarket, many institutions are bound to buy its shares in large quantities simply to maintain the balance of their portfolios.

Balance sheet ratios

The balance sheet can tell you a great deal about the financial health of a company, but it doesn't throw up convenient investment ratios in quite the same way as a profit and loss account. There's one possible exception – the net asset value – which we'll come to later. But there are a number of items an investment analyst or a financial journalist will check.

Borrowings and balance sheet gearing

Back to John Smith & Co. One of the first things to look at is the company's **gearing**: the relationship between the **borrowed**

money and the **shareholders' money** in the business. We've already touched on it briefly but now it can be reduced to a convenient formula.

The borrowings, in the case of John Smith, are the £8,000 bank overdraft and the £30,000 term loan, totalling £38,000. Trade creditors do not count as borrowings in this context, since they are not clocking up interest charges. The shareholders' money in the business is the £49,000 of **shareholders' funds**. The most common way of relating the two is to calculate **borrowings as a percentage of shareholders' funds** – a definition which can be a little confusing because it could suggest that borrowings are a part of shareholders' funds, which of course they are not.

In this case the £38,000 **gross borrowings** are equivalent to 77.6 per cent of the £49,000 figure for the shareholders' interest. This would be fairly high for an established stockmarket-listed company but by no means out of the ordinary for a private company. Sometimes the gearing is worked out on the **net borrowings** (borrowings less cash) instead. In this case the net borrowings are £33,000 after the £5,000 of cash in the bank is deducted and the ratio is 67.3 per cent.

The 'borrowings as a percentage of shareholders' funds' ratio, whether worked out on the gross borrowings or the net borrowings, is referred to as the **balance sheet gearing** to distinguish it from the **income gearing**: the relationship between profits and interest charges that was discussed in the context of the profit and loss account. Both can be useful in estimating whether a company is **over-geared** or **over-borrowed**. High balance sheet gearing matters rather less if a company is exceptionally profitable or if the borrowings are at a very low fixed rate of interest. John Smith is, as it happens, quite highly profitable so interest charges only take a small proportion of profits despite fairly high balance sheet gearing.

Bankers and other lenders always look for a **cushion** for the money they advance. In income terms the cushion is the level of profit out of which the company pays the interest charges. John Smith's profit would have to fall a long way before it was unable to pay its interest, so there is a comfortable cushion for the lender. In balance sheet terms, the cushion is the shareholders' funds. If the company starts losing money, it is the shareholders' funds that will be depleted first, so in John

Smith's case there is (on paper, at least) a reasonable margin before the lender might be at risk of losing his money.

Security for borrowings

The other thing a lender normally requires is **security** for his loan in the form of a **charge** over some or all of the assets of the company. The principle is similar to taking a mortgage on a home. If the borrower fails to keep up his interest and capital payments, the lender – the building society – can sell the house and recover its loan from the proceeds. With a company the charge may be a **fixed charge** on specific assets – its machinery or buildings – or may be a **floating charge** on all the assets of the business including the current assets. The lender has priority for repayment out of the proceeds of selling the assets over which he has a charge. The importance of this in practical terms is that a company, particularly a smaller company, may find it difficult to borrow further money when it does not have enough reasonably saleable assets to provide adequate security for the loan. And since banks will usually take a floating charge when they lend money to a business, the **unsecured creditors** (who are probably mainly the suppliers who have not yet been paid) come at the bottom of the creditors' pile when a company goes bust. They do, of course, still rank ahead of the shareholders.

John Smith's financial position

From John Smith's gearing and from our knowledge of the business we might deduce the following. The company is likely to expand further in the current year, which means it will need yet more money to finance higher levels of stocks and debtors (see below), and it may need to install additional machinery to meet the demand for its paperweights. It generated a cash flow of £12,000 last year and, assuming profits continue rising, the cash flow ought to be higher in the current year. But it is unlikely to be enough to provide all the money John Smith will need. It could probably increase its borrowings a little. But if it were a stockmarket-listed company, it would almost certainly be thinking of raising further equity capital by issuing additional shares for cash. This would reduce the gearing by increasing the proportion of shareholders' money in the business. And quite apart from bringing in money for the immediate needs, by increasing the size of the equity 'cushion' it also prepares the way for bringing in additional borrowed money in the future.

Remember that fast-growing companies tend to use up cash faster than they can generate it from their profits. The expansion means that they are having to tie up more and more cash in higher and higher levels of stocks and debtors: their **working capital** need rises rapidly. A company that expands too fast may be described as **overtrading** (trading beyond its financial resources). It can go bust simply because it runs out of cash to pay its bills, even though it may have been operating at an 'accounting' profit.

Investment analysts therefore check the accounts to see if a company has adequate resources to finance its business and whether it would be able to raise any additional money needed. In the short run, a **rights issue** to raise further money from the sale of shares (see Chapter 9) often depresses the price of the shares because it increases the number in issue.

While looking at John Smith's borrowings, we would also check whether they are long-term or short-term and whether

SHELL TRANSPORT
Oil and chemicals producer
Good value

Ord price: 720p	Market value: £23.9bn
Touch: 719-721p	1994-95 High: 758p Low: 621p
Gross divd yield: 4.7%	PE ratio: 16
Net asset value: 434p	Net debt: nil*

Year to 31 Dec	Turn-over £bn*	Net income £bn*	Stated Earnings per share (p)	Net Dividend per share (p)
1990	73.9	3.61	39.8	20.1
1991	74.4	2.40	25.0	20.9
1992	73.1	3.01	32.6	21.9
1993	83.7	3.00	33.0	24.0
1994	84.3	4.07	45.0	27.1
% Change +1	+36	+36		+13

* Royal Dutch/Shell Transport combined

Market makers: 20   Normal market size: 75,000
Last **IC** comment: 18 November 1994, page 55

Table 4.3 Company performance and the main investment yardsticks. Source: *Investors Chronicle.*

they are at fixed or variable rates of interest. The overdraft
has to be counted as short-term and the interest rate will be
variable. The term loan, we might learn from the notes, has to
be repaid over seven years, which would normally be classed
as 'medium-term'. The interest rate could be fixed or variable
– the notes should say. But nowadays you need to be a little
careful, because a large company may have borrowed floating-
rate money and **swapped** it for fixed-rate, or *vice versa*. It
could also have bought a **cap** or some other hedging instrument to limit its exposure to rising interest rates on
floating-rate borrowings (see Chapters 15 and 17). Companies
are getting rather better at giving detail of arrangements of
these kinds in the notes to their accounts, but you cannot
always rely on it.

Net assets per share

Next, look at the £49,000 figure for shareholders' funds: the
book value of the shareholders' interest in the company.
Often this value is expressed as an amount per share or a **net
asset value per share** (**NAV**). Divide the ordinary shareholders' funds by the number of ordinary shares in issue
(£49,000 divided by 40,000 shares) and you get £1.225 (or
122.5p as it is usually expressed). It corresponds, in this case
though not always, with the £1 the original investors subscribed for each share plus the 22.5p of retained profits
attributable to each share.

It is very important to grasp what this NAV figure means.
The £49,000 of shareholders' funds on which it is based is very
much an accounting figure and does not usually tell you anything much about the value investors are likely to put on the
company in the stockmarket, which normally depends far
more on the profits the company is capable of earning. First,
John Smith & Co has no intention of closing down the business, selling the assets, paying the debts and returning what is
left to shareholders. Even if it did, what was left would be
very unlikely to amount exactly to £49,000. The paperweight-
making machinery **stands in the books** at £27,000, but would a
buyer necessarily pay exactly £27,000 for a used paperweight-
making machine? It is highly unlikely. Would stocks of raw

materials and half-finished or finished paperweights actually bring in £50,000? Again, unlikely.

When a long-term investor buys shares, what he is really buying is the right to a flow of income (by way of dividend) in the future, and generally he is buying shares in companies which he hopes will provide a rising income. If the income rises there is a good chance that the capital value – the market value – of the shares he holds will rise too.

Some companies are capable of providing an increasing flow of earnings without owning anything much in the way of assets. A successful advertising agency, say, might rent the offices it operates from and hire its photocopiers, typewriters and other equipment. Apart from a few sticks of office furniture and whatever cash it had accumulated from its profits, it might own virtually nothing. Its 'assets' are the people who work for it, its reputation in the business and its client connections – items which do not normally appear in a balance sheet. Yet the stockmarket might put a high value on the shares purely because of the profit-earning potential. This is why a yardstick that relates to earnings rather than assets – the price earnings ratio – is the main one investors use.

Asset-rich companies

But there are certain types of company where the assets or a fair proportion of the assets can be reasonably accurately priced and easily sold. Companies whose main business is owning property, owning shares in other companies (**investment trusts** – see Chapter 21), or which have a lot of cash or investments in the balance sheet are the main examples. Others in this category are companies carrying on a trade which involves owning large amounts of property: some stores groups, hotel companies and breweries which own large numbers of pubs.

In these cases the **net asset value** can and does affect the price investors will pay for the shares in the stockmarket. The shares are commonly described as standing **at a premium to** (above) the net asset value, or **at a discount to** (below) the net asset value. The size of the premium or discount is expressed as a percentage. If XYZ Holdings has net assets per share (or an NAV) of 100p and the shares stand at 90p in the market, the shares are at a discount to assets of 10 per cent. If the market price is 108p, the shares stand at a premium to assets of 8 per cent. For taxation and other reasons, the shares of **property investment companies** and single-tier investment trusts normally stand at a discount to assets except at times of market euphoria.

Readily saleable assets are most important when takeovers are in the air. A company with high earnings but few assets may try to acquire an **asset-rich company** to give it more substance. And the company at the receiving end of the bid will argue (not always successfully) that the takeover price should be at least as high as the value of its assets.

Return on assets

This brings us to another commonly used ratio: a company's **return on assets**. It is a measure of the profits the company earns relative to the capital employed in the business. As such, it can be used as a measure of the efficiency of one company against another, though it needs using with care. And it is not specifically a stockmarket measure: it does not reveal anything about the return the company earns on shareholders' money. It measures the return on all money used, whether derived from loans or from the shareholders. A company such as our successful advertising agency, with very few assets, will be earning a very high return on capital employed, simply because very little capital is employed. The return on assets is used mainly to compare one company with another in the same or a similar business.

To calculate the return on assets you take the profit before tax and before the interest on longer-term debt and express it as a percentage of shareholders' funds (less goodwill) plus long-term loans, deferred tax and minorities (see Chapter 5).

The return on assets figure can sometimes provide useful clues for a **stockmarket predator**: a company on the look-out for other companies it might take over. Suppose a retail stores group which owns most of its shops is showing a return on assets of only five per cent. Clearly, it is not a very efficient trader: it could make this level of return simply by renting its shops to other retailers. It is earning very little profit from the trading operation. A predator might reckon he could take over the retail stores group and vastly improve the return it earned by supplying more retailing flair. And it might be possible to recoup part of the costs of the takeover by selling some of the properties or selling them and leasing them back (a **sale and leaseback** transaction – see Chapter 20).

5

Refining the figurework

There are a few more terms relating to company accounts that will crop up fairly frequently in the press commentary and the best way of illustrating what they mean is with another sample balance sheet (see opposite).

This time we have taken a more mature company: call it Jones Manufacturing. Its assets are in the millions rather than the thousands. It owns the buildings from which it operates: note the £3m item for properties included under fixed assets. And, partly because it has been ploughing back a proportion of its profits over many years, its shareholders' funds are a substantial £11m.

Goodwill

The first item that may be unfamiliar is the £1m entry against the heading **goodwill** which might also appear as **intangible assets**. There are two main ways in which this is likely to have arisen and the notes to the accounts should make this clear. First, the company might own trade marks or patents which are not physical or **tangible** assets like plant and buildings, but which have a value nonetheless. These might be classed under the general heading of goodwill or might be shown as intangible assets. Secondly, Jones Manufacturing might have purchased other businesses and paid more for them than the net value of the physical assets they owned. In this case, the difference between the price paid and the value of the net assets acquired might be accounted for as a **goodwill item**. The important point about goodwill is that investment analysts

Refining the figurework

Jones Manufacturing
Consolidated balance sheet at 31 December

	£'000	£'000
FIXED ASSETS		
Land and buildings	3,000	
Plant and machinery	5,600	
		8,600
GOODWILL		1,000
INVESTMENTS IN ASSOCIATED COs		3,000
CURRENT ASSETS		
Stocks	5,000	
Debtors	3,500	
Cash at bank	500	
	9,000	
CURRENT LIABILITIES		
(Creditors: amounts due within one year)		
Trade creditors	3,000	
Tax payable	600	
Dividend proposed	400	
Bank overdrafts	800	
	4,800	
NET CURRENT ASSETS		4,200
TOTAL ASSETS LESS CURRENT LIABILITIES		16,800
CREDITORS (AMOUNTS DUE IN MORE THAN ONE YEAR)		
Term loans	800	
9% Debenture stock 2004	2,800	
6% Convertible Loan Stock 2008	1,500	
		5,100
PROVISIONS FOR LIABILITIES AND CHARGES		500
NET ASSETS		11,200
MINORITY SHAREHOLDERS' INTEREST		200
JONES MANUFACTURING		
SHAREHOLDERS' INTEREST		11,000
Represented by:		
SHARE CAPITAL:		
Issued ordinary share capital		
(20p ordinary shares)	1,500	
Preference share capital		
(£1 shares)	500	
RESERVES		
Profit & loss account		
(revenue reserves)	5,400	
Share premium account	1,650	
Revaluation reserves	1,950	
SHAREHOLDERS' FUNDS		11,000

will normally exclude it when calculating a company's net asset value, which strictly ought to be expressed as **net tangible asset value**. And companies themselves tend to write off against their reserves the goodwill arising on acquisition. More of this later.

The next item is **investments in associated companies** or **interests in associates**; sometimes associates are also called **related companies**. The definition of an **associated company** is open to interpretation. But in general it would be a company which was not a subsidiary, but in which Jones Manufacturing had an interest amounting to between 20 per cent and 50 per cent of the share capital and over whose affairs it exerted some management influence. In other words, Jones Manufacturing does not hold the shares in the associate simply as an unrelated investment, as it might own a holding of government stock.

There is probably some trading relationship between Jones Manufacturing and its **associate**. The associated company might, say, be an important supplier of components to Jones, or it might be an important customer for Jones's products – in either case it could be of benefit to Jones to be able to exert some influence over the associate's affairs. In accounting terms, the interest in the associated company will normally appear in the balance sheet at a figure representing Jones Manufacturing's share of the net assets of the associate. If the associated company or companies had net assets of £10m and Jones Manufacturing owned a 30 per cent stake, the figure in Jones's balance sheet would be 30 per cent of £10m, or £3m. An interest in an associate is different from a mere **trade investment**: a shareholding in a company with which there is probably no particular management involvement or influence.

Varieties of debt

Jones Manufacturing's **sources of finance** are also more varied and a little more complex than those of Smith & Co. There is a bank overdraft, though small in relation to the company's size. But there are three types of medium-term or long-term debt under the heading of **creditors due in more than one year**. First comes the familiar term loan: again fairly small at £800,000.

The other two items – the **debenture stock** and the **convertible loan stock** – are in a different category of borrowings, because they are **securities** issued by the company rather than loans from a bank. Much as the government does when it borrows by issuing a gilt-edged stock, Jones Manufacturing has raised money by creating different forms of loan stock and selling them to investors: the familiar principle of issuing an 'IOU' note in return for cash. These stocks, once issued, will normally be traded in the stockmarket. Investors who paid cash to the company for them when first issued can either wait till the date they are due to be repaid by the company, or can sell them to other investors in the stockmarket. Both in this case pay a fixed rate of interest.

The **debenture stock** will probably be secured on specific assets of the company. Provided the assets are of good quality, it should thus be a safe form of investment for buyers. It is a long-term borrowing. It is not due for repayment until 2004, and when first issued it may have had a **life** of 25 or 30 years – possibly more.

The convertible loan stock is almost certainly an **unsecured loan stock**. It is not secured on the assets of the company, and to this extent it is a little less safe than the debenture. But its most important feature is that it is **convertible**. At some stage of its life, and probably right from the outset, it can be exchanged for ordinary shares according to a pre-arranged formula. This gives it some of the attributes of a loan and some of the attributes of an ordinary share, though in legal and accounting terms it is a loan. Until it is converted, it pays a fixed rate of interest like the debenture stock. Once it is converted into ordinary shares, the shares are identical to the other shares in issue and receive the same dividend.

If the stock is not converted into shares during the **conversion period**, it may revert to being a simple unsecured loan stock, paying the fixed rate of interest until it is eventually repaid in 2008. Whether or not holders of the stock exercise the right to convert it will depend on how successful Jones Manufacturing is. The **conversion terms** were probably pitched originally at a level somewhat above Jones Manufacturing's share price at the time of issue (the **conversion premium**). If the share price at the time had been 80p, the terms of the loan might have stipulated that £1 nominal of the loan could be nverted into one ordinary share, meaning that anyone who paid £100 for £100 nominal of the loan would be paying £1 for a share if he exercised his conversion rights. Five years later, if Jones had increased its profits and dividends at a good rate, the share price might have risen to, say, 180p. At this level there is clearly a value in the right to exchange £1 nominal of loan for a share worth 180p.

Because of this **conversion value**, the price of the convertible loan stock itself would have risen in the stockmarket. Investors would have been prepared to pay more than £100 for £100 nominal value of the loan, when they knew that each £1 nominal could be converted into a share worth 180p. The calculations that give the likely price of a convertible loan stock in the stockmarket, relative to the price of the ordinary shares, are quite complex. In general a convertible loan rises in value to reflect the rise in value of the ordinary shares, but rises at a slower percentage rate than the ordinary shares. On the other hand, it normally provides a higher and more secure yield than the ordinary shares, at least in the early years until the dividend on the ordinary shares catches up. For the company the main advantage of the convertible loan is that the interest rate it needs to pay will probably be lower than for an ordinary unsecured loan stock. Investors will accept the lower interest rate because of the possibility of capital gains if the share price rises and the market value of the convertible stock follows it. The convertible also represents a form of **deferred equity**. If the company had issued ordinary shares instead, its earnings and dividends would immediately be spread over a larger number of shares: the earnings would be **diluted** over the larger capital immediately.

Convertible stocks with considerably more complex features are also commonplace nowadays, particularly in the case of issues made through euromarket mechanisms (see Chapter 17) and you find preference shares (see below) that are convertible into ordinary shares as well as loans that are convertible. One particular type of convertible needs mentioning here: the **premium put convertible** which also surfaced in an even more tortuous form as the **convertible capital bond**.

The 'premium put' feature is an option for the investor which allows him to require the company to buy the stock back at a premium over its issue price after, typically, five years if the share price has not risen sufficiently to make conversion worthwhile. Take the example of a convertible capital bond issued by food group Sainsbury. The stock carried a low **coupon** of 5 per cent. But the investor could sell it back to the company at £133.28 per £100-worth after five years to take his total annual return to 10.26 per cent. The conversion price into Sainsbury shares was 262p but effectively the Sainsbury price had to rise to 349p to make conversion a better option than selling the stock back to the company at £133.28p for every £100 issued. As it happened, the Sainsbury share price rose rapidly and the stock was converted. Other companies such as the advertising group Saatchi & Saatchi found that a 'premium put' stock constituted a time bomb. If their trading fortunes turned down and the share price fell, investors would ask for the stock to be redeemed at a time when the company was least well placed to raise the money to redeem it.

The **premium put** feature appeals to euromarket investors who are generally bond-orientated rather than equity-orientated. The disadvantage for the issuer is that he is not sure when issuing the stock whether he is raising permanent capital or whether he will have to find the money to redeem the issue at a premium after a few years.

Diluting earnings and assets

By issuing the convertible loan, Jones Manufacturing can offset the interest cost (the cost of **servicing** the loan) against tax, whereas dividends on ordinary shares or on convertible preference shares would have to be paid out of taxed income. By the time the loan can be converted, earnings should have risen significantly and the company's asset value should also have risen. Investment analysts and journalists sometimes refer to **fully-diluted earnings per share** and **fully-diluted assets per share**. This means they have calculated what the earnings per share would be on the assumption the stock was converted and current earnings (adjusted for the disappearance of the interest charge on the convertible) were spread over the larger number of shares. They have also done the same sums for the NAV (see below). As we have seen, companies may issue convertible preference shares (see below) instead of convertible loan stocks. They convert into ordinary shares in much the same way, but the dividend on the convertible preference is not tax-deductible as the convertible loan stock interest is.

Provisions

There are two other unfamiliar items. The **provisions for liabilities and charges** of £500,000 has to be knocked off the assets figure before arriving at a net asset value. It may consist mainly of **deferred tax**, which is tax that might become payable in the future but is not yet a sufficiently certain liability to be provided for under current liabilities. It would also include sums the company had earmarked to meet certain known future costs, such as the cost of closing down or reorganising one part of the business.

Minority shareholders

The second item, **minority shareholders' interest**, was mentioned in Chapter 4. Where Jones does not own all the shares of all of its subsidiaries, this figure represents the value of the shares in these subsidiaries held by other parties. Since this value does not belong to the shareholders in Jones it has to be deducted before reaching a net asset value.

Capital commitments

Two further items which could affect the balance sheet in the future appear in the notes to the accounts but not in the accounts themselves. One is **capital commitments**. This is expenditure on assets which the directors have authorized or contracted for but which has not yet taken place. It can be useful in giving an idea of the company's investment plans and whether these would be covered by the cash flow.

Contingent liabilities

The other is **contingent liabilities**. Jones Manufacturing might provide a **guarantee** for the bank borrowings of one of its associated companies. Or there might be a legal case pending against Jones, in which the other side is claiming £500,000 of damages, though Jones denies liability. In both cases Jones does not expect any liability to arise, but it might. So the liabilities are not provided for in the accounts themselves but the company notes that they might arise in the future.

Preference shares

Back to the balance sheet itself. The make-up of shareholders' funds is also more complex than in the case of Smith & Co. First, Jones Manufacturing has two classes of share capital: **preference shares** as well as **ordinary shares**.

Companies with **preference share capital** often have it for historical reasons, though issues of preference shares (particularly convertible preference) have regained popularity in recent years. Various mutations of preference capital may also crop up in the financing of young businesses which are not quoted on a stockmarket and in the financing of management buy-outs (see Chapter 11). Preference shares usually pay a fixed dividend and in this respect are more like a loan stock than an ordinary share. But the dividend has to be paid out of profits which have borne tax, whereas interest on a loan stock is allowable against tax. Against this disadvantage, preference shares will not normally be counted in the **gearing** of a company whereas loan stocks will. And they are safer in that the company risks being closed down if it cannot pay interest on its loans whereas it could miss dividends on the preference shares without the same risk.

Preference shares are part of **shareholders' funds** but not part of **ordinary shareholders' funds**. They are **share capital**, but they are not **equity share capital**. They do not share in the rising prosperity of a company, because their dividend is fixed and does not increase with rising profits. But they are entitled to their dividend before the ordinary shareholders get anything, so the dividend is safer than that of an ordinary share. And if the company should be **wound up** (closed down), preference shareholders are normally entitled to be repaid the par value of their shares (usually but not necessarily £1) before the ordinary shareholders get anything. This is assuming there is something left after loans and all the other debts of the company – which rank before preference shares – have been repaid. Preference shares do not normally carry votes unless the dividend is **in arrears** (the payments have not been kept up).

One technicality you may come across occasionally: certain types of preference share issued by subsidiary companies rather than by the parent company, but guaranteed by the parent, may have more of the characteristics of a loan than of share capital and may need to be treated as a liability rather than as capital in the consolidated accounts.

Less usual types of share

We have only shown preference shares and ordinary shares, but there are various other less common forms of share capital that companies may issue. These are variations on the theme of equity or preference. **Deferred ordinary shares** probably do not **rank for dividend** until converted into ordinary shares at some future date. **Preferred ordinary shares** will get a minimum dividend before the ordinary get anything, and probably share in ordinary dividends thereafter. **Participating preference shares** may be similar; they get a fixed dividend plus an extra dividend on top that depends on profits. **Convertible preference shares** convert into ordinary shares, and so on.

Par values

Look next at the **equity capital**. Note that Jones Manufacturing has **issued ordinary share capital** of £1.5m, but that this is divided into units of 20p each. In other words, each pound of nominal capital is divided into five shares, so there are 7.5m shares in issue, each with a **nominal** or **par** value of 20p. The meaning of the par value sometimes causes problems. It has nothing to do with the price at which the shares may be traded in the stockmarket and for most practical purposes you can forget it – American companies often have ordinary shares (known as **common stock**) with **no par value**.

Many British companies have shares of 25p par value and the other common denominations are 5p, 10p, 20p, 50p, and £1. But this is relevant mainly for certain accounting purposes and for a technical **Companies Act** requirement that companies may not issue shares at prices below their par value. What interests investors is the price at which a share is quoted in the stockmarket, and it is perfectly possible to have a 5p share quoted at 400p or a £1 share quoted below its par value at 80p.

Authorized and issued capital

One other facet of a company's capital crops up in press reports, particularly of take-over offers. As well as the figure for **issued capital** (the nominal value of the shares in issue) you will see references to **authorized capital**. This is the maximum amount of capital that the company has authorization from its shareholders to issue. Jones Manufacturing might have an authorized capital of £3m, divided into £500,000 of preference capital (all of which is issued) and £2.5m of ordinary capital. Since only £1.5m of ordinary capital is so far issued, there is £1m of **authorized but unissued capital** in existence, equivalent to 5m 20p shares. The directors can thus issue a further 5m shares without needing to get shareholders' permission first. And, in fact, 1.5m of these unissued shares are already earmarked for the eventual conversion of the convertible loan stock.

If a company wants to issue more shares than it is authorized to do, it must call a meeting of shareholders and get them to vote in favour of an increase in the authorized amount. This might crop up if Jones Manufacturing wanted to take over another company by issuing 6m of its own shares in exchange for shares in the target company. Unless Jones's own shareholders agreed, the deal could not go through. It may also crop up when a company wants to make a **rights issue** or a **scrip issue** (see Chapter 9).

Because of the takeover possibilities, many shareholders – particularly the big institutions – are unwilling to vote a company a big increase in authorized capital unless they know for what purpose the new unissued shares are required. Where the authorized capital exceeds the issued capital by a large amount, the directors of the company have considerable discretion. Shareholders may be happier if they know their permission would be required before the company could, say, radically change the balance of its business by issuing shares to take over another concern. This is one of a number of ways shareholders may exercise control over the companies they invest in.

Warrants

Apart from shares there is another type of quasi-security that a company may issue, which will be referred to in the notes to the accounts but which will not appear as share capital in the balance sheet. This is the **warrant**. A company may issue warrants which give the holder the right to **subscribe** at a fixed price for shares in the company at some future date. The **subscription price** will usually be fixed above the current price of the shares when the warrant is issued, so at this stage any value in the warrant is simply hope value.

Suppose a warrant is issued which gives the right to subscribe for one share at 180p at some point in the future. The current share price is 150p and there is no **intrinsic value** in the warrant. But if the share price should rise to 250p, there is a clear value in the right to subscribe at 180p for a share that could immediately be sold for 250p, and the price of the warrant itself will reflect this value. The principle is much the same as for a **traded option** (see Chapter 18 for a fuller explanation). But a warrant gives the right to subscribe cash for a new share the company issues. An option gives the right to buy an existing share from its present owner and does not affect the finances of the company itself. American terminology sometimes confuses this distinction, however. Warrants are traded in the stockmarket much like shares themselves.

Warrants are sometimes issued to improve the attractions of a loan stock and are often referred to as an **equity sweetener** or **equity kicker**. Fixed-interest loans are unpopular in periods of high inflation, but if subscribers to a loan are given, say, one warrant for every £3 of loan, they have an interest in the increasing prosperity of the company, as reflected in its share price. When warrants are issued in this way, they are afterwards normally traded separately from the loan. Arriving at the theoretical value of a warrant, relative to the price of the ordinary shares, is a pretty technical process and best left to the experts. The actual value at a given time is set by the balance of buyers and sellers in the market, as with a share.

Profit and loss account reserves

Jones Manufacturing's **profit and loss account reserves** (they used more commonly to be called **revenue reserves**) at £5.4m are considerably larger than its issued capital. This points to some years' worth of **ploughed-back profits (retained earnings)** which are added to the profit and loss account reserve in the balance sheet each year. If the company went through a temporary bad patch in which it did not earn any profits it could, if it chose, use part of these ploughed-back profits of previous years to pay a dividend (always assuming it also had enough cash). And in a loss-making year the revenue reserves will be depleted by the amount of the net losses plus the cost of any dividends paid.

Share premium account

The **share premium account** is part of shareholders' funds, but needs rather more explanation. It arises when the company issues new shares at a price above their par value (and in the case of an established company, the shares will almost always be worth more than their par value and new shares will be priced accordingly). Assume that in the past Jones had decided to raise money by offering new ordinary shares to its existing shareholders (a **rights issue** – see Chapter 9). Its share price at the time was 110p and it issued the new shares at 80p. Since the shares have a par value of 20p, each new share was being sold at a **premium** of 60p to its par value. So for each new share sold the company added 20p to its nominal capital and accounted for the additional 60p by adding it to share premium account.

The share premium account has a special position in law in that it cannot be **written down** without the permission of the courts (it could not be used to cover **operating losses**, for example, without this permission). Since it arises from the issue of capital, it is treated rather as if it were part of the company's capital – part of the 'cushion' of equity that provides protection for creditors.

Revaluation reserves

Revaluation reserves are usually created or added to when the company revalues some of its assets upwards, probably the properties that it holds as fixed assets. Suppose Jones had commissioned a professional **revaluation** of its buildings which showed them worth £1.95m more than their book value. It would have increased the value of properties in the accounts by £1.95m and added £1.95m to capital reserves to show that this extra value (the **surplus over book value**) belonged to the shareholders. Balance sheets must balance.

The revaluation of properties is often referred to in the context of takeover bids. If a company owns properties that were last revalued ten years ago (not Jones Manufacturing in this instance), a press report might say: 'the book net asset value [of the company being bid for] is 250p per share against the offer of 275p per share. But if properties are now worth £3m more than the book value, the net asset value would rise to 310p and the offer would look to be on the low side'. Thus the writer is mentally adding £3m to the value of properties, increasing capital reserves (and therefore shareholders' funds) by a like amount, and working out his net asset value figure on the result. He would apply the same arithmetic if the company owned investments that were worth more than the figures at which they were **stated in the books**.

Adjusting the net asset value

Finally, the **net asset value** for Jones Manufacturing. There are two complications. First, goodwill is normally excluded to produce a figure for **net tangible asset value**. Second, the preference shares are not part of the ordinary shareholders' funds, and also have to be excluded from a calculation of assets attributable to the ordinary shares. (See table on the next page.)

The whole question of the accounting treatment of goodwill is in a state of flux. In the past companies have usually written off goodwill against reserves when they have incurred it via a takeover. But this has the effect of reducing shareholders' funds, which can cause problems. Some companies have

	£'000
Shareholders' funds (as stated in the accounts)	11,000
less	
Goodwill	1,000
	10,000
less	
Preference capital	500
Ordinary shareholders' funds	9,500
Divide by the 7.5 million shares in issue	
Net tangible asset value per ordinary share	126.7p

attempted to compensate by including as an asset the value of well-known **brand names** they own, which they may describe as **intangible assets**, though in effect this value is only another form of goodwill. Most investment analysts will exclude goodwill from net asset value calculations, however it is presented or described.

In the United States, companies show goodwill on their balance sheets but have to **amortize** it each year just like a physical asset. In other words, they have to make a deduction from their published profits to write down the book value of the goodwill each year. This can result in significantly lower profits than for a comparable UK company which writes its goodwill off to reserves. Some internationally-minded UK companies produce an addendum to their main accounts showing how the figures would look under **US GAAP** (the generally accepted accounting principles in the US). The main difference between the UK and US variants usually relates to the treatment of goodwill.

In 1995 the **Accounting Standards Board** was still studying the most appropriate method of accounting for goodwill in the UK. Many companies were against the adoption of US practice, arguing that goodwill might be rising in value rather than falling. They did not like the implications of US practice for their published profits. A possible compromise was a system where UK companies would show the goodwill on their balance sheets but would not need to amortize it if they could demonstrate that it was holding or increasing its value.

Back to Jones Manufacturing. As an added sophistication, we can work out the **fully-diluted** net asset value per share for Jones. Take the £9.5m adjusted ordinary shareholders' funds (after excluding goodwill and preference capital). Add in the nominal value of the convertible loan stock – £1.5m – since this will cease to exist as a liability when converted and therefore shareholders' funds will increase by £1.5m. Then divide the result by the enlarged number of ordinary shares: 7.5m plus the 1.5m arising on conversion. The result: £11m divided by 9m shares = £1.222 or 122.2p. So conversion of the loan stock will **dilute** assets per share from 126.7p to 122.2p. A fairly minor **dilution** as it happens, but worth bearing in mind.

6

Equities and the Stock Exchange

What is the **London Stock Exchange**? It is the sole stock exchange in Britain, with its headquarters in Throgmorton Street in the City of London. Major regional cities used to have their own trading floors. But all of the **regional exchanges** are now merely branches of the London Stock Exchange, and trading floors where market members dealt with each other face to face – even the London trading floor – are now obsolete. In place of the old physical marketplace are the dealing rooms of the individual securities houses, linked with each other by telephone and computerized information systems. **Dealing** in shares and bonds takes place over the telephone between these dealers' offices.

The dealing is by no means confined to the securities of British companies and bonds of the British government. London is also the major centre for dealing in overseas securities. This international aspect is reflected in the exchange's full name – The International Stock Exchange of the United Kingdom and the Republic of Ireland Limited – adopted when it merged with **ISRO**, a body representing London dealers in international bonds, at the end of 1986.

Of London's financial institutions, the Stock Exchange has altered more than most in recent years and it is still changing. The most significant changes took place on 27 October 1986 in what was known as **Big Bang** day. The Big Bang process involved changes not only to the exchange's trading methods but also to the structure and ownership of its member firms. Since the Stock Exchange is a mixture of the old and the new, we will need to look back at some of these changes to understand the trading system as it has evolved today.

Securities traded on the London Stock Exchange

The securities traded on the London Stock Exchange have expanded in recent years – enormously, in the case of overseas securities – but the mainstays have not changed. The exchange is the main market in which **ordinary shares** in companies (**equities**) and **government bonds (gilt-edged securities** or **gilts**) are bought and sold. These are not the only types of security traded. Various types of bond issued by companies (usually known as **industrial debentures**, **industrial loans** or **corporate bonds**), **convertible loan stocks**, **preference shares** and more esoteric pieces of paper such as **warrants** are also traded. The market in **traded options** used to be part of the Exchange but is now amalgamated with the **Liffe** financial futures market. And the term **fixed-interest market**, used mainly to cover gilt-edged securities, also embraces loans issued by local government in the UK and by certain overseas governments as well as fixed-interest corporate bonds.

The total value of shares listed in the market – £775 billion at end-1994 for UK and Irish companies listed in London – is known as the **market capitalization**. The **turnover** figure – £606 billion for UK and Irish equities in 1994 – needs treating with care. In London each transaction counts twice. Mr Smith sells shares which initially go to a marketmaker and are ultimately bought by Mr Jones. The value of the sale and of the purchase will be counted as separate items under turnover. The same applies to the measurement of **bargains** (a Stock Exchange transaction is called a 'bargain', whatever price you pay). In 1994 a total of 9.4m equity bargains was recorded. London ranks third to New York and Tokyo in terms of market capitalization.

In addition to its business in domestic shares, the London Stock Exchange is the largest market for trading in international equities, using an electronic price quotation system called **SEAQ International**. Shares in any company listed on a stock exchange approved by the London Stock Exchange can be traded via this system. The total value of trades in 1994, at £719 billion, was somewhat larger than that in domestic shares.

The Stock Exchange is both a **primary market** and a **secondary market**: a market where new securities are issued for cash and a market where existing securities are sold by one investor to another. In 1994 some £20 billion was raised by the first-time sale of shares by new or existing UK and Irish companies and the figure rises to around £25 billion if domestic company bonds and other securities are included. In 1994 a further £33 billion or so was raised by UK and Irish companies by the sale of eurobonds formally listed on the London market, though trading in these bonds is outside the domestic market (see Chapters 13 and 17).

Who owns shares and who deals

Despite encouragement from privatization issues for the private investor, today's Stock Exchange is dominated by the **financial institutions**. In the 1950s **private investors** owned more than 60 per cent of all shares directly. By 1993 their holdings represented less than 18 per cent of the total. Institutions (mainly the pension funds and insurance companies) owned almost 62 per cent of all shares in 1993, against some 30 per cent thirty years earlier. But, reflecting the internationalisation of securities ownership and trading, **foreign investors** have been the fastest-growing category in recent years, with more than 16 per cent of the London equity market in 1993 against only 7 per cent in 1963.

When it comes to **trading volumes**, private investors are still less significant than in terms of ownership. In terms of bargains they accounted for almost two-thirds of the total in 1994. But this is misleading, since their bargains tend to be small. Their deals accounted for under 8 per cent of the total in terms of value while UK institutions accounted for over 73 per cent and foreign investors for almost 18 per cent. Because their bargains are small, private individuals pay average **commission rates** of 1.1 per cent whereas the average for institutional business undertaken on commission is 0.28 per cent. Private individuals contributed over 32 per cent to total commission revenue in 1994 against roughly 57 per cent from institutional deals. But it is not difficult to see where the market perceives its best interests. Large institutional deals are not necessarily more expensive to undertake and process than the small private-client deals and can therefore be vastly more profitable.

Figures for **share ownership** in Britain can therefore convey a very distorted picture of investment activity. Thanks largely to privatization issues and the arrival on the stockmarket of former building society Abbey National, the number of individuals owning shares direct rose from around 3m in 1980 to a peak of 11m or so in 1991 (it has fallen a little since). But a majority of these shareholders own small amounts of shares in one or two privatization stocks, rarely if ever use a stockbroker and are largely irrelevant to stockmarket activity. The number of active or substantial private investors is probably numbered in the hundreds of thousands rather than the millions.

Layers of the market

More than one market comes under the aegis of the London Stock Exchange, and the terminology can become confusing. Until 1980 the London Stock Exchange was the sole market. Companies whose shares or other securities were traded there were **listed** on the Stock Exchange, and still are. The 'listing' refers to a **Listing Agreement** that companies have to sign, which governs some aspects of their behaviour and their reporting to shareholders. At end-1994 there were a little over 2,000 UK and Irish listed companies. In addition, the shares of many overseas companies are listed on the London exchange as well as in their country of origin.

In 1980 the Stock Exchange introduced a **second-tier market** called the **Unlisted Securities Market** or **USM**, though by 1995 it was scheduled for closure at the end of the following year. It was designed to provide a nursery for smaller or more recently established companies, which might eventually aspire to a listing on the Stock Exchange itself. The costs of entry were somewhat lower, and the criteria a little less strict: normally a two-year profit record would be required before entry as against three years for the Stock Exchange, which is sometimes referred to as the **main market**.

Companies whose shares are traded on the USM are not 'listed', though they have to sign a very similar agreement. Their shares are usually described as being **quoted** on the USM, though the term 'quoted' is loosely used to cover listed companies as well. The USM is run by Stock Exchange member firms and for most purposes is treated as being part of the Stock Exchange: USM stocks are traded in exactly the same way as listed companies. The decision to close this market was not welcomed in all quarters. Venture capitalists, in particular, had sometimes found it useful for launching private companies they had earlier backed and thereby getting their money back.

Partly as a replacement for the USM in its original guise (in later years it had become more and more similar to the main market) the Stock Exchange planned to launch in June 1995 a new small-company market called the **Alternative Investment Market** or **AIM**. The idea was to cater for the funding needs of young or developing companies and efforts were made to keep the costs down and make the rules as simple as possible. Some companies were expected to migrate from the USM to AIM. Other AIM constituents might be companies whose shares were previously dealt under the Stock Exchange's Rule 4.2. This allowed dealing on a **matched bargain** basis (see

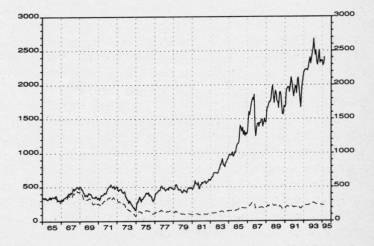

Figure 6.1 The solid line shows share price performance over 30 years, as measured by the Financial Times Ordinary Share Index. Performance does not look quite so impressive when share prices are adjusted for inflation (lower broken line). Source: *Datastream International*.

glossary) in shares of companies that were neither listed nor quoted. And other AIM constituents would be companies new to the Stock Exchange altogether.

But most 'junior' markets face a common problem. Cut back too far on the regulation and scandals erupt which damage the credibility of the market. Step up the regulation and the costs deter companies from joining. There is also a perennial problem in stimulating sufficient trade in the shares of small companies to ensure a reasonably liquid market.

In 1987 the Stock Exchange had launched an earlier version of a small-company market known as the **Third Market**. But it proved short-lived, closing after a few years. This was a fairly loosely-regulated market, aimed at companies of the type sometimes previously traded on the freewheeling **Over-The-Counter** or **OTC** markets. The OTC markets were never part of the Stock Exchange. They were 'unofficial' and the Stock Exchange did not like them. Dealing in the OTC markets used to be conducted over the telephone by **licensed dealers in securities**, who had satisfied the minimal requirements of the Department of Trade and Industry to be allowed to deal in securities with the public. There was no central marketplace and no very effective supervision or regulation; safeguards for investors were minimal. But the Financial Services Act of 1986 effectively put paid to the OTC market in its previous form. The new rules made life very difficult for a marketmaker who was not a member of a recognized investment exchange.

Why trading systems changed

To understand how the Stock Exchange works today it is easiest to look briefly at the largely defunct system that was replaced in the course of the Big Bang.

Before October 1986, there were two classes of Stock Exchange member and members were generally grouped into firms or partnerships. There were the **jobbers** who operated as **marketmakers**. They operated a **book**, buying and selling shares on their own behalf (**taking positions in shares**) and hoping to make a profit on the difference between their buying and selling price. This difference was known as the **jobber's turn**. Jobbers were not allowed to deal with the public. They could deal only with stockbrokers or with each other. They operated during trading hours from **pitches** (stalls) on the Stock Exchange floor.

The **stockbroker** was the agent who executed the public's buying and selling instructions and was remunerated via a **commission** calculated on the value of the deal. Mr Smith (or a major institution) wanted to buy 500 ICI shares. He contacted his broker with the instruction. The broker or one of his trading staff went to the jobbers on the trading floor and bought the shares from the firm which offered the most favourable price. The theory was that this **single-capacity** system (single-capacity because a jobber could act only as principal and a broker only as agent) provided a valuable safeguard for investors. Competition between jobbers prevented their overcharging. And the broker as agent had only his client's interests at heart.

But the system was expensive. The Stock Exchange imposed a scale of **minimum commissions**, which all brokers had to observe and was pitched at a level to provide a living for the least efficient. In addition, the investor was meeting the cost of the jobber's turn.

The system had other drawbacks. The market was **under-capitalized**, because it was difficult under a partnership structure for jobbers to raise the finance required to take large **positions** in stock and provide **liquidity** for the market by always being ready to buy or sell in large quantities. The big investing institutions could not deal easily in the quantities of stock they required. The supposed competition between jobbers was often illusory. And dealing in the shares of some major British companies was moving towards the more liquid New York market.

Trigger for change

The impetus for change came eventually from the government. The Stock Exchange, under threat of legal action on its alleged **restrictive practices**, voluntarily agreed to abandon its fixed commission structure.

The **New York Stock Exchange** (NYSE) had abandoned fixed commissions in 1975. From that year commissions on large deals were by negotiation, and the level of commission on large deals dropped sharply. British brokers realized they would see their income slashed under **negotiated commissions** and the larger ones demanded the right to operate as **market-makers**, hoping to recoup the loss on commissions from the profits on making a book in shares. Thus the old **jobber/ broker distinction** broke down. The Stock Exchange also announced that its rule against outside ownership of Stock Exchange member firms would be abandoned. This opened the way for banks and other cash-rich UK and overseas institutions to acquire broking and jobbing businesses and provide them with the finance they would need.

Takeover of Stock Exchange firms

From these changes arose the market that we know today. Between 1983 and 1986 most of the major firms of jobbers and brokers (with the notable exception of brokers Cazenove) arranged to sell out – generally at very inflated prices. Sometimes the new bank or merchant bank owners put together several Stock Exchange firms to form a powerful **securities house**. Most of the larger groupings planned to operate as **marketmakers in equities** as well as **agency brokers**. At the same time it became clear that a number of large American and Japanese houses would be applying for membership of the London Stock Exchange. Changes in the pattern of trading in gilt-edged stocks were being planned at the same time (see Chapter 13).

Computers and the London trading system

Today's market needs to rely heavily on computer information systems to accommodate the large number of **equity market-makers**. These marketmakers operate as principals – make a book in shares for their own profit – much as the old-style jobbers did. There were 35 marketmakers immediately after the Big Bang and 30 today. They operate from trading floors in their own buildings, scattered round London. They feed the prices at which they are prepared to deal in the different shares into a computerized system called **SEAQ (Stock Exchange Automated Quotation system)**. This was planned initially as a **price information system** rather than an **automated dealing system**. The dealer uses the SEAQ screen to see who is offering the best price in the stock that interests him. He then phones the chosen marketmaker and arranges the deal. The rule is that the marketmaker must be prepared to deal up to a certain stated number of shares at the price he has quoted though he can, of course, adjust his quoted prices after he has done the deal. With larger deals above this stated number, the deal is subject to negotiation. Later, in 1989, a fully automatic system for executing small transactions was introduced under the name of **SAEF (SEAQ Automatic Execution Facility)**. And a computerized trading system for the whole market, which will cut out the need for arranging deals by telephone, is now mooted.

While the principle of the London market is competition between marketmakers in all shares, this has proved unrealistic in the case of some very small or infrequently-traded companies. For these there might be only one marketmaker or there might be no marketmakers quoting continuous prices. Here, a system called **SEATS (Stock Exchange Alternative Tracking Service)** displays the marketmaker's quote (if any) and firm orders from member firms.

You will sometimes see London's trading system described in the press as a 'quote-driven' system. In other words, marketmakers quote the price at which they are prepared to deal and the investor may buy or sell if he wants to. Some other stock exchanges operate an 'order-driven' system. Buyers and sellers state what they want to buy or sell, and at what price, and the market serves to match them. The SEATS system in London is effectively more of an order-driven system and the possibility of the London market as a whole moving towards an order-driven system is sometimes discussed in the financial press. There are also periodic rumblings as to whether the London Stock Exchange should maintain its virtual monopoly of share dealing in Britain or whether outsiders should be allowed to quote prices in competition.

Marketmakers, brokers and some big institutional investors will all have SEAQ screens in their offices. The screen will show them the marketmakers who are offering the most favourable prices in the share they are interested in at given time. The Stock Exchange used to provide an additional screen-based information service called **TOPIC** carrying news of company events, developments in the financial sphere and share price movements but this is now operated by an independent company, ICV, which provides a service called TOPIC3.

The Stock Exchange itself provides a **Regulatory News Service** or **RNS** which disseminates news of company profit announcements, share issues and the like: information that companies are obliged to file under Stock Exchange rules. And the Stock Exchange also provides data-feeds of market trading information to subscribers and, as part of its **Sequence** programme, is developing a variety of further information services. Via its own computers it is able to monitor trading activity and investigate unusual price patterns which might suggest **insider dealing** ahead of major company news items or attempts to rig the market.

Commission deals or net prices

Under the London trading system, major investing institutions have a choice. They can use a broker as an agent, in which case the broker executes the purchase or sale with the marketmaker offering the best price (possibly his own firm's marketmaking arm). In this case the institution is liable for commission, though at a negotiated rate, as well as bearing the cost of the marketmaker's turn. Or the institution can have its own SEAQ screen and deal direct at a **net price** with the marketmakers, in which case it avoids commission costs. Immediately after the Big Bang a high proportion of UK institutional business was being undertaken direct with marketmakers at net prices. In 1994 it was a little under one third. Private investors do not, of course, have the option of dealing direct with marketmakers.

The relationship between institutional investors and the markets is rather different today from in the pre-Big Bang years. The broker's job as agent was (and is) to get the best deal for his client. But the relationship between an investor and a marketmaker is **adversarial**. The marketmaker wants to sell at the highest price possible. The investor wants to buy at the lowest price possible. They are on opposite sides of the fence. With marketmakers and brokers now under one roof there is an inevitable temptation – doubtless honourably resisted in many cases – for the securities house to recommend purchases of shares which it has on its books. It is one of the invitable **conflicts of interest** of the system.

Marketmakers, brokers and securities houses

Stock Exchange members today fall into a number of categories. First there are the **marketmakers**. They have a duty to make a continuous market in the shares in which they have opted to deal. Then there are **broker dealers** who may supply clients with shares they hold on their own books, but have no obligation to make a continuous market. There are strict rules to ensure that they do not supply clients with shares from their own stocks that could have been bought more cheaply from a marketmaker. Both types may also act as **agency brokers** (like the old-style stockbrokers), executing clients' buy and sell orders with the marketmakers and charging a commission on the deal. Some members confine themselves entirely to the agency role.

The bigger brokers generally form part of large financial

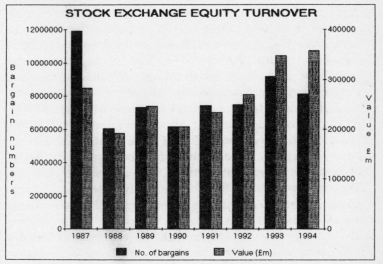

Figure 6.2 Turnover in shares of British and Irish companies on the London Stock Exchange. The number of trades ('bargains') has never regained the 1987 boom level, but the value of shares traded is now higher than in 1987. Source: *London Stock Exchange.*

groups which offer a wide range of banking and financial services. Barclays de Zoete Wedd (BZW), for example, combines brokers de Zoete & Bevan and former jobbers Wedd Durlacher. But the **securities house** is owned by Barclays Bank, the clearing bank, and is in effect its investment banking arm. Other groupings had their origins in a broking firm alone and built up their marketmaking know-how from scratch.

The structure poses some problems with terminology, particularly for financial journalists with memories of the pre-Big Bang days. Journalists often tend to talk of **brokers** and refer to them by their original names even when they are part of a larger grouping. But the term **securities house** has gained ground when referring to the large concerns. **Marketmaker** is normally used when referring to the specific function of making a book in shares.

The financial conglomerates

The terminology becomes clearer if you look at the services the integrated financial groups can provide. Clearing banks offer most forms of financial service. Prior to the Big Bang their share dealing had to go through an independent broker. Today, Barclays and National Westminster are heavily into the securities markets though Lloyds in particular has resisted the temptation to get deeply involved. Merchant banks offer many of the same services, except for **retail banking**: dealing with the public via a branch network. They undertake **foreign exchange dealing**, **eurobond dealing**, **new issues** of shares on the stockmarket and **underwriting** of securities issues. Many have extensive **investment management** business: they manage investments on behalf of the pension funds in particular. Their **corporate finance** arms advise companies on capital raising and help to plan their takeovers and takeover defences. They may of course – as in the case of BZW – be subsidiaries of a clearing bank. In addition to the traditional British banks, overseas securities houses and investment banks are now strongly represented in the London market.

Even before the Big Bang, the larger brokers had diversified some way beyond pure agency broking business and overlapped with the merchant banks in several areas: notably new issues, investment management and – up to a point – advice to companies. They have been joined in these activities by overseas investment banks and securities houses. **Investment research** on industries, individual companies, interest rates and economic prospects has long been a vital service provided particularly to institutional investors to try to secure their business. The **investment analysts** who prepare it are a useful source of information for financial journalists as well, and much press comment is influenced by their views.

Conflicts of interest

Integration of many different functions within a single financial grouping has its advantages: most types of financial service can be provided by a single organisation. But it is not without its problems. Paradoxically, several of these disciplines ought to be kept well clear of each other. The investment management arm must not know if the corporate advice arm is counselling ABC Industries on a planned takeover of XYZ Holdings. If it knew, it could make large profits by buying the shares of XYZ before the bid became public. The marketmaking arm must not know if Myopic Mutual Assurance has approached the agency brokerage arm to acquire a couple of million pounds' worth of shares in ABC, though the information would assist the marketmaker considerably in adjusting the price it quoted. The marketmaking arm must not learn of the intentions of the fund management arm, nor of ABC's plan to take over XYZ. And so on.

To deal with the possible **conflicts of interest** and to convince the outside world that no improper use is being made of information available in different parts of the organization, safeguards are required. Securities houses have **compliance departments** or **compliance officers** with a brief to ensure the confidentiality rules are observed. Within the organization there are **Chinese Walls**: barriers that are supposed to exist between different arms of a securities house to prevent information from passing between them. Sometimes they are invisible walls. Sometimes the different arms are physically separated. Cynics claim they've never met a Chinese Wall that did not have a grapevine growing over it. Or, more succinct if less politically correct, that there's no Chinese Wall without a chink.

The post-Big Bang realities

From the more sober viewpoint of the 1990s it is difficult to recall, let alone to comprehend, the euphoria that accompanied the Big Bang changes. Brokers were televised breaking out the champagne on the steps of their offices in the early morning as they prepared to go in and do battle in the new competitive marketplace. Dealing volumes would, the marketmakers somehow came to believe in the warm glow of the Thatcher boom, expand to give them all a good living. Frenetic dealing in shares would itself create value.

The excesses of the time are reflected in the six-figure salaries and Porsche cars offered to top investment analysts and dealers and in the new phrases that crept into the language. **Golden hallos** were the lump sum cash inducements paid to attract top staff and **golden handcuffs** were the financial arrangements made to lock them into their jobs.

While dealing boomed in the months immediately after Big Bang, reality soon intervened with a bath of cold water. **Dealing volumes** for UK shares collapsed with the October 1987 stockmarket crash and it was 1993 before they had regained the 1987 level in terms of value. In terms of bargain numbers they had never got back near 1987 levels by 1994. Many securities houses were forced to cut costs and draw in their horns and some withdrew from the market entirely. Hindsight confirmed what many had feared at the time: the new financial conglomerates had generally overpaid vastly for the businesses they took over. The smiles were confined to the partners of the old-style brokers who had had the sense to take the cash and run.

The proliferation of marketmakers after the Big Bang did, however, result in greatly increased competition and initially in a reduction in **spreads** between buying and selling prices for shares. The abolition of fixed commissions brought a reduction of 50 per cent or more in commission rates on large deals. Both factors made dealing cheaper, so investors – in true market fashion – initially dealt more actively in the months leading up to the 1987 crash so that they paid as much in the long run. But small investors often paid more than previously, as the minimum commission charged on small bargains often rose sharply. Excess profits on institutional business were no longer there to subsidize the small man.

With this exception, the Big Bang brought fewer changes for the private investor than for most market users. His order still goes through a broker to whom he pays commission. But the problems of very high minimum commissions on small deals were somewhat eased in due course as new style brokers sprang up (sometimes sponsored by banks and even building societies) offering low-cost 'no-frills' or **execution only** share buying and selling services. The execution-only service cuts out the traditional hand-holding and advice, providing a share-dealing and settlement service, pure and simple.

Stockmarket technicalities

The change which the private investor will notice most has come far more recently with the abandonment of the London Stock Exchange's traditional equity market **account system** in favour of **rolling settlement**. Trading in gilts was and remains for **cash settlement** (in practice this means payment the day after you buy the stock).

For the old equity market account system, the year used to be divided into two-week Stock Exchange accounts, plus four three-week accounts which usually covered the Bank Holidays. The normal account thus ran from the Monday of one week to the Friday of the following week. A buyer of shares did not have to pay (and a seller did not get the proceeds of the sale) until **settlement day** or **account day**, which was ten days after the end of the relevant account. A speculator could thus **deal for the account**. If he bought at the beginning of the account and sold before the end, he would never have to pay for the shares. He would simply receive or pay a cheque for his profits or losses.

That has now disappeared. In 1994 the Stock Exchange introduced ten-day **rolling settlement**, which meant that an investor normally paid or was paid for his shares ten days after he bought or sold them. It was proposed to bring the rolling settlement period down to five days by the middle of 1995.

When an investor buys or sells a share, he is sent a **contract**

note which gives details of the transaction and payment becomes due on settlement day. Once the contract note has been sent, the broker deals with the subsequent paperwork – and the system has hitherto been largely paper-based, even if computers are used to generate the paper. Purchases and sales have to be registered with the company whose shares are involved and the company eventually issues a **share certificate** to the new owner. British company shares are thus **registered securities** (though the identity of the real owner is sometimes cloaked in a **nominee name**). It is a Companies Act requirement that a company keep a **register of shareholders**, and the public has the right to inspect the register on payment of a fee. In some countries shares in **bearer** form are more common. The certificate alone is proof of ownership.

Settlement of share trades (transfering stock and money between buyers and sellers) currently takes place via a Stock Exchange computerized system called **Talisman**. To cut out the time-consuming processes involved in paper-based registration of shares, the Stock Exchange had been developing a new electronic system called **Taurus**, but this was abandoned after vast sums of money had already been spent. In place of Taurus, the Bank of England is now sponsoring the development of a new electronic settlement and registration system called **Crest**.

Bullish and bearish

Much of the old Stock Exchange terminology survives the market changes. Somebody who sells shares he does not own in the hope that the price will fall and he will be able to buy them more cheaply before he has to deliver has undertaken a **bear sale** or a **short sale**. The investor is **short** of the shares – he does not own them – at the time he sells them. Short selling can be a dangerous game. If the price rises instead of falling, there is theoretically no limit to the price that might have to be paid for the shares that are required for delivery. Marketmakers have to sell shares they do not own in the course of their daily trading. The disappearance of the account system makes it more difficult for private individuals, though there are now opportunities for betting on a price fall with traded options or even via stockmarket index betting systems run by traditional 'bookies'.

The term **bear** (see Chapter 7) is used not only to cover a short seller but anyone who expects the market to go down. By extension, a **bear market** is a falling market and a **bearish** news item is one that might be expected to cause the market to fall.

The opposite of a bear is a **bull**, who expects prices to rise. A **bull market** is a market on a long-term rising trend and **bullish** news is news that is likely to push prices up. **Long** is (self-evidently) the opposite of **short**. Somebody who is **long** of a particular share owns the share in question – possibly with the implication that he holds large quantities which he intends to sell rather than holding for the long term. A **stale bull** is somebody who bought shares in the hope of a price rise, has not seen the rise and is tired of holding on.

Bid and offered prices

Though the newspapers normally quote only a **middle price** for a share, we have seen that the marketmaker quotes a price at which he will sell and a price at which he will buy. The marketmaker's selling price is the **offered price** (the higher of the two, and the price at which the investor will buy). The marketmaker's buying price is the **bid price** (the price at which an investor can sell to him). The difference between the two is the **spread** or **turn**. Different marketmakers may quote a different range, depending on the state of their books and whether they want to encourage investors to buy from them or sell to them. Thus you might see:

	MARKETMAKER A	MARKETMAKER B
Offered	102p	103p
Bid	100p	101p

The spread is the same in both cases (though it need not be). The likelihood is that marketmaker A is long of the particular share. He wants to encourage investors to buy from him so that he can square his book, so he is prepared to sell to investors at 102p. Marketmaker B is probably short of the share, so he will only sell at the higher price of 103p to discourage still more investors from buying from him shares that he does not have. But he is prepared to offer investors 101p if they will sell to him, thus hoping he can pick up the shares he needs to square his book. An investor who wanted to buy would naturally get the best price from marketmaker A and one who wanted to sell from marketmaker B. The difference between the lowest offered price and the highest bid price (in this case 1p) is known as the **touch**.

The Stock Exchange publishes a **Daily Official List** of prices of all shares traded on the Stock Exchange or the Unlisted Securities Market. But since it gives the highest price and the lowest price at which dealings took place during the day, the spread is unrealistically wide. In an adjusted form, however, these **official prices** are relevant for some tax purposes, particularly probate. Of more interest is the information in the Official List on prices at which deals actually took place. Details of price, size and time of transactions allow the day's performance to be tracked.

7a

What moves share prices
a: In 'normal' times

'Observers attributed the lacklustre tone to the absence of any market-affecting news.'

Share prices had been slipping slightly, activity was very low, and the reason – we are told – was that there was no reason on this particular day for things to be otherwise.

The quotation comes from a report on the French stockmarket, but might have been written about other markets, too. News – good or bad – is what brings out the buyers and sellers. Without the buyers and sellers, there is no **activity**. Markets thrive on activity and for the professionals, the brokers and marketmakers who derive their living from market activity, no news is very definitely bad news.

But in London, where shares of over 2,000 UK companies are traded, there is no such thing as a day without news. The daily **stockmarket reports** which feature in the financial pages record both the ups and downs of the markets and the movements of individual shares. At their best, when they give background information on reasons for price movements, they are essential reading. At their most turgid, they are simply a list of price movements in narrative form, stretching the writer's imagination to find synonyms for 'rose' and 'fell'. Most of what they contain is self-explanatory, but a few technical terms crop up. More serious, the general tenor may be difficult to grasp without some knowledge of the influences that move share prices.

Looking at the stockmarket from a 1995 perspective, there has still been no movement in share prices to compare in terms of drama with the events of 19 and 20 October 1987. On those two days the London equity market fell 20 per cent. Since stockmarket crashes contain useful lessons for the future, we will look in the second part of this chapter at the facts behind the stockmarket's fastest ever bust. But the events of Autumn 1987 will be easier to understand if we look first at the influences that operate on share prices in more normal times.

Bull and bear markets

The stockmarket crash of 1987 and the recession which arrived at the turn of the decade came as a cold bath to investors who imbibed their market lore in the heady climate of the earlier 1980s. The Thatcher boom of the 1980s (or the Lawson boom, depending on where you choose to put the credit or the blame) had lulled investors into a false sense of security. They had forgotten the health warning that investment products must carry, to the effect that share prices may go down as well as up. By the summer of 1987, the London equity market had enjoyed a long **bull phase** – in other words, rising share prices had been the rule for a number of years. If you adjust share prices for inflation, they had been rising in **real terms** since 1982. If you ignore inflation, share values had been on a rising trend since 1975. There had been ups and downs along the way, but the trend had not been broken.

This was unusual. Previously, for most of the post-war period share prices had followed a regular cyclical pattern of **bull markets** (prices in a sustained rising trend) followed by **bear markets** (where prices were falling). The highs and lows of each cycle generally mirrored the **stop-go** pattern of the British economy itself. The stockmarket **peaks** and **troughs** normally preceded those in real economic activity, because stockmarket prices are always looking forward a step. In the depths of a recession, share prices begin to rise to reflect the coming upturn. At the height of a boom they tend to become weak in anticipation of the next downturn. But over the post-war period as a whole, the movement in prices was upwards until the 1973–75 financial crisis brought a horrendous stock-market collapse with prices falling to scarcely a quarter of their previous peak.

While business cycles did not disappear in the 1980s, the

stockmarket had been less cyclical, helped for much of the time by a boom in the value of financial assets which sometimes seemed almost independent of underlying economic performance. The crash of 1987, though it brought a sharp halt to the bull market of the 1980s, in practice wiped less than a year's growth off share prices. It was remarkable more for the speed with which it happened than for the size of the fall. The recession of the early 1990s was the real price paid for the excesses of the 1980s, and its effects were felt far more widely across the economy. But the stockmarket suffered far less seriously than other areas such as the residential and commercial property markets. Though share prices underwent a couple of severe dips and several more minor ones, they were generally on an upward trend between 1988 and 1993, with the stockmarket looking forward to economic recovery long before it was discernible to the man in the street.

Stockmarket movements need to be seen on at least three levels. First, there is the long-term trend of the equity market, secondly the short-term fluctuations up and down within this trend, and thirdly, the movements of individual shares within the movement of the market as a whole.

Share prices reflect earnings growth

Investors buy **ordinary shares** mainly because they expect share values to increase. Over a long period, what causes share prices to increase is the increasing **earning power** of companies, and their ability to pay higher **dividends** out of these increased earnings. But in the short run a lot of other factors can distort the picture.

An example helps. Suppose that companies on average pay out half of their earnings as dividends and the average **yield** on ordinary shares is 4 per cent and the average **PE ratio** is around 17. Suppose also that on average companies are increasing their earnings and dividends by 10 per cent a year. Share prices might be expected to rise by 10 per cent a year to reflect the underlying growth in profits and dividends.

Different values put on earnings

Over a long period this may well happen. But the example assumes that investors always expect – again on average – that ordinary shares will yield 4 per cent and that they will be prepared to buy shares at a price equal to 17 times their current earnings. In practice there will be some times when they expect higher yields and others when they will accept lower yields. Some times when a PE ratio of 17 looks too high and others when it may seem on the low side.

Why is this the case? It is easier if we now come down to a single company. Call it ABC Holdings and assume it is totally typical of the market averages: the ABC shares at 100p offer a yield of 4 per cent and stand on a PE ratio of 17. If its earnings and dividends grow at 10 per cent a year, a buyer of the shares can expect a 14 per cent a year overall return: 4 per cent of income and 10 per cent of capital gain from the rise in the share price. But suppose something happens to alter the outlook for ABC's future profits: it comes up with a new product that should help raise the future growth rate from 10 to 12 per cent. Earnings will now rise faster in the future than had been expected. And, all else being equal, investors will be prepared to pay a higher price for the shares today because they are buying a more rapidly rising flow of future earnings. The share price might rise from 100p to 110p, where the yield drops to 3.7 per cent and the PE ratio rises to 18.7. The share has been **re-rated**.

When interest rates change

Now take a totally different aspect, which we touched on in Chapter 1. ABC Holdings at 100p yields 4 per cent and stands on a PE ratio of 17. With expectations of 10 per cent a year growth in earnings, the overall return is 14 per cent if the share price rises in line. An expected overall return of 14 per cent might look about right if, at this time, investors could get a redemption yield of 11 per cent on long-dated gilt-edged securities. It would not look nearly so good if interest rates rose so that gilt-edged stocks offered a risk-free 14 per cent. Investors would want a higher return on the ordinary share, so its price would have to fall. Nothing has necessarily happened to alter the outlook for ABC's profits. But the price falls because the returns available on other forms of investment have increased.

So the price of any individual company's shares – relative to others – will reflect the growth prospects of that company and therefore the **overall return** investors can expect. And the prices of ordinary shares as a whole will be affected by returns available on alternative forms of investment.

While these forces are always at work, they are not always so easy to spot in the reports of short-term price movements. Investors do not necessarily sit down and work out their assumptions on relative growth rates or returns available elsewhere before buying a share. But prices in the stockmarket reflect a balance of the (often instinctive) views of many thousands of investors. And it is noticeable that the ratings of individual companies do reflect their perceived growth prospects and that, over a long period, there is a remarkable correlation between movements in the yields on equities and those on fixed-interest investments.

Thus in a period of buoyant economic activity and rising company profits, the equity market as a whole might be expected to show a rising trend (though it will anticipate what is happening in the economy). And when we come down to the particular, any news about a company which adds to expectations of future growth will cause the share price to rise, and events which might depress earnings will cause it to fall, relative to the market as a whole.

Re-rating: up and down

The aim of investment analysts and managers, and of commentators in the financial press, is to find companies which are **undervalued** relative to their growth prospects. The writer who spots that a company is due for an **upward re-rating** before others realize that its earnings prospects are better than expected is (if he is right) offering his reader the chance of a capital profit. It is, of course, equally important to spot companies whose growth prospects are diminishing and whose shares are likely to be **re-rated downwards** – astute investors will want to sell before the share price adjusts downwards. But warnings of this nature are a lot less common in print than the **buy recommendations**. And press commentators along with most other investment advisers are much less adept in forecasting major turning points in the market as a whole than they are at predicting price movements in individual shares.

Don't necessarily expect a press warning ahead of a major fall in the stockmarket.

If share prices in the long run depend on a combination of company profits and alternative investment returns, in the short term they can be moved by a variety of other factors. Many of these are purely technical. Investment comment draws a distinction between **fundamental** influences (those relating to company profits or assets) and **technical** influences (mainly those affecting the share price without reflecting on the trading position of the company itself). Here are some of the more important ones:

Company profit announcements

Surprisingly, you will see from market reports that a share price often falls when a company reports good profits. A market report probably talks of **profit-taking**. The reason is as follows. In the weeks ahead of the **profit announcement** the share price rises as investors buy in expectation of the good figures. By the time these figures arrive, there is no reason for the speculators to hang on any longer, so they sell to take their profits. It is another example of the stockmarket **discounting** news well in advance.

Press recommendations

If the press (or a firm of brokers) **tips** a share, the price will usually rise. It will rise furthest if the shares are a **narrow market** – in other words, the recommendation relates to a company which does not have a great number of shares in issue or available on the market. In this case a small amount of buying would push the price up, whereas a recommendation for a large and widely traded company such as British Gas might have relatively little impact on the price.

Don't assume, however, that all the price rise that follows a press recommendation is the result of share buying. **Market-makers** read the press too, and when they see a share recommended they will tend to move up the price they quote in anticipation of likely buying. Thus investors often find they can buy a share only at a price considerably above the one quoted when the recommendation was made.

Marketmakers' manoeuvres

You'll sometimes see reports such as 'marketmakers were short of stock, and prices rose as they balanced their books'. This simply means that marketmakers had sold shares they did not own – they went **short** – and later they had to buy the shares they needed to deliver to clients. This buying moved prices up.

Marketmakers thrive on activity and when there is little activity they may attempt to stimulate it artificially. For example, at a time when there was little news to encourage investors either to buy or sell, they might move their quoted prices down to attract buyers and generate some action. However, there are now many more marketmakers than before and their competitive dealing can also chase share prices a long way up or down when investors' moods change.

Bear operations

It is not only marketmakers that sell shares they do not own. Speculators in the market may also **go short** in expectation of a price fall. They sell shares in the hope they can buy them at a lower price before they have to deliver. The profit on a successful short sale is the difference between the two prices – though, as we saw, the manoeuvre is more difficult for private investors now that the fortnightly account system has gone.

It is a dangerous manoeuvre. If the speculators get it wrong and the price rises rather than falling, there is no limit to their potential loss. They might sell shares at 100p in the expectation of a fall in the price to 80p. Suppose instead that there is a takeover bid for the company which forces its price up to 200p. They now have to buy shares at 200p to deliver the shares sold at 100p.

Short sellers have to buy to fulfill their contractual obligations to deliver the shares. If marketmakers sense there has been widescale short selling of a particular share they may deliberately move their quoted prices up, forcing the **bears** (those who had been trading on expectation of a price fall) to buy at an inflated price. This is known as a **bear squeeze**. Quite commonly you will see reports that prices rose on **bear covering**, even when the general trend of prices had been downwards. This simply reflects the forced buying by speculators who had earlier sold short and does not necessarily indicate a reversal of the market's downward trend.

A **bear raid** occurs when speculators descend on a company and deliberately try to force the price down, partly by short selling but possibly also by circulating unfavourable rumours about the company. They hope to buy the shares cheaply once the price has dropped. Bear raiders are, of course, vulnerable to being caught in a bear squeeze.

Technical corrections

Markets seldom continue up or down in an unbroken line. After a period of rising or falling prices you often see references to a **technical correction** or to the market **consolidating**. If prices have been rising for a long period, there will often be a break as some investors sell to take their profits and prices temporarily fall. They may well continue on up after the **shakeout** has taken place. A similar process takes place in reverse on the way down. The market tends to move in fits and starts, with investors pausing for breath at various points on the way up or down.

Chartist influences

There is a theory that you can predict from past price movements what a share price (or the market as a whole, as measured by one of the indices) is likely to do in the future. Whether you believe in this theory or not, you cannot ignore the fact that at times it has a strong impact on share prices. Commentators who base their forecasts on these theories are known as **technical analysts** or **chartists** (because they use charts to plot the price movements).

The theory is not as silly as it might sound. Suppose the share price of ABC Holdings had, over the past few months, fluctuated between 100p and 120p. This would suggest that each time the price dropped as low as 100p there were investors who considered it cheap at this price and were prepared to buy. Each time it rose as high as 120p a fair body

of investors considered it was becoming expensive and therefore sold. So 100p and 120p became recognized as **resistance
levels**.

If subsequently the price dropped significantly below 100p
or rose significantly above 120p, this would suggest that something had happened to change investors' perception of the
shares. The chartist would not need to know what had happened but simply that the price – reflecting the balance of
opinion among buyers and sellers in the market – had broken
out from a resistance level and might be expected to continue
in the direction it had taken until a new resistance level was
reached.

This merely illustrates the principle – in practice the chartist
projections may be based on considerably more complex
analysis. And nowadays share prices are probably plotted with
the help of computers rather than on graph paper, and the
computer can be programmed to give buy and sell prompts at
appropriate points.

Since most **chartists** work on broadly similar theories, their
predictions can be self-fulfilling. If all chartists reckoned the
ABC Holdings share price had breached a significant resistance level when it rose through 120p to 125p, all who
followed the theory would duly jump in and buy and the price
might be carried up to, say, 140p. Chartist techniques are also
widely used in other markets such as gold and foreign exchange.

Interest rate and currency movements

We have seen that a rise in interest rates will depress the price
of gilt-edged stocks and may also depress equity prices by
raising the returns available on other investments. But it will
have different impact on different kinds of company. It might
depress, say, housebuilders more than the average because
higher interest rates mean higher mortgage costs and could
deter housebuyers. It would depress highly-geared companies
which use a lot of variable-rate borrowed money, because
higher interest costs will depress their profits. It might actually
help companies which are sitting on large amounts of cash and
will therefore earn a higher interest income. But, all else
being equal, higher interest rates raise the cost of borrowing

for consumers and for industry and may be expected to damp down economic activity, which is bad for company profit prospects. This is quite separate from the purely technical factor that higher interest charges may depress share prices because of the higher returns available elsewhere.

The effect of **currency movements** is also complex. A fall in sterling, bringing the prospect of higher interest rates to defend the pound, will usually hit gilt-edged prices and might be expected to have a knock-on effect on share values. But a lower level of sterling improves British industry's competitive position in home and export markets and thus improves profit prospects. So sometimes a weakening in sterling will depress bond prices but boost ordinary shares.

Weight of money argument

Share prices tend to rise when there are more buyers than sellers. If there is a lot of money available for investment in stockmarkets, prices will tend to rise – hence the **weight of money** factor.

It used to be fairly simple to calculate. **Pension funds** and **insurance companies** have about £27 billion a year to invest. This is spread mainly between gilt-edged stocks, UK ordinary shares, UK property and overseas investments. Calculate how much will be needed to subscribe for new gilt-edged issues (if the government is a net borrower at the time) and how much will be absorbed by buying new shares expected to be issued on the stockmarket. Allow for the proportion invested in property and overseas and what is left is available to buy existing gilt-edged stocks or equities. If it exceeds likely sales from other quarters (private individuals are normally sellers on balance), prices should rise.

Today's sums are more complex, partly because of the freedom to invest overseas without penalty since exchange controls were suspended in 1979. But more important, it is very difficult to estimate likely overseas investment in UK stockmarkets. There are so many options for UK and foreign investors nowadays that weight of money calculations are no guarantee of future equity trends in any one market.

Too many shares

When a company raises capital by issuing new shares or issues shares in a takeover, the price will often fall. This is simply because initially there are not enough buyers around to absorb all the new shares. And if it is known that there are owners of large blocks of shares who want to dispose of them (possibly **underwriters** left with shares they do not want – see Chapter 8) the price may be weak until these have been disposed of. You will see references to large blocks of shares **overhanging the market**.

Politics

As a general rule, particularly in the run-up to an election, evidence that the Conservatives are doing well will boost gilt and equity prices and evidence to the contrary will depress them. This is not always totally logical. Rightly or wrongly, in the past the Labour party has been associated in many minds with high inflation and high interest costs, though ordinary shares have often performed well under a Labour government. Sometimes share prices will rise in anticipation of a Conservative win, but fall on heavy profit-taking when the expectation is fulfilled. Betting on elections can be dangerous.

Sentiment

This is the indefinable factor. On some days investors feel cheerful and decide to buy. It may be good political or economic news, it may simply be that the day is sunny or England has won a game of cricket. But one strong and consistent influence on the London stockmarket is the performance of share prices across the Atlantic on **Wall Street**. A big rise or fall on Wall Street – and to a lesser extent in Tokyo – is often reflected in the behaviour of equities in London. Sometimes this is logical. The same political or economic news has an impact on both markets, and a movement in the returns available on Wall Street will affect expectations elsewhere; many of the same shares are in any case traded on Wall Street and other markets. But sometimes the Wall Street rise or fall simply influences **sentiment** in London. Though, for London, the Wall Street link is probably the strongest, the crash of October 1987 (with its knock-on effect on all world markets) demonstrated how quickly market movements now travel across most frontiers.

Takeovers

We have left **takeovers** to last because at times they dominate stockmarket thinking. The assumption is that if Company A bids for Company B it will need to pay above the current market price of Company B shares, though in practice the Company B share price often rises as a result of leaks or inspired guesses in the weeks before a bid is announced.

Actual takeovers, and rumours of takeovers, raise the prices of individual shares. Investors' thinking becomes obsessed with takeovers and they look for other possible bid candidates and force up the prices by buying the shares. The equity market as a whole is carried upwards by the takeover fever.

Price rises on takeover talk seem to fly in the face of the idea that a company's earnings prospects determine the value of its shares. This is not so. The bidder is simply paying a price that takes account of the expected earnings growth of the victim company over the next two or three years, the earnings he expects to be able to squeeze out of his victim (possibly with the help of creative accounting), or the possible cost savings from eliminating overlapping activities and jobs. Thus for any share there are at least two possible values. What it is worth in the market on its own earnings prospects. And the price a bidder might have to pay, which pre-empts a few years of earnings growth or which is based on the potential for **asset-stripping** (see glossary) or selling off the constituent businesses. Shareholders in the victim company get jam today rather than jam tomorrow.

7b

What moves share prices
b: In the crash of '87

Investors have short memories. After every major crash in financial markets we read that lessons have been learned and taken to heart. The same mistakes could not be made in the future. Do not believe a word of it. Within ten years or so the crash is no more than a faint folk-memory. The same mistakes are resurfacing, perhaps in slightly different form. Once financial markets get a head of steam behind them, nobody wants to hear the words of caution. After the 1974–76 collapse in the commercial property market, for which the groundwork was laid by excessive bank lending, we were told that the same thing could never happen again. Between 1984 and 1990 the banks increased their property loans sevenfold. By 1991 the bloated commercial property market had collapsed and the banks were preparing to account for their multi-billion pound property loan losses. It therefore does no harm to remember what a crash in the financial markets is like, even if it is too much to hope that the lessons will prevent similar happenings in the future.

For investors nurtured on the bull market of the 1980s the roof fell in on Monday 19 October 1987. And it was not only investors who suffered falling roofs. The Friday morning of the previous week, a once-in-a-century freak storm had devastated much of southern England, causing widescale property damage but also disrupting transport and all forms of communication. On that day the Stock Exchange in London had barely functioned. Many securities dealers had not arrived for work. The Stock Exchange's SEAQ price information system was out of commission much of the day and such dealing as

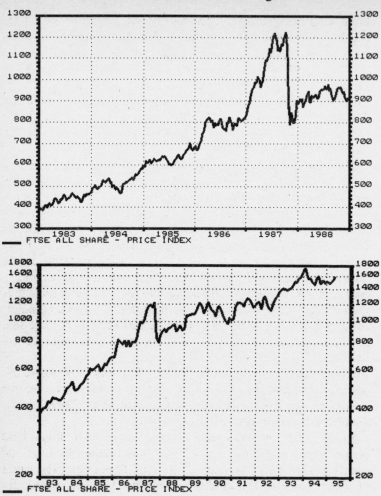

Figure 7.1 How history lends perspective. The top chart shows the boom in share prices in the 1980s which paved the way for the dramatic bust in October 1987. The bottom chart shows exactly the same thing, but has been updated to 1995 and uses a logarithmic scale. The '87 crash seems barely more than a blip. Be careful with charts: they can be designed to deceive. Source: *Datastream International.*

took place reverted to old systems of direct contact. No Stock Exchange indices were calculated in London that day.

America was spared the storm, but nasty things had been

happening on Wall Street. On Saturday 17 October the *Financial Times* led with a story headed 'Wall Street ends two worst weeks with record daily fall'. The Dow Jones Industrial Average – the most commonly used index of the American market – had fallen over 17 per cent from its August peak. On Friday 16 October alone it had dropped almost 5 per cent. The *Financial Times*'s market report commented 'It was not simply that the stockmarket fell. . . . It was more: last week the US stockmarket lost its optimism'.

Had London been fully functioning that Friday, and had share price indices been calculated, some indication of what was to come this side of the Atlantic might have filtered through. As it was, London was worried; but there was little sense of market cataclysm that weekend. Monday's *Financial Times* led with a story 'Bull yields to bear as Wall Street accepts the party's over'. But it was writing mainly of the United States. In Britain, the biggest ever sale of government-owned shares was about to take place: the £7.2 billion offer of the government's stake in British Petroleum. Monday's paper contained a piece on the BP sale headed: 'A test for the bull market's resolve'. In Britain we were still talking of bull markets.

By Tuesday the worldwide bull market was history. At the close on Monday 19 October the London market was down almost 10 per cent from its close the previous Thursday, as measured by the FTA All Share Index.

But on that Monday the United States had again held centre stage. The Dow Jones Industrials crashed by over 500 points to 1738.42: a one-day fall of over 22 per cent, the worst of which happened after the London market had closed. By Tuesday's close London was a further 11.4 per cent down for a two-day fall of 20 per cent. And, with only modest occasional rallies, it continued down well into November. At its nadir the FTA All-Share Index was down 36.6 per cent from its July 1987 peak. Other markets worldwide had suffered a similar fate. On Monday 19 October and the following day the Tokyo stockmarket lost 17 per cent and the Australian market was down almost 28 per cent. Hong Kong could not be measured at this point. The market had closed.

Once the full extent of the market rout was apparent, the economic gurus were out in force to rationalize the week's

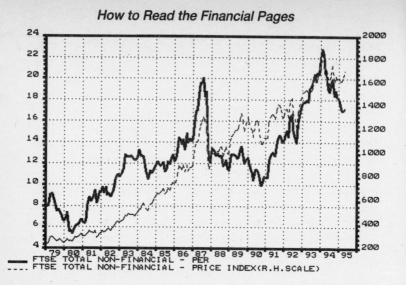

Figure 7.2 The average PE ratio on shares of industrial and commercial companies (solid line and left-hand scale) rose to 20 in 1987 as share prices (broken line and right-hand scale) boomed and lost contact with the fundamentals of company earnings. PE ratios returned to more normal levels with the subsequent crash in share prices. Source: *Datastream International.*

events. The instability in the financial system as a result of world trade imbalances, and particularly the budget and trade deficits in the United States, was apparently to blame for the mayhem in the world's financial markets. The economists singularly failed to explain why, since these imbalances had been present for some considerable time, the crash had not happened before.

There was in fact a far simpler and, at least with the benefit of hindsight, more accurate explanation of the week's events. Most speculative booms in stockmarkets end with a bust: what sparks the fall is almost irrelevant. Professor J K Galbraith summed up the phenomenon in his book on an earlier and ultimately far more serious stockmarket crash in the United States, *The Great Crash 1929*. '. . . it was simply that a roaring boom was in progress in the stock market and, like all booms, it had to end. . . . When prices stopped rising – when the supply of people who were buying for an increase was exhausted . . . everyone would want to sell. The market wouldn't level out; it would fall precipitately'. On Monday 19 October 1987, this happened again on Wall Street – and in London and across the world.

The price falls in the 1987 crash were as nothing compared to the bear market of 1973–75, when share prices fell to around a quarter of their previous peak. It was the speed of the fall that created the drama. A decline in share prices that in previous decades might have taken place gradually, over a year or more, was telescoped into a day or a few days. Again, many explanations have been advanced for the suddenness of the fall, and computers (or the men and women who programme them) were singled out for a large share of the blame.

There was much talk of the perils of **programme trading**, though the phrase appeared to mean different things to different commentators. In the United States widescale arbitrage habitually took place between the cash market and the financial futures market, with computers signalling the minor discrepancies in pricing between the two that offered the chance of a profit (see Chapter 18). **Portfolio insurance** was also common in the States. This is a tactic by which major institutional investors may seek to lock into the profits on their portfolios. It can involve operations in the futures or options markets (the value of the futures or options positions rises if the value of shares in the portfolio falls). It can also involve a set programme for turning part of the share portfolio into cash if prices fall more than a certain amount. And on top we have the familiar **chartist** theories (see previous chapter) whereby a price fall can itself signal a larger price fall and stimulate selling which makes the prediction self-fulfilling.

All of these factors and more were probably at work on Wall Street during the crash. The interaction of the stockmarket and the futures market meant that a fall on one stimulated selling on the other, which in turn led to further selling on the first. And the use of semi-automatic programmes made the spiral twist even more rapidly down.

But perhaps this form of computerized trading (which in any case was not widespread in London at that time) was the least significant aspect of computers in the crash. More important was the instant dissemination of information across the world by electronic message and computer screen. The trader knew instantly what was happening in other financial centres and marked down share prices in his own in consequence. As panic spread through the world's financial centres it became clear that instant information had negative as well as positive features.

So much for the technicalities. Why had share prices been poised for a fall? If we take the London market in isolation (and many of its features were mirrored overseas) the charts tell much of the story. Look first at Figure 7.2, plotting the FTA All-Share Index (excluding financials) since 1983. Share prices had been climbing steadily through to the end of 1986. In the first half of 1987 the rate of increase accelerated (a typical feature of the late days of a bull market) as more and more investors or speculators climbed on the bandwagon, attracted by the profits made from the market in recent years. By its peak in the middle of July, the index had climbed 48 per cent from its beginning of the year level. Then look at the other (solid) line, showing the average price earnings (PE) ratio on the FTA 500 non-financials index.

The immediately striking point is that though on balance PE ratios were rising up to the end of 1986 – again, this tends to happen in a bull market – they were not rising anything like as fast as share prices. In other words, company profits and earnings were rising rapidly, providing part-justification for the increase in share prices. But the rise in share values in the first half of 1987 finally lost contact with the **fundamentals**. Company profits did not rise 48 per cent in half a year, as shares did. Outright speculative fever had taken hold. If we look at Figure 7.3, showing average dividend yields against average redemption yields on gilt-edged stocks, we get another facet of the same picture. Up to the end of 1986, company dividends had been increasing fast enough to prevent a great drop in yields despite booming share prices. In 1987 share prices shot ahead of dividend growth and dividend yields fell sharply to below 3 per cent on average. In the process, as the chart shows clearly, the traditional relationship between gilt-edged returns and dividend yields was sharply distorted.

Thus, in 1987, share prices totally lost contact with the fundamentals – earnings, yield and alternative investment returns – which are the ultimate support for share values. When prices began to fall, there was nothing to stop the rout until a rational relationship with the fundamentals was re-established.

In fact, for all the drama, the crash did no more than return share prices to their value of a year earlier, when the final speculative fever had taken hold. The crash was a vindication – not a negation – of the theory that company profits and dividends determine share values in the long run.

What of the aftermath? Company profits and dividends continued to grow after October 1987. The economic collapse, which many felt that the crash foretold or would cause, simply failed to happen over the following eighteen months. Shares again began to look quite attractive on the fundamental criteria. The crash was a pure stockmarket phenomenon: a bust following an excessive speculative boom. That is not to say that it did not have its economic effects. The authorities in Britain, it is argued, were terrified of any action that might provoke further mayhem on the markets. They therefore failed to act soon enough to damp down an over-heating economy, with the result that the 1980s boom ran totally out

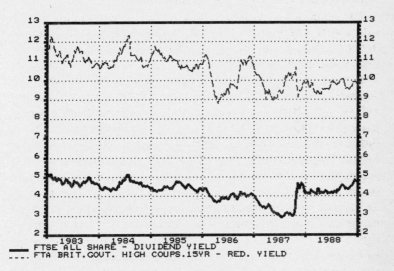

FTSE ALL SHARE - DIVIDEND YIELD
FTA BRIT.GOVT. HIGH COUPS.15YR - RED. YIELD

Figure 7.3 The average dividend yield on shares (solid bottom line) normally maintains a relationship with the yield on gilt-edged stocks (broken line). But in 1987 the final stages of the share price boom pushed dividend yields below 3 per cent and distorted the relationship. This relationship returned to a more normal pattern after share prices collapsed and dividend yields therefore rose again. Source: *Datastream International.*

of control and the reaction – the recession of the early 1990s – was correspondingly more severe. But that is another story.

Even in the short term, however, the crash had left its scars. It largely destroyed the illusion that the City could sustain its extravagant lifestyle with ever more frenetic dealing in shares. There was little more talk of expansion in the equity trading rooms; cutbacks became the norm. The **liquidity** of the market had been exposed as an illusion. The events of 1987 showed that shares were easy to buy and sell while prices were rising. But once the fall began, those who hoped to get out fast found they were lucky if they could get through to their broker or to the marketmakers. The trading system introduced in the Big Bang was already in need of revision.

Could a crash on a similar scale happen again? It will already be clear that our own answer is 'yes', though it is most likely to come after a period of feverish speculative activity in the markets. Before the 1987 crash the British government had encouraged such speculative fever, by hyping privatization issues and by offering the taxpayer's assets to the public at below their worth. The illusion of the stockmarket as a source of instant profits had been created. It fuelled the boom that preceded the bust.

If such speculative fevers could be prevented in the future, perhaps crashes could be prevented as well. But once the stockmarket gets a head of steam behind it, nobody wants to miss the fun. Everybody holds on for the last five per cent of profit as the market approaches its peak, and everybody succumbs to the delusion that he or she will be able to spot the warning signs of the downturn ahead of the herd. The 1987 crash showed what happened when investors put this delusion to the test of reality and, in the event, all rushed to sell at the same time.

8

Stockmarket launches

When the stockmarket is buoyant you can expect a spate of new companies **coming to the market** – achieving a **quote** for their shares for the first time – encouraged by the high valuation that will be put on their shares and by investors' readiness to buy them.

The term 'new companies' is perhaps misleading. They are not new businesses, but businesses which are new to the stockmarket. For the first time their shares can be bought and sold on the stockmarket. The larger ones may apply for a **listing** on The Stock Exchange itself (the **main market**). Smaller or younger companies (or companies which wished to **float** only a small amount of their share capital) used to apply for a quote on the **Unlisted Securities Market (USM)**, also run under Stock Exchange auspices. For a time the very small or new companies had the option of a **Third Market** in which their shares could be traded, but it was not a success and had a relatively short life. And by 1995 the Stock Exchange was also running down the USM with a view to closure. For the smaller companies a new **Alternative Investment Market** known as **AIM** was proposed, due to begin operating in the summer of 1995.

For many individual investors, applying for shares in **new issues** is their first introduction to Stock Exchange affairs. They may apply for shares with the intention of holding onto them as an investment. But they also **stag** new issues by applying for shares in the hope that these can be sold at a profit as soon as **dealings begin** (we will see later why this is often a good bet). First, the mechanics of a new issue.

Type of launch

There are four main ways a company may float its shares on the market (flotations attract nautical metaphors just as takeovers attract marital ones, and a new issue may also be described as a **launch**):

- The **offer for sale**. Shares are offered for sale to the public, partly via the medium of the newspapers which carry a **prospectus** with details of the company (a prospectus is a legal requirement when shares are marketed) plus an **application form** for the shares. This is the method of most interest to the general public and we will look at it in detail later.

- The **placing**. In this case the company achieves an initial spread of shareholders by arranging privately to sell shares to a range of investors: usually several hundred of them. The placing is usually arranged by the company's broker and most of the shares will probably be placed with his clients. The general public who are not clients probably do not get a look-in at this stage. After the placing, permission is given for the shares to be traded on the stockmarket, and anybody can buy in the normal way. Many USM issues – where the quantities of shares sold might have been fairly small – were made via a placing.

- The **intermediaries offer**. Shares are offered for sale to financial intermediaries for subsequent allocation to their clients. Again, investors who are not clients of the intermediaries in question cannot buy at this stage but have to wait until the shares are traded on the market.

- The **introduction**. This is less common. It happens when a company already has a large spread of shareholders and simply wants permission for the shares to be dealt in on the stockmarket. An introduction does not involve the raising of capital or the marketing of shares – though it could pave the way for raising additional capital in the future – and it is the cheapest way of coming to market. When a company moved up from the USM to the main market it was probably by way of an introduction.

With the exception of introductions, combinations of these

various issue methods may be possible. Thus, for smaller issues the shares might be marketed via a combination of offer for sale and placing, or placing and intermediaries offer. For medium-sized flotations, placings would be allowed only if combined with an offer for sale or intermediaries offer. And for a large flotation (over £50m) the Stock Exchange would insist on an offer for sale. There are criticisms nonetheless that too many issues nowadays are closed to the general public because the offer for sale mechanism is not employed.

Who is raising money?

In any report of an offer for sale, a placing or an intermediaries offer, one of the first points to focus on is: who gets the money from the sale of the shares? The shares may come from one of two sources:

- Shares being sold by the existing shareholders – perhaps the founders of the company who built it up from its inception. In this case the cash raised goes to these original shareholders, not to the company.
- New shares created by the company. In this case the cash from the sale of the shares goes into the company's own coffers, not to its original owners.

In practice, the shares made available may be a mix. Some are existing shares sold by the owners and some are new shares sold to raise cash for the company. Be a little cautious if you see that all the shares are coming from existing shareholders and that they are disposing of a large part of their holdings. Why have they decided to cash in at this point? There may be a valid reason, but you would want to know.

Pricing an offer for sale

Offers for sale to the public are of two main types: **fixed-price offers** and **tender offers**. The fixed price offer is the more common. How is the price fixed?

Every issue requires **sponsors**. Traditionally, an issue would be sponsored by a broker or both a merchant bank and broker might be involved. More recently, other types of institution –

such as accountants – may apply for permission to act as sponsors. And on the new AIM market the role of **nominated adviser** is substituted for that of sponsor. Normally – though not always – a company coming to market makes in its prospectus a forecast of profits and dividend for the current year, as well as giving details of its historical profits. Working with these figures, the sponsors will look for existing quoted companies in a similar line of business. By reference to the **ratings** (**PE ratio** and **yield**) these companies enjoy – and adjusting for the superior or inferior **growth prospects** of the newcomer – it should be possible to fix the appropriate rating, and therefore the price, for the shares of the newcomer. (See also **book-building** in glossary).

Two points should be borne in mind. The sponsors want to make sure the new issue gets off to a good start: in other words, when trading begins in the shares the price in this **aftermarket** should not be below the offer for sale price and preferably should rise some way above. So they will try to pitch the shares at a price a little below what they are likely to be worth. Too far below and they will be accused of failing to get a sufficiently good price for their client.

Secondly, the company itself almost certainly errs on the side of caution in arriving at its profits forecast. There is nothing worse for a market newcomer than to fail to meet its **prospectus forecast**. So the forecast will be pitched some way below what the directors expect profits to be.

The first point means that – unless the sponsors have got their calculations badly wrong or the stockmarket drops sharply between the price being fixed and the start of dealings – the shares are being sold at less than their likely value and there is therefore a very good chance of a quick profit for **stags** who manage to secure an allocation of shares. The second means that you should not take too seriously the reports which appear later when the company publishes its first profit figures after going public. They are often headed 'XYZ Holdings exceeds forecast' as if this implied unexpectedly good performance. The truth in most cases is that investors should have been worried if the company did not exceeed its forecast. It had planned to do so.

The tender offer

Some companies are almost impossible to value – for example, there may be no comparable quoted company – and in these circumstances a **tender offer** can make sense. Investors are invited to apply for the number of shares they want and asked to state what price they are prepared to pay above a stipulated minimum. Assuming the issue is **fully subscribed** – applications are received for at least the total number of shares on offer – the sponsors will calculate at what price all the shares available can be sold. This becomes the **striking price** and anybody who applied for shares at this price or above has a chance of getting some. The shares are allocated at the striking price, even to those who bid at a higher price. Those who bid below the striking price get none.

The striking price will not always be the highest possible price at which all the available shares can be sold. As this becomes a bit complicated, an example helps. Suppose XYZ Holdings offers 10m shares to the public and invites tenders at a price of 120p or above. Applications were received as follows:

No of shares applied for at each price	Price	Cumulative total of shares that could be sold at each price
2,000,000	140p	2,000,000
3,000,000	135p	5,000,000
5,000,000	130p	10,000,000
2,000,000	125p	12,000,000
4,000,000	120p	16,000,000

The right-hand column shows that, at a price of 130p, all of the 10m shares available could be sold, since there were applications for 5m at 130p, 3m at 135p and 2m at 140p. So 130p would be the highest possible striking price. But the sponsors may decide they would rather sell at a slightly lower price to ensure the shares get off to a good start when dealings begin. So they fix on 125p as the striking price. Since there were applications for 12m shares at this price or above, not all the applicants will get all the shares they asked for.

Oversubscription and allotments

Sponsors pitch their price at a level that they expect will attract applications for more shares than are on offer. Or, with a tender offer, they may settle for a striking price below the highest possible. If they are right and there are applications for more shares than are on offer, the offer is **oversubscribed**. Press reports normally give the extent of the oversubscription.

Then comes the problem of deciding who gets shares, and how many: the **allocation** or **allotment**. This depends on policy and on the extent of oversubscription. It may be decided to hold a **ballot** of all applicants, with the successful ones receiving a standard allocation, whatever they applied for. Or those applying for large numbers (over 100,000, say) may have their applications **scaled down** to, perhaps, 10 per cent of what they asked for. Those applying for fewer than 100,000 might each get 100 shares, or might be put in a ballot with the successful ones getting 300 shares each and the remainder nothing. It depends on the spread of shareholding the company and its sponsors want (the big initial privatisation offers from the government for companies such as British Gas tended to be structured so as to favour small investors).

Underwriting an issue

Most new issues are **underwritten**. This means that big investors – particularly institutions – agree for a fee to buy any shares which are not bought by the public if the offer is **undersubscribed**. The vendors – the company or its original shareholders – are thus sure of getting their money. The merchant bank sponsoring the issue takes a fee (a percentage of the value of the shares on offer) and pays part to **subunderwriters** – investors who agree to take a certain maximum number of shares if required to do so. **Underwriting fees** are a useful source of income for merchant banks and investing institutions and the City does not like tender offers (which are not invariably underwritten).

It is unusual for the underwriter or subunderwriters to be called on to take up shares. But if an offer for sale is undersubscribed and **left with the underwriters** you may see references in the press to shares **overhanging the market**. This may mean that underwriters, who were forced to take up more shares than they wanted, will want to sell them (**lighten their holdings**). The share price is unlikely to rise far until these shares overhanging the market have been sold and end up in **firm hands**: with investors who want to keep them.

For the most dramatic case of an **issue flop** we need to go back to 1987 and the sale of the government's £7.2 billion stake in British Petroleum in October that year. This was not technically a new issue, as BP's shares were already listed on the Stock Exchange. Rather, the government was disposing of its own large shareholding in the company via a **secondary issue**. But the issue coincided with – and probably helped to cause – the stockmarket crash of that month. As the share price in the stockmarket fell below the offer price, most of the shares were left with the underwriters and subunderwriters, who suffered massive losses. They would have suffered still worse losses if the Bank of England had not effectively re-underwritten the part-paid shares by offering to buy them at 70p – a startling case of government subsidy for the private sector securities houses of Britain and North America. And, as a reflection on the financial sophistication (or lack thereof) of the British public, it is worth noting that over a quarter of a million people applied to buy the government's BP shares at the offer price, even when it was clear that BP shares could be bought at a much lower price in the stockmarket.

Sometimes, as in the BP case, underwriters earn every penny of their fees. But there has been mounting criticism of the City's underwriting system, though probably more in relation to underwriting rights issues (see Chapter 9) than new issues. The standard fees of 2 per cent of the issue proceeds for most non-government issues are, the critics argue, a form of cartel. They pay insufficient attention to the differing degrees of risk in different issues. Supporters of the system argue that the pricing of the issue should help to even out the risk factor.

The offer for sale timetable

The sponsors of an issue want as little time as possible to elapse between fixing the price of an issue and the receipt of

LONDON RECENT ISSUES: EQUITIES

Issue price p	Amt paid up	Mkt. cap (£m.)	1994/95 High	Low	Stock	Close price p	+/-	Net div.	Div. cov.	Grs yld	P/E net
150	F.P.	507.9	165	154	Albright & Wilson	162	−1	RN6.0	1.5	4.6	18.0
§10	F.P.	16.1	13¼	12	Bath Press	12¼	–	–	–	–	–
–	F.P.	20.5	201	198	Beale	200		HN5.9	–	3.7	–
–	F.P.	28.5	126	123	Colleagues	126		–	–	–	–
§128	F.P.	15.6	135	130	Dailywin	130	−1	RN6.0	2.2	5.8	6.8
§125	F.P.	21.1	131	128	GET Group	128		N–	–	–	11.1
100	F.P.	30.0	101	100	Geared Inc Inv C	100		–	–	–	–
§135	F.P.	17.0	138	126	Golden Rose	127		–	–	–	–
100	F.P.	152.0	96	95	HTR Inc Gth Sp Inc	95		–	–	–	–
100	F.P.	92.7	103½	102	Do. Zero Div Pf	103		–	–	–	–
–	F.P.	21.8	87	83	Inv Tst of Inv Tsts	84		–	–	–	–
–	F.P.	2.91	59	55	Do. Warrants	56		–	–	–	–
35	F.P.	21.4	36	33	MCIT S Cap	33		–	–	–	–
35	P.P.	23.4	36	36	MCIT S Inc	36		–	–	–	–
–	F.P.	0.36	5	3	Melrose Warrants	3½		–	–	–	–
476	170	6,121.6	193	163½	*Natl Power (P/P)	171½	−½	FN15.45	2.6	4.0	13.1
150	F.P.	15.8	160	150	Photobition	153		RN6.0	2.0	4.9	11.1
512	185	4,034.9	206	176½	*PowerGen (P/P)	187	+1	FN15.0	3.2	3.6	11.1
–	F.P.	78.3	498	493	Schroder I G Uts	495		–	–	–	–
–	F.P.	24.0	101½	100	Throg DI Zero Pf	101		–	–	–	–
–	F.P.	4.40	11¼	10½	Wessex Trust	11		–	–	–	–
145	F.P.	65.3	183	170	Zotefoams	180	−2	W4.65	2.1	3.2	18.2

* Note: Issue price 10p higher for institutional and overseas investors.

Table 8.1 Information on new issues. Source: *Financial Times*.

applications. They are vulnerable if the market falls in the interim – as with the BP issue – and the shares on offer consequently look overpriced.

Normally a **pathfinder prospectus** is made available to major investors and the press some days ahead of the issue. This contains the details of the company and the offer, so that investors can assess them, but leaves blank the vital information on price and prospective yield and PE ratio. This information is then filled in just before the prospectus is published. Applications then have to be in, usually within a matter of days, and the basis of allocation is announced a few days later.

Allotment letters go out to successful applicants as soon as possible after the basis of allocation is decided, and unsuccessful applicants get their money back. The Stock Exchange fixes a date on which official dealings in the shares will start. In the *Financial Times* the prices of shares in newly-floated companies are listed for a time in a special table in the 'Companies and Markets' section of the paper under the heading **London recent issues: equities**.

The major **denationalization** or **privatization issues** – British Telecom, British Gas and the like – worked to a longer timetable because of the size of the issues and the number of unsophisticated investors they were expected to attract. And when there are a lot of companies coming to market, the timetable may in any case vary a little.

Grey markets

In practice, shares may be traded in a **grey market** before shareholders get their allotment letters or even before the basis of allotment is known. The Stock Exchange was disparaging of unofficial grey markets which used to be run by non-Stock Exchange members. Dealings are risky, because applicants do not yet have shares, so there is no guarantee there that they can or will deliver. But in the case of the TSB Group (Trustee Savings Bank) launch, the Stock Exchange's own **official market** got under way before many applicants knew whether or not they had been allocated shares, to the considerable annoyance of many of them. And with British Gas the start of official dealings was deliberately set a week before allotment letters could be received. One reason was supposedly the risk of the Exchange's (then fairly new) computerized systems collapsing under the strain unless the start of dealings was staggered.

Part-paid shares

Most shares are **fully paid**. In other words, suppose we are talking of 20p shares being sold at 100p, the buyer or subscriber pays the whole 100p at one go. But sometimes – mainly with the privatization issues and in the case of some gilt-edged stocks (see Chapter 13) – the price is paid in two or more instalments. This means the vendor gets his money spread out over a period rather than in a single lump.

Thus when XYZ Holdings launches, it might decide to sell its shares at 100p but ask for 30p immediately, a further 30p in six months and the remaining 40p in a year. When only 30p has been paid, the shares will be **part paid**. The *Financial Times*'s **London recent issues: equities** table shows the amount paid for each share in a column headed **amount paid up** (in pence). Usually the entry is 'FP' for fully paid, but not in every case.

Part-paid shares are speculative because they are **highly**

geared. Suppose investors think the right price for XYZ shares is 130p: a 30p premium on the issue price of 100p. In their 30p-paid form, the shares might also be expected to stand at a premium of 30p, so the market price is 60p. This means that anyone who was allotted the part-paid shares at 30p has a 100 per cent profit on his outlay to date, though the shares are only thought to be worth 30 per cent more than their issue price. But it works the other way round, too. If the shares are thought to be worth only 90p against an issue price of 100p, in their 30p-paid form they might be expected to stand at 20p. At that point a subscriber has lost a third of his outlay to date. The problems of the BP issue in 1987 were exacerbated by the fact that only 120p of the 330p sale price was payable immediately, and the value of the part-paid shares roughly halved at one point.

New issue fraud

Multiple applications for shares in an offer for sale are, at best, discouraged and in the case of the privatization issues those making multiple applications were threatened with prosecution. Some applicants, including a few moderately prominent figures, were actually prosecuted. A multiple application is when one person fills in a number of different application forms, perhaps with different names and addresses, hoping to get more shares or increase his chances of getting some shares. It is most likely to happen with a popular issue that is expected to be **heavily stagged** and where there is an almost certain profit when the shares begin trading.

The issuing bank's normal way of discouraging multiple applications is to threaten that all cheques sent in will be cashed. If the multiple applicant has borrowed heavily to stag the issue, he is paying large interest charges until he gets the money back in respect of his unsuccessful applications. The government – perhaps because it was selling state assets at less than their true worth to attract the public into its version of popular capitalism – decided that one handout per person should be the limit and adopted the prosecution route for anyone who attempted to grab more.

9

Rights, placings and scrip issues

There is an old principle, enshrined in British company law, that when a company issues new shares to raise cash, those shares should be offered first to the existing shareholders – the owners of the business – in the form of a **rights issue**. This is the principle of **pre-emption rights**.

By and large the principle still holds, but in recent years it has been eroded at the edges. The rights issue process is lengthy and cumbersome, some companies and their banking advisers argue. Companies should be free to take advantage of temporary windows of opportunity in the financial markets by issuing shares as and where they see an opening. Companies in America have considerably more freedom in this respect and the principle of pre-emption rights counts for little. American companies may issue shares *en bloc* to a securities house, which subsequently sells them through its marketing network. This, it is claimed, is faster and cheaper for the company. And the people who make these claims are frequently the banks and securities houses which would earn most from this method of share distribution.

But there is a paradox here. How can a procedure be good for a company if it is not good for the existing shareholders who own the company? Echoes of this debate surface from time to time in the financial columns of the press. Generally the big investors – the insurance companies and pension funds – will argue strongly for the existing rights issue system. But they have compromised by allowing companies to make small issues of shares without going through the rights procedure. You will frequently see in companies' annual reports that they

RIGHTS OFFERS

Issue price p	Amount paid up	Latest Renun. date	1994/95 High	Low	Stock	Closing price p	+or-
340	102	–	196pm	165pm	Cadbury Schws Cv Ln	195pm	+6
175	Nil	20/4	21pm	6pm	Cookson	20pm	+6
335	Nil	–	73pm	64pm	Dalgety Cv Ln 1995	64pm	–2
90	Nil	11/5	31pm	25pm	Horace Small	31pm	+2
90	Nil	15/3	4pm	1pm	Shorco	1pm	
50	Nil	10/4	4pm	2pm	Torex Hire	2pm	–1⁄2
39	Nil	–	1¹⁄2pm	1¹⁄2pm	Unit Group	1¹⁄2pm	
52	Nil	20/4	14pm	7pm	Wyko	14pm	

Table 9.1 Stockmarket prices for 'rights'. Source: *Financial Times*.

ask investors to vote them the powers to make limited share issues to buyers other than existing shareholders. It may be described as 'disapplication of the statutory pre-emption rights'.

Thus, anything we say about traditional methods of issuing new shares for cash must be read with a note of caution. Rights issues are still the norm, but **placings**, **open offers** and **vendor placings** are also frequently encountered. It is the rights issue, however, that we need to look at first.

Mechanics of the rights issue

The **rights issue** procedure – 'rights' because existing share-holders have the first right to put up the new money – goes like this. The company announces it intends to raise a particular amount by creating and selling new shares. The new shares will be offered to the shareholders in proportion to their existing holdings. And they will virtually always be offered at a price below that of the existing shares in the market, to give shareholders an incentive to put up money for the new shares. If they are offered at a price way below the existing price – say, at half the market value – the issue would be described as a **deep discounted** rights issue or as having a very large **scrip** element (see below). But this is the exception rather than the rule. Discounts of 20 per cent or so are more common.

This is a point that often causes confusion. You will come across phrases in the press like: 'XYZ Holdings is offering shareholders one new share for every five held at the very favourable price of 200p against a market price of 400p' or

146

'XYZ Holdings is making a rights issue on very attractive terms to investors'.

This is usually sheer nonsense. The shareholders already own the company. The company cannot offer them anything that is not theirs already. The price at which the new shares are offered is a technicality, provided they are offered to existing holders. Investors are not getting anything on the cheap. An example illustrates the point.

Adjusting the price

Suppose XYZ Holdings, whose shares are quoted in the stockmarket at 260p, decides to raise £40m by creating and selling 20m new shares at 200p each. The shares are offered to shareholders in the ratio of two new shares for every five existing shares they hold (a 'two-for-five' rights issue). For an investor who decides to take up his rights, this is how the sums go. For every five shares worth 260p each that he holds, he buys two new shares at 200p each. The average value of his shares after the issue would be 242.9p:

5 existing shares at a market price of	260p =	1300p
2 new shares for cash at	200p =	400p
Total for 7 shares	=	1700p
Value of 1 share	(1700p/7) =	242.9p

If all else were equal, 242.9p (call it 243p for simplicity) would be the price at which the XYZ shares would stand in the market after the rights issue. In other words, the market price would adjust down from 260p to 243p to reflect the fact that new shares had been offered below the previous market price. In practice, the general level of the stockmarket and the prices of individual companies are constantly moving up or down, so the sums may not be quite so clear cut. But the principle holds good.

It follows from this that the right to buy new shares at below market price has a value in itself, which is why it needs to be offered first to existing shareholders. A shareholder who simply ignored the rights issue would start with 5 shares at

260p worth 1300p in total and end with 5 shares at 243p after the price adjustment, worth only 1215p. In practice, when the shareholder does nothing the company will normally sell his entitlement to the new shares on his behalf and send the proceeds to him.

Cum-rights and ex-rights

When a company announces a rights issue, it says that the new shares will be offered to all shareholders on the company's **register of shareholders** at such-and-such a date. But since it can take time for purchases and sales to be reflected on the register, the Stock Exchange adopts its own different cut-off date. Anybody buying existing shares in the market before this date buys them with the right to subscribe for the new shares (**cum-rights**). Anyone buying on or after this date does not have the right to the new shares – this remains with the seller. The date is the day on which the shares go **ex-rights** for Stock Exchange dealing purposes, and it is therefore the day on which the market price will adjust downwards – from 260p to 243p in the example. After this date the share price in the Stock Exchange Official List and in newspapers will be marked for a time with an **xr** to tell buyers that they are not acquiring the right to subscribe for the new shares.

Dealing in rights

The rights to subscribe for new shares can be bought and sold in the market in much the same way as shares, and the value of the rights will be roughly equivalent to the **ex-rights price** (the price which has been adjusted downwards to take account of the issue) less the subscription price for the new shares. In the example, the right to buy for 200p a new share which will be quoted in the market at 243p ex-rights will be worth about 43p (243p minus 200p), though technical considerations can affect this a little. Shareholders who do not want to put up money for new shares will sell their rights and thus end up with some cash plus a smaller proportionate stake in the company.

Shareholder has 5 shares at 260p	= 1300p
	———
Sells rights to two new shares at 43p	= 86p
Retains 5 shares at adjusted price of 243p	= 1215p
	———
Has cash and shares of	1300p
(adjusting for rounding-up errors)	———

The rights themselves are a short-life high-geared investment rather like an **option** or **warrant** (see Chapter 18), and often appeal to gamblers. Suppose XYZ's ex-rights share price rose 10p from 243p to 253p: an increase of 4 per cent. The value of the **nil paid** rights (the subscription price for the shares has not been paid) might be expected to rise from around 43p to around 53p: an increase of 23 per cent. Like all gearing, it works in reverse and the value of the rights can disappear entirely if the XYZ share price suffers a sharp fall.

The *Financial Times* carries in its 'Companies and Markets' section a table of **rights offers** showing the prices (technically the **premiums**) quoted for rights to buy new shares. It gives the price at which the new shares are being issued (which would be 200p for XYZ), the proportion of this price which has already been paid (if any – see Chapter 8) and the highest and lowest price at which the rights have traded. You can see that the percentage swings can be very large. The **pm** after the price simply means that the price is actually a premium which the buyer pays for the right to subscribe to a new share.

The price for the new shares in a rights issue is normally pitched sufficiently far below the market price to allow a bit of leeway in case the share price falls in the interim – investors will not put up money for the new shares if they can buy existing shares more cheaply in the market. Nevertheless, to make sure the company gets its money, the issue will normally be **underwritten** – institutions agree for a fee to put up the money for any shares the company cannot sell (see Chapter 8). As we have seen, the standard 2 per cent underwriting fees in rights issues come in for periodic criticism.

Deep-discounted issues

To XYZ Holdings it makes little difference if it issues 20m new shares at 200p each or 40m at 100p each. It still raises the

£40m it needs. And if it pitches the **subscription price** at 100p against a market price of 260p for the existing shares, there is very little risk that the market price might fall below the subscription price and prevent the new shares from being taken up. A **deep-discounted rights issue** such as this would therefore not need to be underwritten – a considerable cost saving. In practice, very few companies follow the deep-discounted route. The reason usually given is that there is a slight tax disadvantage for some shareholders in the deep discount process. The City, for which **underwriting fees** are a useful and normally an easily-earned perk, does not encourage deepdiscounters.

> 'Prudential Corporation, Britain's largest life assurance company, yesterday surprised the stockmarket by seeking £357m from its shareholders through a rights issue.
>
> 'The market was even more surprised when the Pru revealed that the issue would not be underwritten. A rights issue not underwritten is rare and the Pru's current issue is by far the largest of its kind to date. Its terms are one new share at 600p for every five held and it will involve the issue of 60,257,503 new shares.' (*Financial Times*, 2 May 1986)

When XYZ's market price is 260p the company is being no more and no less 'generous' if it offers new shares at 100p than at 200p. Remember the principle. The company belongs to the shareholders and there is nothing they can be given that they do not already own. The only benefit they may derive is if the **dividend per share** is maintained on the increased capital, which has the same effect as a dividend increase. This is a totally different decision, but it is often confused with the rights issue itself. If XYZ was paying a 10p per share gross dividend before the issue, the yield on the shares at 260p would have been 3.8 per cent. If it paid the same dividend per share after a two-for-five rights issue at 200p, the yield at the **ex-rights price** of 243p would rise to 4.1 per cent.

Other share issue methods

As we have seen, the rights issue is far from dead, but other methods of issuing new shares for cash are also reasonably common. The ones you are likely to read about include:

- The **placing**. This works in much the same way as a placing used as a method of bringing a new company to market (see Chapter 8). New shares are created and the company's financial adviser will sell them direct to a range of investors. The shares will probably be offered at a price a little below the market price, but not as far below as in a rights issue. Sometimes, all the new shares might be offered to investors on an overseas stockmarket. In the 1980s companies and their advisers frequently presented this as a way of gaining a wider geographical range of shareholders – useful to a company's international standing, they claimed. In practice, the overseas buyers who acquired shares below the market price frequently sold them rapidly and at a profit to UK investors (a process known as **flowback**). The guidelines imposed by institutional investors would normally allow a placing of only a small proportion of the company's capital unless there were **clawback** arrangements for existing shareholders (see below).

- Placing and **open offer**. This can be described in slightly different ways. Essentially, new shares are created and sold conditionally (usually at a small discount) to large investors, mainly the institutions. But existing shareholders have the right to take up the new shares at the same price instead. So the new shares will end up with the purchasing institutions only to the extent that existing shareholders decide not to take them up. Thus far, the result from the company's point of view is much the same as with an underwritten rights issue. The arrangement for the institutions to purchase the shares serves the same purpose as a conventional underwriting agreement: the company knows that it will get its money.

  But note that this does not produce the same result as a conventional rights issue for all shareholders. A holder who does not take up his entitlement under the clawback has no **rights** to sell for cash. The benefit of new shares at below market price goes to somebody else.

- The **vendor placing**. Suppose Company A wants to buy a division of Company B, and wants to use its own shares to pay. Company B, on the other hand, wants cash, not shares in Company A. Company A could, of course, make a conventional rights issue to raise the cash to pay Company B. But it might be quicker and simpler to issue new shares to the required value to Company B and at the same time make arrangements for all these new shares to be bought by institutional investors for cash. This would be a vendor placing (the shares are placed with institutions on behalf of the vendor). The purchaser thus pays in shares but the vendor receives cash. Again, the institutional shareholder rules place an upper limit on the size of transaction that can be undertaken in this way without the new shares being offered to existing shareholders by way of clawback.

- The **euroequity** issue. A company uses a securities house or a number of securities houses to market the new shares that it creates to investors in a range of overseas countries via the international market mechanisms (see Chapter 17). Such operations by UK companies will tend to be limited by the pre-emption rules.

- The **bought deal**. Instead of placing shares with a number of investors, a company can invite bids for all the shares from the **securities houses**. The securities house offering the highest price gets the business and pays cash for the shares, hoping to make a profit by selling them via its distribution network to a range of investors. This might be described as a 'primary' bought deal, and in Britain its application is limited by the pre-emption rules. But the principle of the bought deal is not limited to new shares a company creates. A company which held a large investment portfolio of other companies' shares that it wanted to dispose of could invite offers for the lot (a 'secondary' bought deal). Both types of business can be very profitable for the securities houses, though they are also very high risk – the buyer could lose heavily if the share price dropped between its buying the shares *en bloc* and selling them to the final purchasers. The operation requires large amounts of capital – one of the reasons why British securities houses need big financial backing to be able to compete with their American counterparts. Equally important, it demands a large efficient marketing department with a wide spread of investor contacts.

The dangers of the bought deal procedure were underlined in 1990 when merchant bank Kleinwort Benson paid

£138m (or 99p per share) to Burmah Castrol for its 29 per cent stake in Premier Consolidated Oilfields, hoping to distribute the shares quickly at a profit. Instead, the price fell heavily and Kleinwort eventually got out at 78p for a loss of £34m on the operation.

> 'Granada is to finance the purchase of Laskys by issuing 10.8m new shares. The entire issue has been taken up by Salomon Brothers, the US investment bank, in a bought deal, a common US stockmarket tactic which is increasingly being imported to the UK.
>
> 'Salomon has paid 282p a share, just 2p less than Granada's 284p closing price on Wednesday. This was a smaller discount than would have been necessary in a conventional vendor placing, Granada said.' (*Financial Times* 17 October 1986)

● **Euromarket convertible issues.** Companies can issue 'deferred equity' to international as well as domestic investors by issuing a convertible bond via the euromarket mechanisms (see Chapter 17). In the past, some companies tried this route as a way of avoiding the institutional rules for new share issues. But the limits on the amount of new capital that could be offered to investors other than existing shareholders now apply to convertible issues as well as direct issues of shares.

Pre-emption rights and the institutions' rules

In the case of a placing, a vendor placing or, particularly, a bought deal, the price for the new XYZ shares would probably be far closer to the market price than in the case of a conventional rights issue. But it will still normally be at some discount to the ruling market price. And this is where the controversy arises. It makes no odds, as we've seen, whether XYZ choses to offer its new shares at 200p or 100p as long as they are offered first to existing shareholders. But if they are offered below market price to investors who are not already shareholders in XYZ, there is a transfer of value from existing shareholders to the new buyers, which is a totally different matter.

The pension funds and insurance companies are the major

existing shareholders in most larger companies, and they have not taken kindly to seeing their birthright eroded. They have therefore argued that most or all of the new shares sold via these techniques should be offered to existing shareholders as a **clawback**.

In practice, as we have seen, they have had to compromise. Their rules – which are reinforced by the authority of the Stock Exchange – lay down that a company may not issue new shares for cash, without offering them first to existing shareholders, if the new shares represent more than a certain proportion of existing capital or are issued at a discount of more than a certain amount. In 1995 the rule was that new shares issued for cash, and by-passing existing shareholders, must not add more than 5 per cent to the company's capital in a single year or more than 7.5 per cent over a rolling three-year period, or be issued at a discount of more than 5 per cent to the market price. For vendor placings the institutions have their own slightly less restrictive guidelines. Here, in 1995 the limit on issues without clawback was 10 per cent in a year and at a discount of no more than 5 per cent. Even at these levels, issues over a period of years to non-shareholders can significantly dilute the existing shareholders' interest and the institutions are not entirely happy with the situation.

'The purchase of Celebrated, owner of four English hotels, is to be satisfied by the issue of 61.2m new ordinary shares in Norfolk which will represent 21 per cent of the enlarged equity.

'Morgan Grenfell is placing the shares conditionally with investment clients but existing shareholders are to be offered them for 25p each. Norfolk's shares closed yesterday at 29p, down 1½p' (*Financial Times*, 27 January 1987)

The scrip issue

From the new, back to the old. There is one further type of share issue that any reader of the financial press has to understand: the **scrip issue** or **capitalization issue**. It arises almost by historical accident, but poses a pitfall for the unwary. It is sometimes referred to in the press (and, even less excusably, by companies themselves) as a **free issue** or a **bonus issue**, again conjuring the vision of shareholders receiving something for nothing. In the case of the traditional scrip issue, this is misleading nonsense.

The historical accident is the fact that the nominal value of the share capital of British companies is distinguished from other funds belonging to shareholders and that the shares themselves therefore have a **par** value: 5p, 10p, 20p, 25p, 50p, £1 or whatever. The equivalent unit of **common stock** in American companies may not need to have a par value.

A scrip or capitalization issue in the UK is the process whereby a company turns part of its accumulated **reserves** into new shares. Suppose ABC Company's shares stand in the market at 800p and its **shareholders' funds** look like this:

	£m
ORDINARY SHARE CAPITAL (in 20p shares)	100
PROFIT AND LOSS ACCOUNT RESERVES	600
REVALUATION RESERVES	300
SHAREHOLDERS' FUNDS	1,000

Because the company has accumulated considerable **profit and loss account reserves** by ploughing back profits over the years, the £100m of share capital gives little indication of the total size of the shareholders' interest. Also, as profits have risen so the share price has risen, to the point where – at 800p – it is **heavy** by British standards. In many other countries, shares which each cost the equivalent of tens or hundreds of pounds are common. Britain has the tradition of units with a smaller value and shares are considered to become less easily **marketable** (less easy to buy and sell in the stockmarket) when the price pushes up towards £10 or so.

So ABC might decide to convert part of its reserves into new shares. Suppose it decides to use £100m of its profit and loss account reserves for this purpose. It creates £100m nominal of new shares (500m shares, since they are 20p units) and uses £100m of the profit and loss account reserves to make them **fully paid**. The new shares are distributed to existing shareholders (in this case in a one-for-one ratio) and the shareholders' funds after the operation look like this:

	£m
ORDINARY SHARE CAPITAL (in 20p shares)	200
PROFIT AND LOSS ACCOUNT RESERVES	500
REVALUATION RESERVES	300
SHAREHOLDERS' FUNDS	1,000

All that has happened is that £100m has been deducted from one heading (profit and loss account reserves) and added to another (ordinary share capital). It is a **book-keeping transaction**, pure and simple, and in no way affects the value of the shareholders' interest in the company nor does it raise money for the company. Shareholders' funds remain unchanged at £1,000m.

Adjusting the price for a scrip issue

In our example the shareholder now has two shares where he had one before. But since the value of the company has not changed, the market price will simply adjust to reflect the issue. Previously the shareholder had one share worth 800p. After the issue he has two shares worth 400p each. The greater number of shares in issue and the less heavy price may make them slightly more marketable.

A scrip issue need not be in the ratio of one-for-one (also referred to as a 100 per cent capitalization issue). It could be one-for-ten (a 10 per cent issue), two-for-five, two-for-one and so on. The complication in each case is that the market price has to be adjusted for the issue. If the issue were one-for-ten, the market price would come back from 800p to 727.3p. The investor starts with 10 shares at 800p, worth 8,000p in total and he ends with 11 shares. Dividing the 8,000p by 11 shares gives a price of 727.3p.

As with a rights issue, the Stock Exchange sets a date after which a buyer of ABC's shares in the market will not acquire the entitlement to the new shares resulting from the scrip issue, and that is the day the price adjusts downwards. After the adjustment the letters **xc** will appear after the price, meaning **ex-capitalization**.

If a scrip issue by itself is significant only in a technical sense it can, like a rights issue, have implications for the share-holder's income. If ABC makes a one-for-one scrip issue and wants to pay out the same amount of money by way of dividend after the issue, it will have to halve the rate of dividend per share. The shareholder who received 10p on one share gets the same income from 5p on two shares after the issue. If ABC holds its dividend at 10p per share, it is effectively doubling the payment. Occasionally, companies increase their dividends by paying a constant amount per share, but making regular small scrip issues such as one-for-ten.

How scrip issues complicate comparisons

With a one-for-one scrip issue, when the market price halves, it is not easy to miss what is happening, though brokers still get calls from clients asking why their shares have performed so badly. A one-for-ten issue, with a comparatively minor downwards adjustment in the price, is far easier to miss. When tracking the performance of a share price over the years, the investment analyst or journalist has to **adjust** for every scrip issue. Not only must the price be adjusted. Previous years' earnings and dividends per share will also need adjustment. Suppose ABC earned 25p per share and paid a 10p gross dividend for the year before it made its one-for-one scrip issue, at which time the share price was 800p. In the year after the scrip issue the earnings per share were 15p, the dividend was 6p and the share price has touched 550p. What has really happened?

All of the earlier year's figures have to be adjusted for the issue:

One share at 800p	=	two shares at 400p
25p earnings on one share	=	12.5p per share on two shares
10p dividend on one share	=	5p dividend on two shares

Therefore, in comparing the previous year's performance with the latest one, we are comparing **effective** or **adjusted** earnings per share of 12.5p with the latest year's 15p, and an effective or adjusted previous year's dividend of 5p with a current one of 6p. The share price has risen from the **equivalent**

of 400p to the current 550p. Net asset values must be adjusted in a similar way.

Discussions of company performance in the financial press are thus studded with words like 'effective', 'adjusted' and 'equivalent', and reflect this particularly irritating technicality of British company practice. In theory, all figures should also be adjusted for a rights issue at below market price, though practice varies. Certainly, a deep-discounted rights issue (which really contains strong elements of a scrip issue as well as a money-raising issue) requires adjustment.

Less common forms of scrip issue

Two other quirks of the scrip issue process crop up from time to time. Sometimes, companies give their shareholders the option of receiving their dividend in the form of a scrip issue of new shares in place of cash. In the past the new shares would have been issued only to the value of the net dividend (the dividend after basic rate tax has been deducted). But more recently we have seen the **enhanced scrip dividend**, where the company offers a larger value in shares than in cash to persuade shareholders to opt for the former. Under the changes to the tax credit system that we looked at in Chapter 3, this could offer tax advantages to the company: it does not have to pay Advance Corporation Tax on a scrip dividend. But there are objections. In effect, a company that pays most of its dividend in shares rather than cash is making a smallish disguised rights issue – boosting its cash resources by avoiding a cash outflow – often without adequately explaining the reasons. It was sometimes felt that this encouraged companies towards laxity in their cash management by removing the need to ensure that the cash was there for the annual dividend.

Secondly, in some of the government **privatization issues**, shareholders who retain their shares for a specified period were promised a **loyalty bonus** in the form of a scrip issue. In this case the issue does have a value since it does not go to all shareholders alike. Those who receive the extra 'loyalty' shares are increasing their proportionate stake in the company at the expense of the other shareholders who do not qualify.

10

Bidders, victims and lawmakers

Takeovers are the jam on the bread and butter of normal investment business. When Company A bids for Company B, it will almost always be at a price above that which Company B commands in the market on its own merits. Therefore there are instant profits for shareholders of Company B. Moreover, the **market professionals** have a strong vested interest in takeovers. They generate high share dealing **volumes**, and activity is the lifeblood of brokers and marketmakers. They generate big fees for the **merchant banks** who advise the companies involved in the takeover. And there are spin-off benefits for the accountants, solicitors and other professionals drawn into the affair. The City has a strong vested interest in a high level of takeover activity and there will be fierce resistance to efforts to curb it.

In the press, takeover activity is covered at several levels. There are the takeover tips: 'buy shares in XYZ Holdings; a predator is sniffing round'. There are the blow-by-blow accounts of disputed takeovers which can occupy many column-inches week after week. And there are the occasional more thoughtful pieces questioning whether frenetic takeover activity harms Britain's economy and dissecting some of the less desirable tactics employed. Much of this is self-explanatory, but a little background is needed.

Take the last point first. **Takeover activity** tends to go in waves and often reaches its peak when share prices are close to their peak after a prolonged bull market. At these times takeover considerations can almost totally dominate stockmarket thinking as a form of collective fever takes hold.

Everybody is looking for the next takeover victim, buying its shares and forcing prices up. The process becomes self-fuelling. Financial journalists catch the fever like everybody else. Remember this when reading the financial pages: some of the comment on share prices loses all contact with fundamental values.

The justification put forward for takeovers is that they increase **industrial efficiency**. Sleepy companies are gobbled up by more actively managed **predators** which can get better returns from the victim company's assets. In some cases this may be true. But there is little if any consistent evidence that takeovers improve industrial and commercial performance in the long term. Contested takeovers are almost unknown in Germany and Japan, two of the strongest industrial performers. Takeovers may, however, suit the biggest owners of British companies: the insurance companies and pension funds. Finding it difficult to exert positive influence to improve management in the companies they invest in, they may welcome a takeover aproach from an actively managed company that will do the job for them.

Opposition to excessive takeover activity that sometimes finds its echo in the financial pages homes in on other arguments. The threat of takeover induces short-sighted attitudes in company managements. They will not undertake long-term investment if the cost threatens to depress profits before the benefits appear. Depressed profits depress the share price and make the company vulnerable to takeover. Institutional investment managers, too, are being forced to take a short-term view of their performance: **short-termism**. If they are judged over a three-month period on the performance of the investments they manage, they will be inclined to back a takeover which shows them short-term profits.

How accounting blurred the issues

Finally, there are criticisms of the way that the outcome of takeovers has been presented in accounting terms in the past. The profits of the combined group were often presented in an unduly rosy light. This was frequently achieved under the system of **acquisition accounting** by making large **provisions** at the time of the takeover to cover reorganisation costs and even future trading losses of the company acquired. Effectively, these provisions were treated as a deduction from the value of the assets acquired. Company A paid £50m for Company B, which had £30m of net assets. Company A then made provisions of £10m to cover reorganisation costs and future trading losses, reducing the net value of the assets acquired to £20m. Since Company A had paid £50m for net assets of £20m, it had paid £30m for goodwill which it immediately wrote off against reserves. The £10m provisions never affected Company A's profit and loss account and by using up the provisions it could present Company B as making a contribution to profits from day one. The reality may have been that it was loss-making at this point.

Accounting's standard-setting body, the **Accounting Standards Board**, was concerned by these abuses and two new accounting standards – **FRS 6** and **FRS 7** – look set to eliminate them. In future, if Company A wants to make provisions against reorganisation costs or future trading losses in Company B, these provisions will have to go through the profit and loss account of the combined group after the takeover. In other words, published profits will be reduced by the amount of the provisions and the outcome of the takeover will be presented in a more realistic light.

At the same time the new standards greatly restrict the use of another way of accounting for takeovers – **merger accounting** – which could also sometimes present an unrealistic view. Note that except in this context the word **merger** does not normally have a precise technical meaning (see below).

Takeover mechanics

Takeovers in Britain are fought within the framework of formal rules, rather like the moves of medieval combat. As with most rules, frequent revisions of the detail are needed as new techniques emerge. We will come to the more important ones later, but the point to grasp at the outset when reading of any takeover is that a form of corporate democracy prevails. Company A gains **control** of Company B by persuading the holders of at least 50.01 per cent of the Company B **votes** to sell to it or accept its offer. If it already owns some shares in Company B it may require fewer votes to take it to the magic control point. Most companies have a one-vote-per-ordinary-share **capital structure**, so in practice Company A usually has to secure over 50 per cent of the Company B shares.

Within this general rule there are numerous permutations. The first thing to look for in the press report is whether the bid is agreed, defended or contested:

- The directors of Companies A and B may have met and decided that a merger is in the interest of both parties. In this case the bid for Company B will be **agreed**, though this is not a guarantee that it will succeed. The shareholders, not the directors, have the ultimate word. An agreed bid between two companies is often referred to as a **merger**.

- Company A may announce that it is bidding for Company B and the Company B directors may decide to try to fight off the bid. In this case it is **defended** or **contested**. It is certainly **hostile**.

- Two or more companies may bid at about the same time for Company B, which perhaps does not want to be taken over by either of them, or might back the bid from Company C against that from Company A. This will be a **contested** bid. A company at the receiving end of an unwelcome bid often searches for a **white knight**: an alternative bidder that would be acceptable to it and might keep it out of Company A's clutches.

While the directors of a company that is bid for have a duty to act in the best interests of their shareholders, it would be unrealistic to suppose that they always entirely ignore their own interests. A bidder who would allow them to keep their jobs after the takeover might have greater appeal than one who would want to substitute its own management. On the other hand, directors who are ousted after a takeover frequently walk away with very large cash sums – **golden handshakes** – in compensation for early termination of their employment contracts (see Chapter 12).

Form of the offer

When Company A bids for Company B, it has several options. It can make a:

- **Cash offer**. In this case it simply offers a certain amount in cash for each Company B share. Shareholders in Company B who decide to accept have no further interest in the combined group. But acceptance counts in much the same way as if they had sold their shares for cash in the stockmarket, and they may be liable to **Capital Gains Tax** on profits.
- **Paper offer**. Company A offers to swap its own shares in a certain proportion for those of Company B. This will also be referred to as a **share exchange offer**. Company A might offer three of its own shares for every five of Company B. If the Company A shares stand at 360p in the stockmarket, this puts a value of 216p on each Company B share. Sometimes a bid will provide a mix of cash and paper.

In a paper offer, instead of offering its own shares Company A might offer to swap some other form of security for the Company B shares. It might offer 216p nominal of Company A 6 per cent convertible loan stock for each Company B share, again valuing them at 216p if the convertible is worth its nominal value (there can be heated arguments on this point). Or it might offer a mix of convertible and shares, or a choice between the two. When the bid terms become very complex, involving rare and wonderful forms of security, these securities are sometimes referred to as **funny money** (see glossary). When a company issues massive quantities of its shares in a succession of takeovers, the press sometimes talks in terms of a **paperchase** or makes references to **wallpaper**.

In the case of a paper offer from Company A for Company B, acceptance by Company B shareholders does not count as a disposal of their shares for tax purposes. But they will be liable for tax if they subsequently realize profits from the sale of the Company A securities they had received in exchange.

Note that with any paper offer, the value of Company A's shares in the stockmarket determines the value of the offer for each share in Company B, and therefore the chances of the bid succeeding. Company A thus has every incentive to keep its own share price up, and its friends and associates may help its chances by buying its shares to **support** the price (see below).

In a paper offer, the bidder will often establish a floor value for its bid by arranging **underwriting** for the shares it offers. Take the share exchange offer we looked at earlier. Company A offers three of its own shares for every five in Company B. With Company A at 360p Company B shares are valued by the offer at 216p. But Company A arranges with institutions that they will agree to buy any new shares it offers at, say, 340p cash if the recipients want to sell or perhaps it offers a 340p cash alternative from its own resources. So a shareholder in Company B who accepts the Company A offer knows he can take 340p in cash, which gives an **underwritten cash value** for the bid of 204p per Company B share. Of course, if the Company A share price stays high after the bid, he would do better if he wants cash by taking the new Company A shares and selling them in the stockmarket.

Market purchases

So far we have assumed that a takeover simply involves an approach by Company A to the shareholders of Company B outside the stockmarket. But in many cases Company A will use the stockmarket as well. It will perhaps build up a stake in Company B by buying shares in the stockmarket before it makes a formal offer. Or, once an offer has been made, it will increase its chances of success by buying the shares of Company B in the market – the shares it acquires via **market purchases** can then be lumped together with acceptances by Company B shareholders to reach the magic control figure.

But there are rules governing market purchases in the course of a bid (see below), and Company A has to be careful. By buying in the market it may force up the Company B share price, which can make it more difficult or more expensive to gain control.

Rules of the game

Takeovers are policed by the **Panel on Takeovers and Mergers** (the **Takeover Panel**) which applies the **City Code on Takeovers and Mergers** (the **Takeover Code**). The Takeover Panel has always been a non-statutory body with the main City institutions represented on its board, though it now has the backing of the Securities and Investments Board and relevant Self-Regulating Organisations and thus a new range of sanctions if it requires them. It has generally been one of the better examples of **self-regulation** at work. With a full-time executive, it can give quick judgements on contentious points arising in a takeover, and these are generally respected by the parties involved. In the more legalistic atmosphere which has evolved since the Big Bang there is perhaps a greater tendency for the contestants to bring their lawyers with them to discussions with the Panel, but there have been very few legal challenges to Takeover Panel decisions. Certain aspects of takeovers are also governed directly or indirectly by the **Companies Acts**.

The Takeover Code has been expanded over the years to incorporate points raised by specific cases which have a general application. You do not have to understand all its ramifications to follow a press report of a takeover. But the rules can play an important part in some of the big contested bids and a general understanding of the principles, which are relatively simple, is useful.

Underlying the Takeover Panel's approach is the principle that all shareholders should be treated equally when one company tries to gain control of another. This is a counsel of perfection, but at least some of the worst abuses have been eliminated. In the bad old days of the jungle, before the Panel existed, one company might pay a high price for a controlling interest in another company, but make no offer to the remaining **minority shareholders**, who were left out in the cold. Those closest to the market would have the best chance of knowing what was going on and selling at the higher price. Therefore, much of the rulebook is concerned with preventing control from changing hands until all shareholders can see what is happening.

The trigger points

When a company acquires shares in another, it may come up against **trigger points** which affect its subsequent actions.

A company which builds up a stake of **30 per cent** in another is obliged to make a bid for all the shares in the target company unless specifically exempted by the Panel. This is because 30 per cent is pushing close to **effective control**: it is difficult for anyone else to bid successfully when one party has a stake of this size. So a **mandatory bid** follows acquisition of a 30 per cent stake. You will often see in the press that one company has built up a stake of 29.9 per cent in another: just below the level that triggers a bid.

When Company A builds up a stake of 30 per cent in Company B, the price it offers the remaining shareholders must usually be at least as high as the highest price it paid over the previous year. If in the course of the bid it buys Company B shares at a price above the bid value, it will have to increase the bid. In a voluntary bid, if the bidder acquires (or has acquired) 10 per cent or more of the voting rights during the previous 12 months, the offer will have to include a cash alternative at the highest price paid over the twelve months. In a voluntary bid where this 10 per cent has not been acquired, the bid must be on terms at least as favourable as the highest price paid over the previous three months.

There are also provisions designed to limit the speed with which Company A can acquire shares in the market before it has announced a firm intention to make an offer. With some exceptions, it is not allowed to buy more than 10 per cent of the voting rights in a seven-day period if this would result in its holding more than 15 per cent of the votes in total. When a company goes over a 15 per cent holding in another company, it must notify the Stock Exchange and the company concerned. These rules give the directors of Company B a breathing space in which to advise their shareholders on whether or not to sell (and if not, why not), and allow smaller shareholders as well as professional investors who are close to the market to decide whether to take advantage of the price the predator is paying. A **dawn raid** is when a company swoops on the stockmarket to buy a stake of up to 15 per cent in another company in double-quick time. Another means of acquiring a sizeable holding quickly, though it is less common, is to invite shareholders to tender shares for sale, up to the maximum required.

Conditions to be met

Takeover bids are **conditional** upon a number of factors. In other words, the bid may lapse unless the conditions are met.

The most important conditions are those regarding **acceptances**. Normally the offer will lapse unless the bidder gets over 50 per cent of the victim. Between 50 and 90 per cent it has the option of letting the bid lapse or declaring it **unconditional** – except in a mandatory bid, where the offer must go unconditional at 50 per cent. Above **90 per cent** the bid has to become unconditional. The **Companies Acts** allow the bidder to acquire any remaining shares **compulsorily** when it already has over 90 per cent of the shares it bid for.

The other required condition built into a takeover is that the bidder must withdraw if the bid is referred to the **Monopolies Commission** or the European Union competition authorities. If called on to do so, the Monopolies and Mergers Commission – to give it its full title – will investigate a proposed takeover and can report against it, usually on the grounds that it would seriously diminish competition. Whatever its finding, its researches normally hold up a takeover for more than six months, and few potential predators are prepared to wait. The **Office of Fair Trading** recommends whether a particular bid should be referred to the Monopolies Commission, though the Industry Secretary has the last say. Policy in this area is not always wholly clear.

There are also important trigger points for **disclosure of shareholdings** in another company (most of these apply outside takeovers as well). Any person or company acquiring **3 per cent** or more of another company (this trigger point used to be **5 per cent**) must declare the holding to the company. You will often see references in the press to the fact that one company has acquired over 3 per cent of another, perhaps presented by the writer as a prelude to a possible bid. Following the Guinness affair (see below), the Takeover Panel tightened its rules to require disclosure of transactions which resulted in a stake as small as **one per cent** in the parties to a bid or which resulted in changes to stakes of over one per cent, once the bid had been announced.

Sometimes in the past, when Company A wanted to prepare the ground for a bid for Company B, it would persuade its friends, Companies C and D, to buy Company B shares, effectively **warehousing** them on its behalf. Nowadays, Companies A, C and D would be held to be **acting in concert** (or would constitute a **concert party**) and their shareholdings

would be lumped together for the purposes of the various disclosure and trigger points. In practice it may be difficult to
prove that parties are acting in concert, particularly when the
beneficial owners of shareholdings are obscured behind overseas **nominee names**. Such activities might also be criminal
insider trading.

Share price support

We have seen why it is vital for the bidder to maintain its own
share price if it is offering shares. But there are limits – in
theory at least – on what can be done by way of support.

First, all **associates** of the bidder must declare their dealings
in the shares of either party. The most common forms of associate are the merchant bank advisers and funds under their
control.

Secondly, any buyer – even if he is not an associate – will
have to declare his holdings if they pass one of the trigger
points for disclosure.

Thirdly, the company itself must not support its own share
price with company money. This revolves on a **Companies Act**
provision that companies may not, except with the permission
of their shareholders and in very closely defined circumstances, give **financial support for the purchase of their own
shares**. It was the main point at issue in the Guinness scandal
(see below).

Again, the practice may diverge some way from the theory.
In the course of a bid, **friends** of Company A may try to help
by buying shares in Company A to boost its price and selling
those in Company B to depress it. The friends could include
friendly institutions and are often referred to as a **fan club**.
Whether or not the help is given in the expectation of future
favours (in which case the company might be deemed to be
giving financial assistance for the purchase of its own shares) is
often difficult to establish.

In the United States **arbitrageurs** or **arbs** have made a business of acquiring large share stakes in takeover situations.
Sometimes they would simply gain by buying shares in the victim and selling at a profit. Less legitimately, it is suspected
that some might offer their services to support or depress a
particular share price to aid or frustrate takeover ambitions.

Though they have never been so active in Britain, they cropped up frequently in accounts of the Guinness affair (see below).

The bid timetable

To prevent bids from dragging on interminably, there is an established **bid timetable**. The Takeover Panel sets a time limit of 60 days for an offer or series of offers from the same party to remain on the table, starting from the day the **formal documents** go out. If the bidder cannot gain control within this time, he has to wait a year before making another attempt. However, if a second or subsequent competitive bidder emerges, it in turn has 60 days and its deadline also becomes the deadline for the first bidder.

A takeover often starts with a sustained rise in the price of the victim company's shares (yes, for all the insider dealing penalties, it is by no means always the case that a bid remains unheralded until it is declared. However, legitimate buying by the prospective bidder could account for the movement, while some forthcoming bids are not too difficult for the market to spot in advance).

Then Company A announces to the Stock Exchange and press that it is bidding for Company B, usually giving the terms. Company B, if it resists, will usually rush out a statement describing the bid as inadequate and wholly unacceptable, and telling its shareholders to stay firm.

Some time later Company A posts its formal **offer document** to Company B shareholders, giving details of itself and of the offer and – with a paper offer – stressing its own management strengths, the (possibly dubious) **industrial logic** of the offer and the advantages of acceptance. Company B studies the offer and comes out with a formal **defence document**, knocking down the Company A arguments and extolling its own virtues, usually with the help of profit and dividend forecasts and, possibly, asset revaluations.

Salvos of this kind may be fired by both parties several times during the course of the affair. The more important ones are reported in the press. By the **first closing date** of the offer, Company A must decide – if it does not already have control – whether simply to keep the offer open in the hope of further **acceptances**, raise the bid if it clearly needs to offer more or let it **lapse** if it does not fancy its chances of winning. If it lapses, any acceptances that have been received become void. Offers may be raised several times during the affair. Alternative bidders may appear at any point to complicate the decisions. Throughout, Company A and any competitive bidders may be buying Company B shares in the market and friends or associates of all the parties may be supporting the price of their respective protégés (such actions are generally subject to public disclosure). But by the **final closing date** the bidder must announce that the offer is **unconditional** as to acceptances – the bid goes through if the other conditions are met – or allow it to lapse.

Throughout the **offer period** the price of Company B's shares in the stockmarket will give some indication of the expected outcome. If it lags just a little behind the value of the latest bid it can mean that the bid is expected to succeed. If it jumps ahead, the market is probably expecting a higher offer, though it could just possibly be that Company B has justified a higher price for its shares on their own merits.

The United States scene

The takeover scene is considerably rougher – as to the tactics permitted and employed – in the **United States** than in Britain. The Takeover Panel has been effective in preventing widespread use in the UK of some of the more questionable American techniques. **Greenmail** – a form of corporate blackmail – is a prime example. A company builds up a large stake in a potential takeover candidate. It threatens to bid or sell the stake to another prospective bidder unless the target company buys the stake from it at an inflated price – possible, because of the greater freedom to buy their own shares enjoyed by American companies.

The **poison pill** bid defence is another American tactic which has also cropped up only in its milder forms in the UK. The target company builds in a tripwire to make itself less attractive to a bidder. It might, say, create a new class of stock which becomes automatically redeemable at a high price in the event of a successful takeover.

Geared or **leveraged** takeovers have also been less common in the UK where the bidder was a UK company, though the idea enjoyed some popularity in the late 1980s. A bid is made using a high proportion of borrowed money. The resultant company is very highly-geared and forced to concentrate on short-term profitability to meet the interest charges (see Chapter 11). Sometimes these bids involve borrowing money by the issue of **junk bonds** – bonds which offer a high rate of interest but which would not normally count as being of investment quality because they are issued in large quantity by relatively insubstantial companies.

We have already seen how the **arbs** took positions in takeover stocks. But a series of high-profile arrests and court cases in the United States subsequently suggested that their success was based more on **insider dealing** – acting on confidential information, often unlawfully purchased – than on successful prediction, and their activities were consequently curbed.

Leverage and level playing fields

Cross-frontier takeovers are usually for cash; shares are rarely a widely accepted currency outside their country of origin. Thus British companies have made major acquisitions for cash in the United States in recent years, and most large overseas bids for British companies are for cash. British companies at the receiving end of hostile takeovers from overseas have frequently complained about lack of **reciprocity** and the lack of a **level playing field**: the predator companies may be protected from hostile takeovers in their country of origin, though perhaps more by patterns of shareholdings and by local custom and practice than by specific legislation.

Overseas bids for British companies are frequently highly **leveraged** and a trend towards bids made with borrowed money was reinforced domestically by the growth in **management buy-outs** and **management buy-ins** (see Chapter 11), some of which were aimed at stockmarket-listed companies in the late 1980s. There was at that time no shortage of cash from the banks to back management teams dissatisfied with the share price performance of their company (or somebody else's company) who reckoned they could do better by buying it and taking it private. If the company was listed, this involved making a takeover offer to its existing shareholders.

However several high-profile leveraged acquisitions of this kind – including the takeover of the Magnet joinery and kitchens business and the Gateway supermarket group – went badly wrong and extensive capital reconstructions were required. The climate was therefore a lot less conducive to this kind of leveraged operation in the 1990s – even had market conditions been right – though buyouts of private companies retained their popularity.

The Guinness affair

No review of takeovers is complete without a glance at the *cause célèbre* that filled so many column-inches of the financial press from late 1986 and is still frequently referred to in the 1990s: the £2.6 billion **Guinness** bid for whisky giant Distillers in 1986.

Drinks group Guinness was competing with the Argyll supermarket business to take over Distillers, which backed the Guinness offer. The Guinness offer was mainly in shares and its value – and therefore Guinness's chances of beating Argyll – depended heavily on the Guinness share price. Having been below 300p in January 1986, the Guinness share price staged a remarkable rise to over 350p at one point. The value of the Guinness offer surpassed that of Argyll's offer and Guinness won the day.

The revelations which followed the appointment of **Department of Trade inspectors** to investigate Guinness's affairs at the begining of December 1986 made it clear that there had been a massive support operation to boost the Guinness share price. More serious were the allegations that Guinness had used its own money in one way or another to recompense those who bought its shares on a large scale and boosted the price: by paying them fees, by making large cash deposits with them or by guaranteeing to cover any losses they might suffer on the shares. Resignations and sackings – at Guinness itself and at its then merchant bank advisers, Morgan Grenfell – preceded the DoT inspectors' findings. Criminal charges against some of the main players followed later and three of them served sentences in Ford open prison. By 1995 their convictions were being reviewed on the basis of new evidence which, it was claimed, had not been made available to the defence at the time of the trial.

The Guinness affair provided a field day for the financial press and – taken with allegations of insider trading elsewhere in the City – considerable embarrassment for a government which had been selling the benefits of stockmarket investment to the public. The government had probably worried unduly. A cynical public is, rightly or wrongly, not often greatly surprised by suggestions of share rigging and insider dealing in the City.

11

Venture capital and leveraged buy-outs

The 'small is beautiful' cry has been heard frequently in British business over recent decades, and various initiatives have emerged to provide finance for smaller companies and start-up enterprises. Several of the more serious national daily papers regularly carry features on small businesses.

Bank loans and overdrafts traditionally provide the finance for businesses in their very early years and the stockmarket allows more mature companies to raise debt or equity capital. But between the two, it is argued, lies a **financing gap**. Businesses which are too large or too fast-growing to subsist on bank finance, yet too small to launch on the stockmarket, may be held back by lack of funds. In particular, smaller businesses find it very difficult to raise equity finance as opposed to loans.

Management buy-outs

We have seen, too, the phenomenon of the **management buy-out** or **MBO**. A group of managers within a large industrial company, say, decide that they would like to own the particular part of the business they run and to operate it as an independent entity. It may suit the large company to sell it to them if the division in question is peripheral to its main business. Alternatively, managers might put in a bid for parts of a business when the parent group has got into trouble and landed in the hands of the receiver.

Sometimes, too, an existing business is acquired with a view to putting in a new management team not previously associated with it who will have a stake in the operation (a

management buy-in). A variation on this theme occurs when a new management team links with existing managers and employees to acquire the business. The name for this operation – **buy-in management buy-out** – may, we suspect, have been chosen mainly for its usual acronym of a **BIMBO**. Finally, in another variation, the managers of a listed company may decide they would like to run and part-own the whole of the enterprise they currently manage on behalf of the public shareholders (see below).

But in all cases we have described, the managers themselves rarely have the money to acquire an established business and they require help in the form of outside equity and loan finance.

Venture capital and development capital funds

To satisfy these different financing needs, there has been rapid growth in **venture capital funds**: organizations which provide finance – sometimes a mixture of equity and loans, but often just one or the other – for unquoted companies. Many of the venture capital funds are offshoots of existing financial institutions: clearing or merchant banks, insurance companies or pension funds. In 1995 there were 110 full members and 100 associate members (the latter providing advice rather than finance) of the **British Venture Capital Association**, the umbrella body for these funds.

The biggest venture capital organization in the UK, however, has a longer history. It is **Investors in Industry** or the **3i** group, whose original venture capital arm was known as Industrial and Commercial Finance Corporation (ICFC) and was founded shortly after the last war. Originally wholly-owned by the clearing banks and the Bank of England, but now with a Stock Exchange listing following flotation of part of the capital, it currently provides most forms of banking and finance service, other than overdrafts, and in 1994 had gross assets of over £3.6 billion. It has financed almost 12,000 businesses during its life, and will consider requests for quite small amounts of money as well as very large sums.

The typical **venture capitalist** puts up money for a growing business or to finance a management buy-out in return for a proportion of the share capital. Individual funds rarely want control of the companies they back, and where the funds required are large the financing may be **syndicated** among a number of venture capitalists. Each puts up part of the money and collectively they may control the enterprise they finance.

The original entrepreneurs, or the managers in the case of a buy-out, thus concede a large part of their ownership of the business in return for the money that they needed to buy it in the first place or the additional finance they need if it is to grow. Often their eventual stake in the business is geared to how well it performs (a **ratchet** arrangement). The venture capitalists usually want to cash in on their stake in successful businesses after five years or so and at this point will want an opportunity of selling the shares – a **take-out** – possibly via a **stockmarket launch** of the company. Alternatively, the company may seek a **trade buyer**: another company that is prepared to offer a good price for the business. In the most successful buy-outs the managers who backed the venture may emerge as millionaires within a relatively short period as the revamped business is floated on the market or sold to a trade buyer within a few years.

There are failures as well as successes in the management buy-out business, and the returns that venture capital funds seek are quite high – perhaps in the region of 30 per cent – to compensate them for their failures. While the participating venture capital fund (or funds grouped under a lead fund where the finance is syndicated) may provide only the equity portion of the money required, they will probably also organize the bank loans that complete the package. You might read in a description of a £10m buy-out that £3m of the money required was provided as equity by a venture capital fund and that the remaining £7m came from a bank loan.

With a large buy-out the structure could be more complex with, say, 30 per cent of the money coming as equity from venture capital funds, 60 per cent coming as **senior debt** from a consortium of banks and 10 per cent provided as **mezzanine debt**. This mezzanine layer is a form of halfway house between debt and equity: debt offering a high return which may also include some rights to share in equity values. The ratio between debt and equity will vary with market conditions. In a recession where business confidence is low the proportion of equity may need to rise as the banks will be less willing to take risk. Be a little careful, too, when you read that 30 per cent of the money for a buy-out was provided as **equity**. The term is used in a somewhat loose sense in the buy-out world. It is unlikely in practice that all of this 30 per cent was subscribed as ordinary capital. For structural and taxation reasons it is more likely to have been provided by the venture capitalists as a mixture of ordinary share capital and preference capital or subordinated loans. It is, however, all risk money.

Most of the major venture capital funds do not consider it worth investigating a **financing proposal** unless the sums involved are quite large and they are generally wary of business **start-ups** (entirely new businesses) where the risk is highest. Occasionally, however, a venture capitalist might be prepared to provide some **seedcorn capital** to see a new project through its very early stages. In general, venture capitalists prefer to provide money to buy an existing business or **development finance** for companies which are already past the initial stage and need more equity if they are to advance to a bigger league. The same is generally true of another type of fund providing capital for unquoted companies – the **Enterprise Investment Scheme** fund – although these funds will sometimes provide finance in smaller quantities.

Leveraged buy-outs and takeovers

Leveraged buy-outs and **leveraged takeovers** were very popular in the United States in the late 1980s and have not entirely disappeared since. Fortunately, perhaps, the principle spread rather late to Britain, just as America was beginning to worry about some of the consequences around the turn of the decade. 'Leveraged' simply means 'geared up' in British terminology.

As we have seen, most buy-outs and buy-ins are geared or leveraged to some extent in that bank loans are used as well as equity capital. But the term 'leveraged buy-out' is used particularly to describe an operation where an investor group, using mainly borrowed money, makes a public takeover bid for a listed company. The amount of equity finance used may be very small. Typically, the debt portion will be in several layers: **senior debt** which is reasonably well secured, some intermediate layers and perhaps an issue of high-yielding high-risk **junk bonds** (see Chapter 10).

A company acquired by way of a leveraged bid (80 per cent and sometimes a lot more of the finance may be in the form of debt) finds that interest charges absorb most of its profits and it is probably under pressure to dispose of parts of its business to raise cash to reduce its borrowings as rapidly as possible. Leveraged buy-outs are a very high risk game whose dangers become more apparent when economic activity turns down, the cost of servicing bank debt rises and it becomes impossible to raise cash by selling parts of the business at acceptable prices. The biggest leveraged operation of the late 1980s was the $25 billion buy-out of food and tobacco group **RJR Nabisco** in the United States. It turned out to be far from an unqualified success.

The biggest attempted leveraged bid for a UK company – Sir James Goldsmith's 1989 attempt to acquire and break up the **BATS** tobacco-to-financial-services group – was eventually abandoned in the face of regulatory hurdles in the United States and lack of enthusiasm in the UK. Experience with leveraged bids for UK listed companies that did go through was far from reassuring, as we saw in the previous chapter.

Enterprise Investment Scheme

Of the tax-favoured schemes to encourage investment in growing businesses, the **Enterprise Investment Scheme** or **EIS** has the longest history. It is a replacement for the earlier **Business Expansion Scheme** or **BES**, which itself first saw the light of day in 1981 as the **Business Start-up Scheme**.

The idea is to encourage higher-earning individuals to sub-scribe for new 'full risk' ordinary shares in private trading companies. Anyone with a sufficiently high income can gain income tax relief on up to £100,000 a year invested in this way. But the income tax relief is only (in 1995) at the lowest rate of 20 per cent and the shares must normally be retained for at least five years to gain the full relief. Thus, an individual with a taxable income of more than £100,000 could use £100,000 a year to buy qualifying shares and his investment would only have cost him £80,000 after the tax relief. Moreover, if he holds the shares for the qualifying period the investor would not normally pay capital gains tax on any profit, while losses he makes (less the original tax relief) would be offsettable against taxable income or against gains elsewhere for capital gains tax purposes. The appeal of the scheme was enhanced in the 1994 Budget when investors were allowed to defer capital gains tax due on profits from other investments if they invested the money in qualifying shares under the EIS. Another important change at the same time abolished the earlier 'interests in land rule' which had disqualified from the EIS any company where land and buildings had accounted for more than half of the assets.

Those who are already directors or employees of a company cannot qualify for tax relief under the EIS when they invest in that company – the idea is to bring in new money from outside rather than give tax relief to those who may already have an interest. But there are provisions to allow **business angels** to invest in a private company and benefit from the EIS, provided they were not already connected with it. These 'angels' are individuals who want to invest in a company and also have something to offer by way of business expertise. They may both invest and become paid directors.

As far as the company is concerned, to rank for the EIS it must carry out, normally for at least three years, a qualifying activity. This broadly rules out a number of financial and investment activities and dealing in securities or property, plus the investment in rented residential property that had been allowed under the BES. The company must not be listed on the Stock Exchange or traded on the USM. The new ordinary shares it issues to EIS investors must not have any preferential rights and the most it can raise under the EIS in any one tax year is £1m (there is a higher limit of £5m for companies engaged in certain shipping activities).

How does the prospective EIS investor locate a suitable company? Ideally he would know of one from his personal experience. In practice, many investors will invest via the medium of an **EIS fund**: a fund set up to invest in a range of qualifying companies. The investor still receives his tax relief and has the advantage of a spread of risk and more or less professional management. Unfortunately, as with many tax-favoured investments, things are not always as rosy as they seem. Investment in unquoted companies, direct or through a fund, carries a fair degree of risk. And there is a danger, as with any form of subsidy, that the price of the product rises to take some account of the tax relief available to the buyer.

Venture capital trusts

As well as relaxing conditions for the EIS, the 1994 Budget also fleshed out the bones of earlier proposals for an entirely new investment vehicle: the **venture capital trust**. A venture capital trust would need to hold at least 70 per cent of its investments in unquoted trading companies: broadly, the same sort of company as would qualify for EIS investment. Not more than 15 per cent could be in any one company. But the trust would not be limited to investing in equity. Up to half of its investment in qualifying companies could be in the form of loans with at least five years to run. If the companies in which it invested subsequently floated on the stock market, the trust could count them as unquoted for a further five years.

The venture capital trust itself would be much like an investment trust and would need to be quoted on the Stock Exchange. Investors in the trust would pay no tax on dividends received or on capital gains arising on disposals of investments of up to £100,000 a year. Probably more significant, if subscribing for new shares issued by a venture capital trust the investor would receive tax incentives similar to those for the EIS. There would be income tax relief at 20 per cent for investments of up to £100,000 a year provided the shares were held for five years, and tax on capital gains from the sale of any asset could be deferred when these gains were reinvested in new shares of the trust, up to this £100,000-a-year limit. However, given the costs of researching investments in smaller, unquoted companies, it seemed likely that venture capital trusts would be set up under the auspices of existing venture capital organisations rather than as stand-alone operations.

Loan Guarantee Scheme

Another government initiative was aimed at helping small companies which had found it difficult to borrow money from normal banking sources, often because neither the company nor its founders could provide the **security** considered necessary for a loan. Most owners of small companies which want to borrow money are required to offer their houses and other assets as security for the debts of the business.

The scheme – the government **Loan Guarantee Scheme** or **LGS** – does not itself provide money for businesses but it removes part of the risk for traditional lenders. A bank can advance a loan of up to £250,000 to an existing small business or £100,000 to a new business starting up, secured on the assets of the business but without personal guarantees from the owners. The bank charges its normal interest rate plus a **premium** of one-and-a-half percentage points on the loan (or half a percentage point if the rate of interest is fixed), which goes to the government to provide the guarantee element. In return, 70 per cent (or 85 per cent for loans to existing businesses) of the value of the loan is covered by the **government guarantee**. Businesses in qualifying inner city renewal areas receive broadly the terms applying to established businesses, even if they are start-ups, and the interest rate is also lower. If the business goes to the wall and the whole of the loan is lost, the government reimburses the lending bank 70 per cent or 85 per cent of its advance.

The LGS has undoubtedly helped some businesses that would not otherwise have got off the ground. Its terms have been frequently amended since it was first established in 1981 and the take-up under the scheme has increased greatly since the last set of changes in 1993. In 1995 the sponsoring government department (the DTI) set in train a thorough review of the scheme with a view to simplification, backed by a consultation paper. The main disadvantage of the LGS is that it supplies loan finance in circumstances where equity is often what is needed, with the result that the business becomes excessively highly geared, which may hasten its demise. Failures among companies taking advantage of the scheme were high in the early years.

12

Pay, perks and reverse capitalism

We have looked at companies, but what of the men and women – and in the mid 1990s it was still predominantly men – who run them? The escalating **pay and perks** of the directors of listed companies had become a major political issue by mid-decade. A little background helps in understanding the increasingly frequent press and television reports on the pay and option profits of board members, particularly in the previously nationalized industries.

The starting point is a paradox that explains some of the confusion on this issue shown by the Conservative government of the day. Capitalism, by and large, is about allowing the owners of capital to enjoy the fruits of their capital. Yet, by amending the tax laws to promote executive share option schemes and the like, the government paved the way for extensive transfers of value from the owners of a business (the shareholders) to the directors and managers (the employees who run the business on the owners' behalf). This process of **reverse capitalism** – taking money from the owners to give to the senior employees – was a curious interpretation of the capitalist ethic.

Press reports tend to focus on massive jumps in boardroom pay or multi-million pound profits made from the exercise of executive share options. But the full picture is often more complex (and sometimes even more startling) than these reports would suggest. By the mid-1990s, the directors of many of Britain's larger listed companies were rewarding themselves in five or six different ways, sometimes more:

- A basic salary

- A short-term performance-related bonus on top of basic salary, probably up to a maximum of 50 per cent of salary.
- Executive share options, which deliver profits when the share price rises.
- Longer-term incentives geared to performance over a three- or four-year period. These might take the form of cash payments or an outright grant of free shares.
- A variety of benefits in kind such as cars, life and medical insurance and, in some cases, company-owned accommodation.
- A pension based on final salary (sometimes with a non-tax-approved top-up scheme where the tax rules limited the amount that could be paid out by the main scheme)
- Various generally less publicized devices such as employee share ownership plans (ESOPs) or phantom options.
- The prospect of a golden handshake if the director is ousted for one reason or another.

How the reverse capitalism package works

Short-term bonuses or **annual bonuses** tend to be linked to a measure of short-term performance: perhaps the growth in earnings per share over the year. They account for many of the wilder percentage jumps in a director's pay – when a good year succeeds a bad one – that the press picks up. Sometimes they are actually paid a year later, when company earnings may have turned down again, making it more difficult for shareholders to discern a link between pay and performance.

The 1984 Finance Act smoothed the way for **executive share option schemes**, and most companies have adopted them. For no payment, a director is granted options over, say, a million shares, usually exercisable (see Chapter 18) at the market price at the time of grant. Normally, he will have to wait three years before the options can be exercised. Suppose the share price was 100p at the time of grant and five years later had risen to 250p. The director has the right to buy a million shares (normally, new shares which the company creates) at 100p each, costing £1m. He immediately sells them at the market price of £2.5m, making a profit of £1.5m. The creation and sale of new shares at a price below that in the market represents a transfer of value from the shareholders of the company to the director concerned.

Longer-term performance-related share schemes have been introduced recently to counter some of the criticisms of executive share options (see below). In a typical scheme, a director receives a gift of free shares if his company beats some pre-ordained performance target over, say, a three-year period. A popular performance trigger is the **total return** provided by the company to its shareholders over the three years, compared with that offered by other companies. Total return is the combination of share price movement with dividends paid. Thus, a large company might compare itself to the other 99 constituents of the Footsie index. If the company is in the bottom 25 companies in terms of total shareholder return, the directors get no free shares. If it is in the top 25, they get the maximum number allowed. In between, the number depends on their position in the league.

The **benefits in kind** are taken for granted nowadays and they excite little comment, but **pensions** are worth a closer look. Most schemes will pay a pension geared to final salary and it is noticeable that directors frequently ensure that their salaries are bumped up substantially in the years leading to retirement. The effect is to give the director a pension considerably larger than the contributions made to the scheme on his behalf over the years would justify. The cost therefore falls indirectly on the other scheme members. Where the tax laws limit the pension a director can receive from a tax-approved scheme, the company frequently contributes on his behalf to a separate non-tax-approved scheme. For pension calculations based on salary, however, bonuses are normally disallowed.

Phantom options and employee share ownership plans (ESOPs) rarely receive the attention they deserve, particularly as it may have been difficult in the past for a shareholder to find out anything about them. A phantom option is an option on non-existent shares – but if that sounds crazy, wait a minute. The company tells the director, say: 'The share price is now 100p. We will grant you phantom options over a million shares, which you can exercise at any time over the next ten years. If, some years later, the share price has risen to 250p and you decide to exercise, we will pay you the difference between 100p and 250p on a million shares. In other words, we will pay you £1.5m'. The effect is much the same as with the example we quoted of a traditional executive share option, but the tax treatment of the profits may be different and no new shares are created. Phantom options are sometimes used legitimately to reward directors of overseas companies who cannot benefit fully from a UK executive share option scheme. They may be used more questionably to generate rewards for directors that shareholders know nothing about in advance.

ESOPs deserve a chapter to themselves. They are **employee share ownership plans** or **employee share ownership trusts**. The type run by large companies is generally the so-called 'non-statutory ESOP', which attracts no special tax benefits. It works like this. The ESOP buys shares in the sponsoring company, financing them with bank loans guaranteed by the company or with loans from the company direct. The shares are bought in the market, so no new shares are created. These shares are then available for allocation to employees as part of a bonus scheme, profit-sharing scheme, option scheme, or whatever. The rules will usually say that all employees can benefit from the ESOP, but in practice they are used predominantly to provide further benefits for directors and senior executives. They are not without risk to the company and therefore to its owners. If the share price falls, the ESOP may end up with shares worth less than the loans it raised and the loss will generally fall on the company in one way or another. This happened with, among others, a container-leasing group then called Tiphook, which suffered a share price collapse and had to write off more than £20m on guarantees for loans to its ESOP.

Golden handshakes also hit the headlines. Directors are often employed under **rolling contracts** of three years (**evergreen contracts**). This means that there will always be three years of their contract outstanding. There is pressure now from institutional shareholders to reduce this to two years, but the process has a long way to go. If a director is forced out, he will be able (virtually regardless of the reason) to claim for most of what would have been due to him had he completed his contract. Companies are usually anxious to avoid litigation and want to wind the affair up as quickly as possible. Thus, even directors who have run their companies into the ground frequently depart with a 'golden handshake' of something approaching three years' salary. Cynical observers have a rule of thumb: the bigger the cock-up, the bigger the payoff (mainly because the company wants to get rid of the director in question with the minimum of fuss).

Objections to incentive schemes

The declared objective behind bonus schemes and the like is to 'incentivize' management so that it produces improved performance from which shareholders and the economy also benefit. This poses a second paradox. Why is it that the highest-paid people in a company need extra payments to persuade them to give of their best?

But there are detailed objections to some of the **incentive schemes** in force today. Annual bonuses focus on short-term performance, may encourage short-term attitudes, and the basis on which they are granted may be far from clear. It is also fairly easy to manipulate earnings per share in the short term, and this is often the measure on which the bonus is based.

Executive share options are open to the objection that they may reward even poor management when the share price is carried up by a bull market – though the company itself has underperformed. They also dilute the interests of existing shareholders and provide little long-term incentive since the director almost always immediately sells the shares he receives from exercise of his options. Institutional shareholders have tried to pressure managements to introduce some further **performance criterion** before options can be exercised, but have left it to companies to select the criterion. As a result, most of them are undemanding. Options can only be exercised if the company's earnings per share have risen faster than retail prices over a three-year period, and the like.

The longer-term share incentive plans were introduced to counter some of the objections to share options though many companies operate the two in tandem. They do encourage a slightly longer-term view on the part of company management and sometimes introduce a more realistic performance criterion than share option schemes. But the criteria are again often relatively undemanding. Since these schemes are fairly new, it remains to be seen whether directors will demonstrate confidence in their company by holding on to the free shares that they are given.

ESOPs are open to the objection that the company is exposing itself to a risk in the movement of its own share price. A second objection is that they are often remarkably opaque – shareholders may know little if anything about them (but see below).

But the overriding criticism voiced of virtually all incentive schemes is that they offer directors a carrot, but no stick. Directors collect extra loot if the company or the share price does well. They do not suffer – as shareholders in the company suffer – if the company does badly. This may, it is sometimes argued in the press and elsewhere, encourage directors to take excessive risks with the company. If it works, they benefit. If it does not, shareholders suffer. And there is always the golden handshake at the end of the day as the ultimate reward for failure.

Limits of shareholder power

Shareholders do not – as of the mid-1990s – have an opportunity to vote on directors' pay levels, and there would be practical difficulties in giving them the right to do so. They can, of course, vote to remove a director, but in practice any pressure to moderate pay is more likely to come from the investing institutions and to take place behind the scenes. There is pressure for companies to give more detail in the annual report on how pay is decided, but the explanations are still frequently indecipherable or too general to be of practical use.

Shareholders are required to vote on the establishment of an executive share option scheme, largely because it will involve the creation of new shares. The institutional shareholders, as we saw, are also seeking to insist on an additional performance trigger.

Bonus schemes, long-term incentive plans, phantom options and the like do not normally require shareholder approval unless they involve the creation of new shares. And there is no requirement under company law for shareholders to approve the establishment of an ESOP.

Where to go for information

The information available on directors' pay and perks is improving – slowly – though the legal requirements remain minimal. A company is required to show in its annual report the total of boardroom pay and to show separately the pay of the chairman and the highest-paid director (if different). The pay of the other directors must be shown in certain bands: the number of directors earning between £100,001 and £105,000, and so on. But in none of these cases do the individual directors have to be named. This has led to some monumental journalistic cock-ups and consequent grovelling apologies in the press. You cannot safely assume that the highest paid director is the chief executive, or that he is necessarily the same person who was highest paid the previous year.

The **employment contracts** of individual directors of a company must be available for inspection at certain times, notably during the annual general meeting and for a few weeks beforehand. Journalists occasionally make use of this facility to do a little digging, the results of which appear in the financial press.

As we saw, shareholders have to be given the details of proposed executive share option schemes and to vote on them. The annual report also has to show the number of options granted and exercised during the year and the number outstanding. But here there has been real progress, which goes far beyond legal requirements. Accounting's **Urgent Issues Task Force (UITF)** has recommended far more extensive disclosure of options in the annual report. While its requirements are not, in this case, mandatory, most listed companies are beginning to adopt them. The recommended disclosure shows option details for each named director and allows the shareholder to calculate roughly what profits he made by exercising options during the year and what inbuilt profit was available to him for the future.

There is also progress on ESOPs, and from the same source. At the time of writing, the UITF was proposing rules on accounting for ESOPs which, once adopted, would make it far less easy for a company to withhold information from shareholders. The ESOP – and the shares in the company that it held – would have to be included in the group accounts and an explanation provided to allow shareholders to see the financial position of the ESOP and who benefits.

Finally, there is pressure from other sources for more information on directors' pay and perks. A committee of the financial community's great and good – the **Cadbury Committee** – produced a code of conduct on the financial governance of company affairs: the **Cadbury Code**. It recommended, inter alia, openness by companies on directors' remuneration, though in terms so general that their effect was weakened. A later committee, the **Greenbury Committee**, was set up specifically to examine boardroom pay and perks in response to the government's embarrassment on the issue. It had yet to report at the time of writing, but was generally expected to recommend greater disclosure rather than legal curbs.

Quis custodiet?

Individual shareholders are generally all too ready to take their directors' advice on how they should vote on company affairs and are rarely in a position to exercise much influence on boardroom pay levels – though there have been attempts. With less than 18 per cent of listed shares they are, anyway, a minor force.

Institutions, with over 60 per cent of listed shares, should be in a far stronger position. But they are frequently reluctant to use their muscle. There are several reasons for this. First, they have a genuine belief in incentives which will produce performance from which all shareholders will benefit. Secondly, they need to work with the City establishment, which will not thank them for rocking the boat. Thirdly, the insurance groups which are major institutional shareholders are mainly companies with boards of directors of their own. These boards have their own pay and perks to consider and might not welcome excessive intervention in the pay affairs of other companies.

Given this vacuum, the Cadbury Committee took a hand. Each company should have a **remuneration committee**, consisting mainly of non-executive directors, who would fix the pay and perks of the executives. The results have been hilarious. Many non-executive directors are executive directors of another company and have very little interest in restraining boardroom pay levels. In addition, they tend to rely heavily in their deliberations on surveys of boardroom pay and perks produced by numerous firms of **remuneration consultants**. It is an unusually brave non-executive director who will insult the executives by suggesting that they should be paid less than the average for companies of a similar type and size. But if every executive director's salary is raised at least to the average by the remuneration committee, then it is a mathematical inevitability that the average itself must rise each year by leaps and bounds. There are strong grounds for thinking that the remuneration committee system has accelerated rather than moderated the explosion in boardroom pay and perks.

Where the press homes in

It is the pay and perks of the directors of previously nationalized companies – British Gas, the water companies and the electricity companies in particular – that have attracted most media attention and the reasons for these specific attacks on the reverse capitalism process need explaining. First, these directors were generally very badly paid by private industry standards when they were running their businesses for the state. Indeed, the prospect of moving over to a private-sector salary scale was a prime inducement for them to cooperate in **privatization** plans. Given the low starting point, the percentage increases in their pay were thus very large and caught the press's eye.

Secondly, share options for the executives were also built in at the time of privatisation. These have delivered far bigger profits for the directors than were ever envisaged, mainly because the businesses have proved far more profitable than had been expected and share prices have thus risen very rapidly. In many cases the government had seriously underestimated the cost savings to be made in the previously state-run businesses – mainly through sacking employees – and had therefore sold them much too cheaply. Via their share options the directors have benefited, whereas the taxpayer has lost out.

The directors claim they are running major competitive businesses and should be remunerated accordingly. Critics maintain they are running monopoly utilities with assured revenues and that there is no valid comparison with directors running competitive businesses in the market place. The debate is likely to rumble on and to be reported in the media for years to come.

Getting down to figures

But what are the private-sector salaries and perks that the utility bosses seek to match? A survey of well over 1,000 companies late in 1994 by remuneration consultancy Monks Partnership showed that as many as 95 per cent of industrial companies operated an executive share option scheme and, in the larger companies with turnover of £400m-plus, as many as 85 per cent paid bonuses to directors on top of salary. Longer-term incentive schemes were being introduced rapidly and almost 40 per cent of the Footsie 100 companies already operated them.

Another survey at about the same time of well over 100 larger companies by Bacon & Woodrow and Remuneration Economics showed that the average basic salary of chief executives of large companies was £317,000. If bonuses, pension contributions, other benefits and national insurance contributions were taken into account, the average cost to the company of employing the chief executive was considerably higher at £533,000 – and this excluded the cost to the company or the benefit to the director from share options.

Finally, a search through the **Datastream** database of market, company and economic information in the first half of 1995 showed that over 20 companies paid at least one director £1m a year or more, excluding share option profits, and a further 86 paid their top-earning director between £500,000 and £1m. Since more than one director in a company may be earning a salary above these levels, the total number of super-earners is certainly higher.

How far will the pay explosion go?

High boardroom pay is frequently defended as the reward for high company performance. In practice, surveys on this issue frequently have problems in establishing a correlation. It is also justified on the basis that 'directors in other countries get more, and we would lose our top entrepreneurial talent if we did not match overseas pay rates'. Again, in practice it is difficult to compare pay and perks across frontiers as there are too many variables. While some UK executives undoubtedly have a value in the international marketplace, very many probably do not. It is not unrealistic to ask – as the press occasionally has the temerity to do – if the performance of British industry would be one jot better or worse if company directors were paid a decent basic salary and 'incentives' were scrapped across the board.

Where will the pay and perks explosion stop? A survey published in 1994 in the *National Institute Economic Review* disclosed that in the years 1985 to 1990, top directors' pay in Britain rose by 10 per cent a year in real terms (after adjusting for inflation) while average earnings rose at a real rate of only 2.6 per cent a year. If we look at more recent experience and take that 1994 survey figure of £317,000 for the average basic pay of the chief executive in the larger company, it represented almost 19 times average earnings for the population as a whole. Moreover, these executives had enjoyed a basic pay rise of over 10 per cent in the latest year, against less than 4 per cent for the population as a whole. If we extrapolate this trend, in ten years time the chief executive would be earning about 35 times the average worker's pay in Britain, and in 20 years it would be 67 times. And these comparisons make no allowance for bonuses, share option profits and the like, which company directors receive.

Further escalation on this scale may not happen. But it is difficult to see what will stop it. The pattern of share ownership and control in Britain means that the owners of companies who foot the bill cannot (or are unlikely to) exert restraint on the directors they elect to manage their businesses. Thus, company directors themselves control the marketplace for their services – and the rates of pay. It is an odd interpretation of the free market philosophy. But the whole phenomenon of reverse capitalism is more than a little odd.

13

Government bonds and company bonds

The government needs an efficient market in its own longer-term debt: this is the part of the stockmarket known as the **gilt-edged market** which we touched on briefly in Chapter 1. 'Gilt-edged stocks' or 'gilts' is simply the term used for British **government bonds** or **government stocks**. The government's agent in this market is the Bank of England, which advises on

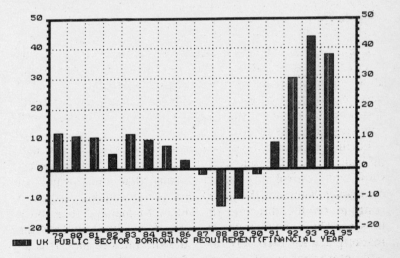

Figure 13.1 How the government's borrowing need shot up in the recession of the early 1990s (at the end of the 1980s the government had been repaying debt). Our chart of the public sector borrowing requirement (PSBR) in billions of pounds explains why net issues of government bonds were so heavy in the early 1990s. Source: *Datastream International.*

debt issues and organizes the selling, servicing, purchase and redemption of government stocks; these stocks are created in the first instance by the Treasury. In 1994 the total **turnover of gilt-edged stocks** was £1,545 billion (almost half representing trades between marketmakers) and the total value of all stocks listed was some £222 billion.

New issues during the year totalled some £32 billion, as new stocks were created to satisfy the government's borrowing need and to replace those that **matured**. Net issues – issues of new stocks less redemptions of existing ones – were around £23 billion. Occasionally in the past the government has been in the happy position of repaying money rather than needing to borrow more and when this happens the size of the gilt-edged market shrinks. This was the case in 1988–1990 when some long-term investors such as insurance companies began to fear a shortage of governmment stocks to invest in and paid increased attention to company bonds. But in the recession of the early 1990s the government's income from taxes and other sources fell while its spending on unemployment benefits and other items rose sharply. In 1993 it borrowed some £51 billion net via the issue of gilt-edged securities.

The high turnover in the gilt-edged market relative to the value of the stocks listed partly reflects massive and frequent **switching** from one stock to another, when a particular stock appears to offer a small interest rate or tax advantage to a particular class of holder. And proposed changes to the structure of the market (see below) could make it still more liquid in the future.

Press coverage of the gilt-edged market is far more restricted than equity market comment. Except for comment of a highly technical nature, there is far less to say. There are no takeover battles. There are no profit announcements affecting individual stocks. The main news that moves the gilt-edged market is news of Britain's economic and financial outlook, boiled down to a view of likely movements in interest rates and inflation. Estimates of the government's borrowing needs, influencing the volume of gilts to be issued in future, and movements in government bond prices in overseas markets also play their part. Individual news items may affect one sector of the gilt-edged market more than another (see below) but comment on price movements in individual stocks is comparatively rare. This is also true of comment on the bonds issued by industrial and commercial companies, which operate in a similar way to government bonds and much of the explanation in this chapter applies to company bonds as well: certainly the basic price mechanism. But a few additional factors affect company bonds and these will be examined towards the end of the chapter.

Given the limited number of influences on the gilt-edged market, the press comment falls into three main categories. There are occasional pieces on the outlook for the fixed-interest market as a whole, usually sparked off by events that could mark a turning point. There are pieces on the Bank of England's intentions and techniques in its handling of the market. And there are the regular but brief daily reports of price movements of government stocks and the reasons for them, amplified where appropriate by news of new issues or changes in the Bank's issue techniques.

News that moves prices

If you remember the basic mechanism described in Chapter 1 – interest rates go up, prices of fixed-interest stocks come down – and if you remember that higher interest rates are one way of supporting a weak currency, much of this comment falls into place. Weakness in sterling generally rattles the gilt-edged market because it is feared that interest rates may have to rise or stay high to defend the pound. Domestically, fears of higher **inflation**, caused by overheating in the economy, or excessive **earnings growth** bring fears of higher interest rates.

However, different factors affect different sectors of the gilt-edged market. If the government seeks to defend the currency by raising short-term interest rates (which immediately affects the cost of borrowing money from the banks) the effect will probably be most marked on the yields expected from government bonds that have a short life to run (see below). This is because a bond with only, say, a year or two years of life before it is repaid has much in common with a bank deposit and the returns on the two different types of investment will influence each other strongly. On the other hand, when investors look at the returns on bonds with a fairly long life – say, ten years before they are repaid – they will probably pay more attention to evidence about inflationary trends in the coming years. This is because they are interested in the **real return** that the bonds offer over their life (the return after allowing for inflation). If evidence emerges to suggest that inflationary pressures will be higher than expected over the coming years, the markets expect that long-term returns will have to rise to compensate investors for the higher inflation, or alternatively that interest rates will need to be higher to restrain inflation. All else being equal, this means that the prices of existing longer-dated bonds must drop until they provide the returns that investors now expect.

Remember that it is vital for investors to spot evidence of a change in expectations of inflation or interest rates. The **overall returns** can be very high for those who buy gilt-edged stocks just ahead of a major turning point when interest rates are about to move sharply down. When this happened in 1982, overall returns (income plus capital gains) for the year were over 50 per cent.

Technical influences on the market

The market is also affected by more **technical** factors. If a large amount of new stock is being brought to the market it may depress prices, because for a time the supply of stock will outpace investors' readiness to buy, though the Bank's methods of selling stock are intended to minimize the effect. A heavy flow of non-gilt sterling bond issues by companies and others may influence the market for government bonds. One other technical aspect of the market is now frequently remarked: investors have the opportunity to take a bet on movements in gilt-edged prices by buying or selling **financial futures contracts** in gilt-edged securities (see Chapter 18). Price movements in the very sensitive **financial futures market** can thus herald trends in the gilt-edged market itself, often referred to as the **cash market** when contrasted with the **futures market**.

Types of security

To understand the more detailed comment, we need to look a little closer at the structure of the market.

While the terms **gilt-edged market** and **fixed-interest market** are sometimes used almost interchangeably, they are not always quite the same thing. Not all government stocks carry a fixed rate of interest, though the vast majority of them do. And not all fixed interest stocks are government stocks. There are loans issued by industrial and financial companies (**corporate bonds**, **industrial loans**, **corporate loans** or **debentures**), loans issued by local government bodies (**corporation loans**) and loans issued in sterling by foreigners on the UK market (**bulldog bonds**). There are also the **convertible stocks** issued by companies, which were discussed in Chapter 5. Measured by the amount in issue, British government stocks predominate, but bonds issued by companies are also significant.

The life of a stock

Most gilt-edged securities are **redeemable**: the government will repay the stock at some point, but there are a few that have no fixed date for repayment. The notorious **War Loan** is probably the most familiar of these **undated** or **irredeemable** stocks.

The **dated** fixed-interest stocks are subdivided according to

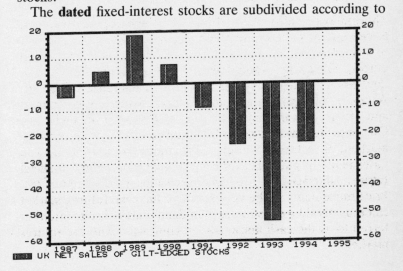

Figure 13.2 The annual volume of government bond (gilt-edged stock) issues, net of redemptions, shown in billions of pounds. A minus figure represents net issues – more than £50 billion of gilts were issued in 1993. The positive figures of the late 1980s represent net repayments of debt at that time. Source: *Datastream International.*

their **life** or **maturity**: how long they have to run until they are repaid. Those with a life of less than seven years (opinions vary – the *Financial Times* chooses five years) are classified as **shorts**, those with lives of seven to 15 years as **medium-dated** and stocks with more than 15 years to run as **longs**. These classifications reflect the current life of the stock, not its life when issued. A 25-year stock issued in 1982 – therefore repayable in the year 2007 – would initially have been in the 'long' category, but by 1995 it would have had a remaining life of under 15 years and would have been classified as a 'medium'. You will see how stocks are classified according to **redemption date** under the heading of 'UK Gilts Prices' in the 'Companies & Markets' section of the *Financial Times*.

How prices are quoted

If you had been looking at UK gilts prices early in 1995 you would also have seen that prices quoted were mainly in a range between about 74 and 130. Though the pound signs are omitted, these are the prices in pounds and fractions of pounds (usually 32nds) for a nominal £100 of the stock. In practice they are **middle prices**, between the buying and selling prices that marketmakers normally quote. Prices and interest rates are, as we saw earlier, expressed in terms of this nominal £100 unit of stock, though it does not mean that buyers or sellers have to deal in round amounts of £100 nominal. But an 11 per cent stock pays £11 of interest on every £100 of nominal value and the stock is normally repaid at this £100 **nominal** or **par value** at redemption. It was noticeable that, in 1995, a majority of stocks were standing above their par value of 100 in the market. This is by no means always the case, but tends to happen when a period of lower long-term interest rates follows a period of very high ones.

The range of coupons

The wide range of interest rates or **coupons** on the different stocks – ranging from under 3 per cent to over 15 per cent in 1995 – gives some indication of the interest rate the government had to pay when they were first issued and hence the very large movements in interest rates over the years. It is not a perfect guide, since stocks are often issued slightly above or below their £100 **par value** (**at a premium** or **at a discount**) and some used to be issued at a larger discount (see below) so that the yield to a buyer even at the outset was significantly different from the coupon rate.

The name is not important

You will also see from the *Financial Times* that stocks have somewhat curious names such as **Treasury**, **Exchequer** and **Funding**. Nowadays, 'Treasury' or 'Exchequer' is chosen as circumstances dictate to help identification if there are stocks of similar coupon maturing in the same year – 'Exchequer' is chosen if there is already a similar 'Treasury' stock. The word 'Loan' in the title indicates that the stock can be held in bearer form.

Regardless of the name, all the money raised goes into a central pool. What is important is the interest rate and the redemption date, which follow the name of the stock. Where two redemption dates are shown, the stock will not be redeemed before the first date and must be redeemed by the second. Thus, Treasury 8 per cent 2002–2006 pays £8 a year on every £100 nominal of stock (carries an 8 per cent coupon) and is due to be repaid (at the government's option) at the earliest in 2002 and the latest in 2006. Treasury 6¾ per cent 2004 carries a 6¾ per cent coupon and will be repaid in the year 2004.

Calculating the interest yield

However, 6¾ per cent is not the yield an investor in Treasury 6¾ per cent 2004 would have received if he had bought the stock early in 1995. The price of Treasury 6¾ per cent in early February 1995 was 88⅛. Since the investor is only paying 88⅛ (or slightly more since the quoted price is a middle price) for this £100 of nominal value, he is getting £6.75 per year in income for an outlay of about £88.13 (decimals are easier to calculate with than fractions). The yield on his outlay is therefore around 7.66 per cent. This is known as the **interest yield**, **income yield**, **flat yield** or the **running yield**. To calculate an income yield, you need to express the annual income as a percentage of the price the investor would have to pay. The sum to calculate an income yield is therefore simply:

$$\frac{\text{Interest rate (6.75)}}{\text{Market price (88.13)}} \times 100$$

giving the answer of 7.66 per cent.

What a redemption yield means

If Treasury 6¾ per cent were an **undated** stock, this would be the end of the matter. But it is to be repaid at its nominal £100 value in 2004. Thus a buyer in early 1995 could say to himself 'I'm paying just over £88 for a stock that will be repaid to me at £100 if I hang on to it till 2004. In other words, I'll see a £12 capital profit in 2004, in addition to the income I've been getting. This £12 is really part of the total return I'll get on the stock if I hold on to it. If I apportion the £12 over the nine years or so that the stock has to run, it works out at about £1.33 a year. So notionally I'm getting an extra £1.33 per year for my outlay of £88.13, which is about 1.5 per cent. This is my **gain to redemption**. If I add it to the 7.66 per cent yield I'm getting from the income, I have a notional combined yield of over 9 per cent.'

In practice, an investor who did his sums this way would have grasped the general principle, but would be wrong on the detail. To calculate the total return requires a compound interest sum and is best done with a computer programme or a sophisticated calculator. But he is right inasmuch as the *Financial Times* quotes two yields for each dated gilt-edged stock. First the **income yield**, then the **redemption yield**, which combines the interest yield with the notional **gain to redemption** or **loss to redemption** (see below). When Treasury 6¾ per cent 2004 at 88⅛ was showing an income yield of 7.66 per cent, in practice it gave a redemption yield of about 8.56 per cent.

With **low coupon stocks**, possibly but not necessarily issued many years ago in periods of low interest rates, the difference between income yield and redemption yield will be greater. Take Funding 3½ per cent 1999–2004. Again taking a price in early February 1995, at 74⅜ it offered an income yield of 4.71 per cent and a redemption yield of 7.30 per cent. These calculations would have been based on the assumption that the government would not repay the stock until 2004, since it would want to hang on as long as possible to a loan that was costing it only 3½ per cent a year in interest.

It is probably easiest to grasp the principles of gilt-edged stocks by taking – as we have done – stocks which stand in the market below their par value of £100 and where there is therefore a gain to redemption for the investor. But, as we saw,

UK GILTS PRICES

	.... Yield				.... 1995	
Notes	Int	Red	Price £	+ or –	High	Low
Shorts" (Lives up to Five Years)						
Exch $10\frac{1}{4}$pc 1995............	10.16	6.43	$100\frac{27}{32}$	....	$101\frac{7}{8}$	$100\frac{25}{32}$
Treas $12\frac{3}{4}$pc 1995‡‡.......	12.39	6.78	$102\frac{15}{16}$	....	$104\frac{7}{8}$	$102\frac{15}{16}$
14pc 1996	13.36	6.82	$104\frac{25}{32}$	....	$106\frac{7}{8}$	$104\frac{25}{32}$
$15\frac{1}{4}$pc 1996‡‡............	14.18	7.07	$107\frac{17}{32}$	....	$109\frac{5}{8}$	$107\frac{17}{32}$
Exch $13\frac{1}{4}$pc 1996‡‡........	12.52	7.09	$105\frac{13}{16}$	....	$107\frac{1}{4}$	$105\frac{13}{16}$
Conversion 10pc 1996	9.65	7.39	$103\frac{5}{8}$	$+\frac{1}{16}$	$103\frac{27}{32}$	$103\frac{3}{32}$
Treas $13\frac{1}{4}$pc 1997‡‡.......	12.17	7.56	$108\frac{7}{8}$	....	$109\frac{9}{16}$	$108\frac{9}{16}$
Exch $10\frac{1}{2}$pc 1997............	10.03	7.59	$104\frac{23}{32}$	$+\frac{1}{16}$	$105\frac{19}{32}$	$104\frac{1}{32}$
Treas Cnv 7pc 1997‡‡......	7.07	7.59	$98\frac{15}{16}$	....	$98\frac{31}{32}$	$97\frac{1}{8}$
Treas $8\frac{3}{4}$pc 1997‡‡........	8.58	7.75	$102\frac{1}{32}$	$+\frac{1}{16}$	$102\frac{1}{4}$	$100\frac{1}{32}$
Exch 15pc 1997	12.98	7.86	$115\frac{9}{16}$	....	$116\frac{3}{16}$	$114\frac{15}{16}$
$9\frac{3}{4}$pc 1998..................	9.35	7.93	$104\frac{5}{16}$	$+\frac{1}{16}$	$105\frac{13}{16}$	$102\frac{3}{4}$
Treas $7\frac{1}{4}$pc 1998‡‡........	7.37	7.93	$98\frac{5}{16}$	$+\frac{1}{8}$	$98\frac{1}{2}$	$96\frac{5}{16}$
Treas $6\frac{3}{4}$pc 1995–98‡‡...	6.96	7.93	$96\frac{31}{32}$	$+\frac{3}{32}$	$97\frac{3}{16}$	$94\frac{13}{16}$
Treas $15\frac{1}{2}$pc '98‡‡.........	12.72	7.97	$121\frac{27}{32}$	$-\frac{1}{32}$	$122\frac{5}{16}$	$120\frac{3}{8}$
Exch 12pc 1998	10.73	8.06	$111\frac{27}{32}$xd	$+\frac{1}{32}$	$112\frac{3}{16}$	$109\frac{21}{32}$
Treas $9\frac{1}{2}$pc 1999‡‡........	9.08	8.04	$104\frac{19}{32}$	$+\frac{1}{32}$	$104\frac{15}{16}$	$100\frac{7}{8}$
Treas Fltg Rate 1999.........	–	–	$100\frac{5}{16}$xd	....	$100\frac{5}{16}$	$99\frac{13}{32}$
Exch $12\frac{1}{4}$pc 1999............	10.79	8.10	$113\frac{17}{32}$	$+\frac{1}{32}$	$113\frac{15}{16}$	$111\frac{7}{16}$
Treas $10\frac{1}{2}$pc 1999	9.70	8.07	$108\frac{7}{32}$xd	$+\frac{3}{32}$	$108\frac{9}{16}$	$105\frac{13}{32}$
Treas 6pc 1999 ‡‡	6.45	8.00	$92\frac{31}{32}$	$+\frac{1}{8}$	$93\frac{1}{4}$	$89\frac{15}{16}$
Conversion $10\frac{1}{4}$pc 1999...	9.50	8.13	$107\frac{29}{32}$xd	$+\frac{5}{32}$	$108\frac{1}{4}$	$105\frac{1}{8}$
Conv 9pc 2000‡‡	8.67	8.03	$103\frac{13}{16}$	$+\frac{5}{32}$	$104\frac{1}{8}$	$100\frac{23}{32}$
Five to Fifteen Years						
Treas 13pc 2000..............	10.84	8.17	$119\frac{31}{32}$	$+\frac{1}{32}$	$120\frac{13}{32}$	117
8pc 2000‡‡................	8.00	8.01	$99\frac{31}{32}$xd	$+\frac{5}{32}$	$100\frac{9}{32}$	$96\frac{9}{16}$
10pc 2001	9.24	8.18	$108\frac{1}{4}$	$+\frac{1}{8}$	$108\frac{5}{8}$	$104\frac{25}{32}$
14pc 1998–1	12.11	8.08	$115\frac{19}{32}$xd	$-\frac{1}{32}$	116	$114\frac{9}{32}$
7pc 2001 ‡‡.................	7.42	8.15	$94\frac{5}{16}$	$+\frac{1}{8}$	$94\frac{23}{32}$	$90\frac{21}{32}$
$9\frac{3}{4}$pc 2002....................	9.03	8.28	108	$+\frac{1}{16}$	$108\frac{5}{8}$	$103\frac{31}{32}$
8pc 2003‡‡...................	8.11	8.25	$98\frac{19}{32}$xd	$+\frac{1}{32}$	$99\frac{1}{4}$	$94\frac{5}{8}$
10pc 2003	9.09	8.31	$109\frac{31}{32}$	$+\frac{1}{32}$	$110\frac{23}{32}$	$105\frac{7}{8}$
Treas $11\frac{1}{2}$pc 2001–4	10.05	8.32	$114\frac{15}{32}$	$+\frac{5}{32}$	$114\frac{25}{32}$	$110\frac{31}{32}$
Funding $3\frac{1}{2}$pc 1999–4.....	4.50	6.84	$77\frac{27}{32}$	$+\frac{11}{32}$	$78\frac{5}{16}$	73
Conversion $9\frac{1}{2}$pc 2004.....	8.81	8.29	$107\frac{13}{16}$	$+\frac{1}{32}$	$108\frac{21}{32}$	$103\frac{5}{16}$

Table 13.1 Gilt-edged price information. Source: *Financial Times*.

early in 1995 the majority of government stocks were standing above 100. Where this is the case the buyer will, of course, register a capital loss rather than a gain when the stock is repaid at only £100. In this case the redemption yield will be lower than the income yield. The income the investor receives over the years has to be high enough to compensate for this capital loss on redemption.

Take another example. Early in 1995, Treasury 13½ per cent 2004–8 stood in the market at 128¼. The assumption with this stock would have been that the government would repay it as early as possible (in the year 2004) because it was paying the high interest rate of 13½ per cent and it could have borrowed money at a much lower rate in 1995. On the assumption of redemption in 2004, the stock offered an interest yield as high as 10.53 per cent but a redemption yield of only 8.91 per cent.

How tax affects the returns

Trading between one gilt-edged stock and another is often driven by considerations of tax. The position could well change in the future, as proposed developments in the gilt-edged market (see below under heading 'The winds of change') may imply changes in the tax regime. So what follows is an outline of the tax considerations as they applied in 1995 – and had for a number of years.

The difference between income yield and redemption yield is very important to investors (though slightly less so than when the highest income tax rates were well above 1995's 40 per cent). This is because capital gains on gilt-edged stocks (and on qualifying bonds issued by companies) are exempt from tax. So a high-tax-paying investor might keep only 60p for every pound of income a stock provided him with, but he would keep the whole of every pound he received by way of capital gain. Look again at Funding 3½ per cent 1999–2004 and see what the return is to an investor paying the top tax rate. He is getting 4.71 per cent of income and a notional 2.59 per cent of capital gain to provide the combined 7.30 per cent redemption yield. Tax affects the sums as follows:

Government bonds and company bonds

	What the investor gets	
	Gross	Net of 40% tax
Income yield	4.71%	2.83%
Gain to redemption	2.59%	2.59% (no tax)
Total return	7.30%	5.42%

So the **net return** is 5.42 per cent. The higher-rate taxpayer would have needed a **gross income yield** of over 9 per cent to give him the same net return if the whole of it was taxed. Look at the Treasury 8 per cent 2003 we examined earlier and do the same sums:

	Gross	Net of 40% tax
Income yield	8.31%	5.00%
Gain to redemption	0.33%	0.33% (no tax)
Total return	8.64%	5.33%

Though this stock offers a gross redemption yield of 8.64 per cent against only 7.30 per cent for the Treasury 3 per cent, it actually provides a lower net income for the high-rate taxpayer because more of the return comes in the form of highly taxed interest and less in the form of capital gain. It was quite common in the past for the government to issue low-coupon stocks at a substantial discount specifically to appeal to high tax payers. However, with the reduction in top income tax rates and with a technical change in the tax treatment of deep-discounted issues in the 1989 Budget, we may not see this type of issue in future.

If we look again at Treasury 13.5 per cent 2004-2008, we can see how the sums work out for a stock standing in the market above its par value. At its early-1995 price of 128¼ it offered an income yield of 10.53 per cent but yielded only 8.91 per cent to redemption. The sums look like this:

	Gross	Net of 40% tax
Income yield	10.53%	6.32%
Gain to redemption	− 1.62%	−1.62% (no tax)
Total return	8.91%	4.70%

Thus Treasury 13.5 per cent 2004–08 provides a considerably lower return after 40 per cent tax than either of the other stocks we have looked at. It helps to explain why the redemption yield is actually higher. But to a pension fund that pays no tax on income it would offer a better return than either of the others. The examples underline an important aspect of the gilt-edged market. No one government stock is quite like another. Different stocks are worth different amounts to different classes of investor.

Remember, however, that redemption yields of any kind are, to an extent, notional. The redemption yield is relevant to the investor if he **holds the stock to redemption**. In the interim its price will be determined by the interplay of buyers and sellers, though on balance it will obviously move closer to 100 as the redemption date approaches. This is known as the **pull to redemption**. But the redemption yield is the main yardstick for comparing one stock with another and for calculating the likely price a borrower would have to pay for raising money via a bond issue at a given time.

Interest rate effects

One more example will help to explain prices in the gilt-edged market (and other forms of bond market) and it will be easier this time if we invent a hypothetical case rather than taking actual stocks. Suppose that in 1995 the government had decided to issue three different stocks. One was short-dated with a life of only three years, one was medium-dated with a life of ten years and one was a 'long' with a life of 25 years. Suppose also that the government reckoned, given the structure of interest rates at the time, that it would have to offer investors a redemption yield of 8.5 per cent on each of the stocks to persuade investors to buy them. Each stock was issued at its par value of 100.

Now, these assumptions are, of course a little unrealistic. It is very unlikely that the yields investors expected would have been exactly the same for a short-dated stock, a medium-dated one and a very long-dated stock. But they serve to illustrate our point. So we have our three stocks which we will call:

	Price	Income Yield	Redemption Yield
Short-dated 8.5% 1998	100	8.5%	8.5%
Medium-dated 8.5% 2005	100	8.5%	8.5%
Long-dated 8.5% 2020	100	8.5%	8.5%

With each of the stocks at a price of 100, income yields and redemption yields are exactly the same because there would at this point be no gain or loss to the investor on redemption.

Now suppose that a year later things have deteriorated in the UK economy. There is evidence of higher inflation in the pipeline and investors demand higher yields to compensate. If the government issued a new gilt-edged stock at this point it would have to offer a yield of, say, 10.5 per cent to persuade investors to buy. What happens to the market prices of our three stocks issued in 1995? The answer is clearly that no investor would buy them at a price of 100 where the redemption yield is only 8.5 per cent. The prices of the stocks will have to fall in the market until they reach a level where investors would buy them. What would this level be? It is the price at which they will offer the 10.5 per cent redemption yield that investors now expect. Again, we are being slightly unrealistic because it is doubtful if investors would expect exactly the same redemption yield from three stocks with different lives and different tax characteristics. But, to illustrate our point, this would be the position if each stock now had to offer a redemption yield of 10.5 per cent (remember that the remaining life of each stock is now a year shorter than when they were issued in 1995):

	Price	Income Yield	Redemption Yield
Short-dated 8.5% 1998	96.55	8.80%	10.5%
Medium dated 8.5% 2005	88.71	9.58%	10.5%
Long dated 8.5% 2020	82.68	10.28%	10.5%

The example shows very clearly that long-dated stocks show

WORLD BOND PRICES

BENCHMARK GOVERNMENT BONDS

		Coupon	Red Date	Price	Day's change	Yield	Week ago	Month ago
Australia		9.000	09/04	89.4500	+0.060	9.11	9.23	9.90
Austria		7.000	05/05	98.6000	+0.110	7.20	7.20	7.43
Belgium		6.500	03/05	92.1200	−0.010	7.66	7.71	7.95
Canada *		9.000	12/04	106.1000	+0.310	8.07	8.05	8.40
Denmark		7.000	12/04	91.5200	+0.160	8.31	8.45	8.85
France	BTAN	7.750	04/00	102.7500	−0.130	7.06	7.20	7.49
	OAT	7.500	04/05	99.9000	−0.280	7.51	7.65	7.81
Germany Bund		7.375	01/05	103.0200	−0.140	6.93	6.92	7.10
Ireland		6.250	10/04	85.2500	−0.250	8.84	8.84	8.82
Italy		9.500	01/05	87.6400	+0.420	11.67†	12.19	13.15
Japan	No 119	4.800	06/99	108.9810	–	2.55	2.61	2.80
	No 174	4.600	09/04	109.0800	+0.190	3.33	3.35	3.41
Netherlands		7.750	03/05	105.1400	+0.080	7.00	6.99	7.26
Portugal		11.875	02/05	100.1000	+0.300	11.84	12.18	12.10
Spain		10.000	02/05	0.0000	–	0.00	11.57	12.24
Sweden		6.000	02/05	73.0420	+0.390	10.56	10.86	11.64
UK Gilts		6.000	08/99	92–29	–	8.02	8.07	8.29
		8.500	12/05	102–09	+1/32	8.17	8.28	8.42
		9.000	10/08	106–08	–	8.22	8.32	8.44
US Treasury *		6.500	05/05	99–04	−14/32	6.62	6.69	7.03
		7.625	02/25	108–14	−11/32	6.95	7.02	7.34
ECU (French Govt)		6.000	04/04	88.2500	−0.160	7.88	8.04	8.33

London closing, *New York closing   Yields: Local market standard.
† *Gross (including withholding tax at 12.5 per cent payable by nonresidents)*
Prices: US, UK in 32nds, others in decimal   Source: MMS International

Table 13.2 Government bonds from different countries, with price and yield information. Source: *Financial Times.*

much larger price movements for a given change in interest rates than short-dated ones. An investor in the short-dated stock who had bought at 100 originally and now needed to sell would have lost some money but not a massive amount. The investor in the medium-dated stock would have lost quite heavily and the investor in the long-dated stock would have fared worst of all. Investors in all three stocks would eventually be repaid at 100 if they hung on for redemption, but in the meantime the losses could be substantial. Thus, investors who are averse to risk and might want to get their money back in a hurry are more likely to buy the short-dated stocks. Those who want to tie their money up for a long time at a known return, together with the more adventurous or those who want to take a deliberate bet on favourable movements in interest rates are more likely to go for the long-dated stocks.

The **pull to redemption** is much greater with a short-dated stock than a long-dated one. When a stock is due to be repaid at £100 in the fairly near future, redemption is the dominant

influence and its price will not fluctuate so widely in response
to movements in interest rates. Nor, as the example shows,
does it need to do so to accommodate investor's changed expectations of the return they should get. It is true that
short-term interest rates can nowadays fluctuate very widely
(perhaps by more than long yields), and will affect short-dated
stocks more than the long-dated ones. Thus, as our example
shows, price fluctuations can be quite marked even at the
short end of the market. But the risk of capital loss is still a
great deal lower than with long-dated stocks. Market reports
will often highlight the different magnitude of price movements at the long and short end of the market. Investors
switch between stocks of different maturities according to the
way they expect long-term and short-term interest rates to
move.

Cum-dividend and ex-dividend

Interest on gilt-edged securities is paid twice a year. So between dividend payments it is **accruing** – building up – until
the moment it is paid. Prices for gilts are now quoted **clean**
(they exclude **accrued income**). But a buyer normally pays for
(and receives the right to) any income that has accrued since
the last dividend date, in addition to the price he pays for the
stock itself. However, if he buys it once the stock has gone **ex-
dividend** (see Chapter 4), the seller keeps the right to the
forthcoming interest payment. Since the date that a stock goes
ex-dividend does not correspond exactly with the end of an interest period, the seller pays the buyer **rebate interest** in
respect of the period for which the buyer will hold a stock but
the seller will receive the interest from the government. Yields
on gilt-edged stocks are always calculated on **clean prices**. If
the tax laws permitted, it would benefit a higher-rate taxpayer
to buy a stock just after it had gone ex-dividend and sell it
shortly before the next dividend payment was due. In this way
he receives no income, on which high rates of tax would be
payable, but receives the benefit in the form of untaxed
capital gain.

This practice, known as **dividend stripping**, has now been
outlawed and the interest is normally taxed as income whether
in fact it is received as interest or as capital gain. However, an

exception is made for investors whose gilt-edged holdings total less than £5,000 at nominal values. These are taxed on an 'income received' basis.

Index-linked and other stocks

So far we've been talking of fixed-interest stocks. But there are, and have been, other types of government stock. In 1994 the government issued a new **floating rate gilt** which met with strong demand and of which £5 billion was in issue by 1995. It pays a rate of interest ⅛ per cent below the LIBID benchmark (see Chapter 15) and the return to the investor therefore varies with movements in interest rates in the economy. Also in 1994 the government issued a short-life **convertible gilt**: convertible not, of course, into shares but into a longer-dated gilt on fixed terms and fixed dates.

There are also the **index-linked stocks**, which provide protection against inflation (act as an **inflation hedge**). They were initially introduced in 1981 for the pension funds, then made available to any type of investor. With an **index-linked stock**, both the income and the price at which it will be redeemed are adjusted to take account of the movement in **retail prices**. In other words, both income and capital retain their **real value**. The price you pay for this protection is a much lower nominal coupon rate.

Say an index-linked stock is issued at its par value of 100, with a coupon of 2.5 per cent. Over the next five years, retail prices rise by 30 per cent in total, meaning that it would cost you £130 to buy goods and services you could have obtained for £100 five years earlier. So the price at which the stock will be redeemed rises to 130. The interest it pays must also rise by 30 per cent to maintain a real interest rate of 2.5 per cent. So the interest rate after five years will be 2.5 per cent on the new £130 redemption value (equivalent to 3.25 per cent on the original £100 nominal value).

Of course, if retail prices were to fall in year six, the redemption value could be adjusted down again from 130 and so could the interest. But in the more likely event that retail prices continue rising (though at different rates in different climates) the redemption value of the stock will continue to rise.

In practice, the redemption value of an index-linked stock

does not match the movement in retail prices (as measured by the **retail prices index** or **RPI**) quite as closely as in the example because there is a time lag of eight months built in so that the size of the interest payment is known before the start of the interest period. This means that the return from the last eight months of the life of the gilt is not indexed and the real return will therefore vary depending on the future rate of inflation. In compensation, the investor is recompensed for inflation in the eight months before the stock was issued. The *Financial Times* quotes two possible real redemption yields, one on the assumption of 5 per cent inflation and the other on the assumption of 10 per cent. The *Financial Times* also shows (in brackets after the name of each index-linked stock) the starting point for the indexation sum on the retail prices index or RPI.

The market price of the index-linked stock is, as with a fixed-interest stock, not directly determined by the redemption value, though this will begin to exert more influence as redemption comes close. Real redemption yields are low (in the 2.3 to 3.9 per cent range early in 1995) partially reflecting the fact that most of the return comes in the form of untaxed capital appreciation. Index-linked stocks are not at their most attractive when **real rates of return** on conventional gilt-edged are high: in other words, when the nominal yields are well above the inflation rate. Index-linked stocks are more popular when inflation fears rise.

> '. . . attention was diverted to the index-linked sector. Election and inflation possibilities, which received a good deal of publicity in the weekend press, touched off renewed hedge buying . . .' (*Financial Times*, 17 February 1987)

Indices for government stocks

Price movements in the fixed interest market are measured on a number of indices. Separate **Financial Times-Actuaries indices** are published for **short**, **medium** and **long-dated stocks** as well as for the **irredeemables**. There is also an **All Stocks Index** for gilt-edged as a whole. There are separate indices for short- and longer-dated index-linked stocks and a third index for index-linked stocks as a whole. The *Financial Times* also publishes its own longer-established **Government Securities Index** with a base of 100 in 1926. Market reports talk of price movements of a **point** or fraction of a point in individual stocks: a point in this context is one pound per £100 nominal.

New issues and dealing mechanisms

The mechanics of issue and subsequent dealing for gilt-edged stocks, as with equities, underwent some changes with the Big Bang. And by 1995 further changes were being canvassed in the interests of a more efficient market and greater competitiveness with government bond markets overseas (see below).

In the past, when a **public offering of stock** was made, a minimum price was usually set and **tenders** were invited at or above that figure. All accepted bidders at tender paid a common price. The price might be due as a single payment, or payment might be made in instalments (see Chapter 8 for a description of **partly-paid stocks** in the equity market, where the procedure is similar).

Stock that did not find buyers at a tender remained in the hands of the government and was subsequently made available to the market by the Bank of England as and when there was a demand for it and when it suited the authorities to make further sales. Stock available for issue in this way is described as a **tap stock** because the supply can be turned on and off as required. A second source of stock that can be used as a **tap** is issues of small **tranchettes** of stock – possibly of a range of different stocks – which are available for sale to the market in the same way. Sales of tap stocks to the market are made via the Bank's dealing room.

However, no issues of stock via the tender method have been made since 1991 and the more recent auction method is now the norm. This was first introduced in 1987 when the Bank undertook an experimental series of **auctions** for selling large amounts of stock, initially as a supplement to the tender method. The main difference between the auction and the tender is the implication, in the auction method, that there is the intention to sell all the stock on offer. Also, competitive bidders are allocated stock at the price at which they bid, rather than at a common **striking price** as in a tender (see

Chapter 8 for a description of the tender mechanism). But for small bids the facility exists for stock to be allocated non-competitively at the average of the accepted competitive bids.

New gilt-edged stocks are created to satisfy the government's financing needs and the market's need for a balance of short, medium and long dates and index-linked stocks. The gilt auction operations by the Bank now take place according to a calendar determined a year in advance, with an indication of the maturity of the stock to be auctioned being given in advance of each quarter.

At times when the government is a net repurchaser of stock – far from being the position in 1995 – the Bank of England may operate **reverse auctions** under which holders can offer to sell stock back to the authorities, who accept the stock offered at the most favourable price. As with the ordinary auction, there would also be facilities for small offers of stock.

Before Big Bang, gilt-edged stocks – once issued – were traded on the stockmarket via the **jobber/broker mechanism** as with equities. Nowadays the **marketmaking function** is undertaken by **primary dealers** known as **gilt-edged marketmakers** or **GEMMs**. They include former gilt jobbing and broking firms but also offshoots of banks and other financial institutions including a number of American, Japanese and continental European firms. These primary dealers have an obligation to maintain a market in all government stocks and have the right to deal direct with the Bank of England. They can bid for available tap stocks when they wish.

> 'Government bonds started well, and the authorities took the opportunity to sell more of the 1994 tap stock issued last week. This checked the market's advance. . . .' (*Financial Times*, 13 January 1987).

The market mechanism is eased by **inter-dealer brokers**, via whom the gilt-edged marketmakers can effectively deal with each other without disclosing their positions to their competitors. The primary dealers have access to a **price information system** via the **SEAQ** screens, but this is more rudimentary than the SEAQ equity service and they rely more heavily on screen-based price information supplied by the inter-dealer brokers. In order to cover their short positions, marketmakers can also borrow (rather than buy) stock from

Stock Exchange money brokers, who have increased in number since Big Bang.

Dealing in gilt-edged stock is for **cash settlement** (payment the next day), and major institutional investors are likely to deal direct at **net prices** with a primary dealer rather than going through an **agency broker**. Small private investors will go through a broker as before (though **commissions** are lower than on equities) or can buy through the National Savings Stock Register (see below).

The winds of change

By the mid 1990s there were fears that Britain's gilt-edged market might be losing out in terms of competitiveness with some overseas government bond markets and change was once again in the air. There were proposals for introducing an open system of **repurchase agreements** or **repos** in the gilt market at the beginning of 1996 – they already exist in some of the more liquid overseas markets.

In effect, repos would allow much easier lending of gilt-edged stocks and borrowing against gilt-edged stocks. Somebody with a bearish view of the market, for example, would be able to sell stock that he did not own and temporarily borrow the stock that he needed to deliver. Alternatively, investors wishing to buy gilts may be able to borrow sterling more cheaply by using the gilts as security. Repos should thus add to the liquidity of the market. In association with the introduction of an open repo market, investors likely to participate (which means mainly corporate bodies) would be able to receive interest on gilts gross by holding them in special accounts at the **Central Gilts Office**. Such investors who are liable for UK tax would have to account for their interest income quarterly (see below).

There were also proposals for reducing the number of individual gilts in issue and concentrating on a smaller number of larger (and therefore more liquid) issues. And settlement procedures were also under scrutiny. There was even talk of introducing a market in **financially-engineered** government bonds, as exists elsewhere. Thus, a conventional bond could be **stripped** into its two components of income and capital, with the rights to the income payments and to the eventual capital repayment marketed as separate securities. Both components would in effect be very much like zero-coupon bonds (see below).

These **strips**, if they are introduced, would imply changes to the tax treatment of government (and probably of corporate) bonds. No longer would it be possible to make the present rigid distinction between (taxed) income and (untaxed) capital gain. A likely solution, canvassed by the Inland Revenue, would be to tax total returns from bonds, however they were split between income and capital gain.

Post Office Register

In Britain, the public has an opportunity to buy certain gilt-edged stocks without going through a broker at all. A selection of stocks is included on the **National Savings Stock Register** and these can be bought through a Post Office. The cost for small transactions will generally be less than the commission payable if you go via a broker, though transactions take longer and the price at which you buy will not necessarily be that ruling at the moment you apply. Stocks bought through the Post Office Register also pay interest **gross**, whereas interest on government stocks is normally paid **net** of basic rate tax to UK investors, as with the dividend on a share. But those who are liable still have to pay the tax at the end of the day.

Corporate bond market

Companies as well as governments often want to borrow money for long periods at fixed rates of interest. And, just like governments, they can do so by issuing fixed-interest bonds which become **securities** of the company. Such bonds could gain in popularity with investors now that the rules for **personal equity plans** or **PEPs** allow these to be used as a tax shelter for company bond as well as share investments (see Chapter 21).

When a company issues a bond, a few additional considerations apply that do not crop up with government bonds. First, a company (even the best company) is not as secure as the government. Investors assume that the government will always be able to pay the interest on its debt and repay the debt at the end of the day. The government can ultimately tap taxpayers for the money it needs. A company, on the other hand, has to be able to earn the profit from which it will pay the interest and must find the cash to repay the debt eventually. Companies, even large and reputable companies, do sometimes get into trouble and even go bust. A bond issued by a company will therefore need to offer a higher return than one issued by the government to compensate investors for the higher risk. A very large and safe company may not need to pay a great deal more than the government would. A smaller and less secure company might have to pay considerably more.

Secondly, investors are prepared to lend to the government for 25 years or so, because they assume that one government or another will still be around in 25 years. They may be more reluctant to lend to companies for such a long period. Very well-established companies or those with assets such as property which investors expect to increase in value may be able to borrow for very long periods. Others may have to settle for somewhat shorter terms.

Thirdly, when the government issues a bond it might issue several billion pound's worth. Since there will be many thousands of investors in any single government bond, the bond will be easy to buy and sell in the **secondary market** without moving the price too much. In other words, it will be very **liquid**. Companies will normally issue bonds for rather smaller amounts and the bonds will not be quite so liquid. Again, investors expect some compensation for this factor in the form of additional return.

Deciding the coupon rate

But the rates of return on company bonds will take the returns on 'risk-free' government bonds as their starting point. If, at a particular time, investors expect a redemption yield of, say, 8.5 per cent on a government bond repayable in ten years' time, what rate of return would the company have to offer? The company's financial advisers, who know the market well, might decide that the company would need to offer 50 **basis points** (half a percentage point) more than the government to attract investors. If the government **benchmark gilt** – the one selected as a yardstick for medium-dated bonds – offers a redemption yield of 8.5 per cent, the company bond would need to offer 9 per cent.

But bond prices can move up and down quite rapidly and it may still be a few days before the company bond is ready for issue. So the company or its advisers might say that the redemption yield on the new bond will be set at 50 basis points over the redemption yield on the benchmark gilt at 3 pm next Wednesday, the day of issue. If on that day the benchmark gilt is yielding 8.65 per cent to redemption, the new company bond will need to offer a redemption yield of 9.15 per cent.

This does not mean that the coupon will necessarily need to be 9.15 per cent. Instead, the company could issue the bond with a coupon of 9 per cent but issue it below its nominal value at a price (roughly 99.04 in this instance) which would provide investors with a redemption yield of 9.15 per cent over ten years. If the company making the bond issue were a smaller or lesser-known concern it would have to offer a higher yield – a greater **spread** over the benchmark gilt: say, 180 basis points. Its cost would thus be 10.45 per cent.

The credit risk

Once issued, company bonds respond to changes in interest rate expectations in much the same way as government bonds. But there is another factor that can affect their market price. Suppose something happens subsequently to affect investors' confidence in the company that issued the bond. A year after the bond issue the company begins making losses and investors start to question whether it will be able to pay the interest. The general level of yields in the market has not changed, let us suppose, and the benchmark gilt is still yielding 8.65 per cent. But buyers of the company bond in the market would now demand a considerably higher return to compensate them for the higher risk that they now perceive.

This means that the price of the bond must fall. Suppose it falls to a price of 70 before investors are prepared to buy it. At this level, with 9 years of life still to run, it offers a redemption yield of 15.37 per cent (provided it does, in the event, pay the interest): no longer 50 basis points over the benchmark gilt yield but 672 basis points above it. If the company returns to profit, buyers of the bond will see a handsome profit themselves. If the company goes bust they might lose the whole of their investment. Buyers of company bonds are not just at the mercy of changes in interest rates. They can be affected by changes in the **credit status** of the company and changes considerably less dramatic than in our example are taking place much of the time.

For this reason, company bonds may carry a **credit rating** issued by one of the independent **rating agencies** (see Chapter 17). This rating aims to reflect the degree of risk and will be amended if the company's fortunes change.

Fixed-interest bonds issued by companies fall into two main categories: those that are **secured** and those that are **unsecured**. With a secured bond, the loan is normally secured on a specific asset or specific assets owned by the issuing company. If the company defaults on the terms of the bond, the asset or assets can be sold to provide the money to repay investors (though the position is slightly complicated by the 1986 Insolvency Act). This gives greater security than if the investors in the bond have to compete with other creditors for repayment if the company should get into trouble. It is similar to the system applying in the residential property market, where a lender to the homebuyer takes a **mortgage** on the property, which allows the home to be sold to repay the loan if necessary.

With an unsecured bond, the investor is relying mainly on the standing of the issuing company and its ability to earn the profits and generate the cash to pay the interest on the bond and repay it at the end of the day. Investors may insist on certain conditions or **restrictive covenants** to strengthen their hand. There might be upper limits on the amount of money the company could borrow and the company might have to stay within certain ratios between profits and interest charges.

All else being equal, a secured bond will normally be slightly cheaper for the issuing company than an unsecured one. In other words, the yield it has to offer to attract investors will be slightly lower. Traditionally, bonds issued in the domestic stockmarket were frequently secured whereas those issued in the **euromarket** or **international market** (see below) tend to follow American practice and are usually unsecured. But the division is not rigid.

Bonds with a difference

There is another type of 'fixed interest' bond that you will come across sometimes, and that is the **zero coupon bond**. Its distinction is that it pays no interest at all during its life. The investor's return comes entirely in the form of a **gain to redemption**. A company issues a bond at, say, a price of 50 and agrees to repay it at 100 in seven years' time. In practice, this is much the same thing as a compound annual rate of interest of 10.4 per cent, but the investor has to wait for seven years to get this 'interest' as a lump sum.

Not all bonds offer a fixed return at all. Companies, like the government, have the option of issuing **floating rate** bonds instead and some types of company – particularly banks and other financial groups – use them a great deal more. The bonds, which are usually known as **floating rate notes** or **FRNs** pay a rate of interest that is geared to a widely accepted yardstick for interest rates such as LIBOR (see Chapter 15). The issuer agrees that the FRN will pay, say, 50 basis points (half of one percentage point) above the rate of LIBOR. In practice this means that the average rate of LIBOR will be taken over, perhaps, a six month period. If average LIBOR was 9 per cent the FRN would pay 9 per cent plus the 50 basis points **spread** or 9.5 per cent in total in respect of that six months' period.

We saw that with a bond that has a fixed coupon, the price in the market has to change to accommodate changes in interest rates in the economy. With an FRN the interest rate itself can change so that the market price does not need to adjust in the same way. The price is likely to stay far closer to its nominal value of 100 and in this sense the risk for the investor is considerably less, as are the possible gains. But if something happened to damage the **credit standing** of the issuing company, the price in the market could, of course, drop for this reason.

New types of bond and FRN are constantly being developed and tailored to investors' requirements at a given time (see Chapter 17). And **convertible bonds** – bonds that may convert into shares – are a long-established part of the financing armoury (see Chapter 5). Nor do bonds necessarily need to be traded on a stockmarket at all. Companies may make **private placements** of bonds that are **placed** with (sold direct to) big investing institutions who will often hold them until they are redeemed.

Tapping the bond markets

At times of high inflation when long-term interest rates are high, UK companies have generally been reluctant to raise capital by issuing long-term fixed-interest bonds. They do not want to commit themselves to paying very high interest rates for 20 years or so when there is a chance that capital might become considerably cheaper at a later date. And many investors are very reluctant to buy fixed-interest bonds when they think that inflation will seriously erode the real value of their capital.

Issues of fixed-interest bonds by companies virtually dried up in the high-inflation era of the 1970s and they have been unpopular at times of high interest rates subsequently. But the generally lower levels of inflation for part of the 1980s and the early 1990s have seen a resurgence of interest in the corporate bond market, reinforced in 1994 by the decision to allow PEPs to be invested in them. For investors, **industrial debentures** or **corporate bonds** have the advantage of offering rather higher returns than the government's own bonds, still with quite a high level of safety.

UK companies are not limited to the domestic stockmarket when they wish to issue bonds. In the **euromarket** or **international market** the larger companies can issue bonds in sterling or in a range of other currencies. And they can also issue foreign-currency bonds in the domestic stockmarkets of a number of other countries, particularly the United States. The euromarkets need a chapter of their own (see Chapter 17). But it is important to note that many of the differences in issue and trading techniques for sterling bonds between Britain's domestic stockmarket and the euromarket have now broken down. Dealers tend to talk of the two markets almost interchangeably.

14

Banks, borrowers and bad debts

Banks occupy a special place in the economic and financial system. Industrial companies may be allowed to go to the wall or come under the control of foreigners. Banks are normally viewed with a more protective eye by the authorities, although there is no such thing as a blanket guarantee of support for a bank in trouble.

Why the special treatment? First, there are not many aspects of economic life that can function without a stable banking system. Secondly, banking is a business that depends on confidence. Allow the confidence to be destroyed and you are a fair way to destroying the banks. Thirdly, banks play a vital role in the creation of money: something that governments like to keep within their control. Fourthly, they play a central role in the operation of payment systems around the world.

To see two of these considerations at work, look back to the events surrounding the collapse of Barings, one of the City's oldest merchant banks, early in 1995. Barings had lost over £800m – considerably more than the total shareholders' money in the business – through wild and probably un-authorized gambles in the derivatives markets of the Far East. The bank was bust. Should the Bank of England step in to save it with taxpayers' money?

After a week-end of intensive discussions with the London banking community (which was not on its own prepared to undertake a rescue while the size of the bill was still unknown) the Bank of England decided against bailing out Barings. On the one side was the desire to sustain the reputation of the

City and confidence in its banking system. On the other, Barings was judged to be a fairly small player and it was not thought that there was great **systemic risk** in allowing it to fail. In other words, the knock-on effect on the banking system as a whole was judged to be fairly small. Later, the main operations of Barings were taken over by Dutch banking group ING which was prepared to pump in cash to replace the missing millions. Consequently, while holders of the bank's shares and other securities lost out, there was no loss to Barings' depositors

Deposits, advances and liquid funds

The best way to understand what is written about banking is to start by looking at what a bank is. At its simplest, a bank takes **retail deposits** from private individuals and others and lends money (makes **advances**) to borrowers. A certain proportion of the money it takes in as deposits is held in **liquid** or **near-liquid** form: as cash or in a form in which it can readily be turned into cash. This is a safeguard in case some **depositors** want their money back. Another proportion will normally be held in the form of investments which are a little less liquid. The remainder can be lent to customers.

Borrowed money and shareholders' money

The detail may vary, but the principle is much the same for most **deposit-taking institutions**, including **building societies** which are really just a specialist form of bank whose business in the past has been to lend mainly to homebuyers. In practice, banks are not completely dependent on retail deposits because they also borrow **wholesale funds** in the money markets, which add to the money they have available to lend.

Like any company, a bank needs some money of its own – shareholders' funds – as well as the borrowed money it obtains from depositors or in the money markets. But banks are very much more **highly geared** than most industrial and commercial companies. They use a lot of borrowed money and relatively little of their own. Let us see how this structure translates into a (simplified) bank balance sheet:

ASSETS

Liquid assets	£100
Investments	£250
Loans to customers (Advances)	£750
	£1,100

Financed by:

Current and deposit accounts	£1,000
Share capital and reserves (shareholders' funds)	£100
	£1,100

The bank in this example has only £100 of its own money against £1,000 of borrowed money from depositors. Its total resources are thus £1,100. It holds £100 (equivalent to 10 per cent of its deposits) in liquid form, a further £250 as investments and lends the remaining £750.

The money creation process

How do banks create money? Assume that the bank in our example attracts a further £100 of deposits. It will hold £10 of this as cash and lend the remaining £90. The customer who borrows the £90 spends it on, say, a piece of office equipment. He pays the £90 to the office equipment supplier, who deposits it in his own bank. This increases the deposits of the supplier's bank by £90 of which the bank will lend £81, holding back £9 in cash form for safety. And so on. Since the money finds its way back into the banking system at each stage, that original £100 of extra deposits in the first bank actually generates – in this case – a further £1,000 of spending power in the economy.

If the proportion of their deposits that banks held in liquid form were lower (8 per cent, say) each additional £100 of deposits would create proportionately more spending power. One of the ways central banks sometimes try to control expansion of the **money supply** (see below) is by varying the permissible ratio between deposits and the amount held as **reserve assets**, which covers cash and certain other near-cash items (**reserve assets ratio**), though this system is no longer used by the Bank of England.

The most commonly quoted measures of money supply in the press in Britain are M_0 ('M nought'), which comprises notes and coins in circulation plus banks' balances at the Bank of England. The broader M_4 measure covers notes and coins plus private sector current and deposit accounts with banks and building societies and private sector wholesale deposits.

A bank works on the principle that no more than a small proportion of depositors will want their money back at any one time and this calculation affects the proportion of deposits held in liquid form (the **liquidity ratio**). And a glance back at the simplified bank balance sheet shows the main ways a bank can get into trouble. If depositors suddenly lose confidence in a particular bank, they may all try to get their money back at the same time and a **run on the bank** develops. This does not mean that the bank is necessarily unsound, but may cause it to collapse all the same. The bank will not be able to get back rapidly the money it has advanced to customers and if it runs out of cash it may be forced to close its doors.

Whatever his problems, a banker is virtually obliged to maintain that his bank is totally sound until he has to close the doors. Any admission of difficulties will worry depositors and make them more likely to withdraw their money. So statements from bankers that everything in the garden is rosy must be treated with a large dose of salt. It may be true, but the banker would be equally obliged to say it if it wasn't.

This illustrates one of the paradoxes on which a banking system rests. Even the soundest of banks is sound only as long as its depositors think that it is sound. It explains why central banks play a vital role.

Rescues, recycling and lifeboats

To prevent a run if the bank is basically sound, the central bank will often organize a **recycling** operation. Banks which are not under any pressure from depositors will be persuaded to make deposits with the troubled bank to replace its vanishing deposits from the public. Such a rescue for third-tier money-lending institutions – euphemistically referred to as **secondary banks** – was organized in the 1973–75 period of

financial crisis or **secondary bank collapse** in Britain. The clearing banks were dragooned into forming a **lifeboat** via which they made money available to secondary banks which had seen their normal deposits melt away.

Capital adequacy requirements

In reality, most of the secondary banks were not sound – their liabilities (what they owed) exceeded the real value of their assets (the money they had lent, much of which they lost). And this brings us to the second way a bank gets into trouble. The bank in our sample balance sheet could not lose more than £100 of the money it has lent without becoming insolvent. If it loses £100 of its £750 of advances, this completely wipes out the £100 of shareholders' money in the business. Any further losses and it will not be able to cover what it owes to depositors. The problems of the Barings bank in 1995 illustrated this process at work.

Again, a banker has to judge what 'cushion' of shareholders' money he needs to allow for any likely losses on his business activities. And the central bank normally makes doubly sure by imposing certain **capital adequacy ratios** which stipulate the amount of its own money a bank needs relative to its total assets. Since a bank that operated with less of its own money and more borrowed money could have an advantage over its competitors (though at greater risk), there have been moves in recent years to impose international standards for capital adequacy (see below).

This **capital ratio** or **solvency ratio** is not a simple calculation: the Bank of England will look at the make-up of a bank's business and decide that the risks that need to be covered are higher for some types of business than others. Mortgage loans on residential property, for example, are judged safer than lending to small businesses. And it will take into account some **off balance sheet risks** that do not appear in the accounts: forms of **guarantee** and **underwriting commitment** the bank may have undertaken or risks involved in **derivatives**. Nor are shareholders' funds the exact measure of the bank's own money that the authorities adopt. In calculating its **capital base** to arrive at a figure for primary capital a bank may be able to include certain **subordinated loans** (see glossary) but will have to make deductions for other items. A **risk asset ratio** shows **primary capital** as a proportion of risk-weighted assets. Capital ratios are part of what are normally described as **prudential ratios**: ratios dictated by banking prudence rather than by the central bank's need to control the money supply via the banking system.

Under the international agreement known as the **Basle Accord**, all banks are required to maintain primary capital equal to at least 8 per cent of their risk-weighted assets (mainly, the loans they make). Above this minimum, central banks may impose whatever ratios they consider appropriate to individual banks within their jurisdiction, to reflect differing degress of perceived risk.

Banking in the 1990s

While the relatively simple business of taking deposits and making loans remains at the core of banking activities, banks are considerably more complex operations nowadays. There are five changes in particular that we need to look at:

- The dependence on retail deposits from the public has been reduced. Today's banks raise large amounts of the money that they need in the form of **wholesale funds** in the money markets (see Chapter 15).
- The process of **disintermediation** that we touched on earlier has brought big changes to the ways that banks operate. No longer do they simply borrow and lend. This is because many of their larger customers, instead of simply borrowing from a bank, raise money by selling **debt securities** in a market instead. To replace interest income that they have lost, banks need to be active in the markets in which securities are issued: underwriting the issue of securities, arranging their sale and distribution, etc. In this way they can earn fee income to replace some of the interest income. In practice, many have also tried to boost their income by more active dealing in securities markets.
- The scale of loan required by major companies is often too large for a single bank to take on board. So **syndicated loans** have become more common. Suppose a company

wants to raise £200m. An individual bank might be reluctant to take the risk of lending this amount to a single customer. Instead, a syndicate of, say, ten banks is put together, each of which contributes £20m of the loan, which is organized by one bank as **lead manager**.

- As we saw earlier, the changes brought about by the Big Bang in Britain allowed banks to own **stockbroking** and **marketmaking** businesses, thus introducing them to aspects of securities trading that had been closed to them before. Some plunged more enthusiastically into the new areas than others.

- Banks have had a central part to play in the development of the mushrooming markets in **derivatives** (see Chapter 18). Derivative products such as futures and options evolved as a way of hedging or reducing risk. Such contracts allow risks to be transferred to those best able to manage them. But the derivatives markets rapidly acquired a momentum as gambling markets where large amounts of money could be made or lost on small movements in the prices of commodities, currencies, bonds, equities and many other financial products. It was gambles in the financial futures markets that brought down the merchant bank Barings in 1995.

Off balance sheet risks

By no means all derivatives business takes place in the public markets. The big commercial banks are major vendors of **over-the-counter** or **OTC** derivatives products. These are products that can be tailored for (and sold to) individual clients. A company wants to arrange a **cap** on its borrowing costs (see Chapter 15) or an interest rate **swap** (see Chapter 17). It goes to its bank. For a fee, the bank sells it the desired product. The bank might agree that it will accept the obligation to pay the interest on a £100m floating-rate loan the company has raised and charge the company a fixed rate of interest instead (a swap). Or it might agree to compensate the company for any rise above, say, 9 per cent in the interest rate on a £100m floating rate loan (a cap). And vastly more complex hedging products than these can be devised.

Selling OTC derivatives products of these kinds had become

very big business for the banks by the mid-1990s and there was considerable comment in the press and elsewhere about the risks involved. What, for example, if interest rates rose sharply and the banks had to pay out under the arrangements where they had contracted to insure against increases in interest rates on floating-rate loans?

In practice, the banks lay off their risks. A bank may agree to pay the floating rate interest on a loan and charge a fixed rate in a swap arrangement. But it will match this commitment by charging a floating rate of interest and accepting responsibility for a fixed rate of interest on a loan for another client. Provided neither client defaults (the **counterparty risk**) the two transactions simply cancel each other out, with the bank taking a small cut in the middle.

But as derivatives became more and more weird and wonderful, observers began to question whether the banks' arrangements for hedging their risks were likely to be proof against all eventualities. So complex were some of the derivative products dreamed up by the **rocket scientists** (mathematical geniuses) whom the banks increasingly employed that few if any in the upper echelons of banking could understand them or the risks they implied. The directors thus became increasingly dependent on the judgement of those rocket scientists and the computerized risk-matching systems that they devised.

The risks inherent in these derivative products are mainly **off balance sheet** for the banks: they do not appear in the main financial statements. For example, if you look at the accounts of **National Westminster Bank** for 1994 you will see that loans made by the bank were shown at about £112 billion in its group balance sheet. Excluded here was a further £871 billion of off balance sheet financial instruments entered into by the bank. This figure was, of course, the 'principal amount' of the contracts (the amount subject to interest rate or exchange rate undertakings) and not the amount at risk. And since many of the risks cancelled each other out, the 'risk weighted amount' was calculated to be only around £3.4 billion.

Such figures are pretty typical of the major commercial banks. But, reflecting international evaluation of derivatives risk, press comment is increasingly homing in on the adequacy of risk-evaluation methods and control systems in the derivatives markets. Predictions of derivative-induced crises in the financial system are not uncommon.

Banking crises and banking cycles

A visitor from Mars who surveyed recent banking history could be forgiven for concluding that it consisted of periodic crises interspersed with relatively short periods of calm. In Britain we have had three major upsets in the past twenty years: the property and secondary bank crisis of the mid-1970s; the Latin-American debt crisis of the 1980s (very much an international problem); and the property and small business loan crisis of the early 1990s.

The secondary banking crisis we have already touched on. The **Latin-American debt crisis** or, in wider terms, the **Third World debt crisis** had its roots in the 1970s when the major commercial banks, particularly in the United States, drew in deposits from oil producing countries which had generated massive revenue surpluses from the oil price increases of that decade. Much of the money was lent to Third World countries – **less developed countries** or **LDCs** in the common banking euphemism – which seemed good business at the time. The total debt of the Third World was put in the mid-1980s at over $1,000 billion. For a variety of reasons – including high interest rates and low prices for basic commodities – many of these borrowers found themselves unable to **service** their loans (meet interest charges and capital repayments).

The outcome was an excellent illustration of the old banking adage that you are at your banker's mercy if you owe him £5 and he is at your mercy if you owe him £5m. A game of poker – for somewhat larger sums – ensued. If the banks admitted they would not get their money back and wrote off their loans, they would be shown to be insolvent or at least they would fail the capital adequacy tests. So they attempted to maintain the fiction that the loans were sound. To do so they frequently arranged a **rescheduling** of the original loans. At best this meant extending the terms of the loan to give the debtor countries more time to pay. At worst it meant lending them more money (which they were unlikely to be able to repay) to meet the instalments of capital and interest (which they could not otherwise pay) on the original loans. Without rescheduling, the debtor countries would be forced to **default** on the loans (fail to keep to the terms) and the lending banks would then be forced to classify the loans as **non-performing**.

The debtor countries in their turn had a difficult choice. If they simply defaulted, they would find it difficult to borrow again in the international capital markets. But the threat of default was a powerful weapon in bargaining with the lending banks.

The game of make-believe that rescheduling made possible was somewhat disrupted in May 1987 when Citicorp, one of the major American lenders, announced a $3 billion **provision** or **reserve** against its Third World loans. This meant it was not writing down the value of specific loans but was accepting that it stood to lose at least $3 billion of its Third World lending. Citicorp could afford to make the provision but it posed problems for some other lenders with less capital who were forced by Citicorp's action to acknowledge realities. The major British banks made similar provisions in due course. The banking emperors were not seen entirely without clothes, but were left looking distinctly chilly in their underpants.

The saga provided several insights into the nature of banking. First, banks do not always write off loans as soon as they suspect that the money is lost. While the banking authorities require banks to provide against losses on a prudent and timely basis, an observer might conclude that they sometimes fudge the realities until they have accumulated enough reserves to be able to afford the write-offs. Banking is not only a matter of confidence. The make-believe element is often important.

Secondly, 'profit' in banking is a more than usually nebulous concept. A bank declares good profits in the years that it makes the loans that will ultimately bring it severe losses. Thirdly, dud loans can sometimes be sold – at a price. In the later years of the Latin-American debt crisis a **secondary market in bank debt** emerged. A bank with non-performing loans to the Republic of Erewhon might decide it would rather take its losses and get shot of the whole business. So it would sell the loans at, say, 50p in the pound to some other financial institution that was prepared to take a gamble on the amount it could recover. The prices at which the debt of different countries traded in this secondary market gave a pretty fair view of bankers' estimates of the likelihood of recovery.

No sooner was the worst of the Latin-American debt crisis out of the way than banks internationally were again lending very heavily for property development and purchase in the late 1980s (see Chapter 20). In Britain, very substantial lending on commercial property was exacerbated by a great expansion of lending to small businesses. In the severe recession of the early 1990s in Britain, property values fell like a stone and numerous small businesses went bust. Many billion pounds worth of lending had to be written off by the British clearing banks alone.

Rescues and reconstructions

There is nothing like a period of high interest rates accompanied by economic recession to expose the financing follies of the previous era. In the early 1990s companies that had expanded over-fast by takeover in the 1980s, and financed on borrowed money, were going to the wall like flies. In some cases there was no choice but to let the companies be wound up. In others, the lending banks decided that they would lose less in the long run by trying to keep the company going, probably with the help of a **capital reconstruction** or **capital reorganisation**.

No two cases were quite alike, so we will take a hypothetical example to illustrate the main principles. Suppose Splurgeandspend Holdings had gone on a takeover spree in the great Thatcherite days of the 1980s and borrowed most of the money to do it. By 1991 the interest rate on its loans had more than doubled and, with the recession, its profits had halved. It faced an interest bill of £150m a year and had profits of only £70m before interest. Result: a pre-tax loss of £80m.

Splurgeandspend's total borrowings at this point were about £1bn. The value of the businesses it had bought in the 1980s had slumped heavily and many of the assets required writing down to realistic values. Once these write-downs had been made, the value of the group's assets would have been £200m less than the money it owed to the banks. It had a **deficiency on shareholders' funds** of £200m. Add to this the fact that

Splurgeandspend was running out of cash and had no way to raise more.

The lending banks knew that, if they closed the business down on the spot, they would get very little for the assets and would lose a large part of their loans. Since some of Splurgeandspend's businesses would have been quite promising in more normal economic conditions, they decided to try to keep the company going. First, they agreed to convert £300m of their loans into shares in the company at a price of 4p per share (the shares had, of course, slumped to virtually nothing in the market). This **equity-for-debt swap** would eliminate £300m of Splurgeandspend's borrowings and therefore also eliminate the interest charge on this amount.

Secondly, they converted a further £200m of their existing loans into a new kind of subordinated loan on which no interest would be payable for five years. Thirdly, they agreed to waive the interest due on the remaining £500m of loans for one year to give the company a breathing space to sort itself out and sell some of its businesses (if it could) to raise cash. Finally, they agreed to make available a new overdraft facility of £30m to provide the company with a little cash to tide itself over.

Splurgeandspend thus has no interest bill to worry about for a year. For the following four years it will pay interest on only £500m of borrowings and thereafter on £700m. It has a chance of survival. But there is a price – banks are not charities. The company's share capital is massively expanded by the conversion of £300m of loans into shares. The original shareholders are left with only 5 per cent of the enlarged capital and are thus virtually wiped out. The rest belongs to the banks. If the company recovers, they will reap the rewards. The major British banks do not usually own shares in companies. But the early-1990s recession left them with quite significant shareholdings in troubled companies that arose through this kind of reconstruction.

The major problem in organising a reconstruction of this kind, if the company has loans from many different banks, lies in getting all the banks to agree. Where the company has a **syndicated loan** from, say, 20 different banks there will often be some banks that want to close the company down immediately and recover what they can. Recognising this problem, the Bank of England developed guidelines known as the **London rules**, designed to persuade banks to give troubled companies a chance of surviving where possible. Some overseas banks with a different lending culture were not always easy to convince.

Banking supervision in Britain

For the first half of the 1980s, banking institutions in Britain (with the main exception of building societies which had their own regulatory structure) were divided between banks and **licensed deposit takers** or **LDTs**, which comprised mainly the less established or second-tier concerns. The distinction was abolished by a new **Banking Act** in 1987 which allowed all but the smallest deposit-taking institutions to call themselves banks provided they satisfied prudential requirements as to the way the business was run (and provided the people running it were judged fit and proper).

A **Board of Banking Supervision** was established under the 1987 Act to provide advice to the Governor of the Bank of England on matters relating to banking supervision. The Governor, Deputy Governor and an executive director of the Bank are ex-officio members of the Board, and there are six independent members. After the collapse of Barings, the Chancellor asked the Board to investigate the circumstances and to identify the lessons to be drawn.

Critics suggest that the Bank has a conflict of interest in that it is supervisor of the banks as well as being the body which advises on (and implements) monetary policy. Cynics ask whether the Bank would really be prepared to advise the government to, say, raise interest rates at a time when this might damage the banks for which it has supervisory responsibility. Should the two roles be separated? Questions on these lines resurface whenever there is a problem in the banking system and, predictably, were aired in the press after the Barings affair.

15

The money markets

Money market reports are an acquired taste. Few readers who
are not in the money business will come completely to grips
with their technicalities. But when the **money markets** are
giving an important signal about likely trends in **interest rates**,
a less technical interpretation of what is going on will probably
appear elsewhere in the financial pages.

Money markets are the responsibility of the **Bank of
England**. The Bank is **lender of last resort** to the banking
system. The level at which it is prepared to lend, and the
terms, can be used to influence the level of interest rates
across the economy.

Nowadays, decisions to change **official interest rates** – that
is, the rates at which the Bank provides funds to the banking
system – are made at the monthly meeting between the Chancellor and the Governor of the Bank. The expectations
generated by this meeting therefore attract a considerable
amount of press comment before the event and the decision
arrived at is widely covered afterwards. The press is also keen
to spot any hint of disagreement between Chancellor and
Governor. Does the politician have a different agenda from
the banker? This should become clearer when notes of the
meeting are published some weeks after the event.

Market rates of interest will reflect demand and supply in
the market for short-term funds, but will also, of course, reflect expectations about future official rate moves. A guessing
game is under way much of the time between the Bank and
the market's professionals, and the authorities have to play
their cards close to their chest otherwise they are offering a

one-way bet to the market. If the professionals know in advance how rates are going to move, they can buy or sell as appropriate, with an assured profit on the operation.

Functions of the money markets

Why are money markets needed? They are a form of short-term counterpart to the long-term investment markets of the Stock Exchange. The Stock Exchange funnels long-term savings into long-term investment. The money markets allow money which is available for shorter periods to be directed to those who can use it, and also have the virtue of transmuting very short-term deposits into money which can be lent for longer periods. Despite their name they are not just a market in deposits but also in a variety of forms of short-term IOU or **financial instrument** which are close to money because they are **marketable**. In other words, they can be turned quickly into money by a sale in the market. We will look at these later.

The money markets fulfil several functions. First, at any one time there will be some banks which have a very temporary shortage of money and others which have a surplus: money has been withdrawn from one bank and deposited with another. A mechanism is needed so that banks which are temporarily short can borrow the funds they need, and those with a temporary surplus can put it to work.

Secondly, banks will in any case want to hold a proportion of their funds in a form which allows them to get at it quickly if needed. This means putting it on deposit with other institutions or buying short-term financial instruments.

Thirdly, while banks derive a large proportion of their sterling funds from the accounts of individual depositors (**retail deposits**), they also borrow in very large amounts from companies, financial institutions and local government bodies which have short-term surpluses of cash to put to work (**wholesale funds**). Likewise, these bodies borrow in the money markets when short of cash.

Finally, a mechanism is needed to iron out imbalances in the supply of money between the **banking system** as a whole and the government. There will be times when the commercial

233

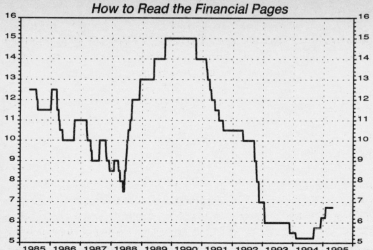

UK CLEARING BANKS BASE RATE - MIDDLE RATE

Figure 15.1 Bank base rates and Britain's recession of the early 1990s. After the 1987 stockmarket crash, fears of provoking further mayhem on the markets led to relaxation of monetary policy and interest rates continued down although inflationary pressures were already building up. When the government was forced to change tack in 1988, interest rates were increased very rapidly, doubling in little more than a year. The move suceeded in reducing economic activity and curbing inflation, but caused a severe recession and devastated the inflated residential and commercial property markets. Rates began to fall back again in 1990, but by 1992 the further reductions needed to revive economic activity proved impossible if sterling was to stay within the ERM. After it dropped out of the mechanism and was effectively devalued in September 1992, interest rates were allowed to continue very rapidly down until inflation fears began to resurface in 1994. Source: *Datastream International*.

banking system is short of money because, for example, individuals or companies are withdrawing funds from their bank accounts to pay their tax bills to the government. But the government can also influence the amount of money available to the commercial banking system via-a-vis the government by selling gilt-edged stocks or treasury bills to the private sector, which has to transfer money to the government to pay for them. However, if these are sold directly to the banks rather than to the **non-bank private sector** (to individuals and organizations other than banking institutions or government bodies) they will not affect broad money supply since they do not act on the liabilities of the banking system.

These **open market operations** can create a shortage of money in the banking system. For example, suppose the government issues gilt-edged stock for sale to the public (see Chapter 13 for the mechanisms). To pay for, say, £500m of stock the public would have to withdraw £500m from its deposits with the banking system. Therefore this money would leave the commercial banks and be paid to the government. All else being equal, a shortage of cash would be created in the banking system which the Bank could use to increase its influence on the commercial banks.

The money markets provide mechanisms to cope with all these differing requirements. They fall into two main parts (we are talking now of the sterling money markets – a market in foreign currency deposits exists alongside them). There is the traditional **discount market** and there are the **parallel money markets**, of which the main constituent is also known as the **inter-bank market**.

The discount market

Although comparable arrangements can be found elsewhere, the **discount houses** are uniquely British institutions which act as a buffer between the Bank of England and the commercial banks. In practice, they operate as specialist banks which make a living by borrowing surplus short-term money from the commercial banks and using it to buy **financial instruments** such as **Treasury bills**, commercial **bills of exchange** and **sterling certificates of deposit** (these are all forms of short-term IOU which we look at later).

The money the commercial banks lend to the discount houses is **at call**. In other words, the banks can ask to have it back when they need it. This could pose a problem for the discount houses if they have already used the money to invest in bills of exchange. So the Bank of England steps in. When the discount houses are short of cash they have the right to sell bills of exchange, Treasury bills and local authority bills to the Bank (**rediscount** them with – sell them at a discount to – the Bank). This amounts to lending by the Bank to the discount houses and provides them with the cash they need. Until recently, this facility was only available to eight discount houses. In 1988 the Bank opened the way for other institutions to enter the discount market and enjoy the same facilities. The newcomers could take the form of traditional discount houses or, alternatively, gilt-edged marketmakers would be permitted to apply to extend their activities to include a money market dealing relationship with the Bank.

Nowadays, the Bank of England publishes its **Minimum Lending Rate** or **MLR** (in the past this used to be published in somewhat different form as **Bank Rate**, and you will still find this term cropping up occasionally). The market participants therefore know the rates at which the Bank will be prepared to deal in the market. The Bank posts the rates at which it has conducted its open market operations immediately after the completion of each round of operations. The major banks quote their own yardstick rate of interest, **base rate**, which is changed when necessary, mainly to reflect changes in official interest rates.

Each working day the Bank of England estimates first thing in the morning the likely size of the shortage or surplus in the money market on that day (a **shortage** is the amount by which the commercial banking system is likely to be short of money and will therefore have to borrow from the government) and may revise this estimate at midday and again at 2 p.m. if necessary. Its estimates go out on the Reuters and Telerate screen information systems. It also publishes during the day the details of how it dealt with the shortage. It may have bought bills of exchange from the discount houses (these are listed in four different **bands**, according to their maturity date). It may have lent money to the discount houses. It may have entered into arrangements to buy securities and sell them back later (**repurchase agreements** or **repos**) which act as a short-term loan.

Bills of exchange

The discount houses got their name because they **discount** bills of exchange: they buy them at a discount to their face value. To see how this market works we need to examine the mechanism more closely.

Bills of exchange are a form of short-term IOU widely used to finance trade and provide credit. The work like this. Company A sells £1m worth of goods to Company B. It 'draws' (writes out) a bill of exchange for £1m which it sends to Company B. This bill is an acknowledgement by Company B that it owes the £1m, and Company B signs it to show that it accepts the debt. The bill may state that the money is not payable until some date in the future: perhaps in three months. The bill returns to Company A.

Company A then has a choice. It can hold on to the bill, in which case Company B will pay it the £1m in three months. Or, if it needs the cash sooner, it can sell the bill to somebody else. Whoever holds the bill when the three months are up gets the £1m from Company B.

Bills of exchange do not pay interest. But if Company A sells the bill before it is due for payment, it will receive less than face value. In other words, it **sells at a discount**. So if the bill is due for payment in, say, three months, the buyer might pay only £97.50 for every £100 of face value. The buyer is thus getting a profit of £2.50 per £100 when the bill is repaid at face value, which is equivalent to receiving interest: the discount is usually expressed as an annual rate of interest. When the Bank of England is said to have bought bills at 10¾ per cent, it means that the Bank bought them at a discount to their face value. Thus if interest rates generally come down, the prices of bills will rise (the discount will be smaller). This is why discount houses may be reluctant to sell them when they think interest rates should come down.

The bill described above is a **trade bill**, issued by one company to another. But a bill may be **accepted** by a bank, in which case it becomes a **bank bill**. By putting its name on the bill, the bank agrees it will pay the amount of the bill on maturity, even if the company which acknowledged the debt should default: it is therefore a form of guarantee. Accepting bills in this way was an important part of the business of the merchant banks in the past, hence the term **accepting houses** which used to be used for the top-tier merchant banks. A bill accepted by a bank, because of the security it offers, sells at the very lowest interest rates. Any monetary sector institution can accept bills, but the Bank of England only buys or lends against bills accepted by **eligible banks**, hence the term **eligible bills**. The Bank maintains a published list of eligible banks; in general these are banks which have a substantial and broadly-based sterling acceptance business.

Bank bills also provide a substitute for overdrafts in big company financing. A company arranges an **acceptance credit**

LONDON MONEY RATES

May 15	Over-night	7 days notice	One month	Three months	Six months	One year
Interbank Sterling	$6\frac{1}{4}$ - $4\frac{1}{2}$	$6\frac{1}{4}$ - $5\frac{7}{8}$	$6\frac{3}{8}$ - $6\frac{1}{8}$	$6\frac{3}{4}$ - $6\frac{5}{8}$	$7\frac{1}{8}$ - 7	$7\frac{9}{16}$ - $7\frac{7}{16}$
Sterling CDs	-	-	$6\frac{5}{16}$ - $6\frac{1}{4}$	$6\frac{11}{16}$ - $6\frac{5}{8}$	$6\frac{13}{16}$ - $6\frac{12}{16}$	$7\frac{7}{16}$ - $7\frac{5}{16}$
Treasury Bills	-	-	$6\frac{1}{4}$ - $6\frac{3}{16}$	$6\frac{7}{16}$ - $6\frac{3}{8}$	-	-
Bank Bills	-	-	$6\frac{5}{16}$ - $6\frac{1}{4}$	$6\frac{9}{16}$ - $6\frac{1}{2}$	$6\frac{13}{16}$ - $6\frac{11}{16}$	-
Local authority deps	$6\frac{5}{16}$ - $6\frac{3}{16}$	$6\frac{5}{16}$ - $6\frac{3}{16}$	$6\frac{7}{16}$ - $6\frac{5}{16}$	$6\frac{13}{16}$ - $6\frac{11}{16}$	$7\frac{1}{8}$ - 7	$7\frac{9}{16}$ - $7\frac{7}{16}$
Discount Market deps	$7\frac{1}{2}$ - $6\frac{1}{2}$	$6\frac{5}{16}$ - $6\frac{5}{16}$	-	-	-	-

UK clearing bank base lending rate $6\frac{3}{4}$ per cent from February 2, 1995

	Up to 1 month	1-3 month	3-6 months	6-9 months	9-12 months
Certs of Tax dep. (£100,000)	3	$5\frac{3}{4}$	$5\frac{3}{4}$	6	$6\frac{1}{4}$

Certs of Tax dep. under £100,000 is $2\frac{1}{2}$pc. Deposits withdrawn for cash $1\frac{1}{4}$pc.
Ave. tender rate of discount 6.2097pc. ECGD fixed rate Stlg. Export Finance. Make up day Apr 28, 1995. Agreed rate for period May 24, 1995 to Jun 25, 1995, Schemes II & III 7.98pc. Reference rate for period Apr 1, 1995 to Apr 28, 1995, Schemes IV & V 6.733pc. Finance House Base Rate 7pc from May 1, 1995

Table 15.1 Money-market interest rates in London. Source: *Financial Times*.

with a bank, which allows it to issue bills up to an agreed limit. Each bill is accepted by the bank in return for a fee and can be sold at a discount to raise cash for the company. The effective rate of interest may be lower than on other forms of borrowing.

Treasury bills

Treasury bills work in much the same way as commercial bills of exchange, but are issued by the government as means of managing money market conditions. They are sold at a discount, with an implicit rate of interest. Each Friday the discount houses, banks and others **tender** for the bills on offer – the discount houses are obliged to tender for the lot, so that the government is sure of getting its money even if others do not tender. The amount supplied at the weekly tender varies to reflect the prospective balance of other flows between the government and the market.

As well as sterling bills, the government makes regular monthly issues of Treasury bills denominated in **ECU** (the **European Currency Unit**). The main purpose of this programme is to assist with the management of the UK's foreign exchange reserves. At the same time it will encourage the development in Britain of a market in ECU-denominated instruments.

Certificates of deposit

Certificates of deposit (CDs) are a method of **securitizing** bank deposits. A company with spare cash deposits £500,000 with a bank. It agrees to lock the money away for a year, thus getting the best interest rate. The bank issues the company with a certificate of deposit for the £500,000, stating the rate of interest payable and the date when the deposit will be repaid. If the company needs its cash before the year is up, it can sell the certificate of deposit in the money market. The buyer acquires the right to receive repayment of the £500,000 bank deposit (plus interest) when the year is up. Certificates of deposit may, like Treasury bills and eligible bills, be bought and sold by banks and other money market participants, including the discount houses. But unlike Treasury and eligible bills, CDs cannot be used by the discount houses in their operations with the Bank of England, whereby the market obtains funds through the Bank's open market operations.

The virtue of the certificate of deposit is that the bank (in our example) has acquired a deposit for a year and knows it will have a year's use of the money. But the company which lent for a year and received the CD can in practice have its money back at any time by selling the CD.

The parallel money markets

We started with the discount market because it illustrates how the Bank of England can influence interest rates. But banks wanting to borrow and lend money in the wholesale markets are not confined to dealing with the discount houses. They also operate in the **parallel money markets** – the markets in which banks, local authorities, institutions and companies can borrow from or lend to each other without going through the discount house mechanism. The most important of these markets is the **inter-bank market**, where banks and others deal with each other, often through a money broker who puts the parties together in return for a commission. The market divides further into the sterling inter-bank market and the inter-bank market in foreign currencies, particularly the dollar.

There has been enormous expansion in the use made of the

money markets by large companies in recent years. And the 1989 Budget introduced changes which help to break down the distinction between money markets and the established debt securities markets (Stock Exchange and euromarket) by allowing the issue of financial instruments with a life of up to 5 years. Thus a company wishing to borrow for five years should have the choice of following the securities market route or the money market route. Whereas the securities markets are open to private investors, the wholesale money markets are very definitely a 'professionals only' area.

Commercial paper and MTNs

Commercial paper is an example of the **securitization** process. For companies it offers an alternative to bank borrowing or to an existing form of short-term security: the bill of exchange.

In essence, commercial paper is just another form of unsecured short term IOU, issued in bearer form. It is normally issued at a discount rather than paying interest, with a maturity of up to a year. In Britain the average life of commercial paper has been close to 40 days hitherto.

The sterling commercial paper market got under way in London in May 1986 and initially was open only to very large established companies. These conditions have subsequently been relaxed, opening the way for medium-sized companies to tap the market.

The issue process goes as follows. A company wanting to tap the market gets a bank to set up a programme for it: say, £200m. This defines the maximum amount that the company may have outstanding at any one time. At the same time **dealers** are appointed. When the company wants to raise cash it alerts the dealers, or the dealers may take the initiative by telling the company that there is demand among investors for paper of a particular maturity. The dealers, who are constantly in touch with potential investors, find buyers for the paper. The paper is sold at a discount to its face value which provides the equivalent of a rate of interest. The buyers may be institutions or companies looking for a short-term investment.

When the original issue falls due for repayment, further issues can be made to replace it. Thus, though it is a very short-term market, by **rolling over** issues in this way companies may use it as a medium-term source of finance. In addition to the sterling commercial paper market there is an active international equivalent the **eurocommercial paper market** where companies can similarly set up programmes, perhaps allowing them to issue in a number of different currencies.

There is also now a longer-term form of money market borrowing in the **medium term note** or **MTN**, which has a life of one to five years. Like commercial paper, it has its euro-market equivalent in **euro medium term notes or EMTNs**.

Multiple option facility

The **multiple option facility** or **MOF** is another form of arrangement for tapping the money markets which was popular in the late 1980s and might possibly see a resurgence. It emerged in various shapes but a typical arrangement might have been as follows.

A company got one particular bank to put together a panel of banks who agreed to make available a certain amount of loans – say £150m – for a period of five years. The rate of interest, which would be variable, was set at such-and-such an amount above the benchmark rate of interest when the loans were taken up (say, 20 basis points over LIBOR – see below). This £150m was what was known as the **committed facility** or **standby facility**.

Another group of banks was put together, comprising the original banks plus others which were recruited. They formed a **tender panel**. When the company decided it needed cash, the tender panel banks were invited to bid to provide the funds. Those that were flush with cash at the time would have responded, and the bank or banks bidding the lowest rate of interest would have made the loans to the company. If none of the tender panel banks bid at a rate below that on the standby facility, the company would have resorted to raising the money via this standby. Thus it was sure of getting its cash when needed.

The loans made under this arrangement would probably have been short-term: say, for three months. But as one loan fell due for repayment new loans could have been arranged,

WORLD INTEREST RATES

MONEY RATES

May 15	Over night	One month	Three mths	Six mths	One year	Lomb. inter.	Dis. rate	Repo rate
Belgium	$4\frac{1}{2}$	$4\frac{13}{16}$	$5\frac{1}{8}$	$5\frac{5}{8}$	$5\frac{3}{4}$	7.40	4.00	–
week ago	$4\frac{3}{4}$	$4\frac{13}{16}$	$5\frac{7}{16}$	$5\frac{5}{8}$	$5\frac{5}{8}$	7.40	4.00	–
France	$7\frac{3}{4}$	$7\frac{3}{8}$	7	$6\frac{3}{4}$	$6\frac{1}{2}$	5.00	–	8.00
week ago	$7\frac{11}{16}$	$7\frac{3}{8}$	$7\frac{13}{16}$	$7\frac{3}{8}$	7	5.00	–	8.00
Germany	$4\frac{1}{2}$	$4\frac{5}{8}$	$4\frac{5}{8}$	$4\frac{5}{8}$	$4\frac{13}{16}$	6.00	4.00	4.51
week ago	$4\frac{7}{16}$	$4\frac{5}{8}$	$4\frac{1}{2}$	$4\frac{5}{8}$	$4\frac{5}{8}$	6.00	4.00	4.51
Ireland	$6\frac{1}{16}$	$6\frac{3}{8}$	$6\frac{1}{2}$	$6\frac{13}{16}$	$7\frac{7}{8}$	–	–	6.25
week ago	$5\frac{15}{16}$	$6\frac{3}{8}$	$6\frac{11}{16}$	$6\frac{15}{16}$	$7\frac{3}{8}$	–	–	6.25
Italy	$10\frac{3}{8}$	$9\frac{3}{4}$	$9\frac{7}{8}$	10	$10\frac{3}{8}$	–	7.50	10.26
week ago	$10\frac{3}{8}$	$9\frac{3}{4}$	$10\frac{1}{2}$	$10\frac{11}{16}$	$11\frac{1}{16}$	–	7.50	10.31
Netherlands	$4\frac{3}{8}$	$4\frac{7}{16}$	$4\frac{1}{2}$	$4\frac{5}{8}$	$4\frac{13}{16}$	–	5.25	–
week ago	$4\frac{1}{2}$	$4\frac{7}{16}$	$4\frac{1}{2}$	$4\frac{1}{8}$	$4\frac{13}{16}$	–	5.25	–
Switzerland	$3\frac{1}{2}$	$3\frac{7}{16}$	$3\frac{1}{2}$	$3\frac{1}{2}$	$3\frac{3}{4}$	6.625	3.00	–
week ago	$3\frac{1}{8}$	$3\frac{7}{16}$	$3\frac{5}{8}$	$3\frac{7}{16}$	$3\frac{1}{2}$	6.625	3.00	–
US	6	6	$6\frac{1}{16}$	$6\frac{1}{16}$	$6\frac{1}{8}$	–	5.25	–
week ago	$5\frac{15}{16}$	6	6	$6\frac{1}{8}$	$6\frac{1}{2}$	–	5.25	–
Japan	$1\frac{3}{8}$	$1\frac{5}{8}$	$1\frac{5}{8}$	$1\frac{3}{8}$	$1\frac{7}{16}$	–	1.00	–
week ago	$2\frac{1}{16}$	$1\frac{5}{8}$	$1\frac{3}{8}$	$1\frac{3}{8}$	$1\frac{7}{16}$	–	1.00	–
■ $ LIBOR FT London								
Interbank Fixing	–	$6\frac{1}{16}$	$6\frac{1}{8}$	$6\frac{3}{8}$	$6\frac{1}{4}$	–	–	–
week ago	–	$6\frac{1}{16}$	$6\frac{3}{8}$	$6\frac{1}{4}$	$6\frac{7}{8}$	–	–	–
US Dollar CDs	–	5.86	5.91	5.95	6.05	–	–	–
week ago	–	5.86	5.94	6.07	6.32	–	–	–
ECU Linked Ds	–	$6\frac{1}{16}$	$6\frac{1}{16}$	$6\frac{1}{8}$	$6\frac{1}{16}$	–	–	–
week ago	–	$6\frac{1}{16}$						
SDR Linked Ds	–	$4\frac{1}{8}$	$4\frac{3}{16}$	$4\frac{1}{32}$	$4\frac{3}{32}$	–	–	–
week ago	–	$4\frac{1}{8}$	$4\frac{5}{8}$	$4\frac{1}{4}$	$4\frac{3}{8}$	–	–	–

$ LIBOR Interbank fixing rates are offered rates for $10m quoted to the market by four reference banks at 11am each working day. The banks are: Bankers Trust, Bank of Tokyo, Barclays and National Westminster.

Mid rates are shown for the domestic Money Rates, US$ CDs, ECU & SDR Linked Deposits (Ds).

Table 15.2 A world view of money market interest rates. Source: *Financial Times.*

so for the company it provided the equivalent of medium-term borrowing at a competitive rate of interest. The 'multi-option' refers to the fact that the arrangement allowed for the money to be raised in a number of different forms, which might have included straight loans, acceptances (bills of exchange), foreign currency loans and so on.

Risk hedging

The money markets are also the home of many different types of instrument for limiting exposure to interest rate movements (**hedging** the interest rate risk). A **cap** is really an interest rate option. Say the benchmark interest rate is currently 9 per cent and you reckon a rise to over 11 per cent would seriously damage your business. You can buy a cap from a bank, under which you will be reimbursed for the effects of any increase in the benchmark interest rate above 11 per cent.

A **floor** is an option that works the other way. Suppose you agree with your bank that you will pay a minimum interest rate of 7.5 per cent, even if market rates drop below this level. The bank will pay you for agreeing this floor, in the same way as you pay the bank for providing a cap. So the proceeds from selling a floor can be used to offset at least part of the cost of a cap. An arrangement that includes both a cap and a floor is known as a **collar** or **cylinder** – it can be used to limit the interest you might have to pay within fairly narrow bands. Companies use these and similar instruments quite extensively to limit their interest rate exposure.

Perhaps **swaps** or **interest rate swaps** should be included in the same category of hedging instruments. For a description of how they work, see Chapter 17.

Interest rate indicators

You will find in the *Financial Times* a list of the interest rates for deposits and different types of short-term financial instruments under the heading of **London money rates**. For each, a range of maturities is covered. Thus, in the case of inter-bank deposits there is a rate for overnight money, for money deposited at seven days' notice, for a month, three months, six months and a year. You can plot the rates quoted for different maturities to produce a **yield curve**. Typically, this is a rising curve, showing that money deposited for short periods earns lower interest than money deposited for six months or a year. But when interest rates are expected to drop, there may be a **negative yield curve** with a lower rate of interest on money deposited for a year than money deposited for a month.

The London money rates table shows the rates of interest on **inter-bank deposits**, **sterling certificates of deposit**, **local authority deposits**, **discount market deposits**, **Treasury bills** and **bank bills**. Both buying and selling rates are given. A bank will offer to borrow money (or sell financial instruments) at the lower rate and lend (or buy financial instruments) at the higher rate. The margins between the two rates in these wholesale markets are generally very fine.

Note that the **inter-bank rate (sterling LIBOR)** is a far better measure of short-term swings in interest rates than the **bank base rates**. Base rates are changed relatively infrequently, and normally to reflect changes in official interest rates by the authorities. The inter-bank rate is the constantly changing measure of the cost of money in large amounts for the banks themselves.

In addition to sterling interest rates, the *Financial Times* provides a table of short-term money rates in the other major economies together with the rate of US dollar LIBOR. Interest rates for eurocurrencies (see Chapter 17) are also provided.

The rates of interest on **floating rate bonds** are usually geared to the inter-bank **offered** rate: the rate at which banks will lend wholesale to each other. A bond might carry a rate of interest of, say, 50 **basis points** above the inter-bank offered rate. A hundred basis points is equivalent to one percentage point, so 50 basis points is 0.5 per cent. But the rate on an overdraft to a private individual will be related to base rate and expressed as so many **points** above base rate. A point in this case is a full **percentage point** so five points over base means 16 per cent when base rates are 11 per cent.

Thus the **London Inter-Bank Offered Rate** or **LIBOR** (see Chapter 17) is the usual benchmark rate of interest for wholesale funds, and is the rate in relation to which other floating rates of interest are set. **LIBID** is the equivalent **bid** rate or rate at which banks will offer to borrow. **LIMEAN** (pronounced 'lie-mean') is the rate mid-way between the bid and offered rates.

16

Foreign exchange

If stockmarkets sometimes behave irrationally, they are a model of sanity compared with the **foreign exchange** or **forex** markets in which currencies are bought and sold: exchanged for other currencies. Not only are the swings in the value of one currency against another both frequent and dramatic. They also have vital implications for the economic prospects of the countries concerned and often for the prosperity of the whole free world economy. It is no surprise that currency stories migrate so frequently from the technical **foreign exchange reports** to become lead items in the financial pages.

Precisely because the influences that move currency values are often so irrational, these stories can be difficult to understand without some knowledge of the background. Perhaps the easiest approach is to look on the major trading countries as if they were companies quoted on the stockmarket and on their currencies as if they were company shares.

Official intervention

As with shares, the value of each currency is determined by the balance of buyers and sellers in the market, at least since **floating exchange rates** were adopted in the early 1970s. But just as share prices may be **supported** by friends of the company, the value of currencies can be affected by **official intervention**: buying and selling by **central banks** to try to strengthen or weaken a currency. Where a currency is ostensibly floating but in practice being kept close to a particular

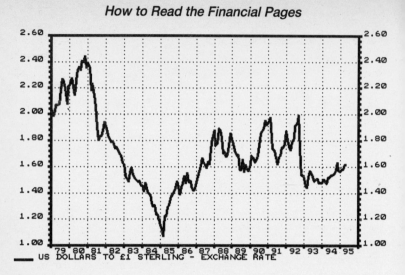

Figure 16.1 Fluctuations in the sterling/dollar exchange rate have borne little relationship to the economic realities as one currency or the other moved too far up or down. Our chart shows the number of US dollars to the pound, which in the first half of the 1980s swung between $2.4 to £1 and little more than $1 to £1. Source: *Datastream International*.

value or **parity** in relation to other currencies by central bank intervention, commentators talk of a **dirty** or **managed float**.

But there is a limit to how far a currency value can be manipulated against the trend of market forces. If the central bank is using its **foreign exchange reserves** to support its country's currency when most other participants in the market are selling because they conclude from economic fundamentals that its value should fall in relation to other currencies, the central bank will in due course exhaust its available reserves, be forced to abandon the support operation and the value will then drop in any case. The market forces predominate. Successful intervention often requires concerted action by the central banks of a number of countries (see below). But even this will ultimately fail if the economic fundamentals are out of line.

The market forces

What are these market forces? Again, there is a parallel between a company and a country. If a company is trading successfully and increasing its earnings, all else being equal its share price will rise. Successful countries which run a **current account balance of payments surplus** – sell more goods and services to other countries than they buy from abroad – and which keep inflation at a low level will also usually see their own currency strong or rising in value over time.

The effect of interest rates

Even if it is not trading spectacularly well, a company can try to make its shares more attractive to investors by increasing the dividends it pays. A country can also try to increase the attraction of its currency to international investors by increasing its **domestic interest rates**. This increases the returns investors can earn by depositing money in the country concerned or by buying bonds in that country. Suppose Britain is increasing its interest rates to attract overseas investors. To invest in Britain they will need to convert whatever currency they hold into pounds to deposit in Britain or buy British bonds. So they will be buying pounds, and when there are more buyers than sellers the currency should rise.

So far so good. But investors in the stockmarket will not buy a share if they are certain its value is going to drop, almost regardless of the income it offers. The income is of little use if the benefit is going to be wiped out by capital losses on the shares. The same applies to a currency. If international investors think the pound is going to fall heavily in value, they will be more inclined to sell it than buy it and the interest rates Britain is offering will only have limited effect. This process was very clearly demonstrated in September 1992 when successive rises in interest rates could not maintain the value of the pound sufficiently for it to remain within the **Exchange Rate Mechanism** of the **European Monetary System** (see below). Interest rate changes can and do influence the value of a currency and much of what the press writes about currencies is concerned with the way countries are adjusting – or being pressured to adjust – domestic interest rates to adjust the value of their currency. But interest rates are only one factor.

Swings in market sentiment

Increasingly, the vital factor is that indefinable element: **market sentiment**. If investors become enthusiastic about a share, they will buy it. Its price will rise and those who bought will show profits. This in turn may attract other investors to buy, the price rises still further and the process becomes self-fuelling. The same thing happens with currencies. Either longer-term investors or short-term speculators (or probably both) become enthusiastic about the dollar and buy it. Its value rises, which encourages still more investors to put their money in the dollar, so it rises still further. And the process can be self-perpetuating – until something happens to change sentiment or encourage investors to take their profit. When this happens, international investors can sell just as frantically as they previously bought, and the value of the currency can fall as fast as it had earlier risen.

The result is that currency swings can **overshoot**. That is, they can go much too far in one direction or another, creating havoc for businesses which trade internationally: they can never be certain what price they will receive for their goods when translated into their own currency. Here the analogy between stockmarkets and currency markets breaks down. In the stockmarket individual share prices can be carried ridiculously high or ridiculously low by swings in market sentiment. But at the end of the day there are some reasonably objective yardsticks: what the company earns and is capable of earning; the dividends it pays and therefore the yield it offers. Ultimately these **fundamentals** tend to reassert themselves and bring investors back to earth.

In the currency markets the fundamentals frequently exert less influence in the short term, so that the currency moves much further than is needed merely to adjust to trading realities. In the very long run the fundamentals will reassert themselves, but before this happens such overshooting may cause serious damage to a country's trading prospects.

How do we measure currencies?

There is another important difference to allow for before we can look more closely at the way currency questions are covered. In the British stockmarkets we measure securities prices in standard units: pounds and pence. But a currency is measured in terms of other currencies and all are moving relative to each other. The pound may be strengthening against the dollar but weakening against the German mark. These **exchange cross rates** – values of each of the major currencies in terms of each of the others – are listed daily in the **currencies and money** pages of the *Financial Times*, as are the values of major currencies in terms of the pound and of the US dollar, in somewhat more detailed form. Note one complication: by convention the markets always talk of 'so many dollars to the pound' rather than 'so much of a pound to the dollar', even when talking of the value of the dollar rather than the pound. So the dollar's value in sterling terms is expressed as, say, $1.6235 to £1 rather than £0.6160 to $1.

In reports of currency movements there are two main ways currency values are expressed: in terms of another specific currency or in terms of a **trade-weighted index** where they are measured against a **basket of currencies**. In the second case,

Figure 16.2 The solid line shows the trade-weighted value of the pound since the Conservative government came to power in 1979. The strength of the early 1980s, boosted by North Sea oil revenues and high domestic interest rates, was not long sustained. In contrast, the broken line shows the trade-weighted value of the German mark. Source: *Datastream International.*

taking the value of the pound as an example, an index is constructed of the currencies of the main countries with which Britain trades, each weighted according to its importance in trade with Britain. This is expressed not as a monetary value but as an index with a base of 100 in 1990. Thus, on a particular day the pound might rise against the dollar from $1.6200 to $1.6300 (you get more dollars for a pound, so the pound has strengthened) but fall from 85.0 to 84.9 on the trade-weighted index. Overall, the pound was a little weaker against all currencies, but the dollar was weaker still so sterling improved against the dollar.

This is often rather badly reported in the media. You may read or hear that sterling rose one cent against the dollar whereas the reality was simply that the dollar was falling against most currencies and fell one cent against the pound. Again, the *Financial Times* shows sterling's value on the trade-weighted index (also known as the **sterling index** or the **Bank of England effective exchange rate index**) and similar indices for other major currencies. Dollar, yen, German mark, Swiss franc and French franc values are frequently quoted.

The fundamentals

We have seen that the value of a currency might be expected – all else being equal – to rise if the country concerned is earning more from abroad than it is spending abroad. Other countries are having to buy its currency to buy its goods and it is adding to its **foreign exchange reserves**, which are roughly equivalent to a country's bank balance. A country may hold its reserves in the form of other currencies, **special drawing rights** (see glossary) or gold.

In theory, as the value of a country's currency rises in relation to other currencies, its goods become more expensive for foreigners to buy. So gradually it sells less abroad, earns less foreign exchange, and – all other things being equal – the currency begins to weaken until its goods become cheaper again and the cycle recommences. A country earning a surplus may also take deliberate steps to prevent its currency from rising too high: reducing interest rates to make the currency less attractive to foreign investors and to stimulate domestic demand so that more goods are consumed at home, more are imported and fewer exported.

In practice the phenomenon of **overshoot** means that self-correcting mechanisms may be rendered ineffective or only work with considerable delay. The problem is that there is no such thing as the 'right' value for a currency against any other currency. It can be argued that if the exchange rate is $1.60 to £1, an item which costs £1 in London should cost $1.60 in New York: the **purchasing power parity** argument. But such considerations clearly did not apply in the 1980s when the value of £1 fluctuated between more than $2.40 and little more than $1.00, which obviously did not reflect movements in the relative prices of goods in New York and London. Instead, when the dollar stood at $2.40 to £1 American goods were very cheap for the British and at just over $1.00 to £1 they were exceedingly expensive. Currency volatility exaggerates trade imbalances which in turn increase volatility.

Cross-border investment flows

We have talked so far mainly about the flows of money between countries that result from their trading performance. These are the **current account** flows which reflect what a country earns from selling goods and services overseas and what it spends in buying goods and services from overseas.

But there are also **capital account** flows, which we have encountered briefly in the form of speculative funds moving in and out of a country as a bet on a rise or fall in the value of its currency. Not all capital flows are purely speculative, however: they can also represent long-term investment in a country from abroad. And they can have a long-term effect on the values of currencies. Take an example. In the first half of the 1980s, the US dollar was rising for much of the time despite an escalating balance of trade deficit which passed $100 billion in 1985. This was mainly because of large inflows of investment funds from abroad, particularly from Japan, attracted by relatively high US interest rates. But in 1985, balance of payments worries plus concerted efforts among central banks to curb the dollar's strength proved all too effective and the currency began to fall even more rapidly than it had risen.

Why should countries worry if their currency becomes too strong? A strong currency can have beneficial effects such as reducing the cost of imported goods. Particularly in the case of a country like Britain, which imports much of the raw materials that it needs, the lower cost of imports helps to keep domestic inflation down. On the other side of the coin, a weak pound means higher import costs and, all else being equal, faster rising prices in Britain.

But if a currency becomes too strong, it can wreak havoc with the domestic economy. Manufacturers find that their products become too expensive to compete with those of other countries in export or home markets, so domestic manufacturers suffer severely. This happened in Britain in the early 1980s.

In the first half of 1995 yet another bout of currency turmoil saw the dollar plummetting and the German mark and Japanese yen soaring. In Germany the authorities welcomed the stronger mark as a means of curbing domestic inflation. By contrast, the damage to home-based businesses was of great concern in Japan.

Where trade imbalances and currency excesses require concerted action, they may be addressed by a meeting of the finance ministers of the major trading nations. These countries – The United States, Japan, Germany, France and Great Britain – are referred to as the **Group of Five** or **G5** and become the **Group of Seven** or **G7** with the addition of Canada and Italy.

The European Monetary System

It is difficult to look at the position of sterling in the 1990s without looking first at the **Exchange Rate Mechanism (ERM)** of the **European Monetary System (EMS)** and the European Union's aspirations to move eventually to full **monetary union**. The first step was concerted action to stabilize currencies between the European Union countries and this was the thinking behind the formal linking of currencies in the EMS.

The Exchange Rate Mechanism works as follows. Start with the **ECU**, the notional European currency constructed from an amalgam of the currencies of all European Union members. Each country's currency is represented in the ECU with a weighting that roughly reflects the country's economic size. Thus Germany has the largest economy and the **German mark** has the heaviest weighting within the ECU. A movement in the value of the German mark against, say, the dollar will therefore have a greater effect on the dollar value of the ECU than a movement in any other currency.

Each currency starts with an exchange rate against the ECU: its **central rate**. Most currencies were – before July 1993 – allowed to diverge only about 2.25 per cent up or down from this central rate and from the central rates of other currencies in the system (in practice, this second discipline was usually the stricter). Some currencies which would have had problems with this discipline were allowed a divergence of about 6 per cent up or down (in theory, about 12 per cent in total but in practice less than this because other currencies might be moving in the opposite direction). Thus, if at any time the strongest currency in the system and the weakest one threatened to diverge more than was permitted against each other, the central banks of the two countries would need to take remedial action to bring them back into line.

If this happened, the central banks of the two countries

BANK OF ENGLAND JAPAN ,90=100 – TRADE WEIGHTED
BANK OF ENGLAND USA ,90=100 – TRADE WEIGHTED

Figure 16.3 Trade-weighted values of the US dollar (broken line) and the Japanese yen (solid line). It is not too difficult to see why Japanese manufacturers were worried about losing their markets after the yen's further spurt in value in 1995. Source: *Datastream International.*

would sell the strong currency and buy the weak one. In practice, a country whose currency was moving out of line might take action before this by buying or selling its own currency or raising or lowering short-term interest rates.

If measures such as these failed to keep a currency within bounds, the EMS members might be forced to agree a formal **revaluation** which re-set the particular currency's central rate within the ERM. But this was regarded very much as a last resort.

Britain, which had frequently run a considerably higher **inflation rate** than most other EC members, hoped to gain from the discipline imposed by this formal currency linking which it joined on 8 October 1990 with the wider 6 per cent fluctuation limit. To hold its position within the ERM it would have needed to get its inflation rate in line with that of other EC members, since high inflation normally leads to depreciation of the currency. The hope in Britain had been that membership of a system dominated by the stability of the German mark would ultimately bring the benefits of low inflation that Germany had enjoyed. It was also hoped that the protection afforded by the ERM mechanism would allow Britain gradually to reduce its domestic interest rates and emerge from recession without sparking a run on sterling. In the event, the UK succeeded in cutting both its inflation rate and interest rates to a level consistent with other members of the ERM.

Unfortunately, this was not enough to allow sterling's continued membership. Germany's own position was affected by the way it chose to integrate the former East Germany. One consequence was that Germany felt obliged to impose considerably higher interest rates than normal to control domestic inflation. Because of Germany's dominant influence, this in turn imposed high interest rates on the whole ERM structure. The consequences were serious for Britain whose inflation rate had been brought under control but which then badly needed to pull itself out of the severe recession that the earlier government medicine of high interest rates had caused. The domestic situation in Britain therefore seemed to demand a further reduction in interest rates to stimulate economic activity but a cut in rates relative to the other European countries would cause sterling to weaken and might make it impossible for the pound to maintain its position in the ERM.

In the event, the pound did leave the mechanism in September 1992 (see below).

The ERM is meant to be only a stage on the road to full **European Monetary Union** (which gives us yet another acronym: **EMU**). Ultimately EMU means closer cooperation in economic and monetary policy between EC member countries, the establishment of a European central bank, the locking together of national currencies and eventually the substitution of a single European currency for these currencies. Arguments for and against Britain's ultimately abandoning sterling in favour of a single European currency are likely to remain the subject of fierce political controversy.

Sterling and currency upheavals

Sterling's problems have been those of weakness for much of the post-war period. But not always. In the early 1980s a combination of North Sea oil revenues, a high oil price and high domestic interest rates in Britain saw sterling climbing strongly and not only against a then-weak dollar. At one point the dollar exchange rate went above $2.40 to £1. The strong currency helped to curb Britain's domestic inflation. But it proved a severe blow for the country's manufacturers who found themselves unable to compete on price in home or export markets. Much manufacturing capacity was destroyed in consequence: some of it inefficient and deserving to go, some of it probably not.

But the strength was relatively short-lived and by the middle of the decade a strong dollar and weak sterling saw a pound buying little more than a single dollar. An improvement in government finances resulted in some strengthening of the pound again in 1987 and 1988, but then rising inflation and mounting balance of payments problems intervened. As we have seen, in October 1990 the government decided with some misgivings to aim for stability via ERM membership.

The events of September 1992 when sterling was obliged to drop out of the ERM have passed into financial folklore. Whatever the British government maintained, the speculators thought that the pound must fall: either through a formal devaluation within the ERM or by dropping out of the

POUND SPOT FORWARD AGAINST THE POUND

May 15		Closing mid-point	Change on day	Bid/offer spread	Day's high	Mid low	One month Rate	%PA	Three months Rate	%PA	One year Rate	%PA	Bank of Eng. Index
Europe													
Austria	(Sch)	15.8663	−0.0926	587 - 738	16.0861	15.8380	15.8432	1.7	15.796	1.8	-	-	106.7
Belgium	(BFr)	46.3727	−0.2333	574 - 879	46.8970	46.2810	46.3227	1.3	46.1927	1.6	45.5777	1.7	109.2
Denmark	(DKr)	8.8067	−0.0279	014 - 120	8.8815	8.7970	8.8142	−1.0	8.8177	−0.5	8.7861	0.2	109.6
Finland	(FM)	6.8880	−0.0345	830 - 930	6.9760	6.8800	-	-	-	-	-	-	87.0
France	(FFr)	7.9066	−0.03	022 - 110	7.9936	7.8951	7.915	−1.3	7.917	−0.5	7.8449	0.8	108.1
Germany	(DM)	2.2566	−0.0129	556 - 575	2.2883	2.2533	2.253	1.9	2.2447	2.1	2.1994	2.5	111.3
Greece	(Dr)	363.390	−2.901	254 - 527	368.344	362.967	-	-	-	-	-	-	68.2
Ireland	(I£)	0.9768	−0.0016	760 - 775	0.9812	0.9753	0.9764	0.5	0.9762	0.2	0.9765	0.0	97.5
Italy	(L)	2566.90	−50.05	415 - 965	2624.11	2523.92	2574.4	−3.5	2587.9	−3.3	2640.9	−2.9	69.0
Luxembourg	(LFr)	46.3727	−0.2333	574 - 879	46.8970	46.2810	46.3227	1.3	46.1927	1.6	45.5777	1.7	109.2
Netherlands	(Fl)	2.5262	−0.0117	252 - 271	2.5594	2.5226	2.5222	1.9	2.5129	2.1	2.4638	2.5	108.9
Norway	(NKr)	10.0289	−0.0691	234 - 344	10.1876	10.0191	10.0202	1.0	9.9966	1.3	9.8693	1.6	98.5
Portugal	(Es)	236.395	−1.446	217 - 573	240.603	235.060	235.53	4.4	238.7	−3.9	-	-	95.7
Spain	(Pta)	194.838	−0.847	729 - 947	197.773	194.136	195.268	−2.6	196.113	−2.6	199.763	−2.5	80.9
Sweden	(SKr)	11.4685	−0.1047	588 - 781	11.6338	11.4460	11.4709	−0.3	11.4753	−0.2	11.4945	−0.2	78.8
Switzerland	(SFr)	1.8868	−0.0056	857 - 878	1.9079	1.8831	1.882	3.1	1.8718	3.2	1.8206	3.5	111.2
UK	(£)	-	-	-	-	-	-	-	-	-	-	-	84.1
Ecu†	–	1.2160	−0.0076	153 - 166	1.2307	1.2143	1.2157	0.3	1.2144	0.5	1.2053	0.9	-
SDR†	–	1.01965											
Americas													
Argentina	(Peso)	1.5608	−0.0111	605 - 611	1.5782	1.5596	-	-	-	-	-	-	-
Brazil	(R$)	1.3876	−0.0189	866 - 886	1.4055	1.3862	-	-	-	-	-	-	-
Canada	(C$)	2.1205	−0.0008	198 - 212	2.1355	2.1133	2.1225	−1.2	2.1237	−0.6	2.1131	0.3	83.5
Mexico	(New Peso)	9.2583	−0.0425	178 - 988	9.3224	9.2165	-	-	-	-	-	-	-
USA	($)	1.5600	−0.0124	597 - 602	1.5774	1.5587	1.5597	0.2	1.5578	0.6	1.541	1.2	89.9
Pacific/Middle East/Africa													
Australia	(A$)	2.1281	+0.0039	270 - 291	2.1295	2.1257	2.1307	−1.5	2.1352	−1.3	2.1523	−1.1	80.6
Hong Kong	(HK$)	12.0622	−0.1004	594 - 649	12.1996	12.0533	12.0582	0.4	12.0488	0.4	11.9819	0.7	-
India	(Rs)	49.0449	−0.3757	214 - 683	49.5780	49.0110	-	-	-	-	-	-	-
Israel	(Shk)	4.7257	−0.0274	209 - 304	4.7675	4.7200	-	-	-	-	-	-	-
Japan	(Y)	135.404	−0.931	304 - 503	137.530	135.240	134.814	5.2	133.569	5.4	127.654	5.7	167.1
Malaysia	(M$)	3.8746	−0.0431	732 - 760	3.9175	3.8723	-	-	-	-	-	-	-
New Zealand	(NZ$)	2.3577	−0.0192	564 - 589	2.3604	2.3551	2.363	−2.7	2.3721	−2.4	2.3862	−1.2	98.4
Philippines	(Peso)	40.1688	−0.2419	283 - 092	40.4303	39.9234	-	-	-	-	-	-	-
Saudi Arabia	(SR)	5.8508	−0.0464	497 - 518	5.9159	5.8462	-	-	-	-	-	-	-
Singapore	(S$)	2.1918	−0.0232	906 - 929	2.2170	2.1900	-	-	-	-	-	-	-
South Africa	(R)	5.7028	−0.0526	007 - 049	5.7635	5.6994	-	-	-	-	-	-	-
South Korea	(Won)	1189.85	−10.6	958 - 012	1200.63	1188.98	-	-	-	-	-	-	-
Taiwan	(T$)	39.7694	−0.238	536 - 851	40.2048	39.7188	-	-	-	-	-	-	-
Thailand	(Bt)	38.5620	−0.3313	402 - 837	38.9850	38.5370	-	-	-	-	-	-	-

† Rates for May 12. Bid/offer spreads in the Pound Spot table show only the last three decimal places. Forward rates are not directly quoted to the market but are implied by current interest rates. Sterling index calculated by the Bank of England. Base average 1990 = 100. Index rebased 1/2/95. Bid, Offer and Mid-rates in both this and the Dollar Spot tables derived from THE WM/REUTERS CLOSING SPOT RATES. Some values are rounded by the F.T.

Table 16.1 Value of the pound sterling in different currencies, for spot and future delivery. Note also the column giving values on the trade-weighted index. Source: *Financial Times*.

mechanism and finding its own level. And, as so often happens, government intervention to support the pound offered them a one-way bet. The authorities were there as buyer when the speculators wanted to sell. On 16 September the pound was at its lower limit within the ERM and at mid-morning the government announced that **Minimum Lending Rate** had been raised from 10 per cent to 12 per cent. But with everybody except the authorities betting on sterling's fall, this failed to lift it from the floor. As a final throw it was announced in the afternoon that MLR would rise again to 15 per cent the following day. Again, it failed to work. Sterling's suspension from the ERM was announced that evening and the MLR rise to 15 per cent was never implemented.

No longer supported, sterling fell 10 per cent more against

the German mark from the level at which it had dropped out of the ERM, and the speculators collected their winnings – able to buy back more cheaply the pounds they had earlier sold short at the higher level. One so-called **hedge fund** (see glossary) had supposedly made $1 billion on the operation. The Bank of Engand, according to the newspaper speculation of the time, had spent some £15 billion in its (ultimately unsuccessful) support of the currency, though only a fraction of this would have been money actually lost. Once attempts to maintain the pound's ERM parity were abandoned, interest rates in Britain were rapidly reduced in a series of steps.

Sterling was not the only currency to suffer from ERM turmoil at the time, though the mechanism ultimately survived, albeit by means of a widening of the margins of the system to plus or minus 15 per cent at the end of July 1993. But by early 1995 currency turmoil was in the air again. Funds were flowing out of the US dollar and into the German mark and the Japanese yen, leading to severe over-valuation of the yen in particular. Japanese businesses were pleading with their authorities to stimulate the economy and act to reduce the yen's strength, while the United States was under pressure to cut its budget deficit and raise its own interest rates to attract funds back in and reduce pressures on the other currencies.

Which currencies will be weakening and which will be strengthening at the time you read this? It is anybody's guess. Movements in currencies are so rapid and sometimes so unpredictable that it is difficult to forecast even a few months ahead where the next major pressure points will be.

Forward markets and hedging

Now that governments have only limited control over the value of currencies, it is up to businesses to protect themselves against the effect of wild swings as best they can. There are various ways they can **hedge** the **currency risk**.

There is a **forward market** in currencies as well as a **spot market**. In the spot market currencies are bought and sold for immediate delivery – in practice, delivery in two days' time – whereas in the forward market they are bought and sold for delivery in the future. You will see that the *Financial Times* table of the value of the pound against major currencies lists a

EMS EUROPEAN CURRENCY UNIT RATES

May 15	Ecu cen. rates	Rate against Ecu	Change on day	% +/- from cen. rate	% spread v weakest	Div. ind.
Netherlands	2.15214	2.09802	+0.00231	−2.51	5.04	-
Belgium	39.3960	38.5178	+0.067	−2.23	4.74	16
Austria	13.4383	13.1755	+0.0129	−1.95	4.45	-
Germany	1.91007	1.87370	+0.00223	−1.90	4.39	-
Spain	162.493	161.735	+0.384	−0.47	2.88	3
Portugal	195.792	196.317	+0.182	0.27	2.13	−2
Denmark	7.28580	7.30807	+0.01957	0.31	2.09	−2
Ireland	0.792214	0.808856	−0.000362	2.10	0.29	−14
France	6.40608	6.55989	+0.01362	2.40	0.00	−20
NON ERM MEMBERS						
Greece	292.867	302.009	−0.047	3.12	−0.70	-
Italy	2106.15	2116.05	−44.56	0.47	1.92	-
UK	0.786652	0.827226	+0.00168	5.16	−2.62	-

Ecu central rates set by the European Commission. Currencies are in descending relative strength. Percentage changes are for Ecu; a positive change denotes a weak currency. Divergence shows the ratio between two spreads: the percentage difference between the actual market and Ecu central rates for a currency, and the maximum permitted percentage deviation of the currency's market rate from its Ecu central rate.
(17/9/92) Sterling and Italian Lira suspended from ERM. Adjustment calculated by the Financial Times.

Table 16.2 The European Union countries and the Exchange Rate Mechanism. Source: *Financial Times*.

spot price and prices for delivery in one month and three months and one year.

The forward price relative to the spot price reflects the **interest rate differential** between the countries concerned. Suppose, say, you hold sterling and are due to pay for goods in German marks in three months' time. You are worried the value of the mark will rise, in which case you will have to pay more in sterling terms. So you might buy German marks today for delivery in three months' time, which means you are **locking in** to a known exchange rate.

Suppose also that you can deposit money in Britain to earn 10 per cent and in Germany to earn only 4 per cent. For three months you have the benefit of the higher sterling interest rate, whereas if you had bought the German marks immediately you would have been depositing the money at the lower German interest rate until it was needed. So the price you pay for the deutschmarks for delivery in three months will be higher than the spot price by an amount that reflects this interest rate advantage – in other words, at the three months' price you will get fewer deutschmarks for your pounds than at the spot price. But if the currency you want to buy forward offers higher interest rates than in Britain, the forward price will be lower than the spot price (at a **discount** rather than a **premium**). These premiums and discounts for currencies in the forward market are shown in the *Financial Times*, together with the annual interest rate differential they reflect.

In practice, hedging strategies in the foreign exchange markets may be a great deal more complex than simply buying or selling a currency forward, though this illustrates the principle. Currencies may be **swapped**, too (see Chapter 17) and banks offer a range of OTC currency hedging products. Currency futures are no longer traded on the Liffe financial futures market in London, though they can be bought on certain overseas exchanges.

Who deals in the forex markets?

Foreign exchange is dealt in by the major banks and by specialist **foreign exchange brokers**, with the dealers operating from the screen-cluttered trading floors familiar from many film and television reports. Dealing is via these screens and telephones: there is no central marketplace.

London, conveniently placed to provide continuity between Tokyo and New York in the time zones, is the largest foreign exchange market. A Bank of England survey of 352 principals and 13 brokers in 1992 estimated the average volume of the London market market at $300 billion per day, with US dollar/sterling and dollar/deutschmark business accounting for 42 per cent of the total. About half of that $300 billion represents forward business, mainly swaps. And about a quarter of the business was estimated to be transacted via automated dealing systems such as that of **Reuters**, where the transaction can be completed on screen without need for contact via telephone or a broker.

Was there really $300 billion of cross-border trade per day that required currency transactions in London? Of course not. More than three-quarters represents dealing between banks. Dealing with non-financial institutions is only 9 per cent of the total. Business with other financial institutions accounted for 14 per cent. Direct business with customers is thus a relatively small proportion of the total and the volume of speculative activity is high. However, each trade-backed transaction may in practice require a number of separate transactions on the exchanges as banks deal to 'lay off' the risk they have taken from the customer. **Arbitrage** (see glossary) evens out temporary disparities between rates for different currencies and ensures that interest rate differentials are reflected in forward rates. Currency dealers justify the vast speculative activity with the argument that it results in a highly liquid market in which necessary trade-backed transactions can be carried out with ease.

While the economists at the banks may seek to make rational forecasts of likely trends in a particular currency, the dealers have a much shorter-term view, taking advantage of temporary swings and anomalies. In the absence of rational reasons for currency swings, they may enlist the help of **chartist** techniques (see Chapter 7a) which indicate likely trends or turning points purely on the basis of chart patterns and profiles. It may add to the volatility of the market if large numbers of participants react to the same chart signals simultaneously.

17

International money:
the euromarkets

By far the biggest **capital market** centered on London is the
euromarket or the **international market**. The two terms do not
mean exactly the same thing, but we will come to the differences later. You do not read a great deal about these markets
day-to-day – except in the *Financial Times* and a few specialist
publications – because they are markets for professionals, they
have no central marketplace and they have not in the past
directly impinged on many private investors in Britain. Yet, in
terms of money raised, they completely dwarf Britain's domestic markets.

To understand the euromarket, start by thinking how markets evolve. A group of people have a need to come together
to barter or sell goods. The market grows initially out of this
need. It is probably informal, and some markets remain that
way. But after a time – and particularly in financial markets –
the participants may decide to introduce a more formal structure and a set of rules. It could help the market to function
more effectively. It could reduce sharp practice and increase
public confidence in the market. It could also, of course, allow
the original participants to frame the rules so as to keep others
out and to ensure that the market provides them with a good
living.

At a later stage, governments may take a hand. Activity in
financial markets can have far-reaching economic implications. The government may feel it needs to exert a
measure of control. It may decide the market needs super-
vising by a governmental body. And so on.

Thus, most countries have domestic financial markets that

are more or less closely regulated – directly or indirectly – by their respective governments. As we have noted, the trend in recent years has been to dismantle a great deal of this regulation – the **deregulation** process – and to throw domestic markets more open to competition. But this has not always been the case. And, when financiers have perceived a need or an opportunity that could not be exploited in the existing regulated markets, they have often tried to find a way round the problem, perhaps by operating in a new 'black' market of their own. The euromarkets have their origin in this sort of process.

The conventional explanation of the euromarkets used to be that they were an informal market in money held outside its country of origin. Thus, deposits of dollars in a European bank would be **eurodollars**, deposits of German marks in a British bank would be **euromarks**, and so on. This money could be borrowed and lent without going through the domestic financial markets of the country concerned and this is what, in fact, happened. Initially, much of the business was in dollars, hence the term **eurodollar market** in the early days.

Nowadays, when people talk about the euromarket they are referring not so much to the origin of the money that is borrowed and lent but more to the structure and techniques of the market in which it is traded. And the 'euro' part of the title is also misleading: the market is a market between banks worldwide. It is by no means confined to currencies held in European banks, or to European currencies. There are **euroyen** and a 'euro' version of the Canadian dollar. The market did, however, have its origins in Europe and more specifically in London, which remains the main centre – a factor that explains the presence of so many foreign banks. If we are drawing a distinction between the euromarket and the international market, we would probably say that the former covers transactions in the currencies of which there is a recognized 'euro' version and the latter term would also embrace dealing outside domestic markets in money or securities denominated in any currency. In practice, the two terms are often used virtually interchangeably.

The important point is that the international market does not belong to any one country, nor is the market as such regulated by any country's domestic supervisors (though London dealers in the market would come within the UK's regulatory structure). Dealing in this international market is not circumscribed by the local rules and regulations of a particular financial centre. To this extent it remains 'informal' or 'unofficial', though market organisations have agreed some rules of their own. If London is the centre of the international market, the market is by no means run mainly by British institutions, nor are British companies among the most important users of the market. American banks and their offshoots are dominant, and to a lesser extent the Japanese.

Restrictions on capital raising by foreigners in the United States domestic markets in the 1960s help to explain the establishment and growth of the international market in London, conveniently situated in the time zones. America imposed limits on the rates of interest that could be paid in its domestic markets and had levied a tax on foreign borrowers which made raising capital in New York uneconomic for them. London, on the other hand, offered a relaxed taxation and regulatory regime as far as the operations of the international market were concerned.

Nowadays, the international market mirrors most of the facilities and forms of security available in domestic markets. Eurocurrencies can be deposited and borrowed for very short periods or for many years. Borrowers can take out the equivalent of a term loan in a eurocurrency. They can issue various forms of bond or 'IOU note' to raise money in a eurocurrency. And because the eurocurrency market is largely unfettered by national restrictions, many of the more innovative forms of financing are first devised in the eurocurrency market and often copied subsequently in domestic financial markets. It is a case of giving the market what it wants or selling the market what you think it will take. Recent years have also seen considerable growth in **euro-equity** issues – issues of company shares via the international market rather than in the domestic stockmarket of the company concerned.

It is important to note the difference between borrowing a eurocurrency and simply borrowing in an overseas financial market. A euroyen loan is a borrowing denominated in yen through the international market structure whereas a **samurai** bond is a yen bond issued by a foreigner in the Japanese domestic market. A **yankee** bond is a dollar bond issued by a

EURO CURRENCY INTEREST RATES

May 15	Short term.	7 days notice	One month	Three months	Six months	One year
Belgian Franc	$4\frac58$ - $4\frac12$	$4\frac34$ - $4\frac58$	5 - $4\frac78$	$5\frac14$ - $5\frac18$	$5\frac{7}{16}$ - $5\frac{5}{16}$	$5\frac{11}{16}$ - $5\frac{9}{16}$
Danish Krone	$6\frac12$ - $6\frac14$	7 - $6\frac34$	$6\frac78$ - $6\frac58$	$6\frac34$ - $6\frac12$	$6\frac34$ - $6\frac12$	$6\frac34$ - $6\frac12$
D-Mark	$4\frac{5}{16}$ - $4\frac{1}{16}$	$4\frac{5}{16}$ - $4\frac{1}{16}$	$4\frac{5}{16}$ - $4\frac{1}{16}$	$4\frac58$ - $4\frac12$	$4\frac58$ - $4\frac12$	$4\frac78$ - $4\frac34$
Dutch Guilder	$4\frac38$ - $4\frac14$	$4\frac{7}{16}$ - $4\frac{5}{16}$	$4\frac{7}{16}$ - $4\frac38$	$4\frac12$ - $4\frac{7}{16}$	$4\frac58$ - $4\frac{9}{16}$	$4\frac78$ - $4\frac34$
French Franc	$7\frac34$ - $7\frac12$	$7\frac34$ - $7\frac12$	$7\frac{9}{16}$ - $7\frac{5}{16}$	$7\frac18$ - $6\frac78$	$6\frac{13}{16}$ - $6\frac{9}{16}$	$6\frac58$ - $6\frac38$
Portuguese Esc.	$9\frac{5}{16}$ - $9\frac{1}{16}$	$9\frac38$ - $9\frac18$	$9\frac78$ - $9\frac58$	$10\frac18$ - $9\frac78$	$10\frac12$ - $10\frac14$	11 - $10\frac34$
Spanish Peseta	9 - $8\frac78$	9 - $8\frac34$	$9\frac18$ - $8\frac78$	$9\frac{7}{16}$ - $9\frac14$	$9\frac{13}{16}$ - $9\frac{9}{16}$	$10\frac38$ - $10\frac18$
Sterling	$6\frac18$ - $5\frac78$	$6\frac18$ - 6	$6\frac{3}{16}$ - $6\frac{1}{16}$	$6\frac{11}{16}$ - $6\frac58$	$7\frac{1}{16}$ - 7	$7\frac{9}{16}$ - $7\frac{7}{16}$
Swiss Franc	$3\frac12$ - $3\frac38$	$3\frac12$ - $3\frac38$	$3\frac12$ - $3\frac38$	$3\frac{5}{16}$ - $3\frac{7}{16}$	$3\frac58$ - $3\frac12$	$3\frac34$ - $3\frac58$
Can. Dollar	$7\frac{13}{16}$ - $7\frac58$	$7\frac34$ - $7\frac12$	$7\frac12$ - $7\frac38$	$7\frac38$ - $7\frac14$	$7\frac{3}{16}$ - $7\frac{1}{16}$	$7\frac{3}{16}$ - $7\frac{1}{16}$
US Dollar	$6\frac{1}{16}$ - $5\frac{15}{16}$	$6\frac{1}{16}$ - $5\frac{15}{16}$	$6\frac{1}{16}$ - $5\frac{15}{16}$	$6\frac18$ - 6	$6\frac18$ - 6	$6\frac14$ - $6\frac18$
Italian Lira	$10\frac14$ - $9\frac34$	$10\frac{5}{16}$ - $10\frac{1}{16}$	$9\frac{3}{16}$ - $9\frac{1}{16}$	$9\frac78$ - $9\frac34$	$10\frac{1}{16}$ - $9\frac{13}{16}$	$10\frac{7}{16}$ - $10\frac{5}{16}$
Yen	$1\frac38$ - $1\frac14$	$1\frac38$ - $1\frac14$	$1\frac38$ - $1\frac14$	$1\frac38$ - $1\frac14$	$1\frac{7}{16}$ - $1\frac{5}{16}$	$1\frac12$ - $1\frac38$
Asian $Sing	$\frac12$ - $\frac38$	$1\frac38$ - $1\frac14$	$1\frac34$ - $1\frac58$	2 - $1\frac78$	$2\frac18$ - 2	$2\frac34$ - $2\frac58$

Table 17.1 Short-term rates for borrowing and lending in curocurrencies. Source: *Financial Times*.

foreigner in the United States domestic market and a **bulldog** bond is a sterling bond issued in Britain by a foreigner. The samurai, yankee and bulldog are not eurobonds.

Syndicated loans

Out of the original short-term market in eurocurrency deposits – the **inter-bank market** – grew the **syndicated loan** market. **Syndicates** of banks would get together under a **lead bank** or lead banks to provide medium-term or long-term loans running into hundreds of millions or billions of dollars – though the currency in which the money was borrowed would not necessarily be dollars. It could equally well be German marks or Japanese yen. By each contributing part of the loan, the individual banks avoided too large a commitment to any one customer.

Eurobonds

Securitization of eurocurrency lending was the next step and the **eurobond** emerged. It is much like the bonds that governments and companies issue in their domestic markets (see Chapter 13), but the documentation and the issue techniques are somewhat different. It is also denominated in one of the eurocurrencies.

There are other differences, too. In Britain, most domestic bonds suffer **withholding tax**. In other words, basic rate income tax is deducted before the investor gets his interest. Eurobond interest is normally paid gross, without any withholding tax. The bonds are also issued in **bearer** form, rather than the **registered** form applying to UK domestic bonds, which gives them attractions for investors who do not intend being over-frank with the tax man (the tax advantages of eurobonds were probably a significant factor in the growth of the market). And the interest is normally paid once a year rather than in two half-yearly instalments, as is normal in the UK. This means that a coupon of 10 per cent on a eurobond is not generally the same thing as a coupon of 10 per cent on a

FT/ISMA INTERNATIONAL BOND SERVICE

Listed are the latest international bonds for which there is an adequate secondary market. **Closing prices on May 15**

	Issued	Bid	Offer	Chg.	Yield
U.S. DOLLAR STRAIGHTS					
Abbey Natl Treasury 6½ 03	1000	95¾	96⅛	+¼	7.22
African Dev Bk 7⅜ 23	500	96	96½	+⅜	7.73
Alberta Province 7⅝ 98	1000	102⅞	103⅛	+⅛	6.65
Austria 8½ 00	400	107	107¼	+¼	6.70
Baden-Wuertt L-Fin 8⅛ 00	1000	105¼	105½	+⅛	6.77
Bank Ned Gemeenten 7 99	1000	101⅝	101⅞	+⅛	6.54
Bayer Vereinsbk 8⅛ 00	500	105⅜	105½	+¼	6.74
Belgium 5½ 03	1000	89⅝	90	+¼	7.17
BFCE 7¾ 97	150	102⅛	102½	+⅛	6.44
British Columbia 7¾ 02	500	104	104⅜	+¼	7.01
British Gas 0 21	1500	13¼	13½	+⅛	7.93
Canada 6½ 97	2000	100	100⅛	+⅛	6.49
Cheung Kong Fin 5½ 98	500	92	92⅝	+¼	8.30
China 6½ 04	1000	91½	92⅜	+⅛	8.01
Council Europe 8 96	100	101¾	102	+⅛	6.43
Credit Foncier 9½ 99	300	108¾	109⅛	+⅛	6.78
Denmark 5¾ 98	1000	98⅛	98½	+⅛	6.50
East Japan Railway 6⅝ 04	600	96⅜	96⅝	+⅜	7.19
ECSC 8¼ 96	193	102⅜	102¾	+⅛	6.54
EEC 8¼ 96	100	101⅞	102⅛	+⅛	6.40
EIB 7¾ 96	250	101⅜	101¾		6.44
EIB 9¼ 97	1000	106	106⅜		6.54
Elec de France 9 98	200	105¾	106¼		6.69
Ex-Im Bank Japan 8 02	500	105¾	106⅛	+¼	6.94
Export Dev Corp 9½ 98	150	107⅝	108	+⅛	6.73
Federal Natl Mort 7.40 04	1500	103¼	103½	+⅜	7.03
Finland 6¾ 97	3000	100½	100¾	+⅛	6.64
Ford Motor Credit 6¼ 98	1500	98¾	99⅛		6.86
Gen Elec Capital 9⅜ 96	300	102⅞	103⅛		6.47
Ind Bk Japan Fin 7⅞ 97	200	101½	102		7.00
Inter Amer Dev 7⅝ 96	200	101⅜	101⅝		6.46
Intl Finance 5¼ 99	500	96	96¼	+⅛	6.51
Italy 6⅞ 23	3500	86⅝	87	+¼	8.25
Japan Dev Bk 8⅜ 01	500	107	107⅜	+⅛	6.85
Korea Elec Power 6⅜ 03	1350	93¼	93⅞	+¼	7.60
LTCB Fin 8 97	200	101½	102		6.98
Matsushita Elec 7¼ 02	1000	101½	101⅞	+¼	7.10
Norway 7¼ 97	1000	101½	101¾	+⅛	6.38
Ontario 7⅜ 03	3000	101½	101¾	+⅜	7.24
United Kingdom 7⅛ 97	5500	103⅜	103½		5.59
Volkswagen Intl Fin 7 03	1000	98	98⅝	−⅜	7.34
World Bank 0 15	2000	23⅜	23¾	+¼	7.31
World Bank 5⅞ 03	3000	93	93⅛	−⅛	6.99
World Bank 8¾ 00	1250	111	111¾	−⅛	6.10
SWISS FRANC STRAIGHTS					
Asian Dev Bank 6 10	100	104¼	105¼	−¼	5.58
Austria 4½ 00	1000	100¾	100⅞	−¼	4.32
Council Europe 4¾ 98	250	101¼	101½		4.25
Denmark 4¼ 99	1000	100½	100¾	−¼	4.12
EIB 6¾ 04	300	108¾	109½	−⅝	5.53
Elec de France 7¼ 06	100	111¾	112½		5.74
Finland 7¼ 99	300	108⅞	109½	−⅝	4.94
Hyundai Motor Fin 8½ 97	100	107	108	+½	5.20
Iceland 7⅝ 00	100	109½	110		5.47
Kobe 6⅜ 01	240	107	107¾	−¼	5.03
Ontario 6¼ 03	400	105	105¼		5.43
Quebec Hydro 5 08	100	91½	92	+¼	5.96
SNCF 7 04	450	112½	113		5.27
World Bank 5 03	150	101	101⅜	+¼	4.85
World Bank 7 01	600	109¾	110¼		5.02
YEN STRAIGHTS					
Belgium 5 99	75000	109⅝	109⅞	+⅛	2.74
EIB 6⅝ 00	100000	117¼	117½		2.76
Ex-Im Bank Japan 4⅜ 03	105000	107⅝	107⅞	+⅛	3.32
Inter Amer Dev 7¼ 00	30000	120⅛	120⅜	+⅛	2.87
Italy 3½ 01	300000	99⅝	99¾	+⅛	3.60
Japan Dev Bk 5 99	100000	110¼	110⅜	+⅛	2.50
Japan Dev Bk 6½ 01	120000	119½	119⅝	+¼	3.07
Nippon Tel Tel 5⅞ 96	50000	105⅜	105⅝		1.83
Norway 5⅜ 97	150000	106⅛	106¼		1.78
SNCF 6¾ 00	30000	117⅝	117⅞	+⅛	2.77
Spain 5¾ 02	125000	114½	114⅝	+¼	3.35
Sweden 4⅝ 98	150000	106¼	106⅜	+⅛	2.23
World Bank 5¼ 02	250000	112⅞	113	+⅛	3.17
OTHER STRAIGHTS					
Genfinance Lux 9⅛ 99 LFr	1000	105	106		7.59

Table 17.2 Information on bonds traded in the international market. Source: *Financial Times*.

UK domestic bond. With the UK bond the investor can rein-vest the interest he receives after six months and earn interest on it for the second half of the year. It means that 10 per cent paid in two instalments is worth the same as 10.25 per cent paid only once a year. Coupons and yields on eurobonds therefore have to be adjusted to express them in the same terms as returns in the domestic market. So you may read of a yield 'equivalent to such-and-such an amount on a semi-annual basis'.

Issue techniques in the eurobond market are complex, and the way they work in practice is often somewhat different from the theory. At the two ends of the transaction you have the company or organisation that wants to raise money via a eurobond issue (and needs to be sure of getting its money) and the end-investor in the bond (perhaps the proverbial Belgian dentist usually portrayed as the typical eurobond investor). Between is an array of banks. A lead bank (or group of banks) puts the issue together and agrees with the company the terms on which it will get its money. These banks need a good distribution network to be able to place a significant proportion of the bonds with investors. Other banks are brought in to take part of the risk of underwriting the issue (in theory, at least). Then there are other banks (the **selling group**) which are not part of the syndicate but which also use their extensive retail contacts to sell the bonds to the end-investors.

Once the eurobond has been issued in the **primary market** it can be traded in the **secondary market**, an over-the counter or OTC market conducted by dealers over the telephone and television screen. In the early days the lead bank is allowed to **stabilize** (i.e, manipulate) the market in the issue by dealing itself. Whether or not it makes a profit on the issue depends on whether it can sell the bonds at a price that does not wipe out the fees it received. The secondary market can at times be a volatile market, partly because dealers (unlike marketmak-ers on the London Stock Exchange) did not have an obligation to make a market. If times got tough in a particular sector they might temporarily pull in their horns and the mar-ket would lose its liquidity.

Two organisations provide clearance and settlement systems for international bonds and money market instruments: **Cedel** in Luxembourg and **Euroclear** in Brussels. The market's self-regulatory organisation – the **International Securities Market Association** or **ISMA** is based in Switzerland but has an office in London.

Variations on the bond theme

The original **straight** eurobond carries a fixed rate of interest. But forms of bond developed which pay floating-rate interest, known as **floating rate notes (FRNs)**. Some banks have issued **perpetual floating rate notes** or **perpetuals** which are never required to be repaid, though the value of these suffered a dramatic market collapse in the 1980s.

The complexities arise in the many variations of these basic themes, introduced to make eurobonds more attractive to issuers or investors (or both). First the borrower must choose what currency he will borrow in; the interest rate would be usually lower in a strong currency (as the German mark usually is) than it would be in sterling, but if the mark rises, the debt could be a lot more expensive to repay. Some bonds (**dual currency bonds**) reduce the currency exposure from the point of view of the investor: he puts up the money in one currency but is repaid in another at a rate of exchange fixed in advance.

Some eurobonds issued by companies incorporate an **equity sweetener**. Either the bond can be **converted** (wholly or in part) into the shares of the issuing company or it comes with **warrants** to subscribe for the company's shares. The principles are the same as those outlined in Chapter 5 in the context of convertibles and warrants issued by domestic British companies. And, as in the domestic bond market, eurobonds may be issued at a **deep discount** instead of paying a rate of interest (**zero-coupon bonds**) or may initially be issued in **part-paid** form.

The real complexities, however, concern the interest rate and the compromises evolved to obtain some of the advantages of both fixed-rate and floating-rate bonds. Floating-rate notes are issued which can **convert** into fixed-rate at the option of the investor (the **debt convertible**) or may become fixed rate if interest rates drop to a predetermined level (the

droplock). Or there may be an upper limit (a **cap**) to the interest rate payable on a floating rate note (a **capped floating rate note**) and sometimes a lower limit or **floor** as well. There are even bonds which pay higher interest as interest rates generally go down. And the investor might have a **put option** or the issuer a **call option**, allowing one or the other to force early redemption in certain circumstances.

Eurocommercial paper

Even in the field of very short-term securities, there are counterparts in the international market to the instruments found in domestic financial markets. You used to read about the **euronote**: an IOU with a life of under a year. Borrowers would arrange with a bank or dealer to sell or take up the notes they issued under arrangements such as the **revolving underwriting facility** (**RUF**) or **note issuance facility** (**NIF**). The borrower could thus issue further notes as he needed the money or as the earlier ones fell due. Nowadays the emphasis is on **eurocommercial paper** (**ECP**) which works in much the same way as commercial paper in the domestic market (see Chapter 15). A somewhat longer-term version is the **euro medium term note** or **EMTN**. An ECP programme may give the borrower the option of raising money in a range of currencies, and a number of British companies have used it.

Euro and domestic markets in Britain

Of late the distinctions between the domestic market and the euromarket in sterling-denominated bonds have been greatly eroded. Much the same firms deal in securities in both markets, and the rules for the issue of domestic sterling bonds on the London Stock Exchange have been relaxed to bring them closer in line with those applying in the euromarket. There have been sterling issues for UK companies divided between a 'euro' and a 'domestic' component, with the domestic part in the form of registered bonds. Many major British companies have issued **convertible loan stocks** and **convertible preference shares** in the euromarket, and for larger companies the choice between the two markets often depends mainly on questions of tax, issue costs and the type of investor they are trying to attract.

While the domestic market is the main one for the issue of **secured loans** (eurobonds are usually unsecured) the 1980s saw rapid expansion of euromarket issues of **mortgage-backed securities** by British-based **specialist mortgage lenders** who competed strongly with the building societies and banks to provide housing finance. Large numbers of individual residential mortgages – typically a thousand or so – would be 'pooled' in a special-purpose company which then issued floating rate notes or bonds to investors at large, thus recouping the money originally lent to homebuyers. The payments of interest and capital by these homebuyers provide for the interest on the notes and for their eventual repayment. The process is a prime example of **securitization**: mortgage loans are transmuted into tradable securities. However, mortgage-backed securities became rather less popular after the early 1990s collapse of house prices in Britain.

Setting the interest rate

The *Financial Times* carries a table of **eurocurrency interest rates**. These follow but do not necessarily exactly match domestic rates within the countries concerned. Rates are given for a range of eurocurrencies for deposits ranging from very short term to periods of up to a year. Needless to say, rates are lowest for the strongest currencies.

The key rate is three-month or six-month **LIBOR**, which stands for **London inter-bank offered rate** (see Chapter 15). This is the rate at which banks will lend in the inter-bank market, and is adopted as the benchmark rate of interest. The interest on floating rate notes is usually set by reference to the average rate of LIBOR and expressed as 'so many **basis points**' (hundredths of one percentage point) above LIBOR.

Euroequities

The distribution networks used by major eurobond dealers to market loan and bond issues to investors are used on a smaller (but growing) scale to market ordinary shares in major internationally-known companies. It may suit a company to raise cash by selling shares outside its domestic capital market when this is too small for its needs. Other companies may wish to attract shareholders in overseas countries where they trade. Such operations are known as **euroequity** issues. British companies that are already listed are generally prevented by the pre-emption rules from using this route to raise further cash – new shares have to be offered first to existing holders.

Size of the international market

For an idea of the size and make-up of the international market, look at the table on this page and the next, based on figures supplied by Euromoney Bondware and Loanware. Bond issues in the International market raised $423 billion in 1994, with the US dollar and the Japanese yen the predominant currencies. Loan facilities were arranged for $281 billion. The relative popularity of bond issues and loans varies with the financial climate: the bond markets were a little shaky in 1994. In addition, new eurocommercial paper programmes to a value of $37 billion were arranged and equities were issued in the international market to a total value of $55 billion.

INTERNATIONAL BOND ISSUES IN 1994

Currency	Fixed rate $bn	Convertible $bn	Floating rate $bn	Other $bn
US dollar	77.0	11.7	70.0	5.0
Japanese yen	59.6	2.2	8.2	1.0
German mark	23.5	0.1	8.1	0.6
French franc	20.6	2.6	1.3	0.2
Sterling	17.9	1.0	12.2	0.0
Italian lira	15.1	1.0	1.4	0.0
Canadian dollar	12.5	0.0	1.4	0.0
Swiss franc	12.4	3.6	1.1	4.6
Dutch guilder	11.7	0.5	0.1	0.0
Luxembourg franc	11.4	0.0	*	*
OTHER	21.2	0.5	2.7	0.0
TOTALS	282.8	22.7	106.6	11.3

All figures rounded. * = Below $50m
Source: *Euromoney Bondware and Loanware*

TOTAL RAISED OR ARRANGED

Year	Bonds $bn	Loan facilities $bn
1985	153.5	145.6
1986	209.8	149.2
1987	168.2	202.1
1988	214.9	293.9
1989	244.3	290.6
1990	212.7	275.4
1991	285.0	222.2
1992	311.9	191.5
1993	441.6	228.4
1994	423.4	280.6

Source: *Euromoney Bondware and Loanware*

Interest rate and currency swaps

The form in which borrowers can most easily raise money is not always the form best suited to their purposes. Company A, say, finds it can easily raise fixed-interest money when it really needs floating-rate funds. Company B, on the other hand, has no problem in raising a floating-rate loan but its real need is for fixed-interest money which would be expensive for it.

The solution may be a **swap** – in this case an **interest rate swap**. Company A issues its fixed-interest bond and Company B issues a floating-rate loan. They then agree to swap their interest payment liabilities. Company A pays the floating-rate interest due on Company B's loan and Company B pays the fixed rate of interest on the Company A borrowing, with some adjustment to reflect the relative strength of the two concerns. By this mechanism, each ends up with money in the form in which it needs it, at a cheaper rate than if it had borrowed what it needed direct.

This is the principle: each company borrows the money in the form in which it has the greatest relative advantage. The mechanisms are in reality more complex. Companies will not normally seek the **counterparty** for the swap direct, but will arrange a swap with a bank, which can either find a counterparty for the deal (taking a small cut in the middle) or may act as counter-party itself. And swaps, once set up, may subsequently be traded or adapted as conditions change in the market.

The second type of swap is the **currency swap**. Company A may be able to borrow on the most advantageous terms in German marks, because its credit rating is high in Germany where it is known. But it needs US dollars. Company B can most easily raise money in US dollars, but it needs German marks. So Company A issues a German mark loan and Company B borrows dollars. They then swap so that each ends up with what it needs, paying the interest on the currency it swaps into. Since each is borrowing where its credit is best, both end up with cheaper funds than if they had borrowed direct in the currency they needed. Again, a bank probably acts as intermediary. With many swaps both interest payments and currencies are exchanged.

It has been estimated that at times as much as 80 per cent of the funds raised in the euromarket are immediately swapped.

Ranking of borrowers

The interest rate paid by a borrower in the euromarket depends partly on the borrower's standing. The main borrowers are governments, public bodies and internationally known companies, and companies known only in their domestic markets may be less well received.

Several organizations, including **Standard & Poor's** and **Moody's** in the United States, provide **bond rating services** which attempt to quantify the credit-worthiness of a borrower. The highest rating is AAA, hence the term **triple-A-rated** for the very safest borrowers. The same organisations provide ratings for short-term debt such as commercial paper.

Tombstones

Banks which are active in the euromarkets like to advertise their success in raising funds for clients. They do so partly by taking **tombstone** advertisements in the financial pages, particularly (in Britain) in the *Financial Times* and the magazine *Euromoney*. These advertisements announce that they appear 'as a matter of record only' (in other words they are not a solicitation to buy securities) and give the name of the borrower and brief details of the loan facility or bond issue arranged plus the names of the participating banks. The lead bank or banks which put the deal together appear at the head of the list and the remainder are normally listed in alphabetical order. The distinctive layout of these advertisements makes it clear why the term 'tombstone' is appropriate.

Press coverage

Domestic stockmarkets are usually hot on information and the press automatically receives details of most issues. The international market is rather different. The deals are between issuers and banks, rather than direct with the public, even though the public may end up owning the securities that are offered. There is no central stock exchange to impose disclosure rules. Details of a deal are frequently only publicized outside the market (see **tombstones**, above) well after it has taken place. Therefore, much of the information on what is happening in this mammoth market has to be picked up by specialist journalists with close contacts among the participating banks, who sniff out the rumours of a forthcoming deal.

The *Financial Times* publishes a table of international bond prices in its 'International capital markets' section from Tuesday to Friday and a shorter table of recent issues on Monday. In the larger table, bonds are broken down between **straights**, **floating rate notes** and **convertible bonds** and the straights are further broken down according to the main currencies of issue. There is also comment on major issues and, on a Monday, some background coverage of events in the international market. Other serious dailies carry less frequent notes on the euromarkets.

The monthly magazine *Euromoney* was set up specifically to cover the international capital market. Weekly news of new offerings, syndicated loan facilities and the rest appears in *International Financing Review*, aimed strictly at the financial community. And a variety of euromarket newsletters and news services are also aimed mainly at the market professionals.

18

Financial derivatives and commodities

Every financial market involves risk for the market user, but there are some markets whose main function is the **redistribution of risk**. On the one hand, they are the riskiest markets of all. On the other, they are markets in which risks can be reduced or eliminated. These are the **options** and **futures** markets, which come under the general heading of markets in **derivative products** or **derivatives**. These markets are not the only places where derivative products are bought and sold. We saw earlier that the banks undertake large volumes of 'over-the-counter' derivatives business direct with their customers in products such as swaps and interest rate caps (see Chapters 14, 15 and 17). But it is the public derivatives markets that are most frequently reported in the press.

The customers who use these markets fall into two main categories: those who want to **hedge** (guard against) a risk to which they are exposed in the normal course of their business. And those who are prepared to accept a high risk in return for the possibility of large rewards: the **traders** or **speculators**.

Following the collapse in February 1995 of the City of London's oldest merchant bank, **Barings**, as a result of losses in the derivatives markets, awareness of derivatives has spread far beyond the readers of the financial pages. But judging from much of the press and television reporting at the time, there is considerable confusion as to what derivatives are. Yet the principle behind derivative products is a very old one. All that is new is the recent explosive growth in the derivative markets and in the range of products that are dealt in them. So let us start from basic principles.

First, why the term 'derivatives'? Answer: because they are financial products derived from some other existing product. Shares, bonds, currencies and commodities such as cocoa or zinc are all existing products. There are markets in which they can be bought and sold. It is not too difficult to understand what they are.

And today there are derivatives based on these existing products. The derivatives give the right (and perhaps the obligation) to buy or sell a quantity of one of these existing products at some point in the future. Or to benefit in some other way from a rise or fall in the price of one of these existing products.

The betting side of derivatives

Perhaps the best approach is to look at derivatives in terms of a bet. Suppose you think that share prices are going to rise. You could, of course, buy shares to make a profit from the rise that you think is coming. But you would need quite a lot of cash for a worthwhile investment. Alternatively, you could find somebody who is prepared to bet against your view of the market: somebody who does not think that the market will rise as fast as you do or who thinks it is going to fall. So you agree with this person that he will pay you £1 for every percentage point by which the generally-accepted stockmarket index rises above an agreed starting point within, say, three months. The other side of the coin is that you agree to pay him £1 for every percentage point by which the stockmarket index might fall below an agreed starting point.

In practice of course, you would probably be betting much larger amounts: perhaps £10,000 for every percentage point by which the index rises or falls. But the attraction of the system is that you do not have to put up much cash at the outset when you make your bet. You will be required to pay a small deposit or **margin** for safety, but if the bet goes against you and the market starts moving in the opposite way to that you had expected, you might be required to provide considerably more cash or else cancel your bet and accept your losses to date. Equally, if the bet is going your way you could decide to take your profits at any time within the three months by cancelling it.

What we have described here is not the way the **futures markets** work in practice. The mechanics are rather different. But the principle and the effect are much as described in our example. There is an opportunity to make or lose very large sums of money very quickly for a relatively modest initial cash outlay. The same principle underlies many of the **over-the-counter** or **OTC** derivative products that are sold by banks rather than traded in a market.

Now take a different approach. Again, you want to take a bet on your belief that share prices will rise. You think that there is a good chance that the stockmarket index will rise by 10 per cent within three months. Suppose the present level of the index is 100. You bet somebody £1 that the index will rise above 104 within three months. For every percentage point that it rises above 104, he will pay you 50p. So if it rises to 110 as you expect, you will collect £3 (50p multiplied by 6) in return for your £1 stake: a £2 profit or a 200 per cent return on your £1 outlay. If you are wrong and the index does not rise above 104, you will have lost your £1 stake money. But that is all that you will have lost.

What we have just described is the principle behind an **option**. Again, the mechanics of a real options market are a little different and the sums involved are usually much larger. But there is an important difference to note between futures and options. In a futures market you can end up losing a great deal more than your original cash stake, as merchant bank Barings found out. But in an options market a buyer of options knows that his loss is limited to his original stake. In our example, the maximum loss is £1 (the potential losses for the person who creates or **writes** the option that you buy can, of course, be much larger).

The insurance aspect

We have also talked throughout in terms of a 'bet', and the options and futures markets can indeed be used for wild betting. But in many circumstances it would be more accurate to talk of our 'bet' as an 'insurance policy'. Suppose our investor is an institution that knows that it will have £5m to invest in shares in three months' time. It thinks that the market is going to rise and there is a risk that it will have to pay a lot more for the shares by the time it has the money available. For a relatively modest outlay today it could buy options on the stockmarket index. If share prices do rise, it will have to pay more for its shares when the £5m is available. But it will have made a profit on its options that it can offset against this higher cost. The stake money spent on buying the options has served as an **insurance premium**. The futures markets can be used to insure against future price movements in the same way.

How forward markets evolved

If the principles behind futures and options are relatively simple, the mechanics are inevitably more complex. Our best starting point is the **forward** commodity markets where the techniques evolved.

To focus on the essential elements rather than the detail of any particular derivative, we will invent a physical product –

LIFFE EQUITY OPTIONS

Option		Calls Jul	Oct	Jan	Puts Jul	Oct	Jan	Option		Calls Aug	Nov	Feb	Puts Aug	Nov	Feb
Allied Domecq	500	33½	45½	53½	5	9½	16½	GEC	300	22	24½	28	5½	8½	12½
(*524)	550	7	18½	27	29	33½	40½	(*317)	330	5	9½	13½	23	25	29
Argyll	330	8	16½	23½	14	19	23½	Hanson	220	20	22½	24½	1½	4½	7
(*331)	360	1	6½	12½	38½	40½	43	(*239)	240	7½	11	13	8½	13½	16
ASDA	80	6	8	9½	2	4	5	Lasmo	160	13	17½	22	4½	6½	8½
(*84)	90	1½	3½	5	7½	9	10	(*166)	180	4	9	13	16	17½	19
Brit Airways	390	24½	31	38½	6½	12	16½	Lucas Inds	180	16½	20½	23	4	9	11½
(*412)	420	6	16	23½	22½	27½	31½	(*190)	200	6	10½	13½	14	19½	22
SmKl Bchm A	500	18	30½	39½	12	20½	26	P & O	600	30	39	49	12½	25	29
(*501)	550	2½	11½	19	49	52	57½	(*610)	650	9	17	26	42½	55½	58
Boots	500	23	33	40½	9	13	21	Pilkington	180	8	13½	17½	6	9	10½
(*519)	550	4½	11	18	43½	44½	49½	(*183)	200	1½	5½	9	19½	21½	22½
BP	420	31½	40	46	3½	8	11	Prudential	330	24	30	35½	6	11½	13½
(*445)	460	7	17½	24½	19	25½	29	(*343)	360	8½	15	20½	21	27	28½
British Steel	160	18½	20½	22½	1	3	5½	RTZ	800	35½	50	66	18½	30	37
(*177)	180	4	8½	11½	8½	11½	14	(*807)	850	13	27	42	48	57½	63½
Bass	550	40	53½	62½	4½	10	18½	Redland	420	27½	36½	44½	8½	17½	20
(*589)	600	10	24½	34½	25½	32	42	(*432)	460	9	17½	25½	31	38½	41
Cable & Wire	390	26	38	45	6	12½	18	Royal Insce	330	15½	23½	32	10½	18	22½
(*413)	420	10	22	29½	20½	26½	32½	(*334)	360	4½	11	19	29½	36	39½
Courtaulds	460	22	34½	43	9½	17½	20½	Tesco	280	18½	24½	29½	5	8	10½
(*480)	500	4½	16	24½	34½	40½	42½	(*290)	300	7	14	19	14½	17½	20
Comm Union	600	24½	37½	49½	14	27	31½	Vodafone	200	13	19	23½	7	10	13
(*607)	650	7	17	27½	45½	58	61	(*206)	220	4½	9½	14½	18½	21	24
								Williams	330	18	23	29½	6½	11½	13½
								(*337)	360	5	9½	15½	24½	29	30½

Table 18.1 How the prices of options on shares are reported.
Source: *Financial Times*.

call it 'commoditum' – and imagine it is a relatively common metal used in many manufacturing processes.

There is a free market in which commoditum can be bought and sold. In the usual way, the price of commoditum will rise or fall depending on the balance between buyers and sellers in this market, and it can fluctuate quite widely. The mining companies that produce commoditum obviously want as high a price as possible for their product. Conversely, the manufacturers who use commoditum in their products want to buy it as cheaply as possible. But both producers and users of commoditum may have one clear interest in common: there are times when both of them will want to reduce the uncertainty as to price. The producer cannot plan his production of commoditum efficiently if he does not know whether he will get £500 or £1,500 per ton when he has stocks ready to sell in six months. The manufacturers who use commoditum in their products cannot budget efficiently if they do not know whether they will have to pay £500 or £1,500 per ton when they next need to restock on commoditum in six months.

So it could pay both sides to reduce or eliminate the uncertainty. How can they do this? One way would be for the producer and the manufacturer to agree today the price at which the one will supply and the other will buy commoditum in six months' time. Suppose today's price for commoditum for immediate delivery (technically, the **spot price**) is £1,000 per ton. Both sides think that the price is more likely to rise than to fall over the coming six months, though the possibility of a fall cannot be discounted. And after much haggling, they eventually compromise on a price of £1,100 per ton for the commoditum to be delivered in six months. The producer commits himself to selling 20 tons at £1,100 per ton in six months and the manufacturer commits himself to buying 20 tons at £1,100 per ton in six months.

Who wins and who loses from this arrangement depends on what actually happens to the price of commoditum in the market over this six months. If the price for immediate delivery has fallen to £900 per ton by the end of six months, the manufacturer will find himself paying £1,100 per ton for something he could have bought in the market at £900 and he will have lost. The producer, on the other hand will have gained. If the spot commoditum price is £1,400 per ton after six months, the producer will have lost by agreeing in advance to deliver at only £1,100 per ton and the manufacturer will have saved himself a lot of money.

However, both sides to the transaction will have removed uncertainty. They will have had a known price on which to base their planning. And it was to provide this certainty that the **forward** markets evolved. A forward market is one where buyers and sellers can establish a price for a product to be delivered at a specific date in the future. We took as our example a transaction in commoditum to be delivered in six months. But it could equally well have been commoditum for delivery in three months or nine months. Thus, in these forward markets, a range of prices will be quoted. We might talk of the price for 'three months' commoditum' (commoditum for delivery in three months), 'six months' commoditum', 'nine months' commoditum' and so on. And we also assumed a single transaction between one commoditum producer and one buyer. In practice, there will be a number of people prepared to offer commoditum for delivery in six months and a number of potential buyers of commoditum for delivery in six months. The price of 'six months' commoditum' will reflect the views of all these potential sellers and buyers.

Into the futures markets

This principle of buying and selling for future delivery has characterized the markets in physical commodities – mainly metals and staple foodstuffs – for generations. It has also been a feature of the foreign exchange market, where prices can be agreed today for foreign currencies that are to be delivered in the future (effectively the parties thus 'lock into' a known exchange rate). But all of this still seems some way removed from the forces that destroyed the Barings merchant bank in 1995.

To understand this, we have to follow the evolution of the markets a stage further. If **forward** markets are a very old concept, **futures** markets are a somewhat more recent one, though the underlying principles are very similar. In the forward markets, buyers and sellers can agree the price for a product to be delivered at any point in the future. It could be for delivery in two-and-a-half months or for delivery in thirty weeks. In futures markets, the agreements are standardized. Suppose we are looking at a market in commoditum futures from the standpoint of a date early in April. We might see that you can buy or sell a **contract** for delivery of commoditum in May, July, September, November or in January of the following year.

Not only the delivery dates are standardized. So are the terms and conditions of the contract. The standard contracts are, let us suppose, for delivery of ten tons of commoditum on one of the dates we have mentioned. The contracts relate to commoditum of a standard quality and purity. Thus, somebody who buys one commoditum contract for September delivery is, in theory, agreeing to take delivery of ten tons of commoditum on a specified date in September. The seller of a September commoditum contract is, again in theory, agreeing to deliver ten tons of the standard grade commoditum on the specified date in September.

How is the price established? Again, it is by the interplay of buyers and sellers in the market, but the mechanics are a little different from the simple forward market. In our hypothetical futures market, participants can buy and sell the September commoditum contract (and, of course, the May commoditum contract, the July contract and all the rest). The price of a September commoditum contract at any given time will thus reflect the balance between buyers and sellers of that particular contract at the time. If, subsequently, more buyers emerge, the price is likely to go up. If more sellers emerge, it will probably go down.

Let us suppose, as with our forward market example, that we are looking at the position from a standpoint at the beginning of April and that the spot price of commoditum at that point is again £1,000 per ton. A contract for immediate delivery of ten tons of commoditum would thus have a value of £10,000 at that point. And let us assume that a contract for delivery in September stands in the market at a price of £11,000. Anybody who buys the September commoditum contract is thus in theory agreeing a price of £11,000 for ten tons of commoditum to be delivered in September. Anybody who sells the September commoditum contract is in theory agreeing a price of £11,000 for the obligation to supply ten tons of commoditum in September.

The important point to remember is that the September commoditum contract is itself a form of security that can be bought and sold in a market. It is not the same thing as the commoditum metal itself. But it is a **derivative** of commoditum whose market price at any given time will be largely influenced by buyers' and sellers' views of the outlook for the commoditum price. Once you grasp this fact, you can see how the principle can be be extended to other types of product. Why not have a futures contract for delivery of a nominal £50,000-worth of a standard type of government bond in September? Or a basket of shares in companies? Or a standard amount of a foreign currency: German marks, for example?

In practice, this is what has happened. **Financial futures** markets in a whole range of financial products have sprung up and expanded enormously in recent years. They are markets which the participants can use effectively to fix the price they will pay or receive for bonds, shares and currencies in the future. As such, they can be used to offset many of the financial risks that crop up inevitably in the course of business. But they can also be used for gambling on a massive scale. We are getting closer to the events that brought down the Barings merchant bank in 1995. But before turning to financial futures, there are a few further fundamental concepts that we can illustrate more easily with our example of commoditum futures.

Where the dangers begin

First, why should a market in derivatives be any more dangerous than a market in the underlying products? Why should it be more dangerous to buy commoditum futures than the commoditum metal itself? Or government bond futures rather than investing in government bonds? The answer is that it need not be more dangerous, but that it very often is. And the main reason is the **gearing** (or **leverage** in the American terminology) built into futures markets.

Let us go back to our September commoditum futures contract. The contract, remember, is for ten tons of commoditum to be delivered in September. And, as of the beginning of April, the price of this contract in the market is £11,000. The vital point, however, is that a buyer of this contract does not have to put up £11,000 when he purchases it. At that stage he only has to put up a relatively small deposit or **margin**. It might be 10 per cent of the value of the contract. In financial futures markets it might be as low as 1 per cent (sellers of contracts, incidentally, will also have to provide a margin).

UK

■ NOTIONAL UK GILT FUTURES (LIFFE)* £50,000 32nds of 100%

	Open	Sett price	Change	High	Low	Est. vol	Open int.
Jun	107-21	107-21	+0-11	108-05	107-15	43254	59920
Sep	107-05	107-08	+0-12	107-23	107-03	12682	85575

■ LONG GILT FUTURES OPTIONS (LIFFE) £50,000 64ths of 100%

Strike Price	CALLS				PUTS			
	Jul	Aug	Sep	Dec	Jul	Aug	Sep	Dec
107	1-02	1-29	1-49	2-15	0-50	1-13	1-33	2-27
108	0-36	0-62	1-18	1-50	1-20	1-46	2-02	2-62
109	0-18	0-39	0-57	1-26	2-02	2-23	2-41	3-38

Est. vol. total, Calls 3990 Puts 2550. Previous day's open int., Calls 24258 Puts 27072

Table 18.2 The Liffe gilt futures contract, and options on the futures. Source: *Financial Times*.

For our example we will stick with 10 per cent. The bulk of the contract price does not become due until the contract matures (in September, in our example). So our buyer of one contract has to put up £1,100 of initial margin. In return, he is exposed to the profit or loss on £11,000-worth of commoditum. Suppose by September the price of commoditum for immediate delivery has risen to £1,400 per ton. The contract for September delivery of ten tons of the metal is now worth £14,000. Our buyer of the contract has made a profit of £3,000 (the £14,000 current value of the contract less the £11,000 he originally agreed to pay for it). But the startling point is that he has made this profit on a cash outlay of only £1,100: the initial margin that he had to provide. His return on this cash outlay is thus about 273 per cent.

In this case everything went well. But what if the commoditum price began falling shortly after he bought the September contract for £11,000 in April? Suppose the price of the September contract was down to £9,900 by early June. On paper, he has a loss of £1,100. This has completely wiped out the initial £1,100 deposit or margin that he provided, and he will have been required to provide further margin – another £1,000, say – to top up his margin after the paper losses. If he could not or did not meet this **margin call** (provide the further cash margin), the exchange would simply have **closed him out**. In other words, his contract would effectively have been cancelled by the exchange and his paper losses would have become real ones. This is why exchanges always insist on a margin and insist that it is kept topped up. It is to ensure that the investor or speculator has always provided a sufficient safety cushion to cover any losses.

In our example, the purchaser of the September commoditum contract might have taken the view that the price fall in June was just a temporary blip and that the price would rise again by September to give him his expected profit. In this case he would have wanted to provide the further margin to 'stay in the game'. But note that futures markets have an element of a poker game. You may be pretty confident that you have a winning hand. But unless you have a big enough cash stake to be able to stay in the game, you could still lose.

Taking profits and losses

Now, our example so far has assumed that the buyer of the September commoditum contract had intended to hold it until it became due in September. But there is no reason why this should necessarily be the case. If the price of the commoditum contract for September delivery had risen to £13,000 by late July, he might well have decided to take his profit at this point. How would he take his profit? By selling an identical September commoditum contract for £13,000 in late July. His profit then (less expenses, of course) is the £13,000 he receives from selling a contract less the £11,000 he had agreed to pay originally to buy one. But in reality, as we saw, he had never had to put up the full price in cash. What happens in practice is that he simply receives a cheque for his profit and the return of his margin.

Thus, no commoditum has changed hands. There has been no transfer of the physical metal from a seller to a buyer. And this is an aspect that newcomers to the futures markets often find difficult to grasp. In practice, futures markets very rarely result in physical delivery of the underlying product (the **London Metal Exchange** is a little different in this respect). They are a mechanism for determining the price of a product at various delivery dates. They are a mechanism for allowing participants to benefit (or lose) from the rise or fall in the price of an underlying product. But they are not generally markets for distribution of a physical product. Gains or losses are settled in cash.

Betting on a market fall

And the markets can be used equally well to profit from a fall in the value of a product as from a rise. Somebody betting on a fall in the value of commoditum (or a rise less than the market was expecting) would sell a contract rather than buying one. Suppose that in April he sold a September commoditum contract at £11,000. And suppose that the price of this contract then duly fell to £9,000 by, say, July. He could then buy a contract at £9,000 and collect a profit of £2,000.

The point to remember is that the contract is the same, whether you are buying it or selling it. In theory, if you buy you are agreeing to take delivery of ten tons of commoditum in September. If you sell, you are agreeing in theory to deliver ten tons of commoditum in September. In practice, you realize your profit or loss by closing your position: doing the opposite of what you had done at the outset. If you had originally bought a contract, you close the position by selling an identical contract. Thus in theory you had originally agreed to take delivery of ten tons of commoditum and by selling a contract later you agree in theory to deliver ten tons of commoditum. The two obligations cancel each other, so no commoditum needs to change hands. Likewise, if you had sold a contract at the outset, you close the position later by buying a contract.

The move into financial futures

The extension of the futures principle to purely financial products was, perhaps, inevitable. It enables participants to take bets on (or protect themselves against) rises or falls in the value of the underlying products. These products might be government bonds, interest rates, currencies or shares. If the principle of an interest rate future sounds a bit odd, do not worry too much about the detail. In effect, a hypothetical futures contract is constructed, whose spot value rises or falls according to whether the interest rate in question moves down or up (the market price of a contract for future delivery is, of course, determined by buyers and sellers in the normal way).

You will often notice in the financial press that commentators report on what is happening in the futures market as a prelude to what might happen in the **cash** market. Suppose there is some news that might be judged good for gilt-edged stocks (UK government bonds). Speculators who want to profit from a rise in gilt-edged stocks might be inclined to buy gilt-edged futures in the first instance, because they will get a bigger percentage profit from any given price movement than they would by buying the gilt-edged stocks themselves in the stock market (the **cash** market). Thus the price of the gilt-edged futures contract might begin moving up and suggest that the prices of gilt-edged stocks themselves in the cash market might shortly follow suit.

COMMODITIES PRICES

BASE METALS

LONDON METAL EXCHANGE

(Prices from Amalgamated Metal Trading)

■ ALUMINIUM, 99.7 PURITY ($ per tonne)

	Cash	3 mths
Close	1811-12	1831-32
Previous	1798-800	1817-18
High/low	1809/1808	1840/1825
AM Official	1808-9	1828-9
Kerb close		1831-2
Open int.	193,973	
Total daily turnover	47,533	

■ ALUMINIUM ALLOY ($ per tonne)

Close	1645-55	1660-70
Previous	1655-65	1670-75
High/low		1680/1675
AM Official	1660-70	1675-80
Kerb close		1675-85
Open int.	2,494	
Total daily turnover	523	

■ LEAD ($ per tonne)

Close	606.5-607	619-19.5
Previous	604-5	617-18
High/low	608/607.5	621/618
AM Official	608-8.5	621-21.5
Kerb close		617-18
Open int.	31,007	
Total daily turnover	5,273	

·onths pr

Table 18.3 Cash and three-months prices for some of the base metals traded on the LME. Source: *Financial Times.*

How options work

The workings of **options** are probably easier to understand at the outset than those of futures, though in both cases the trading strategies followed by professionals in the market may be very complex. Start with a traditional option on shares. An option in this case is the right to buy or the right to sell a share within a stipulated time period at a price that is fixed when the option is bought. Technically, this is an **American option**, but it is the most common kind in Britain. The so-called **European option** is different in that it may only be exercised on a specific date, rather than at any point up to expiry.

Say that you decide at the beginning of April that the shares of XYZ Holdings are likely to rise sharply within the next month or so. The current price is 100p and you think it might well rise to 130p by the end of June. You could, of course, buy 10,000 of the shares for £10,000, and if you are right your 10,000 shares will be worth £13,000 within three months: a profit of £3,000, or 30 per cent on your outlay. But you need to have £10,000 to do it, and though the value of the XYZ shares is unlikely to fall to nothing, you are in theory putting the whole £10,000 at risk.

Instead, you might consider it was worth paying, say, 10p per share for an option that gave you the right to buy a share in XYZ for 105p at any time over the next three months. If the XYZ share price stays at 100p, the option has no value and you lose the 10p **premium** you paid. But this is the most you can lose. If the share price does rise to 130p, then your option clearly has a value and is worth **exercising**: you have the right to buy for 105p a share that you could resell for 130p.

Suppose you had bought options on 10,000 XYZ shares. The total cost at 10p per share would have been £1,000. If you exercise your option to buy the 10,000 shares at 105p and immediately resell them at 130p, your profit is £13,000 less £10,500. So you make £2,500 but against this you have to offset the £1,000 cost of your options. But this still leaves a profit of £1,500 (before expenses) on an outlay of only £1,000, or a profit of 150 per cent: considerably better than if you had simply bought the shares. The point to note is that options are a very **highly-geared investment**. A comparatively small movement in the share price results in a proportionately far larger movement in the value of the option.

Writing options

But there is another side to the bargain. Who was prepared to agree to sell XYZ shares at 105p if you exercised your option? It was probably an owner of XYZ shares who took a different view from you of what the price was likely to do. He took the view that XYZ shares were fairly fully valued at 100p and that he would be prepared to sell at this price or a little above. But instead of selling at 100p today, he could create or **write** an option and charge 10p for it: the option you bought.

If the price of the shares failed to reach 105p, the option would not be exercised and he would hang on to his shares; but he would have an extra 10p per share in the kitty to set against the fall in the share price. If the price rose above 105p and the option was exercised, he would be obliged to part with his XYZ shares at 105p. But he would really be getting 115p, because he has the 10p premium as well. So by getting 10p for the option he has reduced by 10p his possible paper loss if the XYZ share price falls. He has also limited his possible profit if the XYZ price rises, because the maximum he gets is 115p: 105p for the share and 10p for the option. He has written options as a way of hedging his risk: limiting his possible loss but also restricting his possible profit.

Remember that in futures you buy a contract if you are betting on a price rise and you sell a contract if you are betting on a fall. The contract itself is the same in either case. With options, too, you can bet on rising or on falling prices. But in both cases you buy an option: it is the option itself that is different. If you are **bullish** you buy a **call option** which gives you the right to buy shares at a pre-determined price. If you are **bearish**, you buy a **put option** which gives you the right to sell shares at a pre-determined price.

The traditional options to buy or sell shares that we have been describing so far are arranged with one of the stockbrokers specalizing in this business. You can take out call or put options, or **double** options which give you the right to buy or sell.

The traded options market

More prominent today is the London market in **traded options**, now operated by Liffe (see below). The principle of traded options is clear enough if we go back to the example of XYZ Co. You paid 10p for the right to buy an XYZ share at 105p within the next three months. You exercised the option if the XYZ price rose above 105p. If it did not rise, the option **expired** valueless and you lost the whole of your money.

A traded option differs from the traditional type in that you can buy and sell the option itself, much as if it were a share. Again, it has become a tradable derivative product. Suppose after a month the XYZ share price rose from 100p to 110p. The option for which you paid 10p now has **intrinsic value**, because it gives you the right to buy a share at a price (105p) below its current value (110p). So the option itself is now almost certainly worth more than the 10p you paid for it. Reflecting the rise in the share price, it might now be worth, say, 15p. So you could sell it at this point and take your profit without needing to exercise it. If the XYZ share price had fallen, the value of the option would also have fallen, but you would have had the chance of selling and recouping some of your outlay.

In and out of the money

The 10p you paid originally for your XYZ traded option was all hope value or **time value**. There was no intrinsic value initially in an option giving the right to buy a share at 105p (the **exercise price**) when the share price was 100p. In the market jargon, the option was **out of the money**. If, on the other hand, it had been a call option to buy an XYZ share at 105p when the share price was 110p, it would have been **in the money** – it would already have had intrinsic value. An option to buy a share at 105p when the share price is 105p is **at the money** – exercise price and market price of the shares are the same. With put options this works the other way round; the option is in the money when the market price is below the exercise price.

The time value in an option erodes throughout its life. It may be worth paying 10p for the chance that a share price will rise by the required amount some time in the next three months. It would probably not be worth paying the same if the option only had a week to run. So the market price of an option will usually drop gradually with the passage of time unless the market price of the underlying share moves the right way (up for a call option and down for a put).

Hedgers and speculators

The examples that are usually quoted of futures and options market techniques will tend to stress the **hedging** nature of the operation: using these markets to protect against an existing business risk. But where should we draw the dividing line between hedgers and speculators?

Take the futures markets first. In our example of commoditum futures, both parties to the transaction had a position to hedge. The producer was going to have commoditum to sell and wanted to lock into a known price. The manufacturer was going to have to buy commoditum and wanted to lock into a known price. Both were hedging a known risk. If the commoditum price rose, the manufacturer would pay more for his product but he would have a profit on the futures contract he had bought to compensate him. If it fell, the producer would be offsetting a profit from the futures contract he had sold against the lower price he received from selling his physical commoditum.

But our manufacturer could equally well have bought his commoditum futures contract from a speculator rather than a producer. This speculator might never have handled commoditum in his life. He might not even know what it looked like. No matter; he follows the movements of the commoditum market and, because he thinks the price is going to fall, he sells a contract. Since he has no commoditum to sell, his position is unhedged. If he loses on the futures contract, he will not have profits on the physical metal to offset against his losses. In practice, there are various ways he might hedge his position to some degree in the futures market, but we will ignore these. He is taking a very big risk.

If he sold the September contract at £11,000 and the price fell to £9,000 by September, well and good. He has made £2,000 profit on a small outlay. But what if an explosion puts the world's biggest commoditum mine out of action and serious shortages of the metal threaten? The price could rocket. Suppose the price of the September contract more

SOFTS

■ COCOA LCE (£/tonne)

	Sett price	Day's change	High	Low	Open Int	Vol
May	932	-1	938	932	928	517
Jul	941	-3	949	939	29,298	2,113
Sep	962	-2	969	959	23,140	774
Dec	982	-3	990	980	23,463	548
Mar	1004	-3	1009	1001	26,632	283
May	1017	-3	-	-	6,421	257
Total					121,906	4,566

Table 18.4 Prices of cocoa contracts for different delivery dates on the London Commodity Exchange. Source: *Financial Times*.

than doubles to £24,000. He will have to buy a contract at £24,000 to satisfy his obligation to deliver at £11,000: a £13,000 loss. And he has no protection from ownership of stocks of physical commoditum, which would have risen massively in value.

Straight bets of this kind appear to have been behind the collapse of the **Barings** merchant bank in early 1995. In this case the bank's trading operation in Singapore was betting on a rise, not on a fall. So it was buying contracts rather than selling them. It was taking the bets on its own account: so-called **proprietary trading**. And the main 'product' on which it was betting was a Tokyo stockmarket index. It bought futures contracts whose value would rise if the Nikkei index of Japanese shares rose. Instead, pushed partly by the Kobe earthquake, it dropped like a stone. The bets were not taken to hedge an existing holding of Japanese shares. Since the value of the shares represented by the futures contracts was many billions of pounds, it was unlikely that they could have been. Estimates of the bank's losses on futures contracts ranged from £800m upwards and Barings was wiped out as an independent entity.

Naked option writing

While we have seen that the buyer of an option on shares – unlike the buyer of a futures contract – at least knows what his maximum loss will be, even this market can offer massive losses for the **writer** or creator of options. Again, selling options on shares that you own can be a conservative hedging strategy. But **naked option writing** – selling options when you do not have an existing position to hedge – is a very different matter. Perhaps the most dangerous technique of all is naked writing of put options.

Towards the end of London's stockmarket boom of the 1980s, many small investors were wrongly advised that they could make risk-free money by writing deep out-of-the-money put options on UK shares. In other words, for a premium of a few pence per share they contracted to buy, if required to do so, the underlying shares at a price fixed at a level 25 per cent or more below market prices at the time. The possibility that the market would fall that far was judged so remote as to be negligible. Then came the crash of October 1987 (see Chapter 7b) with shares in Britain falling more than 36 per cent from their peak. The option writers were thus obliged to buy shares at a price way above their market value, landing many of them with losses that far outran their total financial resources. Lesson: unless you are a financial institution with very deep pockets, do not write naked options.

Financial futures markets

The **futures market** most closely related to the securities markets is the **London International Financial Futures and Options Exchange** or **Liffe** (pronounced 'life'). It is the third largest in the world, after the Chicago Board of Trade and the Chicago Mercantile Exchange in the United States. Financial futures are a fast-moving business in every sense. New contracts are introduced quite frequently and dropped if they do not attract the requisite interest. In 1995 Liffe provided a market for futures contracts in **long-dated gilt-edged stocks**, **German**, **Italian** and **Japanese government bonds**, **short-term sterling** and **euro interest rates** and the **FT-SE Index**. In addition it offered options to buy or sell futures contracts and, as we have seen, options on the FT-SE index and individual shares.

The members of Liffe are mainly subsidiaries of financial institutions – banks, discount houses, stockbrokers – plus individual traders or **locals** who trade on their own account. Trading works on the **open outcry** system. Traders yell and signal to each other on the floor, creating bedlam during the busy periods.

Just as commodity futures can be used to hedge an existing risk or to take a straightforward bet, so can financial futures. Each contract is structured differently from the others, but the long gilt contract will illustrate the principle.

The size of this contract is a nominal £50,000 and the price is expressed in terms of a notional 9 per cent long-dated stock. If the price of, say, the June contract were $93^{20}/_{32}$ it would be shown as 93–20. The minimum step by which the price can move (a **tick**) is a 32nd of one per cent. Expressed as a proportion of the £50,000 contract value, this is £15.625. The buyer of a contract is theoretically buying a nominal £50,000 of gilt-edged stock for delivery in the future.

If interest rates fall, the market value of the June contract is likely to rise because gilt-edged stocks will rise in value. If the price rose to 96–18, the investor could sell a contract at 96–18 to cancel the contract he had bought at 93–20. This would represent a profit of 94 ticks or £1,468.75. The initial margin on the long gilt contract is £1,000, so anyone who had bought a contract would have a profit of 147 per cent. Financial futures contracts very rarely result in physical delivery. The purchaser of a contract simply closes his position by selling an identical contract and taking his profit or his loss.

The same principle applies to the contracts in interest rates or the FT-SE equity index. By using futures it is possible to hedge against a rise in interest rates: the value of an interest rate contract falls if interest rates move up, much as with a gilts contract. So you buy a contract if you are betting on a fall in interest rates and sell if you expect a rise. The techniques available to the futures trader can be highly complex. But the most important point in terms of press comment is that price movements in the futures market will sometimes give advance warning of likely price trends in the stockmarket itself (the **cash** market) or in interest rates.

Options traded on Liffe

The market in traded options was taken over from the London Stock Exchange by Liffe and it offers options on the shares of over 70 individual companies, including the major privatization stocks. It also offers options on the **FT-SE 100 Index** (the **Footsie** Index). This is the index of 100 leading shares and the option is a way of betting on the movement of the market as a whole.

For each individual company there are options with different **exercise prices**. The *Financial Times* carries a table of them headed **Liffe equity options**. The exercise price is shown in the column immediately following the company name, and prices are given for call and put options at each price. The idea is to have at least one **out of the money** and one **in the money option** for each company. And at each price there are options with differing lives. They normally run initially for three, six or nine months. Once the life of the three-month option has expired, the six-month option will only have three months' life left, the previous nine-month option will only have six months and a new nine-month option will be created. Options in British Telecom, say, have expiry dates in February, May, August and November – only three being available at one time. Others follow a different cycle to prevent all options having the same expiry dates.

The price quoted is the middle price for an option on a single share, but deals are in **contracts** which normally consist of options on 1,000 shares. Under the name of the company is shown the previous day's price for the shares themselves.

Because of the gearing, price swings in traded options can be very large and can happen very fast. There are theoretical models for calculating what the price of an option should be relative to the underlying share price, and professionals deal actively to take advantage of small anomalies. Activity is sometimes very heavy in options of companies in the news – particularly takeover candidates. The *Financial Times* comments on equity options and futures market activity under the heading **Equity futures and options trading**.

Commodity markets

London's main commodity markets divide between the **metals** and the **soft** (foodstuff) commodities. Metals are traded on the **London Metal Exchange (LME)** and the soft commmodities on the **London Commodity Exchange (LCE)**.

Copper, **lead**, **zinc**, **nickel**, **tin**, **aluminium** and **aluminium**

alloy, are traded on the LME, which is the centre of world trading in the non-ferrous metals. Trading is carried out by the **ring-dealing members** who transact their own or their clients' orders on an **open outcry** basis in trading sessions that last five minutes for each metal and take place four times a day. The official price for the metal for the day is the price ruling at the end of the session, though there is also extensive dealing on the telephone before and after the official sessions.

In addition to the ring-dealing members, there are **commission houses** which offer a brokerage service to would-be investors or speculators in commodities. They channel their business through a ring-dealing member (in some cases they may own one).

Trading on the LME is a mix of **physical** and **futures** business. A price is established for each metal for immediate delivery (the **cash** price or **spot** price) and also a price for delivery in three months. Prices may also be agreed for any period between, and nowadays it is also possible to deal up to 21 months ahead. The futures price is for a standard contract (25 tonnes in the case of copper) of metal of a defined grade and there are also official LME traded options on futures contracts. The *Financial Times* shows both the cash and three months prices for the LME metals and the movement on the day. Usually the three months price is higher than the cash price (**contango**) because the buyer is avoiding financing costs for three months. **Backwardation** is the situation where the cash price exceeds the three months price.

The London Commodity Exchange offers futures contracts (and options on futures) in **cocoa**, **coffee** and two grades of **sugar**. There are domestic contracts in **potatoes**, **wheat** and **barley**, and the LCE now also operates a **freight futures** contract. The exchange works on an open outcry system, except that there is an automatic trading system for one of the sugar contracts. Prices can move sharply on reports or rumours of glut or crop failure in the producer countries. The **International Petroleum Exchange (IPE)**, which is a separate organisation but located in the same building, offers futures contracts and options in various petroleum products, of which the main ones are **Brent crude** and **gas oil**.

The **Baltic Exchange** is the traditional market for negotiation of shipping freight, though the freight futures contract has now moved to the LCE.

19

Insurance and the troubles at Lloyd's

Lloyd's of London, the international insurance market, is one of the oldest of the City's institutions. In the past it was a major contributor to Britain's balance of payments but big losses announced in the first half of the 1990s have somewhat changed that. It attracts a disproportionate amount of press coverage nowadays because of the dramatic nature of the problems it has had to contend with. And the first half of 1995 saw further startling developments.

If we go back 25 years, Lloyd's traditionally minded its own business and expected the world outside to do likewise. The interest the press began to take in Lloyd's in the late 1970s was viewed initially as an impertinent intrusion and an unwarranted attack on one of the very pillars of City life. Lloyd's was beyond reproach, particularly from outsiders. But this attitude proved impossible to sustain as news of a variety of scandals percolated through Lloyd's walls and led to heated debate in parliament as well as the press. The debate has intensified in the 1990s for one overriding reason. It no longer merely concerned Lloyd's internal customs and practices. It was about the financial survival of Lloyd's as an institution.

At the heart of the scandals that first attracted the press's attention to Lloyd's was strong evidence that some at least of the market's professionals were enriching themselves at the expense of the outside **names** – the non-working 'investors' whose wealth allowed the market to function. And in a few cases this process constituted outright theft rather than merely time-hallowed market custom and practice. Be that as it may, some of the trading practices in the Lloyd's market have led to massive losses for the investors. And in the 1990s we have had the unedifying spectacle of many of these investors taking action in the courts to recover money from Lloyd's insiders whose incompetence or negligence, they maintained, was responsible for their losses. In the cases that had come to court by the middle of the 1990s the courts were generally responsive to their view.

Underwriting profits and investment income

In outline, the business of insurance is not unduly complicated. We're talking here about **general insurance** – **underwriting** the risk of damage or destruction to ships, aircraft, property and so on – rather than **life assurance**, which is a different kind of business. The insurer charges a **premium** commensurate with his view of the risk he is underwriting, and hopes that all the premiums he receives will exceed all the **claims** he has to pay out. If he is right, he makes an **underwriting profit**. But he does not rely on the **premium income** alone. The money he receives as premiums is earning interest until it has to be paid out in claims, so in addition he is receiving an **investment income** which can help to offset any losses he makes on the underwriting side. Insurance claims often take a number of years to finalize, so he may have use of the money for some considerable time (business where claims may arise a long time after the insurance was arranged is known as **long-tail business**).

Where an insurer is worried by the size of a risk he is underwriting, he can lay off part of his bet (rather like a bookie) by **reinsuring** it with another insurer. Thus the original insurer may say 'I'll bear the first £10m of any loss, the **reinsurer** will take the next £10m, and I'll accept any excess over that'. Part of the original premium obviously has to be handed over to the reinsurer. Many large risks will also be split with a number of insurers from the outset, each one taking a portion of the liability.

The principle is much the same whether the original insurer is a company or a Lloyd's **syndicate**. The greater part of insurance business in the UK is undertaken by insurance companies, particularly the more standard types of business such as household and car insurance. Lloyd's is best known for marine insurance and for insuring the more unusual types of risk.

How names' wealth is put to work

An insurance company relies on the premiums plus the company's own funds to cover the risks it underwrites (though it may also reinsure part of its risk). Lloyd's, though its members also use reinsurance, has traditionally worked on a different principle. This principle is now undergoing some changes, but they will be easier to appreciate if we deal with the traditional pattern first.

For its 1995 underwriting year, Lloyd's had something under 3,000 working members who underwrite the business (accept the insurance risks brought to them) and some 12,000 non-working members who pledge their wealth to meet possible losses. Confusingly, the non-working members are also underwriters and both types of member who put their wealth at risk are known as **names**. The numbers used to be more than double these figures, but many who are still members of Lloyd's have dropped out from underwriting new business. In some cases this is because earlier losses have not left them with the wealth to continue. In others it is because the scale of the losses suffered by the market has simply frightened them off.

The names do not have to put up vast amounts of money. Instead, they stand surety for the risks that are underwritten at Lloyd's. In other words, they pledge the whole of their wealth to meet claims, should this be necessary. They hope that premiums and investment income will outweigh claims and that they will never have to stump up. But if the worst comes to the worst, they might have to sell virtually everything they own to meet losses – though it is possible to insure against this risk, too.

The beauty of the system, when all goes according to plan, is that wealth can be made to work twice over, and sometimes more. To become a name the individual has to be able to show a minimum amount of wealth (excluding his home and certain other assets): £250,000 at the time of writing. But the amounts he has to hand over in cash are very much smaller. So his £250,000 or more of wealth can be, say, invested in stocks and shares and earning a return for its owner. At the same time it is providing the necessary back-up for the insurance risks that are being underwritten.

There were substantial tax advantages in the past, too. Some of the funds used in the insurance market could be compounding up interest after tax at a much lower rate than the individual might have to pay. The reduction in the top rate of income tax to 40 per cent in the 1988 Budget somewhat eroded the tax advantages of being a Lloyd's name. The increase in wealth required (it was previously £100,000) discouraged others. But the losses have been the main factor.

The syndicate structure

In theory, all members of Lloyd's trade as individuals. In practice they are grouped into **syndicates** – there used to be more than 400 of them, now there are under 200 – and one name may spread his risk by belonging to a number of syndicates. A **working underwriter**, who is a Lloyd's profesional, accepts insurance risks on behalf of the syndicate. The business will be brought to him by a **Lloyd's broker**, who represents the client seeking insurance and whose duty is to arrange it on the best terms. The name is introduced to his syndicate or syndicates by a **members' agent** who, in theory at least, looks after his interests. A **managing agent** looks after the organizational side of the syndicate's business. **Underwriting agencies** sometimes combine managing agents and members' agents in one organization. Accounts are drawn up three years after the year to which they relate, because of the length of time required for claims to be assessed. Thus, the results for the 1992 underwriting year were announced in May 1995.

Scandals and regulation

Lloyd's regulates its own affairs under an Act of Parliament. It did not initially come within the scope of the Financial Services Act (see Chapter 22), though by 1995 there were strong pressures for external regulation (see below). The most recent legislation is the Lloyd's Act 1982, introduced in response to the scandals of the late 1970s and early 1980s. The governing **council of Lloyd's** was to include non-working members and nominated members from outside, and a new office of Chief Executive was created (the incumbent to be approved by the Bank of England). Previously, many large Lloyd's brokers (with their duty to the client) had also owned **underwriting agencies** (with a responsibility to members of the syndicates they managed). The brokers were required to dispose of such interests to avoid the obvious **conflicts of interest**. And greater disclosure of outside interests was required of working members.

The scandals these measures were intended to deal with fell into several categories. Brokers were accused of excessive pressure on syndicates to settle dubious claims. Some underwriting agents took on more business than the syndicate was entitled to underwrite, thus exposing it to excessive losses. Reinsurance was arranged with **offshore companies** in which working underwriters had interests they had not declared to the names and which could be highly profitable. There were suspicions of **baby syndicates**, whose members were Lloyd's professionals, to which the most profitable business might be channelled. And many underwriting agents managed **parallel syndicates** – two syndicates alongside each other, with a risk that one might be favoured at the expense of the other.

There were also cases of taking on business which was suspected to be fraudulent, and still worse cases of straightforward theft of names' money. The problem for names who lost heavily in some of these scandals was in establishing that they had suffered as a result of breaches of Lloyd's rules or fraud (in which case they might be entitled to compensation from Lloyd's) rather than poor underwriting alone (in which case they would have to bear the losses unless they successfully pursued a claim for negligence through the courts). In the biggest of these affairs of the time – the case of the PCW syndicates – names were faced with losses running into the hundreds of millions of pounds. But worse was to come.

In the late 1980s, Lloyd's sought to maintain that the scandals that rumbled on related to events that took place before 1982, and that its regulatory house was now in much better order. Sir Patrick Neill, reporting early in 1987 on regulation at Lloyd's, recognized that progress had been made but suggested that there was still a great deal to do and that the market was still weighted far too heavily in favour of working members. His recommendations included a call for more outside nominated members on the council and an **Ombudsman** to whom names could appeal. Both of these measures were implemented, though did not entirely drown the calls to bring Lloyd's within the scope of the Financial Services Act.

Then came the cataclysm. For its underwriting years 1988 to 1992, Lloyd's syndicates clocked up losses of over £8 billion. These were not evenly spread throughout the market. Some syndicates continued profitable or made modest losses. But others clocked up losses running into the hundreds of millions of pounds. Far from receiving cheques from Lloyd's, many names found Lloyd's was demanding cheques to the value of everything they owned (and more) to meet the losses. Family fortunes were wiped out, homes that had been in the family for generations had to be sold (estate agents recognized this 'Lloyd's effect' at the top end of their business). There were suicides among names attributed to their Lloyd's losses. And some names decided that the time had come to band together and fight back through the courts. How had the debacle occurred?

Reinsurance to close

For the answer, we have to delve a little deeper into the syndicate system. Theoretically, a syndicate exists for one underwriting year. Names who are members can decide to drop out at the end of that year and new names can come in for the next underwriting year. But a name who drops out is not shot of the syndicate. No new business will be underwritten on his behalf after he has left. But he remains liable for his share of losses arising from the years for which he was a member until the books are closed for those years – and this, as we saw, is three years after the event.

Now, even after three years a syndicate cannot be sure that it has met all claims that might arise from business written three years earlier. Suppose we are now in 1994 and the syndicate wants to close its books for the 1991 year. It uses a portion of its 1991 income as a premium to insure against any further residual losses that might arise in respect of the 1991 year. Once the responsibility for any residual risks has been passed on by this **reinsurance to close** process, a line can be drawn under the 1991 results and those who were members of the syndicate for that year will know how much they have made or lost.

Well and good, in normal times. Unfortunately, if a syndicate still faces very large or unquantifiable losses in respect of an earlier year, it may prove impossible to reinsure to close. In that case the year in question – 1991 in our example – remains 'open' well after the normal three years are up and for many years the names who were members of the syndicate in 1991 do not know the full extent of their losses. The number of **open years** has been growing – there are more than 470 – and about 90 relate to the early 1980s.

With whom does a syndicate reinsure to close (reinsure its residual risk in respect of a particular year?). Usually it will be the same syndicate in a later year that picks up the risk in return for a premium. And this has led to the accusation that the membership of some syndicates was deliberately expanded by the recruitment of new names in order to provide cannon fodder to help bear the losses arising from the business of earlier years.

The excess of loss spiral

But there was another form of reinsurance that spelled doom for a number of syndicates: **excess of loss** insurance. As a backstop against **catastrophes**, a syndicate would reinsure with another syndicate against the possibility of losses exceeding a certain unlikely amount. Part of the risk might then be reinsured with a third syndicate, and so on. In this so-called **LMX (London Market Excess of Loss)** spiral, a game of pass-the-parcel was taking place round the market, with the possibility that the original syndicate might even end up taking back part of the risk that it had laid off in the first place. Given the rarity of major catastrophes, this excess of loss insurance was regarded as good business by those who took it on at the time.

But the late 1980s and early 1990s proved a bad time for insurers. Costly catastrophes included the Piper Alpha oil rig explosion in 1988, hurricane Hugo in the following year and the storms of early 1990 in Europe. Since many of the risks had simply been reshuffled round the market, a domino effect resulted, with the problems of one syndicate affecting the next one.

In addition, Lloyd's had suffered in another quarter. There were enormous claims, mainly from the United States and often relating to very old policies, in respect of employers' liability for asbestosis claims and for the costs of cleaning up earlier industrial pollution.

Into the litigation era

Some names on the worst-hit syndicates were cleaned out entirely, others refused to pay, **names' action groups** sprang up and the litigation got under way. The names' action groups sued managing agents for negligent underwriting. The agents themselves were insured up to a point under errors and omissions (O&E) policies, but usually did not have enough cover to meet all claims. In any event, they were probably insured with Lloyd's syndicates, so anything they had to pay out simply increased the pressure on other syndicates in the market. An association of names from the Feltrim syndicates which had suffered losses of over £500m won a case in the High Court against more than 50 Lloyd's professional agencies, alleging incompetent underwriting. But while damages of more than £500m might have resulted, there was considerable doubt as to how much they would receive in practice. The pot of money available within Lloyd's was simply insufficient to meet all justifiable claims from names.

The Lloyd's authorities had attempted to head off litigation, which generally showed the institution in a poor light, and to broker out-of-court settlements between the names and those whom the names held to be negligent. They also proposed a global settlement of some £900m for dissident names, provided partly from Lloyd's central funds and partly by underwriting agencies or their insurers. The names turned it down. They asked for more and they also required protection not only against their past losses but also losses that might arise in the future from past business.

Lloyd's proposed 'ring fencing' pre-1986 liabilities by setting up a company called **Equitas** into which the residual risks of those earlier years could be reinsured, thus drawing a line under names' possible losses. In 1995 the scope of the proposed Equitas company was extended to ring-fence losses up to 1992. The problem, however, was that large premiums would have to be paid by the affected syndicates to Equitas in order for it to take the risk on board. Names who had belonged to profitable syndicates naturally resented ideas of a levy on the market as a whole to meet past losses of poorly-managed syndicates.

Corporate capital makes its debut

Meantime, Lloyd's had implemented a business plan that aimed, inter alia, to introduce **corporate capital** to the market. For the first time corporate bodies were allowed to become syndicate members, though they had to provide a higher proportion of their contribution up-front in cash. A number of stockmarket-listed **Lloyd's investment trusts** also sprang up. These raised money from the public and invested in stockmarket securities like a conventional investment trust. But these investments were used as the wealth-backing for membership of a spread of Lloyd's syndicates.

The insurance cycle

Insurance goes in cycles. When the business looks profitable, competition hots up thus keeping premiums down and business gets less profitable until the industry swings into losses. The competition then abates, premiums are able to increase again and the new business becomes profitable. This process applies to the general insurance companies as well as to Lloyd's, but the Lloyd's losses of the late 1980s and early 1990s were something quite outside the normal **underwriting cycle**. They posed questions as to whether Lloyd's could survive in adequate shape to take full advantage of the upswing in the cycle. And in 1995 various newspapers were raising questions as to whether Lloyd's would be able to survive one of the two annual solvency tests it must undergo, though Lloyd's maintained it would meet the requirements.

Lloyd's plays its final card

In May 1995 the Lloyd's authorities played what might turn out to be their final card. In place of the earlier (and rejected) £900m offer of compensation to names, they came up with a much improved £2.8 billion offer. If names accepted it, they would have to agree to give up litigation. Initial reaction was moderately favourable among some of the action groups, though much detail remained to be worked out as to who would get what. And it was clear that even compensation on this scale would cover only a proportion of disputed losses.

Coincidentally, in the same week in May a committee of Members of Parliament published a report highly critical of Lloyd's and suggested that external regulation of the market was essential if it was to regain its credibility.

At all events, any upswing in the underwriting cycle or proposed compensation plan comes too late for thousands of names who have had to cease underwriting because their assets are wiped out. And a Lloyd's joke doing the rounds in the early 1990s still retained its piquancy at the middle of the decade. Question: How do you make a small fortune at Lloyd's? Answer: Start with a large one.

20

Commercial property and market crashes

Commercial property – office buildings, shops, factories and warehouses – has been one of the major avenues for investment by the **insurance companies** and **pension funds**. It is less popular in the mid-1990s than it once was. But together, these two types of institution still hold properties valued at around £56 billion. There is, however, no central marketplace in commercial property. The 'market' is largely organized by the major firms of **chartered surveyors** or **estate agents**. Among the largest are Jones Lang Wootton, Richard Ellis, Healey & Baker and Hillier Parker. These firms and others like them provide a range of property investment services. They advise on property portfolios, often manage portfolios on behalf of institutions, provide valuations, negotiate lettings, purchases and sales and assist in arranging finance for developments.

There are really two **commercial property markets**. There is the **letting market** in which landlords let buildings to tenants. And there is the **investment market** where completed and revenue-producing buildings are acquired by **financial institutions** as long-term investments. The two markets overlap and increasingly the larger institutions are involved in both aspects. They create investments by undertaking **property developments**, letting the completed buildings and holding on to them for the rent they provide.

Property journalists write about both markets: how rents are moving for particular kinds of property, and the prices investors are prepared to pay for revenue-producing properties.

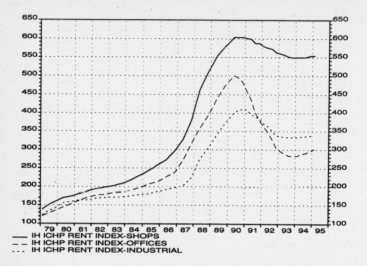

Figure 20.1 How the crash of the early 1990s destroyed the belief that commercial property rents could only rise. Our chart shows the Hillier Parker indices of rental values. Shops (solid line) suffered least badly but rents for office property (broken line) plummeted. Factory and warehouse property (lower dotted line) was in between. Source: *Hillier Parker* and *Datastream International.*

Property as an investment

The commercial property market has always followed a cyclical pattern, but the early 1990s produced the most dramatic bust in living memory, following an over-heated boom in the late 1980s. The values of some City of London offices halved, rental levels and values for most classes of property across the country fell significantly and many of the cherished assumptions of the post-war period were overturned.

By early 1995 it was still far from clear whether property would regain its status as a long-term growth investment. What follows, therefore, is a description of the way commercial property had been regarded until the end of the 1980s – and may again be regarded in the future. We will look later at the causes and implications of the crash of the early 1990s.

For most of the post-war period a commercial property tended to be regarded as a growth investment rather like an ordinary share, though the income comes in the form of **rent** rather than dividend and it requires more management by the investor. However, properties in Britain are often let on **full repairing and insuring leases** which put much of the responsibility for maintenance on the tenant.

Commercial properties are often let on very long **leases** – 99 years used to be common – but nowadays 25 years or less would be the norm and the rent the tenant pays is usually reviewed every five (or even three) years. The owner of the building obviously hopes that the **rental value** of the building (the rent it would fetch if let today in the open market) will rise consistently, but he only collects these increases at three- or five-year intervals when **rent reviews** occur or when the lease comes to an end and is renegotiated.

Properties are normally **valued** as a **multiple** of the rent they produce. Take an office building in London with 10,000 square feet of lettable area and producing a rent of, say, £30 per sq. ft. per year. The total annual income will be £300,000. An investor might be prepared to buy the building at a price which showed him a return of five per cent on his outlay. He is prepared to accept a fairly low initial return because he expects the income to increase in the future, as with an ordinary share.

He is therefore prepared to buy the investment at £6m, which is the price that would show him a five per cent return and is 20 times the rent it produces. This is effectively the 'PE ratio' of the investment, though the property world would talk of buying the building at 20 **years' purchase** of the rent, which means the same thing.

Suppose the first **rent review** is due in five years, and as this time approaches the rental value has risen to £40 per sq. ft. The income from the building if let at its market rent would now be £400,000, though the tenant is still only paying £300,000. But once the rent is reviewed at the end of the fifth year, it jumps to £400,000, which then holds good for the next five years.

Because rent reviews only come at intervals, it is clear that for much of the time the tenant may be paying a rent below the current market value. The rent will **revert** to its market value when the lease runs out and a new one is negotiated or when the rent review in the existing lease occurs. Property journalists thus talk of a landlord expecting large increases in revenue as 'rent reviews and **reversions** occur over the next few years'.

Freeholds and leaseholds

The pattern of property ownership in Britain is complex. The example above is of a **freehold** building, which for most purposes is owned outright by the landlord. But often the interests in the building are split. The original owner of the land may only have granted a lease – for 99 years, say – to the developer who put up the building and who now 'owns' it. In this case the freeholder is the owner of the land, and he charges the developer an annual **ground rent** which used to be a fixed amount but nowadays will probably be adjusted upwards at intervals. The developer becomes the **leaseholder** and his building is **leasehold**. He lets the building to a tenant at a market rent or **rack rent**, and from this he has to pay the ground rent to the freeholder. In practice, ownership of property can be considerably more complex than this with several layers of lease before you get to the tenant who pays the market rent.

Valuation

Valuation of properties – but particularly of leasehold buildings or of **reversionary properties** (properties currently let below the market rent) – can be very complex and is usually undertaken by a chartered surveyor. Since no one property is quite like any other property, he has to work from recent precedents. Suppose investors seem to expect a five per cent return from standard office buildings of the type he is valuing; he adjusts for the different special factors that apply to this building and works out what price would provide a comparable return.

If a property is reversionary – the rent it currently produces is, say, £300,000 but this will jump to £400,000 in a year's time when the rent review occurs – the yield based on the current rent may be very low. However, this yield is often adjusted to produce an **equivalent yield**, which shows what yield the valuer would be working on if the building were let at the market rent.

Finance for developers

We have talked about both investors and **developers** in the property business, though the financial institutions may now fulfill both functions. But long before they got into the development business on their own account, they were the traditional source of long-term finance for property development because they had large-scale funds looking for a long-term home. The 'developer' was usually an entrepreneur with an eye for a good site who would carry out the development but use mainly other people's money to finance it.

In the immediate post-war years, developers of commercial buildings (mainly property companies) normally obtained their long-term finance by **mortgaging** the development to a financial institution when it was completed and let. Insurance companies and pension funds would, typically, provide a loan of two-thirds of the value for 25 years or more at a fixed rate of interest.

As interest rates rose, this became less practicable and various forms of partnership between institution and developer evolved. The most common was the **leaseback** or **sale and leaseback**. The developer identified the site and the possibility of putting up a building. The institution bought the land and provided finance for the development, which was managed by the developer. On completion, the institution granted a lease to the developer, who in turn granted a lease to the tenant at a rack rent. The developer paid a ground rent of, say, 70 per cent of the rental value of the building to the institution. The remaining 30 per cent **top slice** belonged to him. There were numerous variations on this theme, and the developer's rent to the institution would normally rise as the rental income of the building rose. Clearly, if the developer was unable to let the last 30 per cent of space in the building, he had no profit.

Subsequently, various other forms of partnership financing arrangement evolved which split the risk more equitably between the provider of finance and the developer – these may be referred to as **side-by-side** or **partnership** arrangements.

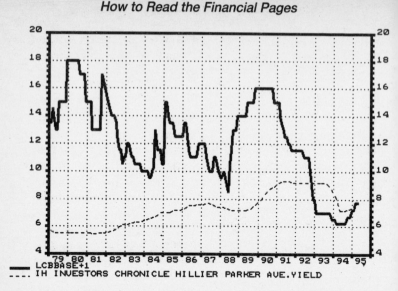

Figure 20.2 Falling interest rates from 1991 and rising property yields temporarily abolished the 'reverse yield gap': the rental yield from property moved above borrowing costs, thus reversing the normal post-war pattern. The solid line shows prime borrowing costs (one percentage point above bank base rates) and the broken line shows average yields for all classes of property. Source: *Hillier Parker* and *Datastream International*.

But increasingly the bigger institutions began to cut out the developer altogether by undertaking their own projects, possibly with the help of one of the large firms of surveyors.

The **sale and leaseback**, incidentally, has also been widely used as a financing method for commercial companies, particularly retailers. Company A might take over Company B, which owns the shops from which it carries out its trade. The shops can then be sold for a lump sum to an institution but Company B continues to occupy them, now paying a commercial rent as a tenant.

The second half of the 1980s saw a big change in financing techniques for property development. The insurance companies and pension funds became relatively less important and far more of the development finance came from the banking system. **Bank loans to property companies** (not all for development) rose by over 1,500 per cent between 1981 and 1991. Much of this lending took the form of **project loans** to the fast-growing property development and trading companies.

The loan was secured on the individual development project. A loan such as this was often made on **limited-recourse** or **non-recourse** terms. This meant that the property company itself was only responsible to a limited extent or not responsible at all for the loan. The banks could only look to the individual development project itself to provide the money to repay them at the end of the day. The larger loans were almost always **syndicated** between groups of banks, each putting up a part of the money. Ultimately, the banks lost heavily on this kind of lending.

The property companies

Apart from the institutions, **property companies** are also significant property owners. These are often stockmarket-quoted companies which either simply hold properties as an investment (**property investment company**) or undertake developments (**property development company**). Many of them do both. An investment and development company usually provides a very secure income, since its revenue comes mainly from recurring rents. A development company whose profits come from selling buildings on completion (a **property trading company**, sometimes known as a **merchant developer**) can be more erratic, since profits can fluctuate widely. It was mainly companies of this kind that got into trouble (and frequently went bust) in the crash of the early 1990s.

Many of the longer-established investment or investment and development companies were originally built up by entrepreneurial developers after the war. Property investment companies tend to be valued on the stockmarket by reference to the **asset backing** for their shares. As with single-tiered investment trusts, the shares usually stand at a discount to the net asset value, except at times of temporary market euphoria. Trading companies which make their profit from selling properties are more likely to be rated on a PE ratio basis and the shares often stand above the asset value when conditions are 'normal' in the property market.

Unitized property

Apart from the shares of property companies, there are a few other avenues for investment in commercial property. There

are specialist **property unit trusts** which own a range of properties. Pension funds or charities can invest in these units to
obtain a stake in a portfolio of commercial property as an
alternative to owning properties outright. But these vehicles
are not open to the public.

The public can, however, acquire a stake in commercial
property by investing in **property bonds**. These are unit-linked
life assurance contracts (see Chapter 21) where the link is to
the value of a portfolio of commercial properties rather than
shares. **Authorized unit trusts** (those in which the general
public may buy units) used to be prohibited from owning
property direct. That has now changed. But while property-
owning authorized unit trusts in theory provide another
avenue for the public to invest in commercial property, there
was not much incentive to start up such trusts in the early
1990s when property was deep in slump. Whether they will
catch on in a big way in the future remains to be seen.

For some time there have been plans to extend the principle
of **unitization** – dividing the ownership of properties among a
number of investors – to single properties. The reason is that
some individual buildings are now so valuable that it is difficult to find even an institution that will buy or finance one by
itself. If the ownership can be divided, however, the problem
is eased. The ownership of the £100m building could be
divided, say, into 100,000 units of £1,000 each, and both institutions and private investors could take a stake.

Most schemes of this type that were researched in the 1980s
subsequently stumbled on legal or tax problems or were
simply abandoned in the crash of the early 1990s. But you will
still sometimes hear references to **PINCs** (**Property Income
Certificates**), **SAPCOs** (**Single Asset Property Companies**) or
SPOTs (**Single Property Ownership Trusts**). There will doubtless be further attempts to find a viable structure for unitising
single properties in the future.

There have also been attempts to market property-based
derivatives. The **London Commodity Exchange** – then re-
joicing in the title of **London Futures and Options Exchange**
or **London FOX** – introduced **property futures** in 1991. These
worked in much the same way as futures based on a stockmarket index (see Chapter 18) but used indices of property
rents and values instead. They allowed bets on commercial

property rents, commercial property values, house prices and building society mortgage rates. But the venture very shortly collapsed in scandal when evidence of fabricated deals emerged.

More successful was the launch in 1994 of **Property Index Certificates** or **PICs** by Barclays Bank. These were bonds issued for two, three, four or five years where the return to the investor was linked to indices of property rents and values. However, PICs were issued in large denominations and aimed at the financial institutions, not at private investors.

Property indices

In writing about property there are several yardsticks that journalists and others use. For **property shares** there is a **property company sub-index** of the FT-SE Actuaries indices. And a number of firms of estate agents produce **indices of rental values** of different types of property, of **movement in capital values** and of the yields on which **prime properties** (the

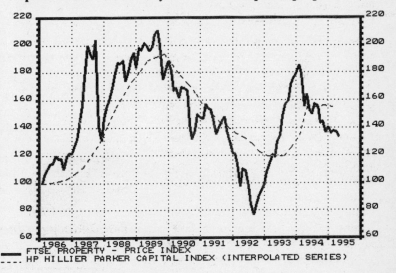

FTSE PROPERTY – PRICE INDEX
HP HILLIER PARKER CAPITAL INDEX (INTERPOLATED SERIES)

Figure 20.3 Property company share prices (solid line) tend to anticipate movements in the value of commercial property itself (broken line). Share prices are also generally more volatile than property values. Source: *Hillier Parker* and *Datastream International*.

best property investments in their category) or average investment-grade properties are changing hands. There are also indices produced by **Investment Property Databank** or **IPD**, an organisation which monitors and analyses the performance of many billions of pounds' worth of commercial property owned by the investing institutions. The other end of the scale from prime property is **secondary property** which may not be of investment grade for the institutions. Normally **shops** show the lowest yield (are the most highly valued), **offices** come next and **industrial properties** which covers factories and warehouses are valued on the highest yields.

Property performance

Commercial property values tend to follow a pronounced cyclical pattern, and often move counter-cyclically to shares (and also sometimes to residential property). The period 1982 to 1986 (while the stockmarket was booming) was very dull in the commercial property market with values showing comparatively little growth. Then in 1987 and 1988 rents and values rose very sharply and were virtually untouched by the October 1987 crash on the stockmarket. By 1989 some worries over the level of bank lending to property companies were beginning to surface: it had reached £22 billion. It subsequently rose to an all-time peak of over £40 billion in 1991. But by then the crash in the property market was well and truly under way.

The crash of the early 1990s

Between 1985 and 1989, the average value of shop property in the UK had risen by 85 per cent. City of London office property had more than doubled in value. The boom attracted enormous amounts of new development, particularly in London offices. When recession struck, the commercial property world thus faced a surplus of space just at the time that prospective tenants were cutting back on their own businesses and their space requirements. With too much space and too few tenants, rental values began to fall. Completing the picture of disaster were very high interest rates which had two effects. Developers faced vastly higher interest bills on their loans from the banks. And the higher returns from bank loans and other investments also meant that investors demanded higher initial yields from property – at a time when yields would have been rising anyway because of the worsened growth prospects for property. In other words, commercial property values had to fall very sharply.

Fall they did. The value of City of London offices dropped on average by over 60 per cent between 1989 and 1992. Shops suffered less badly but on average still lost roughly a quarter of their value. Average yields on all classes of property rose from 7.2 per cent in 1989 to 9.4 per cent in 1991. Rental levels for all classes of property across the country fell on average by 28 per cent from their peak and for City of London offices by half.

The property development and trading companies were faced with buildings that they could not let and therefore could not sell as investments. They had no way of repaying their bank loans, which were clocking up interest charges at a terrifying rate. Even if they could have sold the buildings, values had fallen so far that they would not have produced enough to repay the loans. Many companies of this type, including some of the biggest, went bust. The British clearing banks alone wrote off several billion pounds on their property loans. But the property development and investment companies generally survived because they had the income from completed and tenanted properties to pay the interest on their loans.

The market crash threw up several novel phenomena. The rent review clauses in most leases had an **upwards-only** provision. The rent could rise to the market level at the review point but never fall. So an office tenant who agreed a rent of £60 per square foot in 1989 had to continue to pay £60 psf after the rent review in 1994, even though the real rental value of the building had dropped to £30. This gave rise to the phenomenon of **over-rented properties** – those bringing in a rent above the market rate – which were very difficult to value. The old post-war assumption that rents would always be higher at the review point than five years earlier had, needless to say, gone by the board.

Valuation was made doubly difficult because many parts of the commercial property market virtually dried up and there were few transactions to take as a guideline. Compounding the problem were the very large **inducements** that owners of new buildings were obliged to offer prospective tenants to persuade them to sign a lease. It was not uncommon for the landlord to offer an incoming tenant a three-year **rent-free period** or a large **lump sum inducement** to take a lease at, say, £35 per square foot. That posed the problem of what the real rental value of the building would be without the inducement. And **confidentiality clauses** often prohibited landlord and tenant from disclosing the terms of the lease.

By late 1993 or early 1994 the worst was probably past in the commercial property market. Values had actually staged a recovery as investors turned to property for higher yields than they could get at the time on bonds, and the buying pushed values up. But, at the beginning of 1995, there were still doubts about property's long-term growth prospects until evidence of rising rents emerged. And the scars of the 1990–1993 crash were going to be with the property industry for a very long time.

21

Savings, pooled investment and tax shelters

The public flotations of British Telecom, Trustee Savings Bank, British Gas, the water companies and the electricity companies attracted millions of first-time investors to the stockmarket. But these issues could give a misleading impression of the way the bulk of the British public invests its money.

Direct ownership of shares, in the traditional wisdom, is for those with enough spare cash to afford holdings in a spread of companies, thus reducing the risk if any one of them falls on hard times. Savers who are not yet in this happy position are almost invariably given the following advice: start buying your own home and take out **life assurance**, both as a means of saving and to protect your family. Make suitable **pension** arrangements if you are not a member of an **occupational scheme** (a scheme run by your employer). Smallish amounts of spare cash may be invested for safety, convenience and a reasonable return with your **building society**. Only when you have spare cash after taking care of the necessities should you become more adventurous in your investment policy.

This advice is backed by considerations of tax efficiency as well as safety, though to a lesser extent than in the past. Interest on up to £30,000 of a **mortgage** taken out to buy your main home can be offset against income tax, though since 1995 only at a rate of 15 per cent. Profits on the sale of your main home are free of capital gains tax. For much of the post-war period, home ownership has been regarded as an investment as much as a comfort of life, though this attitude took a heavy knock from the severe fall in house prices over the early

1990s. And the assumption must be that the government – or, certainly, a Conservative government – would continue to reduce tax relief on mortgage interest in the long run.

Life assurance used to offer tax benefits until 1984. There was partial tax relief on the premiums, and there still is for anyone with a pre-1984 policy. New policyholders do not get tax relief.

Pensions, however, remain the best tax bargain of all. Up to approved limits, there is full income tax relief on premiums. And once the premiums are invested by the pension fund it pays no tax on either income or capital gains. The sums invested to provide a pension can thus compound in value far more rapidly than most other forms of investment where income would be taxed. But the pension business has not been without its problems in recent years (see below).

How the British invest their money

This pattern of investment is confirmed by the official figures. By far the largest single item in the wealth of individuals is **housing**. On the latest available figures (for 1993) the value of private housing in Britain was put at £1,116 billion – before deducting the amounts owed under house purchase loans. It had been rather higher before the crash in values in the early 1990s.

Next look at the **financial assets** of individuals: how they hold and invest their money. In the third quarter of 1994, total gross financial assets of the **personal sector** were estimated at £1,632 billion. The most important items were:

	£ billion
Cash and sterling bank balances	184
National savings	51
Government stocks	21
Building society shares and deposits	205
Shares in UK companies	189
Unit trust units	42
Equity in insurance and pension funds	822

Thus the value of individuals' stakes in life assurance and pensions far outweighs any other form of investment. Building society investment comes next and **direct shareholdings** in companies at £189 billion just scrape into third place. This figure for shareholdings has risen in recent years, partly because of privatization issues which attracted many first-time investors to the stockmarket and partly because of a generally rising trend in share prices.

Even so, private investors usually sell more UK shares than they buy each year. And though in 1995 there are nine million or so direct shareholders, many of them simply have a few hundred pounds' worth of shares in British Telecom or British Gas. The government has tried to use its programme of nationalized industry sales as a way of furthering **popular capitalism**, but the prospect of individual investors again becoming a significant direct force in the stockmarket seems remote. Employee share ownership schemes as well as privatization issues may help, and **Personal Equity Plans** or **PEPs** offer tax reliefs for direct share investment (see below). But for the time being, saving via the financial institutions is the order of the day.

The basic personal finance guidance in the press follows the pattern of individuals' savings preferences. The main areas covered are **life assurance**, **pensions**, **house purchase** and **unit trust investment**, with a fair helping of **tax advice**. The schemes on offer from the major life assurance companies are compared. The investment performance – where applicable – of different life assurance savings schemes and of individual unit trusts is recorded. And, as the scope of **Personal Equity Plans (PEPs)** is progressively extended, there is increasing press coverage of this tax-sheltered investment vehicle.

Financial intermediaries in the savings market

This information is aimed at insurance brokers as well as the public. Much life assurance and related savings products is sold through **financial intermediaries**, which in practice normally means **insurance brokers** who frequently (and often misleadingly) also operate under the title of **investment advisers** or **financial consultants**. These are the middle-men between the public and the insurance companies or savings institutions. Since they live from the commission on the products they sell, there is an inevitable temptation for them

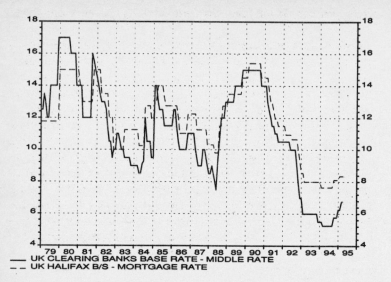

Figure 21.1 Rates of interest on loans to homebuyers are far more commercial today than in the 1970s. The broken line shows the rate charged to borrowers by the Halifax Building Society compared with bank base rates (solid line). Source: *Datastream International.*

to be swayed in favour of the product paying the highest commission, and the independence of their advice is frequently called into question. Along with the insurance companies' own sales forces, they have met considerable criticism over the mis-selling of personal pensions (see below). As an indirect result of the City's new regulatory system, an increasing number of them have in any case tied themselves to one particular insurance company or provider of investment products.

Traditional life assurance

The basic life assurance theme has an infinite number of variations. **Term insurance** is a straight bet with the insurance company: you pay premiums for an agreed period, and if you die during that time the insurance company pays the sum for which your life was insured. If you survive, you've lost the bet (or won it, depending on your outlook) and you get nothing at the end of the period. **Whole life** insurance pays a lump sum when you die, at any age. So your family gets something even if you live to 90.

Endowment asssurance is a savings vehicle for you as well as a protection for your dependents. You pay the premiums, and at the end of the term of the insurance you get a lump sum. If you die earlier, your dependents get a lump sum, as with whole life. The life assurance aspect of the contract is not too complicated: insurance company actuaries can calculate pretty accurately from mortatility tables the risk of your dying before such-and-such an age (though new dangers such as AIDS cause problems) and provide for it in the premium they charge. The premium income goes into the **life funds** of the insurance company, where it is invested and this is where the main uncertainty arises: the return the insurance company will earn on its investments. In the case of a **with-profits policy** the policyholder is entitled to a share of the profits from the growth of the fund.

Two points are worth noting on life assurance investment. First, returns on (particularly equity) investment may turn out to be considerably lower in the 1990s than in the boom days of the 1980s and there are already signs that the with-profits element for policyholders may be less attractive than in the past. Second, many investors who enter into a life assurance contract subsequently find themselves unable to maintain their payments and need to take their money out early. What they receive – the **surrender value** – is usually very low in the early years compared with what they have paid in, partly because the salesman's commission comes mainly out of the early payments. Insurance companies are now being required to give more information on commissions and costs to prospective clients.

Company and individual pensions

Personal pensions are still largely an extension of life assurance, and the major insurance companies provide them. They also run a lot of company pension schemes for smaller and medium-sized groups. Take the company schemes first. These may be **insured schemes**, where the insurance group tells the company what premium it needs each year to provide the eventual level of benefit required. Or the company may hand over the contributions to be invested in a **managed fund** run by the insurance group; the pension scheme is allocated units in the fund pro rata with its contribution, and the value of the units depends on the investment performance of the fund. Or the pension fund may simply employ the insurance company as an **investment manager**, to manage its assets as a separate fund: a field in which merchant banks, brokers and other fund management groups also compete fiercely.

Alternatively, the pension fund can, of course, manage its own investments, as many of the larger ones do. With a buoyant stockmarket and high real returns on investment, many pension funds were showing **surpluses** in the second half of the 1980s and the early 1990s. The value of their investments exceeded what was needed to meet expected liabilities. These surpluses were being reduced in a number of ways – many companies took a **contributions holiday** – and were also being 'raided' by the sponsoring company and by takeover practitioners.

In the past, employees of a company which ran its own pension scheme were normally forced to join that scheme. From 1988 they have been free to make their own arrangements, sometimes known as **personal portable pensions** because they can be taken from job to job. The self-employed already do this if they do not wish to rely on the fairly meagre benefits of the **state pension schemes**. To build up bigger pensions, those in pension schemes may make **additional voluntary contributions** or **AVCs**.

Private sector pension arrangements fall into two main types. Traditionally, company schemes have been mainly **defined benefit** (otherwise known as **final salary**) schemes. An employee builds up his entitlement each year he works for the company and, typically, might receive a pension of two-thirds of his final salary if he has worked for 40 years for the same company by the time he retires. The problem with this type of scheme for the sponsoring company is that it does not know in advance what the pension liabilities will be. This is because it does not know what salaries will be at retirement age or what investment returns will be earned on the contributions over 40 years.

This problem does not crop up with the other type of scheme: the **defined contribution** or **money purchase** scheme.

With these schemes a certain amount of money is contributed each year and invested. When the member retires, his 'pot' of accumulated money is used to buy an annuity to provide him with an income for the rest of his life. But the income does not necessarily bear any particular relationship to his salary in employment. Its size depends on the investment returns earned on his money over the years and the levels of investment yields at the time that the annuity must be bought. Personal portable pensions are of the money-purchase type.

Personal pensions are increasingly used to provide security for loans to an individual or a business. Since part of a pension may be paid as a lump sum and the remainder as a continuing income, the pension terms are designed so that, on retirement, the lump sum repays the loan.

Pensions have, however, been under something of a cloud in recent years. The plundering of his company pension schemes for many hundreds of millions of pounds by the late Robert Maxwell sent a shiver through the pensions business. New legislation introduced in the aftermath of that affair may

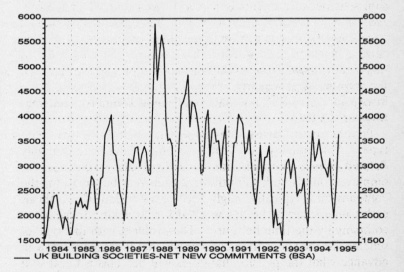

Figure 21.2 Net new lending commitments by the building societies. There is no mistaking the lending splurge of 1988 which helped to push house prices to a new peak and pave the way for the troubles of the 1990s. And look at the fall in new lending once the housing market seized up. Source: *Datastream International.*

slightly improve the security and adequacy of company pension schemes (most of which are reputable and safe anyway) but it has been so watered down that its effects will be limited.

To compound the problems, government encouragement to individuals to make their own pension arrangements has often misfired. The personal pension arrangements on offer from some financial institutions carry high charges and offer very poor returns. Many thousands of individuals have been persuaded to buy such pensions, often opting out from company schemes which offered much better value in order to do so. Some pension vendors who have given bad advice are now to be forced to compensate their victims for the consequences. This major scandal has underlined one salient fact. Pensions are an exceedingly complex area and it is often difficult if not impossible to get competent impartial advice. Walk with extreme care.

Repayment and endowment mortgages

Buying a house with the help of a **mortgage** is usually regarded as a form of savings and mortgages, too, can have a life assurance element. The homebuyer can take out either a **repayment mortgage** or an **endowment mortgage**. With the **repayment mortgage** the amount borrowed is repaid via monthly instalments of interest and capital (more interest and less capital in the early stages and more capital and less interest in the later ones). Repayments are calculated so that the whole of the sum will have been repaid by the end of the term: usually 25 years though, because people move house, the average life of a mortgage in practice is much shorter. The interest rate on mortgages is traditionally variable, so payments have to be adjusted up and down as interest rates change. Changes in the rates are always hot news. But the shock of very high interest rates in the late 1980s and early 1990s encouraged many home-buyers to require (and mortgage-providers to supply) mortgages where the interest rate was fixed, at least for the first few years.

The **endowment mortgage** introduces the life assurance. The money to buy the house is borrowed, usually from a **building society**, and interest is paid to the lender in the normal way. But no capital is repaid. Instead, the borrower takes out an endowment life assurance policy which, when it matures, is intended to provide a lump sum large enough to repay the loan from the building society. Instead of re-payments of capital, the borrower is paying premiums to the life assurance company. These policies can again have a with-profits element so that, on maturity, the loan will hopefully be repaid and there will be an additional sum for the policy-holder. There are many variations on this theme, and the relative tax advantages of the repayment and endowment mortgage are periodically aired in the personal finance columns. But the comment nowadays tends to be more scepti-cal. Too many people are persuaded to take out an endowment mortgage when a repayment mortgage would be more suitable, simply because it earns commission for the ven-dor. And there are increasing doubts whether, with lower investment returns, endowment mortgages will always pay out a large enough sum on maturity to repay the outstanding mortgage loan.

Unit-linked investment vehicles

Move beyond the basic insurance and loan products, and you are next likely to meet the **unit-linked** investment vehicles. These give some of the benefits of stockmarket investment while spreading the risks.

It is inappropriate, as we have seen, for an individual with modest savings to risk them all on the vagaries of one share price – although we were asked to believe that this did not matter when the Government was off-loading previously nationalized industries. It makes sense for those with small amounts of capital or no knowledge of the stockmarket to in-vest in a spread of shares rather than the shares of a single company. Hence **unit trusts** and **unit-linked assurance**. Look at the pages of tables at the back of the *Financial Times*, before the stockmarket prices, and headed **FT managed funds service**, with the main sub-headings **authorized unit trusts** and **insurances**. They occupy several pages and have grown enor-mously in recent years. These are the products that the investment management community is offering the public.

Principles of unit-linked investment

Despite the variety on offer, the principle of **unitized**, **pooled** or **collective** investment is simple. Suppose you and ninety-nine other people each stump up £1 for investment in a new **unit trust**. The managers thus collect £100 in total and use it to buy shares in a variety of companies. Over a period the value of the trust's investments rises by, say, 20 per cent. The original £100 of investments is now worth £120. You own one of the hundred units in issue, so the value of your unit is one hundredth of the total value of the fund. In other words its value has risen from £1 to £1.20 (the actual calculations, allowing for costs, are more complex – see below). How would you sell your unit if you wanted to cash in? You would sell it back to the managers of the unit trust, who will then try to sell it to somebody else. If they cannot do so, they may have to sell some of the trust's investments to raise the money to pay you.

Unit-linked insurance incorporates a similar collective investment mechanism, where the value of the unit is linked to the value of a specific fund or sub-fund of investments, but technically it is a life assurance contract. You hand over your money to the managers. A small proportion of it goes to provide a minimal amount of life assurance cover. The remainder is invested in units of what is technically a **life fund**. If the value of the fund rises, the value of your investment rises, too. What is the point of unit-linked insurance, when you can invest in unit trusts? In the past, there were tax advantages in investing in a life assurance contract. Also, a life fund could invest direct in property (unit-linked schemes invested in property are called **property bonds**) and the scheme could be sold door to door, which was not allowed in the case of unit trusts. The treatment of the two types of investment is now closer in line and property-owning unit trusts are now permitted.

Pricing of unit trusts

The operations of a unit trust are not, of course, quite as simple as in the example. There are charges for the service: typically, an initial charge of 5 per cent or 6 per cent of the value of your investment and an on-going annual charge of 1 per cent or more. Both initial and annual charges have risen over the years, notably the annual rate. So, as with shares, there is not a single price for the units. There is a buying price and a selling price: you buy the units from the managers at the higher 'offer' price and receive the lower 'bid' price when you sell them back. The price spread partially reflects the fact that the unit trust itself has to pay a higher price when it buys shares, gets a lower price when it sells them and will incur dealing expenses. But the spread also includes the initial charge by the managers and various other costs. If a unit trust suffers a large outflow of funds it has some leeway to move bid and offer price down to a lower pricing basis, known as a **bid basis** or **liquidation basis**. Some unit trusts are now structured with no initial charge, but with an 'exit' charge diminishing over a period of years.

Note that performance figures for unit trusts should always allow for the spread. So if the quotation for a particular trust has moved up from 100p-107p to 120p-128p over the year the calculation should allow for the fact that the investor would have bought at 107p and sold at 120p: a gain of 13p or 12.1 per cent, not 20p.

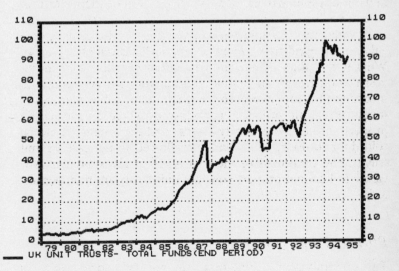

Figure 21.3 The value of funds in the unit trust movement, shown in billions of pounds. The unit trusts have benefited from the PEP tax-shelter in the 1990s. Source: *Datastream International.*

Features of unit trust operation

A unit trust which is marketed to the public needed in the past to be **authorized** by the **Department of Trade and Industry**, though responsibility for authorization has passed to the **Securities and Investments Board**. There are also **unauthorized** trusts which some stockbrokers run for their clients and **unauthorized property unit trusts** are permitted to offer a form of collective investment in property to the pension funds. Advertisements for unit trusts are fairly closely monitored and must contain a **health warning** – a reminder that the unit price can go down as well as up.

When they first launch, unit trusts make a **fixed price offer** for a limited period – you will see the advertisements in the financial pages of the national papers, usually on a Saturday or Sunday. At this time you can apply for units at a known price. The rest of the time you pay the price ruling around the time your application is received. Fund management groups also frequently provide the opportunity for regular savings plans: you arrange to pay so much a month, the money being invested in units when it is received.

Unit trusts must pay out the income they receive on their investments to their unitholders, pro rata with their holdings. But sometimes the investor has a choice between **income units** (where he receives his share of the dividends in cash) and **accumulation units** (where his share of the income is added to the value of each unit). This second option is a convenience but does not offer any tax saving: the income is reinvested net of basic rate tax and any higher rate tax due has to be paid. However, accumulation units are not charged with the cost of reinvestment and the investor also has a better record of his total return when he keeps the same number of units. An alternative is for the investor to be credited with additional units representing the reinvested net income. This may involve paying preliminary charges on the new units.

Now that Personal Equity Plans or PEPs can be used as a tax-sheltered vehicle for holding units in unit trusts that invest mainly in British and European Union companies (see below), unit trust investment via the PEP route should be the first option for investors.

Who offers unit-linked investment?

The *Financial Times* lists over 150 fund management groups offering authorized unit trusts and over 100 offering unit-linked assurance. Variations of the same name frequently crop up in both categories: most of the larger fund management groups offer the whole range of unit-linked products.

Computers make it easy to calculate the value of a trust's investments each day, and hence the unit price. The *Financial Times* listings show, for unit trusts, both **bid** (selling price) and **offer** (buying price)and the price movement over the previous day, plus the **gross yield**. In many cases separate prices are shown for income units and accumulation units: the latter will be higher, because of the reinvested income.

Specialist investment policies

The original idea of unit trusts was to offer a spread of investments across most areas of the stockmarket. Then came more specialist funds, investing according to particular philosophies or in particular areas. Have a look at the trusts run by **M & G Securities**, the doyen of the unit trust business. There is a **general fund**. Then there are funds investing for **high income**, in **smaller companies**, in **recovery stocks** (companies down on their luck whose share price should improve dramatically if they pull round) and so on. And there are trusts investing in specific geographical areas: America, Australasia, Japan and Europe.

The same range of investment policies is evident in the unit-linked assurance funds, normally known as **bonds** (though not to be confused with government or company bonds). In fact, many unit trusts have a **bondized** equivalent: an insurance fund which invests in the relevant unit trust. The prices for the bonds, under the heading of **insurances**, follow the same pattern as those for unit trusts, except that no yield is shown since no income is distributed. With unit-linked assurance, the income from the fund's investments is automatically reinvested in the fund after deduction of tax at the life assurance rate. A life fund is also taxed on capital gains (unlike unit trust funds, which are exempt from gains tax) and this is reflected in the price of units.

Managed funds and switching facilities

Two aspects of 'bond' investment attract a lot of press comment. First, most groups run a **managed fund**. This means that the fund invests in the group's other bond funds and the manager can make a strategic decision to switch the emphasis of the managed fund's investments from one area to another as conditions change. If the London stockmarket looked too expensive he might get out of the group's general UK funds and into, say, its property fund. Second, the individual investor may be given some of the same flexibility. He might buy, say, the property fund, but have the right to switch his investment into another of the management group's funds without incurring the full costs of selling one investment and buying another. This degree of flexibility is, because of the different charging structure and tax position, more difficult to build into unit trust investment.

Note that some insurance brokers will concoct their own investment packages for clients, putting together their own mix of the products offered by the fund management groups.

Offshore and overseas funds

After the **insurances** in the *Financial Times* come the prices for **offshore and overseas funds**. These are not authorized unit trusts, though they operate on the unit principle and many operate under the umbrella of one of the fund management groups that offers authorized unit trusts in the UK. Many of the offshore funds are technically located in the Channel Islands and managed from there, the UK parent group being described as 'adviser' to the fund. Hence management group names with 'C.I.' in the title.

The **offshore funds** operate under the tax regime of the country where they are located: usually more liberal than in Britain. But for a British investor living in Britain there is no tax advantage in investing in them. He will be treated for tax according to the UK rules. Expatriate Britons working, say, in the Middle East and paying little if any UK tax may do better in an offshore fund than in one registered in the UK.

Monitoring performance

Performance statistics for unit trusts and bonds are closely followed. The monthly magazine **Money Management** provides a comprehensive list, showing the value of £1,000 invested over periods ranging from six months to seven or ten years. Performance can vary very markedly, particularly over the shorter periods, and for the intrinsically more speculative funds invested in foreign markets, picking the right country is often more important for the managers than picking the right share, especially at times of wild currency swings. In 1994 – which was not a vintage year for investment – the best performing unit trust turned £1,000 into £1,237 and the worst reduced £1,000 to £529. Most of the winners were specialist Japanese trusts. Many of the losers were trusts investing in emerging stockmarkets elsewhere in Asia, which had earlier enjoyed a boom, then suffered a reaction. An investment policy that was geographically precisely right one year could equally well be precisely wrong the next.

In fact, unit trust investors should be aware that many trusts are marketing-led rather than investment-led. The managers find it easy to market a new trust investing in an area that has recently become fashionable and attracted widespread press comment. But by the time the trust is launched, the best of the growth may be past. For investors the trick is, as always, to get into the areas that will become fashionable before they have done so. Likewise, unit trust sales and the volume of unit trust marketing tend to rise when the stockmarket has been on a rising trend for a long time and everybody has noticed the profits being made. In practice, the market may be near its peak and it could be the worst possible time to buy. Cynical unit trust investors tend to invest **counter-cyclically**. They may buy the previous year's worst-performing trust on the basis that its policy could turn out right the next year. And buy unit trusts in general when the market is low and marketing hype is minimal.

Investment trusts

There is one other – and much older – form of collective investment vehicle which crops up frequently in the personal finance pages: the **investment trust**. An investment trust is a

M & G Securities (0915)H
M & G House, Victoria Road, Chelmsford CM1 1FB
Customer Services/Unit Dealing 01245 390390

Amer & General 5	399.1	422.0	−0.6	0.53
(Accum Units) 5	497.2	525.8	−0.8	0.53
Amer Recovery........... 5	471.8xd	498.9	−1.6	0.42
(Accum Units) 5	542.0xd	573.2	−1.8	0.42
Amer Smllr Cos......... 5	130.6	138.1	−0.6	–
(Accum Units) 5	133.5	141.1	−0.6	–
Australasian.............. 5	146.4	154.8	−1.1	2.08
(Accum Units) 5	179.1	189.3	−1.5	2.08
Capital 5	848.1	896.9	−0.9	2.7
(Accum Units) 5	973.1	1029.1	−1.1	2.7
Charifund 1	701.4xd	708.5	−2.2	5.66
(Accum Units) 1	3332.5xd	3365.9	−10.5	5.66
Commodity 5	376.5	398.2	+0.9	0.52
(Accum Units) 5	552.8	584.7	+1.4	0.52
Compound Growth 5	965.0xd	1020.5	−1.2	3.05
(Accum Units) 5	1025.3xd	1084.3	−1.2	3.05
Dividend 5	41.10xd	43.50	−0.1	4.37
(Accum Units) 5	175.3xd	185.6	−0.6	4.37
Equity Income 5	348.5	368.5	−0.3	4.78
(Accum Units) 5	452.7	478.7	−0.4	4.78
European & General .. 5	520.5	550.4	−0.3	1.23
(Accum Units) 5	658.4	696.2	−0.3	1.23
European Dividend..... 5	74.00	78.30	.....	3.7
(Accum Units) 5	89.10	94.30	.....	3.7
Extra Yield................ 5	422.0	446.3	−1.6	4.86
(Accum Units) 5	1333.5	1410.2	−5.2	4.86
Far Eastern 5	346.3	366.2	+2.5	0.74
(Accum Units) 5	459.7	486.1	+3.3	0.74
Fund of Inv Tsts 5	616.4xd	651.8	−1.2	2.08
(Accum Units) 5	1163.0xd	1229.8	−2.2	2.08
General 5	62.80	66.40	−0.2	3.77
(Accum Units) 5	176.6	186.7	−0.5	3.77
Gilt Income............... 0	60.81xd	60.91	−0.2	7.62
(Accum Units) 0	171.7xd	171.98	−0.55	7.62
Gold 5	62.50	66.10	+1.1	0.85
(Accum Units) 5	73.90	78.10	+1.3	0.85
High Income.............. 5	29.40	31.10	−0.1	4.74
(Accum Units) 5	117.9	124.8	−0.3	4.74
Intl Growth 5	75.50	79.80	+0.3	0.96
(Accum Units) 5	131.8	139.3	+0.6	0.96
International Inc 5	98.90xd	104.6	.....	4.65
(Accum Units) 5	148.9xd	157.5	+0.1	4.65
Japan & Gen 5	41.40xd	43.80	+0.5	–
(Accum Units) 5	44.40xd	47.00	+0.5	–
Japan Smaller Cos.... 5	139.9xd	147.9	+2.0	–
(Accum Units) 5	140.9xd	148.9	+2.0	–
Managed Growth ◆... 5	24.30	25.60	.....	1.72
Managed Income ◆.. 4½	27.90xd	29.30	−0.1	4.23
Midland..................... 5	63.50xd	67.10	−0.1	3.2
(Accum Units) 5	214.5xd	226.9	−0.2	3.2
Pension Ex................ 2	961.3xd	985.4	−2.6	4.28
Recovery................... 5	43.10	45.60	.....	2.56
(Accum Units) 5	70.80	74.90	.....	2.56
Second General......... 5	71.60	75.70	−0.2	3.49
(Accum Units) 5	185.9	196.8	−0.3	3.49
Smaller Cos 5	69.40	73.40	+0.1	3.19
(Accum Units) 5	138.3	146.2	+0.1	3.19
Stlg High Interest 0	25.16	25.25	−0.09	8.28
Treasury ◆ F............. 0	25.04xd	25.09	+0.02	6.31
Trustee 5	42.00xd	44.40	−0.1	4.35
(Accum Units) 5	171.8xd	182.0	−0.4	4.35

Table 21.1 The range of unit trusts offered by a major name in the business. Source: *Financial Times*.

company whose business – rather than making widgets or running laundries – is simply to invest in other companies. It holds a portfolio of investments in the same way as a unit trust or a life fund, thus providing professional management and a **spread of risk**. But you cannot buy 'units' in an investment trust. You buy its **shares**, in the same way as you would buy the shares of an industrial company. Investment trust share prices are thus listed in the share price pages of the *Financial Times* rather than on the unit trust or insurance fund pages.

The value of shares in an investment trust is determined in

exactly the same way as the value of the shares in any other company, by the balance of buyers and sellers in the stock-market. But in making their buying and selling decisions, investors naturally look at the value of the investments the trust owns, usually expressed as a **net asset value per share**, or **NAV** (see Chapter 4) and for technical reasons the share price of an investment trust nowadays is normally below the value of the assets backing the shares. In other words, it stands at a **discount** to the NAV. The size of the typical discount varies with stockmarket conditions.

This poses a considerable problem for anyone wanting to launch a new investment trust. Say he proposed to offer 100 shares to the public at £1 each and invest the £100 he received across a range of companies. The investment trust would have a portfolio of investments worth £100 and the NAV of each of its own shares would thus be £1. But the chances are that the shares would trade in the stockmarket at less than £1. There have been periods in which such a market price might have been only 80p: a discount of 20 per cent to the NAV. In the 1990s, discounts have been smaller. But, even so, few investors want to put up £1 for something which shortly afterwards will be worth less.

Geared and split-level trusts

There are various ways an investment trust can try to reduce or eliminate the discount to the asset value. It may offer special investment expertise in a particular area, which encourages investors to rate its shares more highly, or may attempt to cash in on a current stockmarket fashion. It might have considerable **gearing** – investment trusts can use borrowed money as well as shareholders' money – which means the asset backing for the shares would rise faster than the value of the investment portfolio in a rising market. Or it might organize itself as a **split-level trust**. The principle is that the investment trust's own share capital consists of **income shares** and **capital shares**, the income shares being entitled to all the income from its investment portfolio and the capital shares being entitled to the whole of the rise in capital value of the portfolio over the life of the company, which is limited to a specific period. There are a number of variations on this theme, some of them considerably more complex and involving the issue of several classes of capital. The idea is that, by tailoring different securities to the needs of different investors, their value will be enhanced and the sum of the parts will be worth more than the whole would be if marketed as a single entity. Thus the discount problem can be alleviated.

Unitizing investment trusts

But the surest way for an existing investment trust to increase its total worth is to be taken over or to **unitize** itself. **Unitization** simply means that the investment trust turns itself into a unit trust, substituting units for shares. The unit price is then calculated directly from the value of its investments (and fully reflects this value, which the share price did not). An investment trust is a **close-ended** investment vehicle, because it has a finite share capital. A unit trust is **open-ended** because the managers can create new units or cancel existing ones as demand and supply dictate.

Personal equity plans

The November 1994 Budget widened the scope for a rapidly-growing type of personal investment vehicle: the **Personal Equity Plan** or **PEP**. These PEPs, which were launched from the beginning of 1987, attract much advertising and a commensurate volume of editorial comment in the personal finance pages. The idea of the PEP is to encourage investment in the stockmarket, much as the **Enterprise Investment Scheme** encourages high-earning individuals to invest in shares of unquoted companies. However, the tax incentive comes in a different way and the sums involved are still much smaller.

Individuals are entitled to one 'general' PEP each year and can invest (in 1995) £6,000 in each PEP, which is simply a vehicle for holding shares and other securities in UK and European companies for the individual. In addition, individuals can invest up to £3,000 in any tax year in a separate 'single company' PEP. Income on investments held within the PEP is not liable to tax, neither is there tax on any capital gains. If investments are taken out of the PEP these concessions are lost for the future.

As from the 1995–96 tax year, investments eligible for inclusion in a PEP comprise ordinary shares in UK or European Community companies; qualifying corporate bonds and convertibles of non-financial UK companies; and preference shares in UK and European Community companies. In addition, the whole £6,000 or part of it can be invested in unit trusts or investment trusts which themselves hold at least half of their assets in the form of these qualifying securities. The PEP thus provides a tax-sheltered structure for investment in certain of the collective savings media. Single company PEPs are generally initiated by the company whose shares they hold and – though not limited to this use – can provide useful tax shelter for shares acquired by employees through employee share schemes and the like.

Considerable interest was aroused when the rules were relaxed in the 1994 Budget to allow investment in qualifying company bonds, and bond-holding PEPs were promoted rapidly in consequence. It remains to be seen whether or not this will provide a useful new source of bond finance for UK companies.

As long as the investments remain within the PEP structure they continue to enjoy the tax concessions (within the PEP one share can be sold and another bought with the proceeds without incurring tax liability). The idea, therefore, is that over the years investors will build up portfolios consisting of a number of individual PEPs, each started in a different year.

As an exercise in popular capitalism, the scheme is less than ideal. You may not run your own PEP. It has to be managed by a **professional fund manager** approved by the tax authorities. In practice this means more business for the traditional fund managers: stockbrokers, banks and merchant banks and unit trust groups – though building societies are also allowed to compete. Most of these managers either insist on picking the shares themselves or allow the investor to choose from a very restricted list. The charge for setting up the PEP will probably be 5 per cent or so, which will mop up the first year's income from most equity investments. And some managers will charge fees and commission on share dealing, which cannot be estimated by the client initially. Unit trust-based PEPs can be more efficient in this respect, though there is still an annual management charge.

Tax sheltering with a TESSA

Tax Exempt Special Savings Accounts or **TESSAs** are a somewhat watered down counterpart to PEPS for those who keep their savings in a building society or bank account. Introduced in 1991, TESSAs are special accounts which run for five years, and savers may invest up to a total of £9,000 in the TESSA over that period. Within this limit, up to £3,000 may be invested in the first year with a maximum of £1,800 in any one year thereafter. Provided the savings are kept in the TESSA until it matures after five years, the interest earned is tax-free.

In the past, the interest was due to become taxable in the normal way once the TESSA matured after five years. The 1994 Budget introduced an important further concession. The first TESSAs would be maturing at the beginning of 1996 and it was decided that the capital that had been saved in a maturing TESSA – up to the full £9,000 limit – could be reinvested immediately in a new TESSA where the income would continue to be tax-free for a further five years. The rolled-up income earned in the original TESSA could not, however, be taken into the new one. The £9,000 overall limit remained for the old and any new savings.

22

Supervising the City

Customers in shops have various forms of redress against unscrupulous traders and shoddy products. Users of the City's services have a similar need for protection. So there are safeguards to prevent the investor from suffering at the hands of unscrupulous financial operators. There are rules regarding the nature of the products on offer. And there are rules to govern the operations of the markets themselves and the professionals who trade in them.

The City's **supervisory systems** feature frequently in press reports. The Bank of England's role as supervisor of the banking system was again put under the spotlight by the collapse of the Barings merchant bank early in 1995. And the main supervisory system for investment products, investment advisers and the markets has been in a state of constant evolution since its introduction in the period 1986–88 and has never been long out of the news. It replaced a ramshackle regime that frequently left investors at the mercy of con men like unscrupulous investment advisors and promoters of dubious commodity investment schemes. But it labours under the same disadvantages as all regulatory systems. The abuses that it prevents are not news. When it is forced to move publicly against investment operators, it risks the criticism that it should have prevented the abuse from taking place at all.

Statutory versus non-statutory supervision

There are two main approaches to regulating financial markets: **statutory regulation** and **self-regulation**. Most financial systems have some elements of both. The American system leans towards statutory regulation. A statutory body, the **Securities and Exchange Commission (SEC)**, monitors the issue of securities to the public and the securities markets in which they are traded and reinforces the work of self-regulating bodies such as the New York Stock Exchange.

It is argued that an SEC would not work in Britain. The markets must be policed by those who understand their workings. In America the SEC can attract bright young lawyers as a career stepping-stone. In Britain a comparable body would probably submerge under the weight of civil service bureaucracy. There is special pleading here from the City, which hates outsiders watching its workings, but an element of truth as well.

The British system self-regulatory system

In practice, regulation of the financial system in Britain is a mixture of statutory and non-statutory measures, but with a strong bias in favour of self-regulation. The framework for the system, however, is enshrined in legislation – the **Financial Services Act** which entered the statute book in 1986, though its main provisions came into force considerably later, in April 1988.

The Financial Services Act developed from a report on **investor protection** produced by a shrewd lawyer and adviser to the Department of Trade and Industry, Professor Jim Gower. Under the Act, virtually any person or body wanting to carry on an **investment business** in the UK has to be authorized to do so. The maximum penalty for operating an investment business while unauthorized is two years in jail. The definition of 'investment business' is drawn very widely. It covers brokers, marketmakers, investment managers, sellers of investment products, financial intermediaries of various kinds, commodity scheme operators (a previously glaring gap) and even publishers of investment newsletters and tip sheets. But newspapers were excluded from the provisions, despite a stout rearguard action by the Labour party. And loans (logically enough) do not count as investment products. An organisation providing home mortgages would not come within the scope of the Act, or not in that capacity.

Role of the Securities and Investments Board

With whom do you register for authorization? This is where the complications begin. At the apex of the system stands the **Securities and Investments Board** (**SIB**). The SIB is not a government agency. It is a private company, but with regulatory powers delegated to it under the Financial Services Act. Under this umbrella organization are a series of **Self-Regulating Organizations** (**SROs**) for different types of financial activity. Initially there were five. Now they have boiled down to three. Many organizations need to register with more than one SRO when their activities encompass a range of different investment businesses. Certain professional bodies whose members undertake investment business that is incidental to their main activities – accountants, for example – can apply to be **Recognized Professional Bodies** (**RPBs**) instead of all their members' needing to join an SRO. The markets in which investments are traded do not need recognition as investment businesses if they obtain recognition from the SIB as **Recognized Investment Exchanges** (**RIEs**), though their members still need to be authorized to carry on investment business. The London Stock Exchange is, of course, a Recognized Investment Exchange.

Each SRO had to devise a **rulebook** for members, and has to ensure they observe it. Each rulebook has to be approved by the SIB. At the outset the SIB's own rules had to be approved by the Secretary of State for Trade and Industry, though responsibility for the SIB regulatory structure has now switched to the Treasury. Those who do not or cannot join an SRO have the option of applying direct to the SIB for authorization for investment business, though the SIB strongly encourages applicants to register with the appropriate SRO rather than with itself direct.

The Self-Regulating Organizations

The line-up of SROs in 1995 was as follows:

● The **Securities and Futures Authority** (**SFA**) covers three main activities: dealing in securities, dealing in the financial and commodities futures markets and dealing in international bonds from London. It therefore embraces members of the London Stock Exchange, of the Liffe financial futures market and the commodities markets as well as London eurobond dealers. Prior to their amalgamation in the SFA, there were initially separate bodies for members of the London Stock Exchange and of the futures markets.

- The **Investment Management Regulatory Organization (IMRO)** brings together those managing the main forms of pooled investment: investment trusts, unit trusts and pension funds.

- The **Personal Investment Authority** or **PIA** emerged in 1994 after a lengthy gestation and painful birth. It embraces the supervisory activities of two previous SROs. One of these was the **Financial Intermediaries, Managers and Brokers Regulatory Association (FIMBRA)** which covered insurance brokers and independent investment advisers. This was probably the most important of the bodies as far as the small investor was concerned. The other was the **Life Assurance and Unit Trust Regulatory Organization** or **LAUTRO**. This covered the marketing of pooled investment products by the companies which provided them – an activity that is regulated separately from the investment management side. It thus embraced the retail marketing of life assurance and unit trusts. FIMBRA and LAUTRO have effectively been taken over by the PIA but retain an independent identity in winding down residual business. The PIA thus now covers the retailing aspect of investment products, whatever the distribution channel.

Under the SIB regime, the financial community has to bear the costs of operating its own regulatory systems: a prime appeal for the government but a heavy burden for some financial institutions and ultimately for their customers. The regulators are practitioners with experience of the different businesses involved.

Standards to be applied

What standards does the SIB system impose? Some are self-evident. Those authorized to carry on investment business must be fit and proper – and of adequate financial standing – to do so. Spot checks on a firm's records can be carried out where necessary and a range of sanctions ranging from a rap on the knuckles, through fines, to removal of authorization can be meted out.

The basis of an investment business's relationship with its customer normally needs to be set out in writing. The investment business has to deal fairly with its client. There has to be be a complaints procedure. Unsolicited calls to sell investments (**cold calling**) are normally prohibited except for insurance (as under the previous system) and unit trusts.

Adequate arrangements for segregating clients' money from that of an investment business are required, though in practice this has sometimes been one of the shakier areas. Much pain in the past had been caused by investment managers who collapsed taking clients' money down with their own. And – an interesting provision for brokers and tipsheet writers, though one that would be dificult to enforce – published investment recommendations must be researched and be able to be substantiated.

Compensation arrangements

The London Stock Exchange had long operated a **compensation fund** so that the public could not suffer from the default of a member. Since Big Bang it has been replaced by a somewhat watered-down compensation arrangement. Today, all investment businesses must provide compensation arrangements to protect clients' money up to a certain level should the business go into liquidation. Naturally, neither this provision nor the one requiring research of investment tips insulates the client from losses resulting simply from poor advice.

Where legislation takes a hand

The new self-regulatory structure is designed mainly to supervise those who operate in the investment business. The nature of many of the investments in which they deal is still shaped by legislation.

The affairs of **companies** (both private companies and those whose shares are traded on a market) are largely governed by the **Companies Acts**, of which the latest comprehensive revision is the **Companies Act 1985**. The **Department of Trade and Industry (DTI)** is the ministry responsible for enforcing companies legislation. Companies Acts cover matters such as preparation and submission of accounts, requirements for prospectuses, duties and rights of auditors, safeguards for creditors and shareholders, duties of directors, powers to appoint inspectors into the affairs of a company, and the like. But they also touch on some aspects of securities markets and share trading. **Disclosure** of **3 per cent shareholdings** in a public company (it used to be **5 per cent shareholdings)** is a Companies Act provision. So is a provision which gives a company the power to require disclosure of the investors who lie behind **nominee shareholdings**. The prohibition of **insider trading** (dealing in shares on the basis of privileged **price-sensitive information**) is now covered by the 1993 Criminal Justice Act, but the DTI has powers of investigation under section 177 of the Financial Services Act. The Companies Acts prohibit a company from giving **financial assistance for the purchase of its own shares** except with a lengthy process of shareholder approval: one of the key issues in the **Guinness affair** which surfaced in 1986.

The new accountancy regime established at the beginning of the 1990s under the aegis of the **Financial Reporting Council (FRC)** also has a part to play in companies regulation. In the late 1980s accounting standards in Britain threatened to come into disrepute as lax interpretation of the rules frequently allowed company managements to present the picture they wanted, and to mislead shareholders and others in the process. Not only has one of the FRC's arms, the **Accounting Standards Board (ASB)** considerably tightened up on the rules under which accounts are prepared. Another arm, the **Financial Reporting Review Panel**, can take to task companies which it considers are breaking the financial reporting rules, requiring them to amend their presentation. If they refuse to do so, it can apply to the courts. A sub-committee of the ASB, the **Urgent Issues Task Force**, can give rapid interpretations of disputed issues in the accounting rulebook, again with the threat of court action from the Financial Reporting Review Panel should companies refuse to comply.

The new accounting regime is not statutory. But by a typically British process its decisions have virtually the force of law. Companies are required under the Companies Act to prepare accounts which give a 'true and fair view'. Giving a true and fair view normally implies conforming to the relevant accounting standard, or justifying any departure. Thus, companies that unjustifiably depart from accounting standards in their presentation can be accused of a breach of the Companies Act and the accounting authorities have the power to test the issue in the courts.

The new accounting regime has sometimes been accused of inflexibility – imposing tight rules rather than allowing room for interpretation in the light of individual circumstances – and the issue sometimes surfaces in press comment. After the laxity of the 1980s, some rigidity was probably inevitable. But the proof of the pudding is in the eating. The reliability and usefulness of company accounts has improved enormously in the first half of the 1990s.

Unit trusts had been regulated for many years under the **Prevention of Fraud (Investments) Act**. Now they are authorized and supervised under the SIB regulatory structure.

Other Acts govern the affairs of specific types of business. **Insurance companies** are governed by the **Insurance Companies Acts** as far as the running of the corporate insurance business is concerned – investment management and selling would come under the SIB structure. **Building societies** come under the **Building Societies Act**, the latest version of which has caused considerable confusion about the rules applying when a building society wishes to be taken over by a company or to turn itself into a listed company.

Banks are regulated under the **Banking Act** – a revised Act reached the Statute Book in 1987 – and supervised by the **Bank of England**, though now with assistance from outsiders who serve on the **Board of Banking Supervision**. The Bank has a wider supervisory role which encompasses banking, money markets, foreign exchange markets and the gilt-edged market, but it may make its views felt in any of the markets whose health is vital to the functioning of the City. A key problem in banking supervision is the international nature of the operations of major banks: a key factor in the **Barings** debacle and in the earlier collapse of the **Bank of Credit and**

Commerce International (BCCI) where the head company was registered in Luxembourg.

The **Lloyd's insurance market** governs itself within the powers granted by a specific Act of Parliament. The latest **Lloyd's Act**, which came into force in 1983, tightened up the self-regulatory requirements in response to a variety of scandals. But Lloyd's has fought (successfully, up to 1995) against being dragged within the scope of the Financial Services Act.

Traditional self-regulating bodies

The London Stock Exchange has traditionally regulated its own members, who could be disciplined by the representative **Stock Exchange Council**, and in this respect has probably changed least under the SIB regime. The difference is that the job is now split between the Stock Exchange and the Securities and Futures Authority. Broadly, the Stock Exchange is responsible for matters relating to the running of the market and the SFA for policing the financial health of the market's members. If a stockbroker is 'unable to meet his commitments' (in other words, goes bust), he used to be **hammered** on the Stock Exchange floor. More financially than physically painful, this means the market was told of his default and that he had ceased to trade. Prosaically, the message now goes out on the screens.

The **City Panel on Takeovers and Mergers** (the **Takeover Panel**) was established by City institutions (including the Stock Exchange) in 1968 to police the takeover jungle where most abuses occurred (see Chapter 10). It is not part of the SIB regulatory framework, though with effect from 1988 its powers were beefed up to give its decisions the backing of the SIB's range of sanctions, if required.

Regulatory problems across frontiers

The internationalization of securities markets poses various problems for regulators. First, it is difficult for the supervisors of any one country to monitor effectively the activities of an international securities house, which can switch its 'book' between Tokyo, London and New York in the course of a day.

Secondly, some markets such as the euromarket are truly

international in that they are not attached to any one country. There is no official supranational body with the power to enforce rules on all participants: a cause for concern which crops up periodically in press reports of discussions among leading bankers.

Finally, the international nature of today's securities business can frustrate the efforts of the best-intentioned domestic supervisory authorities. The **removal of exchange controls** in Britain, combined with the use of **nominee names**, means that the British as well as foreigners can deal anonymously in British markets via the medium of a **Swiss bank** and run little risk of detection if they flaunt the rules. It is also very difficult to clamp down on dubious investment schemes selling from overseas to investors in Britain.

The regulatory system in practice

Regulators tread a tightrope. Regulate too severely and the business will go elsewhere. Regulate too loosely, and scandals will erupt which may destroy confidence in the financial marketplace. Britain has a tradition of fairly light regulation in many areas, which has been a significant factor in attracting international business to Britain and maintaining the City as an international financial centre.

There are those who believe that Britain will eventually be obliged to move over to a statutory regulatory body on the lines of America's SEC, particularly in view of the need to harmonize regulation across the European Union. Nevertheless, in its early days the SIB – though not a statutory body – was accused of being excessively legalistic in drawing up its rules and these have subsequently been simplified.

As the SIB was getting into its stride, a major fund management scandal arose. Investors who had handed over more than £100m to be invested by a firm called **Barlow Clowes**, supposedly in safe government securities, discovered that much of the money had been misappropriated and would be lost.

Barlow Clowes investors were a residual casualty of the pre-Financial Services Act regulatory system, when no effective compensation scheme was in force. The SIB emerged with some credit from the affair, having brought it into the open by closing down Barlow Clowes. The SIB also made early use of its powers to close a number of suspect commodity 'investment' firms.

The SIB regulatory structure did not prevent the theft of many hundreds of millions of pounds from the pension funds of companies run by the late **Robert Maxwell** in the early 1990s, though many City institutions must share responsibiity for this disaster. The SROs have, however, been active in fining or closing down investment advisers who failed to obey the rules.

The highest-profile action of the SIB to date, however, concerns the mis-selling of **personal pensions**. An investigation suggested that hundreds of thousands of individuals had been persuaded by salesmen and saleswomen to opt out of occupational pension schemes in favour of taking out personal pensions that were likely to deliver far lower benefits. The government must shoulder a fair degree of responsibility for this situation, having encouraged individuals to make personal pension provision without ensuring that adequate safeguards were in force. But the SIB, if it did not prevent this debacle, has shown itself remarkably tough in addressing the consequences.

Major insurance companies have been fined and forced to send their salesforces back to the classroom for retraining. Moreover, those responsible for giving incorrect advice (or their employers) will have to compensate their victims for the financial loss they are likely to suffer – a process that will probably take years to complete and involve sums running into billions of pounds. Meantime, many financial institutions that marketed personal pensions – and by no means only the insurance companies – are under pressure to make financial provision in their accounts for the cost of meeting their compensation liabilities.

In other ways the first half of the 1990s has been a troubled period for the vendors of life assurance and savings products. A major bone of contention has been the question of **polarization** (see glossary) under which financial intermediaries must decide whether they are independent investment advisers or whether they simply market the investment products of one group. The system has encouraged many one-time independents to link with a particular provider of savings products and raised fears that genuinely independent advice would become even more scarce. Moreover, the 'independence' of supposedly independent advice is itself open to question when the advisers are paid in the form of commission on the products they sell (see Chapter 21).

One success of the regulatory system is the new insistence that buyers of life assurance and investment products should at least be given information on costs and the amount of **commission** that is going to the salesperson. The life assurance industry had long held out against this move. Early in 1995 it was still too soon to judge the effectiveness of this provision or its impact (if any) on savings choices. At that time the PIA was also working on disclosure rules for unit trust sales. Given the enormous complexity of many savings products, it must still be open to question whether most buyers are likely to be directed towards the most appropriate product. And promotional literature is often at best complex and at worst deeply confusing.

When the system is breached

Ideally, a regulatory system prevents misdeeds rather than detecting and prosecuting wrongdoers once abuses have occurred. The fallback for serious cases of financial crime is the state's powers of criminal prosecution. But the British legal system has proved singularly ineffective in delivering convictions in major cases of alleged financial crime.

Frequently (and often unfairly) blamed for this state of affairs is the **Serious Fraud Office** or **SFO**, which has the brief of investigating and prosecuting cases involving serious and complex fraud, particularly where there is a public interest aspect. This would include most of the major cases that are likely to hit the newspaper headlines. In future the SFO is also to take over part of the responsibilities of the Crown Prosecution Service's **Fraud Investigation Group**, which deals with slightly smaller and lower-profile financial cases.

Frauds are often of a complexity that tax the trained accountant, let alone the understanding of a lay jury, and alleged fraudsters usually seem able to obtain the best legal representation however low their fortunes are said to have sunk. There have been suggestions that cases of complex fraud should be dealt with by a judge and expert assessors rather than by a judge and jury, but they have so far been resisted. An added complication is the number of different individuals and bodies that may be picking over the carcass when fraud is alleged in connection with the demise of a company. Liquidators attempting to salvage something for shareholders and creditors may not find it easy to get information when some of those involved face criminal charges. And the existence of criminal charges can hamper the press's own investigative efforts.

You will also frequently read references to the **Fraud Squad**. In practice, most police forces have their experts in financial crime, but the body probably referred to is a branch of the Criminal Investigation Department of the City of London Police. With – in 1995 – almost 30 officers seconded to the SFO and 40-odd at its own Wood Street headquarters in the City, it both investigates Square-Mile crimes itself and passes on high-profile cases to the SFO. The Maxwell investigation started with the City Fraud Squad and moved to the SFO when the scale of the debacle emerged.

23

The financial pages

The British have access to a very wide range of financial reading matter. Much of it comes as an adjunct to more general daily reading: the business and City sections of the national daily and Sunday newspapers. At times of boom in the financial markets the national newspapers derive a large portion of their revenue from financial advertising and the editorial pages of the financial sections expand to reflect the heightened interest.

But any review of the financial press has to start with London's *Financial Times* – the '*FT*'. It sells around 300,000 copies a day of which some 120,000 is overseas circulation. It prints (or will be printing) in two locations in the UK, two in the United States, and in France, Germany, Sweden and Japan. The international editions contain a greater amount of information relevant to the local markets. Back home, it is the City's bible, and on the rare days when the *FT*'s pink pages have failed to appear the City has had a rudderless feel. It is international in outlook with a range of overseas correspondents that much of the British press lacks. The UK edition covers as a matter of course all the major financial markets of the UK and the more important ones overseas. It is a journal of record for news of UK companies. Its news reporting covers the major political, economic, business and financial events worldwide, and its interests extend to the arts and leisure activities. News is put into perspective with the help of background analysis and feature articles. And its statistical information and price coverage of all major financial markets is far more comprehensive than can be found elsewhere. On working days it is now divided into two sections, with the more general domestic and international business and political news in the first part and the specific news of companies and financial markets in the second. On Saturday it is divided into three sections.

In fact, the *FT* is easier to define by what it does not cover than by what it does. First, it does not make investment recommendations as such, though you can read between the lines in the Lex investment comment column and some of the company comment. Secondly, it normally deals in fact rather than speculation. Though its market reporting duly records the rumours that move share prices, it does not always fully mirror the gossipy nature of much City activity. Its nearest American counterpart, the *Wall Street Journal*, is also read in the City: primarily for its coverage of North American business. It has not seriously challenged the *FT* on its home beat.

Not everybody has the time to read a newspaper of the *FT*'s scope each day. The financial pages of the quality press – the *Guardian*, *The Independent*, the *Daily Telegraph* and *The Times* – offer an alternative, covering the main items of business and financial news and dealing briefly with many of the minor ones. A similar formula – news stories, company results coverage, editorial comment and feature articles – surfaces in different guises. While the *Guardian* has a somewhat ambivalent attitude to specific share recommendations, the other three carry regular investment comment.

On Saturdays these quality dailies – like the *FT* – change their spots and devote much of the available space to personal finance coverage: questions of tax, insurance, pooled investments such as unit trusts and family finance planning in general.

A number of Britain's major regional papers – the *Birmingham Post*, the *Yorkshire Post* and *The Scotsman* – follow a similar pattern to the national dailies, though with a bias towards news of local businesses and events.

Below the level of the 'heavy' dailies, the *Daily Mail* and the *Daily Express* have less space to devote to financial coverage, though the *Mail* in particular has at times had significant influence on the stockmarket. The result is a greater emphasis on one or two major financial 'stories'. Both also provide stockmarket reports. The attention to financial news in

London's *Evening Standard* shows that this is regarded as a significant selling point in the battle for readers in the capital. The *Standard*'s financial pages are printed on pink paper – a compliment to the *Financial Times*, though the *FT* has not always regarded it as such.

The heavyweight Sunday papers – *The Sunday Times*, the *Observer*, the *Sunday Telegraph* and the *Independent on Sunday* – start with the assumption that their readers will have picked up the main items of the week's financial news elsewhere. Thus the emphasis is on background analysis of current stories and attempts to get in first with the stories that will hit the financial headlines in the coming week. In this some of them are often helped by financiers (or their public relations advisers) who find it convenient to float a story before the new week's dealings begin in the markets. Not every 'story' necessarily results from journalistic legwork, nor is a partisan approach always entirely absent. All provide personal finance coverage and all at one time or another are active with **share tips**, often of the 'close to the market gossip' variety.

Because of the extensive financial coverage in the national press, Britain supports relatively few stockmarket magazines. The largest and by far the longest established is the *Investors Chronicle*, now under the same ownership as the *Financial Times*. Its strength has traditionally been its very detailed analysis of company profits and company prospects, useful for those who want to monitor their existing investments as well as pick up ideas for new ones. It does make specific share recommendations, but the bulk of its coverage also contains an element of evaluation or advice. Its feature material contains much that is aimed at helping the newcomer to the stockmarkets. It also carries a regular personal finance coverage. Considerably larger in terms of circulation is *The Economist*, but domestic financial markets now occupy a small amount of space in its pages, though its selective coverage of international business issues is strong.

Mirroring the decline in direct stockmarket investment by the individual and the growth of pooled investment schemes, publications on personal financial planning for the individual have blossomed. New magazines spring up and older ones change their names or their owners. Among those seen on bookstalls in the mid-1990s are *Moneywise*, *Inside Money* and

Money Observer (an offshoot of the newspaper). For subscribers, *Money Which* provides advice on financial services
and products. There are also specialist magazines advising on
what mortgage to go for and the like.

These personal finance magazines for the individual should
not be confused with the publications aimed primarily at
financial intermediaries – insurance brokers and so-called
financial advisers – who market investment products to the
public. The leaders here include the monthly *Money Management* and *Planned Savings*, both of which provide detailed
coverage of the performance of unit trusts, insurance funds
and other investment products. *Money Marketing* is a news-
orientated weekly paper that aims for something of the same
market and has attracted several competitors. These papers
for the personal finance business overlap with trade magazines
for the insurance and pensions industries (insurance magazines are legion).

Banking is served by *The Banker*, a monthly magazine
under the same ownership as the *Financial Times*, and the
eurocurrency market by the monthly *Euromoney* and allied
publications from the same stable. The weekly *International
Financing Review* is aimed primarily at the banks and bankers
that put together the big financing packages in the international market, which it records.

Britain has a highly developed trade press. The property
world is served mainly by the long-established weekly *Estates
Gazette*, by *Property Week* (formerly *Chartered Surveyor
Weekly*) and by the news-orientated weekly free-circulation
newspaper, *Estates Times*. Accountancy spawns numerous
publications, of which the monthly magazine *Accountancy* and
the weekly free newspaper *Accountancy Age* are prominent.

Newsletters are a publishing market in themselves. Many
sectors of the financial community are served by a range of
specialist newsletters: taxation, accountancy and eurobond
newsletters in particular. But in addition there is a range of
stockmarket newsletters – **tip sheets** – promoting themselves
directly to the general public.

Some stockmarket newsletters are established, well researched and reputable. But some are distinctly dubious,
backed by claims of successful recommendations in the past

which may fall down on detailed scrutiny. Promotional costs aside, the newsletter publishing business is cheap to get into – little more than a wordprocessor and a telephone is required – and it attracts its fair share of get-rich-quick merchants. You have been warned.

How to read between the lines

Reading the financial pages is one thing. Reading between the lines of the financial pages is a different art. Financial journalists do not always say exactly what they think – often because Britain's very strict libel regime prevents them from doing so. Moreover, they are reporting on a world – the world of finance – which has its own layers of jargon and pseudo-scientific gobbledegook, often disguising the banal nature of what is going on.

To round off our examination of the financial markets, here's a less serious guide to some of the more confusing turns of phrase you might come across in financial reports and the financial press. The interpretations are purely personal and in no way imply that the words and phrases are used in any particular paper or report in the sense suggested here.

The first problem the financial journalist hits is when he wants to put across a warning or express disbelief. Remember, we're talking about money and a surprising number of people take money very seriously: particularly those who hope to make a lot of it or already have a lot of it to lose. Since this definition embraces a high proportion of people in the City, the journalist attacks them at his peril. A casual aside suggesting that the directors of Muggitt Finance put in a bulk order for rose-tinted spectacles before preparing their prospectus profit forecast is enough to have Muggitt's lawyers baying at the gate.

In fact, can a journalist safely suggest that a share is vastly overpriced, even if he is not implying skulduggery on the part of the directors? It's a moot point and he'll often try to find a

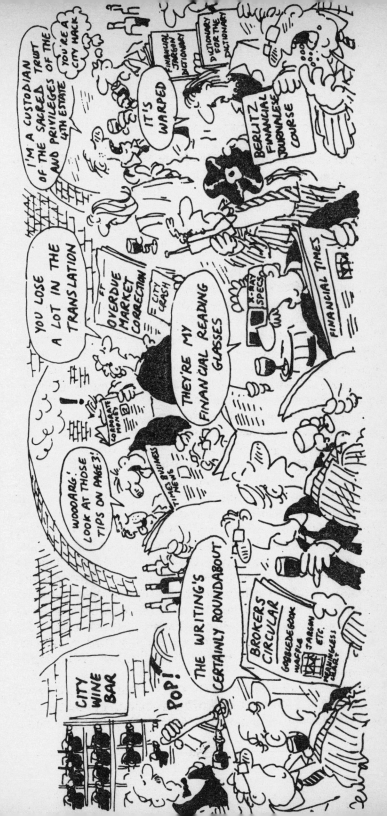

way round it. 'Muggitt's shares have fallen from 300p to 100p so far this year, and holders should consider taking their profits' is one approach. If he simply thinks they're far too high, without the company necessarily being on the skids, he might say 'On a PE ratio of 35, Muggitt Finance is rated well above the sector average; this anomaly is likely to be ironed out in the near future'. He doesn't mean that shares of the other companies in the sector are due for a rise. He means that Muggitt is heading for a fall. 'With the PE ratio at 35, investors should not ignore Muggitt's downside potential' is another way of saying the same thing. 'Not for widows and orphans' simply means 'highly speculative' and occasionally 'not for anyone in his right mind'. It is rather like the definition of a 'recovery stock'. It can mean a share that is going to rise as the company recovers or a company that won't be around very long if it doesn't recover.

When a journalist suggests shares are 'fully valued' he is almost certainly trying to say 'overvalued' without offending the company too deeply. This is not the same thing as describing them as 'fairly valued', which probably means the writer hasn't a clue one way or the other ('a sound long-term hold' also implies that he is sitting firmly on the fence).

There was a journalist in the pre-decimalisation days who spoke his mind and suggested that one company's shares 'standing at 2s 6d' were 'about half-a-crown too high'. His fate is lost in the mists of history.

Comment on individuals is more perilous. For the financial journalist there can be no such thing as a crook, at least until he is safely convicted and behind bars (which, in Britain, he rarely is provided his crime is big enough). The paper's lawyer might just let him get away with 'controversial City financier'. Hence you'll occasionally read pieces like this: 'Speaking from Panama City, Mr Cyril Buck, the controversial financier at the head of the troubled Muggitt Finance group, today strongly criticised the decision by the company's auditors to state that the accounts were prepared on a going concern basis and did not reflect a true and fair view of the company's affairs'. In the vernacular this might be translated as 'Cyril Buck, the spiv at the head of Muggitt, has done a bunk. He's annoyed because the auditors say that the company is bust and the accounts are fiddled.'

Even journalism has had characters of questionable judgement, probably operating at the fringes of the share-tipping end of the market and almost certainly writing for a stock-market 'newsletter' of the kind that claims divine insight into the future movement of share prices. Be a little careful when you read the following: 'Since Rudyard Sharpe took the helm at the end of last year and injected his private business into Salter Way Holdings it is recognised as one of the most dynamic groups in the financial services sector. The shares are a narrow market, but should be bought at prices up to 200p'.

It may be a well-researched and genuine tip. It could equally well mean: 'Ruddy Sharpe flogged his private company to Salter Way at an exorbitant price and is now ramping the shares for all he's worth. That's why he had me to lunch last week. The company's a load of junk but there aren't many shares around so the price will rocket if a few mugs jump in and buy them on my advice. That's why I bought 20,000 myself at 140p last week. I'll sell the moment my readers have pushed the price up to 190p.'

Crooked writers are rare. Two other types of financial commentator can be dangerous to your financial health: the excessively vague and the excessively precise. How many times have you seen a share described in terms like these: 'The shares stand on a PE ratio of 12, which is generous in today's markets'. What does it mean? That the rating is generous to the investor (the shares are priced below their true worth and should be bought)? Or the rating flatters the company (the shares are over-rated and should be sold)? Take your pick.

Then the over-precise, which is most likely to crop up in the research circulars produced by Porsche-powered stockbrokers' analysts but may well be repeated in the financial press: 'The acquisition of Nuggins should contribute around £2.735m to the pre-tax profits of Bloggins Plc next year. Assuming internally-generated sales growth in the range of 11.7 to 11.8 per cent and a 2.34 per cent improvement in the margins of the timber business, the shares at 393p are on a prospective PE ratio of 14.27 and are a medium to strong buy on a seven month view.' Roughly translated, this might mean: 'Your guess as to Bloggins's profits is as good as mine. But our marketmaking arm has a whole load of Bloggins's shares on its books and told me to help shift them. And it's for writing this sort of junk that they pay me £80,000 a year'.

The big institutional investors know which stockbrokers' analysts are worth reading. Most 'research' material goes straight in the bin, and one very large financial institution has a gigantic wheeled tub that goes round the investment department once a week to collect brokers' circulars for the bonfire.

Much of what you read about the City falls into place if you bear in mind a few simple facts. Most financial people the private individual is likely to meet are salesmen of one kind or another. Like salesmen in other fields they'll be tempted to sell you the product that pays them the highest commission or which they happen to have in stock. Like any salesmen, they are not always the best people to advise on the merits of the product.

They have a particular problem when markets are going down or likely to go down. 'Put your money into Bloggins – you won't lose more than half of it' is not an appealing sales message. They have to convince themselves and their clients that markets are going up for ever. Or they devise strategies like 'switching' that generate commission income but fall short of a straight 'buy' recommendation. In either case the message is likely to be wrapped up in further layers of gobbledegook.

Hence: 'Mike Puff, manager of the Duffer group of unit trusts expects to see the equity market rise by 20 to 25 per cent over the year after a weak start, given the relative strength of the UK corporate sector'. This might translate as: 'Mike Puff has as little clue as the rest of us, but he's in the game of flogging investments'.

Or the message from a broker to clients: 'We therefore recommend a switch from Sainsbury to Tesco on income growth grounds. Our charts show that . . . .'. The meaning here could be: 'There's damn all to choose between the two shares, but we rake in the commission each time you sell one and buy the other. We'll recommend you switch back next year'.

Finally, no review of moneyspeak is complete without a glance at that bastion of City tradition: the daily stockmarket report. How often have you seen that shares 'closed narrowly mixed in nervous trading'? The beauty of phrases of this kind is that the words can be used in almost any order with little if any change to the sense: 'closed nervously in mixed narrow trading', 'traded nervously in a narrow mixed close' and so on. Perhaps it means something to somebody. At least it fills column inches and helps to preserve the mystique of the financial markets.

Quick guide to moneyspeak

Here's a quick glossary of some common current terms and phrases you'll meet, with possible meanings.

Overdue market correction A near meltdown of the financial system.

Free market A market in which share prices can be manipulated with relative freedom from official supervision.

Self regulation Regulation of financial markets by the practitioners, for the benefit of the practitioners.

International (or **global**) **market in securities** A system for ensuring that a panic in New York or Tokyo spreads rapidly to London – or *vice-versa*.

Popular capitalism A device for selling shares in state monopolies to some of the people who already own them.

Insider dealer Investors who do not work in the City are 'outsider dealers'.

The shares are acquiring strong institutional backing This is one the boys have decided to ramp up.

Our research report suggests ... In a broker's report on a new issue this may mean that what follows is a few unchecked facts gleaned from the company's own prospectus.

Following the acquisition of Muggitt a phased programme of asset disposals was put in train We got control then asset-stripped it like crazy.

Acquisitive stockmarket-orientated financial conglomerate Paper-shuffling asset stripper.

Acquisitive Antipodean financial entrepreneur Aussie or Kiwi market raider.

Colourful usually linked with the word **entrepreneur**. It is not racist, neither does it usually imply blue blood. **Colourful entrepreneurs** are probably active stockmarket operators. While their tactics pay off they are in the pink. They attract acres of purple prose from the spivvier share tipsters and their competitors go green with envy or white with rage. All too often they overstretch themselves and end deep in the red.

Mr Rudyard Sharpe regards his 18 per cent holding in Nuggins as a long-term investment Ruddy Sharpe is bidding for Nuggins next week.

On a long-term view . . . Looking beyond the next five minutes.

We are responding vigorously to recent consumer complaint In a company report this may mean they are stepping up their public relations budget and running an image-building TV campaign – otherwise carrying on as before.

The accounts give a true and fair view . . . In the auditors' report on a major bank this possibly means that the accounts give a true and fair view except that the £5bn of loans to Latin America are worthless but can't be written off because the bank hasn't the resources.

. . . has been freed from day-to-day responsibility so that he can concentrate on long-term development of the company Has been fired. Employees are sacked; directors leave in a company Mercedes and a flood of euphemisms. When a director resigns for reasons of health, it is not necessarily his current health that is at issue. It is what will happen to his health if he tries to stay.

* * *

'How to read between the lines' is reproduced by kind permission of The Independent, *in which a version of this chapter first appeared.*

Glossary and Index

1 per cent rule 167
212 (*see* **Section 212**)
3i (*see* **Investors in Industry**)
3 per cent rule 167, 342
15 per cent rule 166
30 per cent rule 165–166
50 per cent (significance of) 41,
167
75 per cent (significance of) 41
90 per cent (significance of) 167

above the line 56
accept (of bill) 237
acceptance credit 237–238
acceptances (bills) 237, 242
acceptances (in takeover) 167,
170
Accepting Houses. The old
name for the top tier of
merchant banks in the UK
which used to be members of
the Accepting Houses
Committee. 237
account (Stock Exchange) 111–
113
account day 111
accountants (*see also* **auditors**)
35, 37, 42
**Accounting Standards Board,
accounting standards** 95, 160–
162, 342–343

accounts (company) 39–96
accrued, accumulated income
(on gilt-edged stocks, etc) 44,
207
accumulation units (unit trusts)
328
acquisition accounting 160–161
acquisitions (*see also* **takeovers**)
63
ACT (*see* **Advance Corporation
Tax**)
acting in concert (*see also*
concert party) 167–168
actuary 37–38, 321
**Additional Voluntary
Contributions (AVCs)** 322
adjust (profits, prices, earnings,
dividends, etc.) 56, 147–150,
156–158
administrator, administration.
The 1986 Insolvency Act
introduced a new procedure
known as **administration**. As an
alternative to winding up
(liquidating) an insolvent
company, the court may (with
the support of the creditors)
make an **administration order**,
approving the appointment of
an **administrator**, if it appears
that this may produce a better

result in the long run. The administrator will take over the running of the company, selling off bits to repay debts as and when it appears advantageous. The hope is that the proceeds will be greater than if the company were closed down and the bits sold off immediately, and that it may even be possible for the core of the company to be preserved and to resume normal trading in the future. The procedure has some similarities with the temporary protection from creditors that American companies can claim under **Chapter 11** of their bankruptcy laws.

ADRs (*see* **American Depository Receipts**)

advance (bank) 220

Advance Corporation Tax (ACT) (*see also* **unrelieved ACT**) 52–53

adversarial (relationship) 106

aftermarket (*see also* **secondary market**) 138

agency broker 103, 104, 106–107, 109, 111, 212

AGM (*see* **annual general meeting**)

agreed (takeover bid) 162

AIM (*see* **Alternative Investment Market**)

All-Share Index (*see* **FT-SE Actuaries All-Share Index**)

allotment, allocation (of shares, etc.) 139–140, 142

allotment letters 142

Alternative Investment Market 101, 132, 135

alternative investments. Refers to objects owned at least partly as investments, which would not normally count as financial assets. Examples are: works of art; Georgian silver; antique coins; **busted bonds** (q.v.), etc. Sometimes also referred to as **collectibles**. Alternative investments in this sense have nothing to do with the **Alternative Investment Market** in small company shares.

aluminium 293

American deficit 130, 251

American Depositary Receipts (ADRs). Instead of trading in shares of British companies as such, Americans may buy and sell ADRs, which confer ownership rights to the shares. The shares themselves are held on deposit with a bank. Trading in ADRs rather than the shares cuts the administrative hassle of registering changes in share ownership and avoids the need to pay stamp duty on each transaction.

American Stock Exchange. The smaller of the two Stock Exchanges in New York. The larger, on which the shares of most of the biggest corporations are traded, is the **New York Stock Exchange** (q.v.).

amortization (*see* **depreciation**)

amount paid up 143–144, 149

AMPS (*see* **auction market preferred stock**)

analyst (*see* **investment analyst**)

angel (*see* **business angel**)

annual percentage rate (APR). Organizations granting credit in the UK are required to state the real cost in terms of interest as an annual percentage rate. This is because many of the ways in which interest is expressed in advertisements can be misleading without an APR. An individual who borrows £100 and pays it back in instalments over a year may be quoted a **flat rate** of, say, 12 per cent. But this means he is paying 12 per cent on the full amount for the whole year, whereas after 6 months only £50 will actually be outstanding. The real rate of interest or APR is roughly double.

Annual General Meeting (AGM). General meeting of a company at which normally routine matters are put to the vote of shareholders: acceptance of the accounts, remuneration of auditors, re-election of directors, etc. 41, 49

annuity. A form of pension bought from an insurance company. In the simplest form the buyer pays over a lump sum in return for which he receives a stipulated income for life, consisting part of income on the money paid and part of return of the capital. Whether or not it turns out to be good value depends on how long he lives.

application form (in share issue) 136

APR (*see* **annual percentage rate**)

arbitrage. Taking advantage of differentials in the price of a security, currency, etc., usually in two different markets. If Fastbuck Finance shares are quoted at 200p in London but at the equivalent of 205p in Amsterdam, the arbitrageur

would make a profit by selling in Amsterdam and buying in London. This would tend to make the Amsterdam price fall and the London price rise, and the anomaly would be ironed out. Arbitrage in this sense is an example of the way speculators assist in the smooth running of markets. In the United States arbitrage is often associated with risk arbitrage, which has come to mean taking positions in takeover stocks. (*See* **arbitrageur** or **arb**.) 260

arbitrageurs (arbs) 168–169, 171

Articles of Association. A form of written constitution (technically a contract between the shareholders and the company), required of UK companies. Covers a number of (often standard) items such as borrowing powers, issue of shares, etc. Usually referred to in conjunction with the **Memorandum of Association** which contains information on the company's objects, share capital, etc. (*See also* **Companies House**.)

ASB (*see* **Accounting Standards Board**)

asset-backed securities. The result of securitizing various forms of loan. A company which provides loans via credit cards might issue floating rate notes or other forms of security to investors in the securities markets, the interest and capital repayment being provided by the payments from the credit card borrowers. The most common form of asset-backed

security in the UK is **mortgage-backed securities** (q.v.).
asset backing (*see also* **net asset value**) 78–81, 311, 332–333
asset-rich companies 79–81
asset stripping. Gaining control of a company with a view to selling its assets (often properties) at a profit rather than developing the business as such. Very common among take-over practitioners in the early 1970s. 126
assets 46 *et seq*
associated company, **associate** 55, 84
associates (of companies involved in takeover) 168
at a premium, a discount 79, 93, 199, 259, 333
at call 235
at the money (of options) 288
auction market preferred stock (AMPS). A form of preference share issued by UK companies or their subsidiaries in the US. Though techically share capital, the preference shares have some of the characteristics of a floating rate debt since the 'dividend' is not fixed but varies with money-market rates.
auctions (in gilt-edged market) 210–211
audit 37, 42
audit committee. Already common in different forms in various overseas countries, the audit committee is a committee of non-executive directors that acts as a check on various aspects of the financial governance of a company by the executives. The establishment of audit committees was

recommended by the **Cadbury Committee** (q.v).
auditors 42–43
auditors' fees 42, 52
auditors' report 42–43
authorized capital 91
authorized but unissued capital 91
authorized unit trusts 312, 325, 328, 330
authorized unit trusts (table in *FT*) 325
automated dealing system (*see also* **SAEF**) 104
AVCs (*see* **Additional Voluntary Contributions**)
avoidance (*see* **tax avoidance**)

baby syndicates (Lloyd's) 299
back office (of a broker). Office where the paperwork involved in share transactions is processed.
backwardation (in commodity markets) 294
bad debts. Money a company has lent or trade credit it has advanced, which it will not get back – probably because the creditor has gone bust. The bad debts will have to be written off in the company's accounts.
balance of payments 31, 247, 251
balance sheet 42, 44 *et seq*, 74, 82 *et seq*
balance sheet gearing 50, 74–76
balance sheet total 48
balance the books 22
ballot (in share allocation) 140
Baltic Exchange 294
bands (for bills of exchange) 236
bank bill 237, 243
Bank of Credit and Commerce International 343–344
Bank of England 3, 193, 231, 232–236, 343

Bank of England Index (for sterling, etc.) 250
Bank Rate 236
Banking Act 231, 343
banking crises 222–223, 227–229
banking system 32–33, 35–37, 219–231, 233
banks (*see also* **clearing banks, merchant banks, money market**) 35–36, 219–231, 343
banks (supervision of) 231, 343
bargains (Stock Exchange) 98
Barings 3, 219–30, 274, 290, 343
Barlow Clowes 345
base date (for index-linked gilts indexation) 209
base rates. These are the yardstick rates of interest quoted by the major commercial banks. While these banks are, in theory, in competition with each other, in practice they will normally quote the same rate because their cost of funds is much the same. Lesser-known deposit-taking institutions may need to quote a slightly higher rate to attract funds. Bank base rates are the interest rates most frequently quoted in press reports of interest-rate changes. Base rates are changed rapidly to reflect changes in official interest rates and will signal the cost of borrowing for much of the population. The interest rates on most loans for private individuals and for small businesses are set in relation to base rate. A borrower might pay, say, five or six **percentage points** above base rate on his loan, so if base rate was six per cent he would pay 11 or 12 per cent. What he paid would

change when base rates changed. Likewise, the rates of interest received by depositors would probably maintain some relationship with base rates. Large loans to major businesses are more likely to be geared to **LIBOR** (q.v.) than to base rate, and the interest rate will therefore reflect more directly the cost of money in the wholesale money markets. 234, 236, 244
basic rate income tax 2, 53
basis point (*see also* **point**) 214, 244, 269
basket (of currencies) 249–250
Basle Accord 224
BCCI (*see* **Bank of Credit and Commerce International**)
bear (*see also* **short**) 112–113
bear covering 121–122
bear market 113, 116
bear raid 122
bear sale, short sale 112, 121–122
bear squeeze 121–122
bearer bond 265
bearer security 112, 265
bearish 113, 287
beat the index 74
bed and breakfast. Stock Exchange technique whereby an investor sells particular shares on one day and buys them back the next morning. The purpose is normally to establish a loss for capital gains tax purposes – the investor may have capital profits in that year against which the losses can be offset to reduce tax liability.
below the line 56
benchmark gilt, bond. A government stock whose redemption yield is taken as the

yardstick by which redemption yields on company bonds are set at the outset and measured subsequently. There will be a different benchmark gilt for short, medium and long-dated stocks. 215

benefits in kind (for directors) (*see also* **directors' pay and perks**) 184

BES (*see* **Business Expansion Scheme**)

beta. A measure of the volatility of a share. A high beta share is likely to respond to stockmarket movements by rising or falling in value by more than the market average.

bid (*see* **takeover**)

bid basis (liquidation basis) 327

bid price 113, 329

bid rate 244

bid timetable 169

Big Bang (27 October 1986) 7–8, 97 *et seq*

Big Board (*see* **New York Stock Exchange**)

bi-lateral facility, credit line. A loan arrangement negotiated by a borrower with a single bank rather than with a syndicate of banks. The borrower could, however, negotiate separate bi-lateral lines with a number of individual banks.

bill of exchange 235, 236–238

black economy (cash economy). Areas of the economy where transactions go unrecorded (and therefore untaxed). If your local plumber quotes you two prices for a job – one which will include VAT if you want a receipt and a lower one if you pay cash and forego the

paperwork – you are almost certainly contributing to the black economy if you pay cash.

Blue Arrow affair. More accurately described as the National Westminster Bank or County NatWest affair. A major scandal which led in July 1989 to the resignation of the chairman of the National Westminster Bank, several senior executives and various employees of County NatWest, its investment banking subsidiary, and of securities house UBS Phillips & Drew. The scandal concerned a £837m rights issue by employment agency group Blue Arrow, and the various stratagems used by its bankers and brokers to disguise the relatively low take-up of shares by investors.

blue chip 72

Board of Banking Supervision 231, 343

board of directors. The men and women legally responsible for running a company. The structure of the board varies greatly between companies. Directors who are also employees of the company and have management responsibility are **executive directors**. Directors who simply provide experience and advice in board deliberations, and possibly have jobs elsewhere, are **non-executive directors**. The **chairman** presides at board meetings, but is not necessarily top dog in practice unless he combines his role with that of **chief executive**. The chief executive is responsible for the management of the company as a whole and is often the same person as **managing director**; but some companies have both, with the managing director in the subordinate role. (Americans talk of the chief executive as **Chief Executive Officer** or **CEO**.) Other directors may be distinguished according to their area of responsibility: **finance director**, etc. Each company also needs a **company secretary**, responsible for administration of the legally required paperwork involved in running the company. He or she may or may not also be a director. You need to know your company to know who really counts among the directors – titles can be misleading.

boardroom pay and perks (*see* **directors' pay and perks**)

boiler room. Room with numerous telephones from which high-pressure salesmen attempt to sell securities direct to the public. Pejorative term. (*See also* **bucket shop**.)

bond. Forms of medium- or long-term 'IOU' issued by companies, governments, etc., usually paying interest and usually traded in a market. May be secured or unsecured. Interest may be fixed rate or floating rate (*see also* **gilt-edged stocks**, **government securities** and **corporate bonds**, **industrial debentures**, **loans**, **floating rate notes**). Bonds in the UK normally have a face value of £100. Fixed-interest bonds pay a fixed rate of interest on the £100 face value. But the yield or return to the investor depends on the price he pays for the bond in the market. A bond paying 11 per cent interest gives an income yield of around 12.5 per cent to someone who buys it in the market at £88.20. But **redemption yields** (q.v.) are the measure used for the total return from bonds.

bond rating service (Moody's and Standard & Poor's) (*see* **credit rating**)

bondized (insurance) 329

bonds (insurance) 329

bonus issue (*see* **scrip issue**)

bonuses (directors'). (*See* **directors' pay and perks**)

book (in shares) 102

bookbuilding. An exercise sometimes undertaken by financial advisers when a new issue or a secondary issue of shares is to be made. They canvass major institutional investors to establish how many shares each would be likely to take at what price. It may assist in establishing the price for the issue and judging its likely success.

book value 45, 47

book-keeping transaction 156

borrowing costs 25

borrowings, borrowed money (*see also* **debt**) 46, 50, 74–76, 84–87

bought deal 152

BP issue 141

brand names, brands 95

Brent crude 294

British Venture Capital Association (BVCA) 175

broker-dealers 36–37, 107
brokers (*see* **stockbrokers, insurance brokers**)
bucket shop. Operation for 'pushing' (over-promoting) particular shares to the public. The shares concerned are often of dubious quality (*see also* **boiler room**).
Building Societies Act 343
building society 32, 35, 219, 220, 317, 324, 343
bull 113
bull market 113, 116, 127
bull phase 116
bulldog bond 197, 264
bullish 113, 287
business angel 179
Business Expansion Scheme (**BES**) 178
busted bonds (*see* **scripophily**)
buy-back (of shares). Many companies seek permission from their shareholders to buy-back a certain proportion of their own shares in the stockmarket, if or when conditions are favourable. Sometimes the purchase and cancellation of a certain proportion of the share capital can improve the earnings or the asset backing for the remaining shares.
buy-out, buy-in (*see* **management buy-out**)

Cadbury Committee (on the financial aspects of corporate governance). A committee which devised a code (the **Cadbury Code**) aimed at tightening up various aspects of the financial supervision of companies. Its recommendations included the establishment of

remuneration committees (q.v) and **audit committees** (q.v.). 189
call (*see* **at call**)
call option 268, 287
cap (interest rate) 62, 78, 225, 242–243, 268
capital 13
capital account (of balance of payments) 251
capital adequacy 223
capital base 223–224
capital commitments 88
capital expenditure 65
capital gain 13, 14, 200–204
Capital Gains Tax (**CGT**). Tax payable on profits from the sale of most assets, particularly shares. Profits on sale of gilt-edged securities and qualifying company bonds were, however, exempt up to 1995 though the position could be changing. Investors in Britain could realize net gains of £6,000 (in 1995) before incurring a CGT liability. And in calculating liability, the base cost of the asset can be increased in line with inflation from 1982 so that tax is paid only on 'real' profits. The part of the capital gain occurring before 1982 is not taxable. 163
capital gearing (*see* **balance sheet gearing**)
capital loss 14, 201 *et seq*
capital market 261
capital ratio 223–224
capital reconstruction, reorganization 229–231
capital shares 333
capital structure 162
capital value 14
capitalize (*see also* **market capitalization**). Used in a number of senses. Most

common meaning is 'turn into capital'. Reserves are capitalized (turned into share capital) in a scrip issue. Interest on borrowings is capitalized if, instead of being charged against the profit of the year, it is added to the capital cost of the project to which the borrowings relate. Much investment is a process of capitalizing an income flow. If a building produces a rent of £10,000 a year an investor might be prepared to capitalize this income on a five per cent yield basis. This means he will pay a price for the right to receive this rent which gives him a five per cent return on his outlay. So he values the building on a multiple of 20 times the rent, or at £200,000. To capitalize a company sometimes means putting money into it in the form of share capital.

capitalization issue (*see* **scrip issue**)

capped floating-rate note 268

cash (in balance sheet) 48

cash cow. Business or part of a company that regularly generates useful flow of sales and profits, but without much in the way of growth prospects. Milk distribution in the UK was – by coincidence – a prime example in the past though the economics may now be moving against it.

cash earnings per share 65–66

cash economy (*see* **black economy**)

cash flow 44, 64–65

cash flow statement 42, 44, 65

cash market (as opposed to futures) 196, 285, 292, 294

cash offer 163

cash settlement 111, 212

catastrophe insurance (at Lloyd's) 301–302

Cedel 266–267

central banks 245

Central Gilts Office 212

central rate (for currency) 253

CEO (**Chief Executive Officer**) (*see* **board of directors**)

certificate of deposit (CD) 235, 239, 243

chairman (*see* **board of directors**)

Chapter 11 (of the American bankruptcy laws) (*see* **administrator, administration**)

charge (on assets) 76

chartered surveyors 38, 305

chartist, chartism 122–123, 131, 260

chief executive (*see* **board of directors**)

Chinese Walls 109–110

churning. An investment manager 'churns' investments he manages on behalf of clients when he switches too frequently between different shares, simply to generate commission or other benefits for himself or his associates.

City Code on Takeovers and Mergers (*see* **Takeover Code**)

City institutions 31–38

City Panel on Takeovers and Mergers (*see* **Takeover Panel**)

City of London 31–38

claims (insurance) 296

clawback 151, 153–154

clean price (of gilt-edged) 207

clearing banks 36

clearing house. In a futures

market, the body which reconciles sales and purchases, organizes margins and settlement and provides guarantees against default to users of the market.

close a position. The buyer of, say, a contract for a ton of metal for May delivery closes (cancels out) his position if he later sells an identical contract. He no longer has an outstanding liability to take delivery or to deliver. If the user of a futures market fails to maintain his margin, he will automatically be **closed out** by the market authorities who will buy or sell contracts on his behalf to close his original position. 282–283

close-ended 334

cocoa 294

coffee 294

cold calling 341

collar, cylinder. A combination of an interest rate **cap** and an interest rate **floor**, limiting exposure to changing interest rates within a defined range. 243

collateral. Assets pledged as security for a loan.

collateralized mortgage obligations (CMOs) (*see* **mortgage-backed securities**)

collectibles (*see* **alternative investments**)

coming to the market (*see also* **new issues**) 135

commercial lawyers 38

commercial paper. A form of short-term IOU issued to investors by a company or other major borrower, usually at a discount to its face value. Britain now has a commercial

paper market, which was opened to a wider range of companies in the 1989 Budget. 240–241, 268

commercial property (*see* **property**)

commission (stockbroker's, etc) 99, 103–104, 106, 212, 347

commission houses 294

commitment fee. Fee paid by a borrower to a lender for arranging a loan or agreeing to hold funds available for a loan.

committed facility 241

commodities 15, 293–294

commodities futures markets 34, 277 *et seq*

common stock (American term for **ordinary shares**) 90, 155

companies 39 *et seq*

companies (regulation of) 341 *et seq*

Companies Acts 90, 165, 167, 168, 342

Companies Act 1985 342

Companies House. Building in London where legally required information on public and private companies must be filed with the Registrar of Companies. Members of the public can consult the records of any company (in microfiche form) on payment of a fee. Useful source of information for investigation-minded financial journalists and those checking on a company's credit standing.

compensation fund (*see also* **deposit protection**) 341

compliance department, officer. Department or person responsible for preventing improper cross-fertilization between the different businesses grouped in a securities house and for ensuring compliance with the **Financial Services Act**. The system has been likened to putting a dozen rabbits in a hutch and giving one of them a red flag to wave if the others show signs of breeding. 109–110

compulsory acquisition 167

computerized systems 104–106, 131

concert party 167–168

conditional (of takeover offer) 166–167

confidentiality clause (in property lease) 316

conflicts of interest 106–107, 109–110, 299

conglomerate. Diversified and usually large company with a range of different and often unrelated businesses.

consideration. The price paid for something, not necessarily in cash. If Company A issues a million of its shares to Company B to acquire a business from Company B, the shares are the consideration for the purchase.

consolidated balance sheet 44–45

consolidated profit and loss account 45

consolidating 122

consulting actuaries 37–38

contango (futures markets) 294

contested takeover 162

contingent liabilities 88–89

contract (futures, options) 280, 293

contract note (Stock Exchange) 111–112

contracts of employment (directors') 185–186, 188

contractual savings 34, 318–319

contributions holiday (pension fund). A company running a final-salary pension scheme for its employees may be able to take a holiday for a few years from contributing to the scheme if the scheme has more assets than are currently needed to cover estimated liabilities. This may significantly boost the company's profits in the short run. 322

control of company 41, 161–162

conversion period 85

conversion premium 85

conversion terms 85

conversion value 86

convertible 85, 217, 267

convertible bond, loan stock 85–88, 98, 153, 197, 268–269

convertible capital bond 86–87

convertible preference 86–88, 90, 268–269

copper 293

corporate bonds, loans 98, 197, 213 *et seq*

corporate capital (at Lloyd's) 303

corporate finance 36, 37, 108

corporation loans 197

Corporation Tax 2, 49, 52–53

cost of money 16 *et seq*

Council of Lloyd's 299

Council of the Stock Exchange (*see* **Stock Exchange Council**)

counter-cyclical investment 331

counterparty. The person on the other side of a bargain or transaction that you undertake. **Counterparty risk** is the risk that he may default and therefore fail to deliver. 226, 271

country brokers 37

County NatWest (*see* **Blue Arrow affair**)

coupon 27, 198

covenant. Undertaking to observe certain conditions in connection with, say, borrowing money or signing a lease. Used in writing about commercial property to mean 'standing of the tenant'. If Payola Properties lets one of its office blocks to ICI or Unilever, it has a strong covenant – the tenant is unlikely to default on rent payments.

crash (1973–75) (*see* **financial crisis**)

crash (in property market) 314–315

crash (stockmarket crash of 1987) 5, 117, 126, 127–134

Crawford's Directory of City Connections 38

creative accountancy 44

credit card (interest rates) 25

credit rating. Independent agencies, of which the best known are the US firms **Moody's** and **Standard and Poor's**, will assess the credit standing of long- and short-term debt instruments issued by companies. Particularly in the United States, investors rely heavily on these ratings of the safety of bonds and commercial paper before making investment decisions. It is bad news for a company when one of the agencies **downgrades** its debt because of increasing worries about risk. The term **triple-A-rated** is used to describe the very best quality corporate debt. 27, 216, 272

credit risk, status 215–216, 217

creditors (*see also* **current liabilities**) 48, 76, 84

Crest (*see* **settlement**)

crowding out. Describes the situation where the government is borrowing so much money that there is little available for commercial businesses to borrow, or the cost of funds becomes exorbitant.

cum dividend 70, 207

cum rights 148

currencies (currencies and money pages in *FT*) 249

currency futures 209

currency movements (*see also* **foreign exchange**) 9–10, 124, 245–260

currency risk (hedging – *see also* **currency swaps**) 257

currency swaps 259, 272

current account (balance of payments) 247, 251

current assets 46–49

current liabilities 48

cushion (of equity) 75

cyclical stocks. Shares in companies whose business follows a cyclical pattern of improved and diminished profitability. Share prices will tend to follow this pattern or discount it in advance. Examples in the UK are general insurance and housebuilding.

cylinder (*see* **collar**)

Daily Official List 114

Datastream. On-line screen-based system of information on prices (current and historic) for securities, commodities, currencies, etc. Also covers items from company accounts, economic statistics, etc. Information in the database can be searched and manipulated by the user and can be presented in text or graphic form. Most of the graphs in this book are generated from the Datastream system. 191

dated (of fixed-interest stock) (*see* **redeemable**)

dawn raid 166

dealing floors 104

dealing for the account (historically) 111

dealing mechanisms 97

dealings (start of) 135

debenture stock. (In Britain, normally used to describe a secured company bond) 46, 85, 216

debt (*see also* **borrowings**) 27, 46, 50, 84–87

debt and equity 26 *et seq*, 50–51, 220–221

debt convertible 267

debtors 48

deep-discounted bond. Bond issued at a price well below its face or par value of 100. May or may not pay interest (*see* **zero-rated bond**) but much if not all of the return to the investor is in the form of capital gain to redemption (*see also* **discount**) 199, 267

deep-discounted rights issue 146, 149–150, 154

default (on loan) 228

defence document 169

defended takeover 162

deferred equity 86

deferred ordinary shares 90

deferred tax 88

deficiency on shareholders' funds 229

defined benefit (*see also* **pensions**) 322

defined contribution (*see also* **pensions**) 322

denationalization issues (*see* **privatization issues**)

Department of Trade and Industry (**DTI**) 172, 328, 342

deposit protection. Depositors in British banks are offered a measure of protection if the bank gets into trouble. They will be compensated for 75 per cent of deposits lost, up to a maximum deposit of £20,000. Maximum compensation is therefore £15,000.

deposit-taking institution 220–221

depositors 220

deposits (*see* **retail deposits, wholesale deposits**)

depreciation (amortization) 47, 52, 64, 95

deregulation 7 *et seq*, 262

derivatives. Financial instruments that are a spin-off from the basic products and markets. Thus **options** and **futures** are derivatives, as they are a spin-off from shares, bonds, etc. (*See also* **forward market, forward rate agreement, future, option, cap, floor, swap**) 10, 33, 223, 225, 274–294, 312

development finance 177, 309–311

development of property 38, 309–311

dilute, diluted, dilution (of earnings, assets, etc.) 86–88, 96

direct shareholdings, ownership of shares 99–100, 317, 318–319

directors (*see* **board of directors**)

directors' pay and perks 52, 182–192

directors' report 42
dirty (managed) float 246
disclosure of shareholdings (*see also* **3 per cent rule**, etc.) 167, 342
discount. Used in many contexts. Stockmarkets discount future events by reacting to them before they happen. To buy or sell securities at a discount is to buy or sell them at a price below some standard measure of value, which depends on the context: their par value; their offer-for-sale price; their net asset value, etc. In this sense it is the opposite of a premium. To discount a financial instrument is to buy it below its face value, earning a return from the capital gain when it is repaid (*see* **bills of exchange**). A **discount broker** is a broker offering a cut-price service (*see also* **at a discount**) 20–21, 79, 120, 199, 236, 259, 333
discount houses 235–238
discount market 235–238
discount market deposits 243
discretionary. When an investment manager looks after investments for clients on a discretionary basis, the decisions are made at his discretion, not the client's. **Discretionary clients** of a broker are clients whose investments he manages in this way at his discretion.
disintermediation. Cutting out the middle-man: the intermediary. The person with spare cash, instead of depositing it with a bank, lends it direct to the end-user. 8, 224

distribution. Usually a distribution of income and often used as a synonym for dividend.
diversification. A company diversifies when it extends its activities from its original business or businesses (which it presumably understands) to other business areas (which it may not understand so well). Not always a sure-fire recipe for success (*see also* **conglomerate**)
dividend 14, 28, 49, 53–54, 117, 132–133, 150
dividend cover 64
dividend forecast 138
dividend per share 150
dividend stripping 207–208
dividend yield 14, 66–67
dollar (problems of) 246
domestic interest rates 247, 257
double option 287
Dow Jones Industrial Average. Most frequently quoted index of the **New York Stock Exchange**. Covers thirty stocks, mainly industrial companies.
downside. 'The shares have downside potential' – there is plenty of scope for the price to fall.
droplock 267–268
DTI (*see* **Department of Trade and Industry**)
dual currency bonds 267

earning power (of company) 117
earnings per share (**eps**) 63, 67–68, 117 *et seq*
easier. Word beloved of market reporters. If a market eases or turns easier, prices are moving down (probably gently). (*See also* **firm**).
ECU (*see* **European Currency Unit**)

effective (of share price, earnings, dividend etc.) 157
effective control 166
EGM (*see* **extraordinary general meeting**)
EIS (*see* **Enterprise Investment Scheme**)
EIS fund 179
eligible banks 237
eligible bills 237
employee share ownership plan, trust (ESOP) (*see also* **directors' pay and perks**) In theory, one of the methods of helping employees of a company to acquire a share stake in it. In practice, mainly used in the UK for funnelling extra shares to directors or senior executives. May have the additional benefit of making the company more difficult to take over, and is widely used for this purpose in the United States. 185, 187
EMS (*see* **European Monetary System**)
EMU (*see* **European Monetary Union**)
endowment assurance 321
endowment mortgages 324
enhanced scrip dividend 158
Enterprise Investment Scheme (EIS) 177, 178–180, 334
Enterprise Zones. Designated areas of the country where businesses are freed from certain restraints applying elsewhere, notably planning restrictions and (for a time) the need to pay rates.
eps (*see* **earnings per share**)
equilibrium (of price) 22
Equitas (at Lloyd's) 303
equities (*see* **ordinary shares**)
equity (*see also* **debt and equity,**

negative equity). Equity is usually used in the sense of the owner's interest in an asset, with the risks and rewards of ownership that go with it. Thus it stands for ordinary shares, and equity assets are assets attributable to the owners, after all debts are allowed for. If you buy a house for £120,000, using £20,000 of your own money and a mortgage loan of £100,000, you have £20,000 of equity in the house. If its value rises to £150,000, the value of your equity in it rises to £50,000 (the value of the house, less the loan). If the value of the house falls to £80,000, it is lower than the amount of borrowings outstanding and you have **negative equity** of £20,000. 26–28, 46, 50, 177
equity capital (*see* **ordinary share capital**)
equity earnings 53, 55, 62
equity-for-debt swap 230
equity finance 50
equity sweetener, kicker 92, 267
equivalent (of share price, earnings, dividend, etc.) 157–158
equivalent yield 308
ERM (*see* **Exchange Rate Mechanism**)
ESOP (*see* **Employee Share Ownership Plan**)
estate agents (*see* **chartered surveyors**)
euro medium term note (EMTN) 268
eurobond 108, 218, 264–268
eurobond market (*see* **euromarket**)
eurobond market prices (table in *FT*) 273

Euroclear 266–267
eurocommercial paper (ECP)
241, 268
eurocurrency 262–264, 269
eurocurrency interest rates
(table in *FT*) 269
eurocurrency market (*see*
euromarket)
eurodollars 262
euroequity issues 152, 263, 269–
270
euromark 262
euromarket 33, 153, 216, 218,
261–273
Euromoney Bondware and
Loanware 270–271
euronote 268
European Currency Unit (ECU)
238, 252 *et seq*
European Monetary System
(EMS) 247, 252 *et seq*
European Monetary Union
(EMU) 252, 255
euroyen 262
evasion (*see* tax evasion)
evergreen 185
ex-all (xa). Appearing after a
share price, it means a
purchaser buys without rights to
whatever the company is in the
process of issuing: dividend,
rights issue shares, scrip issue
shares, warrants, etc. (*See also*
xr, xc, xd etc.)
ex-capitalization (*see* xc)
ex-dividend (*see* xd)
ex-rights (*see* xr)
exceptional items (*see also*
extraordinary items) 56
excess of loss spiral (LMX
spiral) 301–302
exchange controls (removal of)
345
exchange cross rates (table in
FT) 249

Exchange Rate Mechanism
(ERM) 247, 252 *et seq*
exchange rates 24, 245–260
Exchequer stocks 199
execution-only broking service
111
executive share options (*see also*
directors' pay and perks) 183,
186, 187
exercise price (of option) 183,
286, 288, 293
exercising (an option) 183, 286
exit PE ratio. The PE ratio that
applies at the price at which a
company is sold or taken over.
expiry (of option) 288
Extel cards. Statistical cards on
companies and individual
security issues, produced by the
Exchange Telegraph Co and
providing the figures and
background information needed
to undertake investment
appraisals. A prime working
tool of the investment analyst.
external growth 63
extraordinary general meeting
(EGM). General meeting of a
company at which non-routine
proposals are voted on by
shareholders. Examples of
matters requiring an EGM
would be an increase in
authorized capital or changes to
the company's aims and objects.
extraordinary items (*see also*
exceptional items) 56

face value. Nominal or par
value of a security, rather than
its market value. 27
factoring. A form of off balance
sheet finance which can have
the same effect as a loan. A

factor will undertake to collect debts owing to a company on the company's behalf and meantime make an advance to the company of a proportion of the money it is due to receive.

fan club 168

fees (in eurobond market) 266

FIMBRA (*see* **Financial Intermediaries, Managers and Brokers Regulatory Association**)

final closing date 170

final dividend 49

final salary scheme (*see also* **pensions**) 322

Finance Bill, Act. The legislation which implements the Budget proposals each year in the UK. The detailed provisions of the Finance Bill are normally debated for some months after the Chancellor has delivered his Budget statement.

finance director (*see* **board of directors**)

finance houses. Quasi-banks, often owned by the major clearing banks. The finance houses specialize in hire purchase and other instalment credit, leasing, debt factoring, etc.

financial assets of individuals 318–319

financial assistance for purchase of own shares 168, 342

financial consultants 319

financial crisis (1973–75) 116, 223

financial engineering. Transforming one type of financial product into a different one to suit the needs of a particular type of borrower, lender or investor. The simplest example is an **interest rate swap** (q.v.) where a borrower may raise, say, fixed interest funds but swap them so that he has the use of floating rate money. 212

financial futures (*see also* **LIFFE**) 33, 196, 281, 284–285, 291–292

financial health 44

financial institutions 32, 99, 153–154, 187, 189, 305, 319

financial instrument. A term covering most forms of short- and long-term investment traded in the money markets or the stockmarket: bank bills, certificates of deposit, shares, bonds, etc. 233, 235

financial intermediaries 35, 319

Financial Intermediaries, Managers and Brokers Regulatory Association (FIMBRA) 340

financial public relations 38

financial ratios 58 *et seq*

Financial Reporting Council (FRC) 342

Financial Reporting Review Panel 342

Financial Services Act (FSA) 102, 338

financial services revolution 7 *et seq*

Financial Times (*see* **FT**)

financing gap 174

financing proposal (venture capital) 177

firm, firmer. When a market firms it means that prices are moving up rather than down, though the motion described is probably gentle. If interest rates firm they are also moving up rather than down, but in bond markets this means that prices

of securities will be moving down. (*See also* **easier**.)
firm hands 141
first closing date 169
fiscal year. Year adopted for accounting and tax purposes. In the UK the government's fiscal year runs to 5 April. Companies can choose the year-end they wish, though end-December and end-March are common.
fixed assets 46
fixed charge (on assets) 76
fixed-interest market 98, 196
fixed-interest securities 19–20, 193–218, 264–268,273
fixed-price offer (stockmarket) 137
fixed-price offer (unit trust) 328
fixed rate (*see also* **variable rate, floating rate**) 27, 61
flat rate. Rate of interest, expressed in a way that often disguises the true interest rate (*see* **annual percentage rate**)
flat yield (*see* **income yield**)
float 136
floating charge 76
floating exchange rates 245
floating-rate bonds, notes (**FRNs**) 208, 217, 244, 267, 273
floating rate of interest (*see also* **variable rate, fixed rate**) 27, 61
floor (interest rate) 243, 268
flotation (*see* **new issue**)
flowback 151
Footsie Index (*see* **FT-SE 100 Index**)
forecast (prospectus) (*see also* **forecast profit, forecast dividend**)
forecast dividend 69, 138
forecast profit 138
foreign banks 36
foreign exchange 108, 245–260

foreign exchange brokers 259
foreign exchange market 23, 33, 34, 259–260
foreign exchange reserves 246–250
foreign income dividend. Companies with much of their earnings from abroad and therefore an **unrelieved ACT** (q.v.) problem in the UK may be able to reduce their overall tax liability by paying a dividend out of their foreign earnings which have not borne UK tax. They will not have to pay (or may reclaim) the **Advance Corporation Tax** (q.v.) on the foreign income dividend. Correspondingly, the shareholder who receives the foreign income dividend will not receive any tax credit.
foreign investors 99
forex (*see* **foreign exchange**)
formal documents (in bid) 169
forward exchange rate 257–259
forward market 257, 277–279
forward rate agreement (**FRA**). A form of interest rate hedge which allows a prospective borrower to fix the cost of money he knows he will need to borrow in, say, three months' time. He is thus protected from adverse interest rate movements in the interim, which could otherwise have made the money more expensive when he needed it.
FRA (*see* **forward rate agreement**)
Fraud Investigation Group (of Crown Prosecution Service) 347
Fraud Squad. Usually refers to an overworked branch of the

City of London police specializing in the investigation of suspected fraud (*see also* **Serious Fraud Office**). 348
FRC (*see* **Financial Reporting Council**)
free issue (*see* **scrip issue**)
freehold property 308
freight (futures) 294
friends (of company) 168
FRN (*see* **floating rate bond, note**)
front-end loaded. Used of various forms of regular investment, including life assurance. It means that a high proportion of the charges to the investor are deducted from his early contributions rather than spread over the life of the investment scheme.
FRS 3 (accounting standard) 56
FRS 3 earnings 56
FRS 6 (accounting standard) 161
FRS 7 (accounting standard) 161
FSA (*see* **Financial Services Act**)
FT. The usual abbreviation for the *Financial Times*
FT 30-Share Index, Ordinary Share Index 72
FT-Actuaries World Indices 73
FT-SE 100 Index (Footsie) 73
FT-SE 100 Index (as basis for options and futures) 73, 291, 292
FT-SE Actuaries 350 Index 73
FT-SE Actuaries All-Share Index 72
FT-SE Actuaries Fledgling Index 73
FT-SE Actuaries Gilt-edged Indices 209–210
FT-SE Actuaries Indices 71–74
FT-SE Actuaries Non-Financials Index 72

FT-SE Eurotrack 100 Index 73
FT-SE Eurotrack 200 Index 73
FT-SE Mid 250 Index 73
full repairing and insuring lease 307
fully diluted (*see* **dilute**)
fully-diluted assets per share 87–88, 96
fully-diluted earnings per share 86–88
fully paid 143, 155
fully subscribed 139
fully valued. 'The shares are fully valued' is often a journalist's way of suggesting they might be overvalued. Certainly, he does not think they are cheap.
fund management (*see* **investment management**)
fundamentals 29, 120, 132–133, 248
Funding stocks 199
fungible. The same as and interchangeable with. If a company has a 10 per cent bond 2005 in issue and decides later to make a further issue of a 10 per cent bond 2005, the chances are that the two issues are fungible: they can be treated as a single bond.
funny money. Used to describe complex, weird and wonderful forms of security sometimes devised by companies. A 'part-convertible subordinated index-linked loan stock with warrants attached' would be funny money. 163
futures contract 274–276, 280, 291–292
futures market 196, 274–276, 279–285, 291–294

G5, G7 (*see* **Group of Five, Seven**)

gain to redemption 200, 217

gains and losses (*see* **statement of total recognized gains and losses**)

gas oil 294

gearing (leverage) 50, 60–62, 74–76, 89, 170–171, 281, 333

general fund 329

general insurance 34, 296

gilt-edged market 19, 193–213

gilt-edged marketmakers (GEMMS) 37, 211

gilt-edged securities (*see also* **government bonds**) 13, 15, 19–20, 25, 98, 193–213

gilts (*see* **gilt-edged securities**)

go short 121

go-go fund. A fund which invests in special situations and highly speculative stocks and probably deals very actively in its investments.

going concern basis. The basis on which accounts of a company are normally produced and audited. It assumes the company is viable and is continuing in business. Lower values would normally be put on a company's assets if accounts were produced instead on the assumption the company was going to be broken up (**liquidation** or **break-up** basis). If an auditor feels obliged to point out that he has approved the accounts on a going concern basis, it normally means there is some doubt as to whether the company is, in fact, viable.

gold. Is bought as an investment particularly at times of financial uncertainty. The London Gold Market was traditionally operated by five merchant banks and bullion dealers who twice a day 'fix' a gold price in the light of supply and demand for the metal; but dealing has now been opened up to a wider range of marketmakers.

golden hallo 110

golden handcuffs 110

golden handshake. Lump sum payment made to compensate sacked or redundant employee for loss of office. The more exorbitant payments normally apply in the case of company directors, who generally 'resign' rather than being dismissed. 162, 185–186

golden parachute. Arrangements made in advance by directors of a company to provide themselves with a happy financial landing if ousted in the course of a takeover, etc. Would include long service contracts with big in-built payments on loss of office, etc.

goodwill 82–84, 94–96, 161

government bonds (*see also* **gilt-edged securities**) 13, 15, 19, 98, 193–213, 291

government borrowing (*see* **PSBR, PSDR**)

government guarantee (Loan Guarantee Scheme) 181

government securities (*see* **gilt-edged securities**)

Government Securities Index 210

grain futures 294

Greenbury Committee 189

greenmail 170

grey market 143

gross 54, 63, 213

gross borrowings 75
gross dividend per share 54, 63–64
gross fund. An investment fund such as a pension fund which is not liable to tax and may therefore enjoy its income gross (untaxed).
gross income yield 203
gross up, grossed up 63–64
gross yield 329
ground rent 308
group balance sheet (*see* **consolidated balance sheet**)
Group of Five, Seven (G5, G7) 252
growth by acquisition (*see* **external growth**)
growth prospects 138
guarantee 88–89, 223
Guinness affair 172–173, 342

half-year 42
hammered (of broker) 344
Hang Seng index. The most commonly quoted index of share prices in the volatile Hongkong stockmarket.
headline earnings 56
health warning 328
heavily-stagged 144
heavy (of share price) 155
hedge (*see* **management of risk**)
hedge funds. Very inappropriately-named investment vehicles: they rarely have anything to do with hedging. They are international funds, subscribed to by wealthy individuals and usually run by go-go managers, which attempt to achieve above-average returns by betting heavily on currencies and special situations in any of the world's markets.
They frequently gear-up their bets with borrowed money, and can be a very destabilising influence in the internatonal markets, particularly in currencies.
high income fund 329
high income gearing 62
high PE ratio 68
high yield, yielding 66–67
highly geared 50, 62, 143–144, 220–221, 286
high-tech. A 'high-tech business' should describe a company operating at the frontiers of technology – and sometimes does. Many more mundane businesses try to acquire a high-tech label in the hope of a improvement in their share ratings; this can misfire, as the stockmarket is weak on understanding of technology and when one high-tech company gets into trouble, all those with the same label may see their share prices suffer.
highs and lows. Prices of securities quoted in the newspapers, showing the highest and lowest prices reached, probably over the past year. These highs and lows will have been adjusted for scrip issues, etc. 70, 73
historical cost convention 56–57
historical cost profits (*see* **note of historical cost profits**)
historical dividend 69
historical dividend yield 70
historical PE ratio 70
holding company 45
hostile (of takeover) 162
housing (value of) 4, 318

hybrid financial instruments. Financial instruments which are a cross between two or more traditional instruments. The most common example is the convertible loan, which starts life as a bond but probably turns into share capital at a later date.

imputation tax system 52–53
IMRO (*see* **Investment Management Regulatory Organization**)
in arrears 90
in the money (of option) 288, 293
incentives (for directors) (*see* **directors' pay and perks**)
income 14
income gearing 60–62, 75
income shares 333
Income Tax 2, 52–53, 202–204, 317–318
income units 328
income yield (**running yield**) 19–20, 199–200
independent investment advisers 35, 319–320
indexation. Adjusting in line with an index. Usually the index is the Retail Prices Index (RPI): the most commonly used measure of inflation. The UK government issues index-linked bonds and there are index-linked forms of National Savings (Granny Bonds). An indexed share portfolio is one which seeks to match as closely as possible the composition and performance of a particular stockmarket index.
indexed portfolios 74
index-linked stocks 208 *et seq*
indices (currencies) 249–250

indices (property) 313
indices (stockmarket) (*see also* **FT**) 71–74
inducement (to sign a property lease) 316
industrial debentures (*see also* **corporate bonds**) 27, 98, 197
industrial efficiency 160
industrial logic 169
industrial property 314
inflation (*see also* **indexation, RPI**) 13, 15, 195, 254
inflation accounting 57
inflation hedge 208
initial public offering (IPO). An international term for an **offer for sale** or a **tender offer**, which has recently crept into UK use.
insider dealing, trading 106, 171, 342
insolvency. A business can go bust in two main ways: by running out of cash to pay its bills and other obligations or by having more liabilities than assets (owing more than it owns). 'Insolvent' is sometimes used to cover both cases. It is an offence for a company to trade while insolvent.
institutions (*see* **financial institutions**)
insurance (*see also* **Lloyd's of London**) 34, 295–304, 319–321, 326
insurance brokers 35, 298, 319
insurance companies 34–35, 124, 305, 343
Insurance Companies Act 343
insurance company market 296
insurance cycle 303
insurances (prices in *FT*) 325, 329
insured scheme (pensions) 34, 321

intangible assets 82, 94–96
inter-bank deposits 243
inter-bank market 235, 239 *et seq*, 264
inter-bank rates 244
inter-dealer brokers 211
interest (in profit and loss account) 52
interest rate differential 258
interest rate swap 243, 271–272
interest rates 15 *et seq*, 61–62, 118–119, 123–124, 195–196, 204–207, 232, 234, 235–236, 243–244, 247, 258–259, 269, 271–272
interest yield (*see* **income yield**)
interests in associated companies, related companies 55, 84
interim (dividend) 43–49
interim (profit announcement) 43
intermediaries offer 136–137
internal growth 63
international capital markets (page in *FT*) 273
international market (*see also* **euromarket**) 33, 216, 261–273
International Petroleum Exchange (IPE) 294
International Securities Market Association (ISMA) 267
intrinsic value 92, 288
introduction (to stockmarket) 136
investment advisers 319
investment analyst 37, 109
investment arithmetic 40, 58 *et seq*
investment bank. The closest American equivalent to the British merchant bank. Issues and underwrites the issue of securities, buys and sells securities, provides corporate advice, etc. Some of the traditional British merchant banks which have been taken over by a larger group or turned themselves into integrated securities houses are also now referred to as investment banks.
investment business (authorization for) 338
investment income (insurance) 296
investment management 36, 108, 322, 329
investment management groups 35, 329
Investment Management Regulatory Organization (IMRO) 340
investment market in property 305–308
Investment Property Databank (IPD) 314
investment ratios 58 *et seq*
investment research 37, 109
investment trusts 79–80, 331 *et seq*
investments (interests) in associated companies (*see* **associated company**)
investor protection 38, 338 *et seq*
Investors in Industry (3i) 175
invisible earnings. A country's overseas earnings from dividends, etc., received from abroad and from supply of services rather than physical goods. 31, 295
IOU (I owe you – promissory note) 19
IPD (*see* **Investment Property Databank**)
IPO (*see* **initial public offering**)
irredeemable 191, 197, 200
ISMA (*see* **International Securities Market Association**)

ISRO 97
issue a loan 27
issue flop 141
issued capital 91
issuing house. Financial institution which arranges issues of securities on a market.

jobber/broker mechanism 104, 211
jobbers 102–104
jobber's turn 102
junk bonds 171, 178

kerb market. Unofficial market in securities, commodities, etc, often operating alongside the official market. Once the official trading session has ended, dealers may continue trading in the kerb market, often over the telephone.

lapse (of takeover bid) 170
Latin-American debt crisis 227
launch (*see also* **new issues**) 136
launder (of money). Take dirty money (from thefts, drug trade, etc.) and turn it into clean money by putting it through some process that disguises its origin. Unit trust managers tend to be suspicious of potential investors who pay with a suitcase of used fivers and bank employees (and others) nowadays have a legal liability to report transactions where they suspect money laundering.
LAUTRO (*see* **Life Assurance And Unit Trust Regulatory Organization**)
LCE (*see* **London Commodity Exchange**)

LDC (*see* **less developed country**)
LDT (*see* **licensed deposit taker**)
lead (metal) 293
lead bank, manager 225, 264
leaseback (*see* **sale and leaseback**)
leasehold, leaseholder 308
leases (of property) 307
leasing. Rather than buy the plant and equipment they need, businesses may lease it instead. They use it as if it were their own, but it remains the property of the institution which put up the money to purchase it: often a bank or other financial institution. The user makes regular payments for its use instead of having had to find the cash to buy it at the outset. Leasing used to offer considerable tax advantages, but these have now diminished, nor can it normally be used to disguise a company's true liabilities in its accounts. (*See also* **off balance sheet** finance.)
left with the underwriters 140–141
lender of last resort 232
less developed countries (LDCs) 227
letting market (for properties) 38, 305
level playing fields 171
leverage (*see* **gearing**)
leveraged takeovers, buy-outs 170–171, 177–178
LGS (*see* **Loan Guarantee Scheme**)
LIBID (*see* **London Inter-Bank Bid Rate**)
LIBOR (*see* **London Inter-Bank Offered Rate**)

licensed dealer in securities 102

licensed deposit-taker (LDT) 231

life (of loan, etc.) 85, 197–198

life assurance 296, 317–321

Life Assurance and Unit Trust Regulatory Organization (LAUTRO) 340

life assurance companies 32, 34, 296, 346

life funds 321, 326

lifeboat (for banks) 223

LIFFE (*see* **London International Financial Futures and Options Exchange**)

lighten (share holdings) 141

LIMEAN 244

limited liability 40–41

limit up, limit down. Some overseas markets in futures or securities impose a limit on the amount by which a price is allowed to move in a single day. If the price has reached the upper limit it is described as 'limit up', and as 'limit down' if it has reached the lower one.

liquid 214

liquidation (*see also* **winding up**) 37

liquidation basis (bid basis) 327

liquidator. A liquidator, normally an accountant specializing in this type of business, goes into a company to wind it up (close it down) by selling its assets and distributing the proceeds to creditors in order of preference: the tax authorities and secured creditors rank high. Ordinary shareholders get what is left after all debts have been paid. Usually (except in the case of a voluntary liquidation where a solvent company decides to wind itself up) there is nothing left for shareholders. (*See also* **receiver**.)

liquidity (of market) 22, 24, 103, 134, 214

liquidity ratio (of banks) 220, 222

listed, listing 100, 135

Listing Agreement 100

Lloyd's Act 298–299, 344

Lloyd's broker 298

Lloyd's of London 3, 34, 295–304, 344

LME (*see* **London Metal Exchange**)

Loan Guarantee Scheme (LGS) 180–181

loan stock 27, 46

local authority deposits and loans 243

locals (in futures market) 291

locking in (to a price, exchange rate, etc.) 258, 278 *et seq*

London Commodity Exchange 293, 294, 312

London Futures and Options Exchange (London FOX) 312

London Inter-Bank Bid Rate (LIBID) 244

London Inter-Bank Offered Rate (LIBOR) 244, 269

London International Financial Futures and Options Exchange (LIFFE) 98, 287, 291–293

London Metal Exchange (LME) 283, 293–294

London money rates (table in *FT*) 243

London recent issues (table in *FT*) 142, 143

London Rules 231

London Stock Exchange 32, 33, 36–37, 97–114, 135 *et seq*, 193–194

long (of stock) 113
long-dated gilt-edged (futures contract) 291, 292
long-dated stocks, longs 198, 206, 209
long-tail business (insurance) 296
long-term borrowings 49, 52
longs (*see* **long-dated stocks**)
loss to redemption 200
low-coupon stocks 200
low-geared company 50
low PE ratio 68
low yield, yielding 66–67
loyalty bonus issue 158
Ltd (*see* **limited liability**)

M & A. Stands for mergers and acquisitions, one of the buzzphrases of the late 1980s. Merchant bank corporate finance departments and securities houses make much of their money from mergers and acquisitions work.
M & G Securities (investment management group) 329
M₀ (M nought) 222
M₄ (M four) 222
Macarthy cards. A form of press clipping service which picks up and categorizes press coverage of companies and of business topics. Useful for mugging up on recent company history and developments.
main market (Stock Exchange) 100, 135
Mainstream Corporation Tax 53
make a book 21
managed fund 322, 325, 330
management advisory services 37
management buy-out, buy-in 171–178

management of risk (*see also* **forward market, futures, forward rate agreements, options, caps, floors, swaps**) 33, 242–243, 257–259, 274–294
managing agent (Lloyd's) 298
mandatory bid, offer 165–166, 167
margin. In some markets, particularly futures markets, clients are only required to put up a proportion of the cost of what they buy: a form of deposit known as margin. But this margin will have to be topped up if it is eroded by adverse price movements. A **margin call** is the notice that the margin needs topping up, otherwise the investor will be **closed out**. 275, 282
margin (interest rate). Margin in this sense is much the same as **spread**. If a **floating rate note** pays interest at 50 basis points over LIBOR, the 50 basis points is the **margin** over LIBOR.
marginal. Frequently used in the sense 'marginal tax rate'. In the UK a high-earning individual would (in 1995) pay 20 per cent income tax on a very small first slice of his taxable income, 25 per cent on the next slice and 40 per cent on the top slice. Under the progressive tax system this means he will also pay the top 40 per cent rate on any margin of additional income he earns, and 40 per cent is therefore his marginal rate.
market (*see also* **stockmarket, futures market**, etc.) 7–9, 15–17, 19–24, 29–30
market capitalization. Used of

stockmarkets and of individual companies. The capitalization of the London equity market is the total market value of all the ordinary shares of all the companies listed on the market (usually excluding foreign-registered companies). The market capitalization (strictly, equity market capitalization) of Joe Bloggs Plc is the stockmarket value of all its ordinary shares: the number of shares in issue multiplied by the market price. If Bloggs has 10m shares in issue and the price is 200p, Bloggs is capitalized at £20m. 70, 98

market price mechanism 19–23
market professionals 159
market purchases 164
market sentiment (*see* sentiment)
marketable 155
marketable securities. Covers most forms of security that can be bought and sold in a market: bonds, shares, certificates of deposit, etc.
marketed (of securities) 37
marketmaker 21, 36–37, 102–111, 113–114, 120–122, 211, 225
matched bargain basis 101
maturity 194, 197
Maxwell, Robert 5–6, 323, 346
medium-dated stocks 198, 209
medium- or long-term debt 49
medium-term note (MTN) 241, 268
mediums (gilt-edged) (*see* medium-dated stocks)
members (of a company) (*see* shareholders)
members' agent (Lloyd's) 298
Memorandum of Association (*see* Articles of Association)

merchant banks (*see also* investment banks) 36, 108–109, 159
merchant developer 311
merger (*see also* takeover) 161, 162
merger accounting 161
metals (commodities) 293–294
mezzanine debt 176
middle prices 70, 113, 198
minimum commission 103
Minimum Lending Rate (MLR) 236, 256
minority interests, minorities or **outside interests** 55, 88
minority shareholders 55, 88, 165
mis-selling of personal pensions 3, 11, 324, 346
MLR (*see* minimum lending rate)
MMC (*see* Monopolies and Mergers Commission)
MOF (*see* multiple option facility)
money (*see* cost of money, sources of money, opportunity cost, time value, present value)
money broker 239
money creation 221–222
money market instruments. Forms of short-term investment that are traded in the money markets and easily turned into cash. Examples include **bank bills** and **certificates of deposit** (q.v.).
money markets 23, 32, 232–244
money purchase scheme (*see also* pensions) 322
money raising 27–28
money supply 221–222
Monopolies and Mergers Commission (MMC) 167
Moody's (bond rating service) (*see* credit rating)

moratorium. When a business defaults on a loan, creditors may sometimes agree a moratorium with the borrower. This means they agree not to insist on immediate payment, judging they might get back more in the long run by giving the business time to wind down its affairs in an orderly manner rather than insisting it is wound up immediately.

mortgage (*see also* **specialist mortgage lenders**) 25, 32, 216, 269, 309, 317, 324

mortgage-backed security 269

mortgage payments 25, 317, 324–325

MTN (*see* **medium-term note**)

multinational company. Company which operates in a major way in two or more countries, such as Unilever or Shell.

multiple applications (new issues) 144

multiple of (on a PE ratio of) 67

multiple of rent (property valuation) (*see also* **years' purchase**) 307

multiple option facility (**MOF**) 241–242

mutual 35

naked writer. A writer (creator) of options, who does not own the underlying shares against which the options are written. Naked writing is a very dangerous practice. 290–291

names (at Lloyd's) 295 *et seq*

names action groups 302

narrow market 120

NASDAQ. Stands for National Association of Securities Dealers Automated Quotations – the computerized price information system used by dealers in the over-the-counter market in the United States. The British SEAQ system is closely modelled on it.

National Savings Stock Register 213

NAV (*see* **net asset value per share**)

nearby, nearest month, furthest month. If we are now in January and contracts in a futures market are actively traded for delivery dates in February, April, June, August and October, then the nearest month is February and the furthest is October.

negative equity (*see also* **equity**) 4

negative (inverse) yield curve. Interest rates for deposits or securities of different maturity – three months, six months, a year, five years, ten years, etc. – can be plotted on a graph. When short-term interest rates are higher than longer-term ones, this line will start high and curve downwards. This is a negative or inverse yield curve. (*See also* **yield curve**) 243

negotiated commissions. Have replaced the former fixed minimum commission structure for deals in securities on the Stock Exchange in Britain. Large institutional investors (or those who operate through brokers rather than buying at net prices) are free to negotiate the level of commission they will pay, which dropped sharply for large trades after Big Bang. Small private investors with little bargaining power generally pay much the same as before or sometimes more. 104

net 54, 213

net asset value (NAV) 49, 78–81, 82–84, 94–96, 311, 332–333

net borrowings 75

net current assets (and **liabilities**) 48

net dividend per share 54, 63

net PE ratio 68

net prices 106, 212

net profit, net profit available for ordinary shareholders 53, 55, 56, 62

net return 203

net tangible asset value 84, 94–96

new issues 108, 135–144, 176, 210 *et seq*

New York Stock Exchange (NYSE). The main stock exchange in the United States, on which America's major corporations are listed. Also referred to as the Big Board, or Wall Street where it is located. 103

nickel 293

NIF (*see* **note issuance facility**)

nil paid 149

nil PE ratio 68

no par value 90

nominal value (face value, par value) 27, 90, 198

nominated adviser 132, 138

nominee (name). Shares can be held for convenience (or, often, for secrecy) under the name of a nominee rather than that of the beneficial owner. Thus Fastbuck Nominees might hold shares on behalf of a number of the clients of Fastbuck Finance. UK companies have powers to require the identity of beneficial owners of shares held in nominee names, but the powers are of little use when the nominee is a secrecy-pledged Swiss bank. (*See also* **Section 212**.) 112, 168, 342, 345

non-bank private sector 234

non-equity capital An accounts heading for share capital that is not ordinary shares. In practice, covers mainly preference shares.

non-executive director (*see* **board of directors**)

non-performing (loan) 228

non-recourse loan, limited-recourse loan. Often arises as follows. Company C is set up by Companies A and B (perhaps to undertake a property development). But it is not a subsidiary of either. Company C borrows the funds it needs as a non-recourse loan. The loan is not guaranteed by Companies A or B, and does not appear in their accounts. The lender is lending against the success of Company C's venture and if Company C gets into trouble he has no recourse or very limited recourse to Companies A and B to get his money back – in theory, at least. Much property development lending was undertaken on a non-recourse or limited-recourse basis in the late 1980s. 311

non-voting shares. Some companies issue classes of non-voting ordinary shares, usually so that the founders (who hang on to a fair proportion of the voting shares) can control the company without needing to own over half the ordinary share capital. Others issue different classes of shares, all of which have votes but some have more votes than others. Terms like 'A Ordinary' and 'B Ordinary' are often used to distinguish the different classes.

note issuance facility (NIF) 268

note of historical cost profits and losses. Under accounting standard FRS 3, this statement is required to supplement the profit and loss account where published profits or losses are different from what they would have been if assets had been held at depreciated cost rather than revalued amounts. 42

notes to the accounts 42, 52

occupational pension schemes (*see also* **pension funds**) 34, 317, 321–324

off balance sheet items, finance. Covers a range of items – usually potential liabilities – which do not appear in the balance sheet of the company concerned. Examples of off balance sheet financing used to be leasing (though companies are now meant to show leased assets and the corresponding obligation to make payments in the case of a finance lease), factoring, sale and leaseback finance for property development, non-recourse loans in joint venture companies, etc. Can cause concern when it disguises the

extent of the commitments the company has entered into. Off balance sheet risks are now a major concern in banking, where banks – instead of simply lending money, which would show in their accounts – provide guarantees for securities issued by businesses, agree to underwrite future issues of securities and enter into derivatives transactions. 223, 225–227

offer document 169

offer for sale 136, 137–143

offer period 170

offer price 113, 329

offered rate 244

Office of Fair Trading 167

office property 314

official interest rates 232

official intervention (foreign exchange) 245

official list 114

official market 143

official prices 114

offshore companies 299

offshore funds 330

OFR (*see* **operating and financial review**)

OFT (*see* **Office of Fair Trading**)

oil (North Sea) 255

Old Lady of Threadneedle Street. Coy nickname for the Bank of England, much overworked by some banking writers.

ombudsman (for Lloyd's) 300

open-ended 334

open interest. In a futures market, the number of outstanding contracts that have not been cancelled by a contract in the other direction.

open market operations 234
open offer 146, 151, 153–154
open outcry 291, 294
open year (at Lloyd's) 301
operating and financial review.
The Cadbury Committee (q.v)
on the financial aspects of
corporate governance
recommended that company
annual reports should
incorporate a review explaining
the company's operations over
the year and including an
exposition of its financial
position.
operating profit, loss 52, 93
opportunity cost 17–19, 25
options (*see also* **directors' pay
and perks**) 98, 149, 274, 276,
286–291
ordinary share capital 46, 47,
89, 90–92
ordinary shareholders' funds 89
ordinary shares (*see also* **equity**)
14, 15, 25, 28–29, 41, 98, 115–134
organic growth (*see* **internal
growth**)
OTC (*see* **Over-The-Counter
markets**)
out of the money (of options)
288, 293
outside shareholders (*see
minority interests*)
Over-The-Counter markets
(OTC) 102, 225, 276
overall return 14, 24, 73, 119,
196
overdraft 25, 46, 49
over-geared, over-borrowed 75
overhanging the market 125, 141
over-rented property 315
overseas funds 330
overseas securities and property
32
overshooting 248, 251

oversubscribed 140
overtrading 77
owners of a company (*see*
shareholders)

P&L (*see* **profit and loss
account**)
Panel (*see* **Takeover Panel**)
paper. Securities of one kind or
another (shares, bonds, etc.) as
opposed to cash. Usually used
in the context of a 'paper offer'
in a takeover – the bidder offers
its own securities rather than
cash. 163
paper profit or loss. A profit is a
paper profit until you take it in
cash. If you bought 100 shares
at 200p each and the price rose
to 300p, you would have a
paper profit of £100. But you
are only sure of an actual profit
of £100 if you sell the shares at
300p.
paperchase 163
par value (also expressed as
nominal value and **face value**)
27, 90, 155, 198
parallel money markets 235, 239
et seq
parallel syndicates (Lloyd's) 299
parent company 44–45
parent company balance sheet
44–45
parities 24, 246
park (of shares). When one
company wants to hide the
extent of its shareholding in
another, it may temporarily
(and probably unlawfully) park
the shares with a third party to
avoid the disclosure rules. (*See
also* **warehousing**.)
part-paid 141, 143–144, 149, 210,
267

participating preference shares 90

partnership 41

partnership finance (for property) 309–311

pass (a dividend) 64

pathfinder prospectus 142

pay and perks (*see* **directors' pay and perks**)

PE ratio (*see* **price-earnings ratio**)

peaks 116

penny stocks. Shares quoted in the market at prices of a few pence only – it used to be less than 10p, but the criteria have widened. The idea is that they should be a good speculation because they usually reflect companies that are down on their luck. The company could go bust, but if somebody gets a grip on it and improves its performance, the shares could rise many times in value. However, nowadays most penny stocks are ramped well above their likely worth in the hope of something of this kind happening. They may not be a bargain.

pension fund performance 37

pension funds (*see also* **occupational pension schemes**) 32, 34, 37, 124, 305

pensions. Pensions offered by employers (**occupational pension schemes**) are of two main types: those that offer a pension geared to final salary (**final salary schemes**, **defined benefit schemes**) and those where the pension is related solely to the amount of money that has been contributed (**money purchase** or **defined contribution** schemes). 317–318, 321–324

pensions (for directors) (*see also* **directors' pay and perks**) 183, 184

PEP (*see* **personal equity plan**)

percentages, percentage points. A fertile ground for confusion. If Payola Properties raises a loan at 10 per cent and Fastbuck Finance raises one at 12 per cent, Fastbuck is paying two **percentage points** more for its money (the difference between 10 and 12). But Fastbuck is equally paying 20 **per cent** more for its money than Payola (because 12 is 20 per cent higher than 10). Writers often confuse the two measures. Usually the context makes the meaning clear, but one or two monumental misunderstandings have resulted. (*See also* **basis points**.) 28, 244

performance (of shares, etc) 101, 331

performance criteria (for incentive schemes) (*see also* **directors' pay and perks**) 184, 186

performance funds. Funds which aim for above-average capital growth, usually at the expense of income and by accepting higher risks. The fund may also switch actively between investments.

permanent capital 45

permanent interest-bearing shares (PIBS). Effectively, a form of subordinated debt issued by building societies which they can count towards their capital for capital adequacy calculations. The need arises because mutual institutions do not have the option of raising equity finance in the stockmarket.

perpetual floating rate notes, perpetuals 267

Personal Equity Plan (PEP) 35, 213, 319, 328, 334–336

personal finance 317–336

personal guarantees 41

Personal Investment Authority (PIA) 340

personal loans 25

personal portable pensions (*see also* **mis-selling of personal pensions**) 321–324

personal sector assets 318–319

phantom options (*see also* **directors' pay and perks**) 184–185

physical market. A market (in commodities, say) where deals lead to delivery of physical commodities. In other words, deals are not merely in futures contracts which are closed out by other futures contracts. 294

PIA (*see* **Personal Investment Authority**)

PIBS (*see* **permanent interest-bearing shares**)

PINCs (*see* **Property Income Certificates**)

pitches (marketmakers') 103

placing 136, 146, 151, 153–154, 217

plc (*see* **public company** and **limited liability**)

plough back 46, 64, 93

pm (premium) 149

point, basis point. If UK bonds rise in price by £1, they are described as rising by one **point**. A stockmarket index rises by one point if it climbs from 1001 to 1002. If bank base rates are 10 per cent, an overdraft at 5 **points** over base rate will cost you 15 per cent. But a **basis point** is one hundredth of one percentage point. If **LIBOR** (q.v.) is 8 per cent, a loan at 55 basis points over LIBOR will cost 8.55 per cent. (*See also* **percentages, percentage points**). 74, 210, 244

poison pill 170

polarization. A current buzz-word, brought into prominence by the Securities and Investments Board. The SIB insists on a distinction (polarization) between financial intermediaries which market the investment products of a particular organization and those which are genuinely independent advisers, marketing a range of products from different stables. This has caused considerable annoyance among, *inter alia*, banks and building societies which like to promote themselves as sources of financial advice but have their own in-house investment products to sell. 346

politics (effect on share prices) 125

poll. Votes at company meetings are normally taken initially on a show of hands. If the result is disputed, a poll can be called for – ordinary shareholders normally have one vote per share, and the number of shares voted for and against is counted. (*See also* **proxy**.)

pooled investments (*see also* **unit linked**) 326

popular capitalism 144, 319
portfolio. The collective term for an owner's holdings of shares, loans, etc. **Portfolio investment** covers investment in securities as opposed to direct investment which usually means putting money into plant, machinery, etc. 72
portfolio insurance 131
positions (in shares) 103, 113–114
Post Office Register (*see* **National Savings Stock Register**)
potato futures 294
pound (*see* **sterling**)
pre-emption rights 145, 153–154
pre-tax profit 52
pre-tax profit margin (*see* **profit margin**)
predators (stockmarket) 80–81, 160
preference shares 55, 89–90, 98, 177
preferred ordinary shares 90
preliminary announcement (prelim) 43
premium (*see also* **at a premium**) 79, 93, 149, 181, 199, 259, 286
premium (insurance) 277, 296
premium income 296
premium put convertible 86–87
present value (of money) 18
press recommendation (*see* **tip**)
Prevention of Fraud (Investments) Act 343
price-earnings ratio (PE ratio) 67–68, 117 *et seq*, 130, 132, 138
price information systems 104, 211
price mechanism 22–23, 28–29
price-sensitive information. Information (usually unpublished) that is likely to cause share prices to move. 342

primary capital 224
primary dealers 37, 211
primary market 23, 98, 266
prime properties 313–314
prime rate. Rate charged by US banks to their very best borrowers. Not the same, therefore, as UK base rates – even the best borrowers normally pay a margin over base rate for an overdraft and base rate itself is simply a yardstick.
principal (in a market) 21
private client. Used of brokers' clients to denote individual private investors rather than institutional clients. 99
private company. In general terms, a limited company (with 'Ltd' after its name) whose securities are not traded in a market. It could, however, be an unquoted subsidiary of a **public company** (q.v.).
private investors 99–100, 111
private placement 217
privatization (denationalization) 142–143, 144, 158, 190–191
professional advisers 37–38
professional fund manager 335
profit 13
profit after tax (*see* **net profit**)
profit and loss account 42, 43, 51 *et seq*
profit and loss account reserves 54, 93, 155
profit before tax (*see* **pre-tax profit**)
profit forecast 138
profit margin 59–60
profit on ordinary activities before tax (*see* **pre-tax profit**)
profit-taking 120
project finance. Finance put up

Glossary and Index

for a particular project (say, a property development) and probably secured on that project rather than forming part of the general corporate borrowing of a company. (*See also* **non-recourse**.) 310

programme trading 131
promissory note 19
property 9, 32, 305–316
property bonds 312, 326
property companies 311, 313
property development 305, 311
property finance 309–311
property futures 312, 313
Property Income Certificates (PINCs) 312
Property Index Certificates, (PICs) 313
property indices 9, 313–314
property investment companies 80, 311
property investment portfolio 38
property lending 310–311
property market 38, 305
property performance 9, 306, 310, 314–316
property shares 313
property traders 311
property unit trusts 312
proprietary trading 290
prospective dividend 69
prospective dividend yield 70
prospective PE ratio 70
prospectus 37, 136, 142
prospectus forecast 138
provision (for bad debts, etc) 228
provisions (for liabilities and charges) 88, 160
proxy. A shareholder entitled to vote at the general meeting of a company can appoint a proxy to vote on his behalf. Directors of the company will act as proxies,

or the shareholder could appoint a friend. Before the meeting the shareholder receives a **proxy card** which he can fill in and sign, nominating his proxy and indicating which way he wants his votes cast on the different resolutions.
prudential ratios (for banks) 224
PSBR (*see* **public sector borrowing requirement**)
PSDR (*see* **public sector debt repayment**)
public company. Public limited company, with 'plc' after its name. A company whose securities are traded in a market or which invites the public to subscribe for its securities must be a plc. (*See also* **private company**.) 40–41
public offering of stock (gilt-edged) 210
public relations (*see* **financial public relations**)
public sector borrowing requirement (PSBR) 194
public sector debt repayment (PSDR). Describes the position when the government's income exceeds its expenditure, and it is able to repay existing debt rather than borrowing more. 194
puff (a share). Over-promote the merits of a share, probably in a broker's circular or a press recommendation.
pull to redemption 204–207
purchasing power (*see* **inflation**)
purchasing power parity 251
pushing (of shares). Over-promoting a particular share to investors. (*See also* **ramp**, **puff** and **bucket shop**.)
put option 268, 287

qualifications (auditors') 43

quarterlies. Quarterly results
and dividend declarations
produced by American listed
companies. 42

quotation. Price quoted for a
security, etc., comprising a bid
and offer price.

quote (listing) 135

quote-driven 105

quoted (company, share, etc.)
100–101

rack rent 308

ramp (a share). Over-promote a
share to get the price up.

rank (for dividend) 89

ratchet 176

rating (in stockmarket) (*see also*
credit rating) 66 *et seq*, 138

re-rated 118, 119–120

re-rated downwards 119

readily saleable assets 80

real. The word 'real' in an
investment context normally
means 'adjusted for inflation'. If
your money is earning 10 per
cent interest in a year when
prices rise by 4 per cent, your
real return is around 6 per cent.

real rate of return (*see also*
indexation, real) 20, 196, 209

real terms (*see also* **indexation,
real**) 116

real value 208

receiver. A receiver is put into a
company to recover a specific
debt or specific debts on which
the company has defaulted (or
sometimes comes in effectively
at the request of the directors
when they know the company is
in trouble and likely to default).
His job is to sell assets as

necessary to recover the debt or
debts. Occasionally he may be
able to do this without its
resulting in the company's
closing down, in which case the
company can revert to normal
trading after his departure. But
generally the appointment of a
receiver is the beginning of the
end and the company is
eventually wound up.

recession 5, 6

reciprocity 171

**Recognized Investment
Exchanges (RIEs)** 102, 339

**Recognized Professional Bodies
(RPBs)** 339

recovery stocks 329

recycling (of deposits) 222–223

redeem 19, 27, 197 *et seq*

redeemable 197

redemption (hold to) 204

redemption date 27, 85, 197
et seq

redemption yield 200 *et seq*

rediscount (bill of exchange) 235

redistribution of risk 274 *et seq*

regional exchanges 97

register of shareholders 112, 148

registered securities 112, 265

regulation, regulator (*see also*
investor protection) 38, 164, 231,
337–348

Regulatory News Service (RNS)
106

reinsurance 296

reinsure to close 300–301

related companies (*see also*
associated companies) 55, 84

relationship banking 12

remuneration committee. The
Cadbury Committee (q.v.)
recommended that companies
should set up a remuneration
committee consisting

mainly of non-executive directors to establish the pay and perks of the executive directors. 189–190

remuneration consultants 190, 191

rent 307 *et seq*

rent-free period 316

rent reviews 307–309

rental value 307–309, 314–315

repayment mortgage 324

replacement cost accounting 57

repos (*see* **repurchase agreements**)

repurchase agreements (repos) 212, 236

rescheduling. Rearranging the terms of a loan. Normally involves spreading interest and capital repayments over a longer period when the borrower is unable to comply with the original terms. Sometimes involves lending him further money out of which he will effectively meet the payments on the original loan – this may help the lender to postpone recognition of the fact that he has probably lost his money. 227, 229–231

rescue (for company)

reserve assets 221

reserve assets ratio 222

reserves (*see also* **revaluation reserves, profit and loss account reserves, revenue reserves, share premium account, shareholders' funds**) 46, 64–65

resistance levels (chartism) 123

resolution. Used in the sense of a proposal put to the vote of shareholders at the general meeting of a company. **Ordinary resolutions** covering the more routine matters require a simple majority to succeed. **Special resolutions**, required to alter a company's **articles of association** (q.v.), require 75 per cent of the votes cast to be in favour. This can be important in a takeover. If shareholders representing more than 25 per cent of the votes refuse to accept the offer, the bidder may gain control but will have difficulty in restructuring the victim company if non-accepting shareholders vote against proposals requiring a special resolution.

restrictive covenant 216

restrictive practices 103

retail banking 108

retail deposits 32, 220, 233

Retail Prices Index (RPI). Commonly used measure of inflation. Costs of goods and services are weighted in the index to approximate to a typical family spending pattern. Can be sharply affected by increases in mortgage interest rates or in taxes on expenditure (VAT, excise duties, etc). (*See also* **indexation**.) 208–209

retained profit (*or* **retained earnings**) 49, 54, 64, 93

retentions (*see* **retained profit**)

return (*see also* **overall return**) 13, 15 *et seq*, 26

return on assets 80–81

Reuters 259

revaluation (of currency) 254

revaluation (of properties) 94

revaluation reserves 94

revenue reserves 54, 93

reverse auction 211

reverse capitalism (*see also* **directors' pay and perks**) 182
reverse takeover. When a small company takes over a larger one, or when the company being taken over will effectively be the dominant force in the combined group.
reverse yield gap. Describes the gap between the yield on bonds and on equities when the bond yield is the higher. Or the gap between borrowing costs and rental yields on properties, when the cost of borrowing is higher. It is a 'reverse' yield gap because, in the days before inflation took hold, 'risky' shares would have yielded more than 'safe' bonds, and property yields would have been higher than borrowing costs. 133, 310
reversionary properties 308
revert, reversions 307
revolving underwriting facility (RUF) 268
RIE (*see* **Recognized Investment Exchange**)
rights issue 77, 91, 93, 145–150, 153–154
rights offers (table in *FT*) 149
ring-dealing members 294
risk (*see* **management of risk**)
risk asset ratio 224
risk capital 28, 50
RNS (*see* **Regulatory News Service**)
rocket scientist 226
roll up. Instead of making regular interest payments on a loan, a borrower may sometimes be allowed to add the interest to the capital amount outstanding. This **rolled-up** interest is thus

effectively paid at the same time as the loan is repaid.
roll over 241
rolling contract (of employment) (*see also* **directors' pay and perks**) 185
rolling settlement 111
RPB (*see* **Recognized Professional Body**)
RUF (*see* **revolving underwriting facility**)
Rule 4.2 101
rulebook (of SROs) 339
run (on a bank) 222
running yield (*see* **income yield**)

SAEF (**SEAQ Automatic Execution Facility**) 105
sale and leaseback 80–81, 309, 310
sales (*see* **turnover**)
samurai (bond) 263
SAPCO (*see* **single asset property company**)
savers, savings 25, 32, 317–336
scaled down (of share applications) 140
scrip dividend 54, 158
scrip issue (**capitalization issue**) 91, 146, 154–158
scripophily. Collecting old share or bond certificates (**busted bonds**) which normally no longer have any value as securities but appeal for their historic associations or artistic merit.
SDR (*see* **Special Drawing Rights**)
SEAQ (**Stock Exchange Automated Quotation system**) 104–105, 211
SEAQ International 98
seasoned equity. Ordinary shares which have already

traded for a time on a market and established a price level.

SEATS (Stock Exchange Alternative Tracking Service) 105

SEC (*see* **Securities and Exchange Commission**)

second-tier market (USM) 100

secondary bank 222

secondary banking collapse 223

secondary issue. Rather like an **offer for sale**, but the shares being offered are already listed and the further shares offered to investors come from their existing owner. The government's sale of its shareholding in British Petroleum in 1987 was a secondary offer. 141

secondary market 23, 98, 214, 228, 266

secondary property 314

Section 212 The section of the 1985 Companies Act that gives a company powers to require shareholders hiding behind nominee names to declare their identity.

secured loan, bond 216, 269

securities 13, 28, 46, 85, 98, 213

Securities and Exchange Commission (SEC) 338

Securities and Futures Authority, The 339–340

Securities and Investments Board (SIB) 165, 328, 339 *et seq*

securities houses 8, 37, 104, 107–111, 152

securities markets 23

securitization. If an investor lends money to a borrower, he is simply making a loan. If, instead, he puts up the money in return for an IOU (I owe you) note which he can later sell to somebody else, the loan has been **securitized**: turned into a marketable security. (*See also* **asset-backed security**, **mortgage-backed security**.) 239, 240, 264, 269

security (for loan) 76, 180–181, 216, 269

seedcorn capital 177

self-regulation 165, 337 *et seq*

Self-Regulating Organizations (SROs) 339–340

sell at a discount 237

selling group 266

semi-annual (of interest) 266

sentiment 125–126, 248

senior debt 176, 177

Sequence programme 106

Serious Fraud Office. Official department dealing with larger or more politically sensitive fraud cases. 347

service (a debt). Meet the interest payments and capital repayment schedule of a loan. 87, 227

settlement. The process of clearing the paperwork that follows the purchase or sale of stocks and shares. The client has to pay or be paid, has to deliver or receive share certificates, and purchases and sales have to be reconciled between the different marketmakers and brokers. These are **back office** operations and high share dealing volumes can bring logjams. In an attempt to speed up the settlement process and make it cheaper, a paperless electronic share registration system is proposed under which share certificates do not have to change hands each time shares are bought and sold. The Bank of England is sponsoring the development of a system called CREST. The Stock Exchange had earlier attempted to develop a system called TAURUS, which was abandoned after vast sums had been spent. TALISMAN is the Stock Exchange's existing computerized settlement system for marketmakers. 112, 212

settlement day 111

SFO (*see* **Serious Fraud Office**)

shakeout 122

share (*see* **equity, ordinary shares, preference shares,** etc.)

share capital 89

share certificate 112

share exchange offer 163

share ownership, share-owning democracy 99–100

share premium account 93

share prices (in newspapers) 68–74

shareholders 28, 41

shareholders' funds 49, 50, 75, 89, 155–156

shareholders' interest (*see* **shareholders' funds**)

shareholders' rights 41–42, 162, 187–189,

shell company. A company, normally with a Stock Exchange quotation, which is now relatively inactive and has little by way of earnings or assets. Former plantation companies, whose estates in the Far East have now been nationalized, are a prime example. An entrepreneur with a vigorous private company will sometimes gain control of a shell company

and inject his private business into it, thus gaining a ready-made stockmarket vehicle. This process is described as a **shell operation**.

shop property 314

short (of stocks, etc.) 112, 121–122

short end of the market (gilt-edged) 207

short sale, bear sale 112, 121–122

short sellers, selling 121–122

short-term borrowings 49, 52

short-term sterling interest rates (futures contract) 291

short-termism 160

shortage (in banking system) 236

shorts, short-dated (of gilt-edged) 198, 207, 209

SIB (*see* **Securities and Investments Board**)

side-by-side finance (for property) 309–310

single asset property company (**SAPCO**) 312

single-capacity 103

single-company PEP 334

single property ownership trust (**SPOT**) 312

sinking fund. A form of reserve in a company's accounts, to which it allocates sums to cover the eventual repayment of a loan or the eventual expiry of a lease. (*See also* **wasting asset**.)

smaller companies fund 329

soft commissions. Commissions for financial services paid in kind rather than in cash. Before the Big Bang, brokers who derived large commissions from institutional clients under the fixed commission structure often gave part of the money back by providing customized research or paying for screen information systems for the use of the client. Though the competitive system following the Big Bang was meant to eliminate soft commissions, there are signs that they are creeping back.

soft commodities 293, 294

soft loan. A loan on terms more favourable than those applying to a normal commercial borrowing. Sometimes used to assist worthy projects – business start-ups in areas of high unemployment, etc.

solicitors (*see also* **commercial lawyers**) 35

solvency. Being in a state to meet your obligations and pay your bills. (*see also* **insolvency**)

solvency ratio (of banks) 223

sources of money, finance 45, 84–87

Special Drawing Rights (SDRs). A form of artificial money created by the International Monetary Fund. Countries may hold part of their official reserves in the form of SDRs which can therefore be used for payments between countries – in this sense they can be a substitute for gold. 250

special resolution (*see* **resolution**)

special situation. Usually used to describe a company whose shares could rise sharply if a particular set of circumstances comes to fruition. Sometimes used of potential takeover stocks but more commonly of **recovery situations** – companies which have been in trouble but whose shares could rise sharply in value if management succeeds in turning the company round. Some funds specialize in investing in special situations.

specialist mortgage lenders. A new breed of mortgage providers for house purchase, who recoup the money they advance by floating **mortgage-backed securities** (q.v.) in the securities markets. 269

speculators. The old distinction between long-term investors and speculators has largely broken down. Many investors are speculators up to a point. Speculation normally implies taking above-average risk and often suggests short-term investment decisions. Though frequently maligned, speculators provide a useful service in most markets by taking advantage of any short-term anomalies in prices and thus preventing prices from getting out of line with each other. They may be less beneficial when they completely supplant genuine investors in a market. (*See also* **arbitrage**.) 274, 289–290

split (share split). If a share price becomes too **heavy**, the shares may be split. Instead of having one 20p share standing in the market at 900p, the investor ends up with, say, two 10p shares worth 450p each. The effect may be similar to that of a scrip issue, but the technicalities differ. In the case of a share split, the par value is reduced, and no capitalization of reserves is involved.

split-level trust 333
sponsors (to an issue) 137–138
SPOT (*see* Single Property Ownership Trust)
spot price, spot market 257, 278, 294
spread (between bid and offer price) 23, 110, 113
spread (interest rate). Sometimes used to mean the margin a borrower pays above one of the benchmark interest rates. When LIBOR is 10 per cent, a borrower paying a spread of 30 basis points over LIBOR pays 10.3 per cent. 215, 217
SRO (*see* Self-Regulating Organization)
stabilize (price of new issue) 266
stag, stagging 135, 138, 144
stale bull 113
stand in the books at 78, 94
stand in the market at 22
Standard and Poor's (bond rating service) (*see* credit rating)
standby facility (*see* committed facility)
start-ups 177
state pension schemes 322
statement of total recognized gains and losses. A statement required under accounting standard FRS 3 which effectively shows the change in the book value of the company over the year before allowing for dividend payments. Thus, if the company had earned profits of £5m after tax and had incorporated a £2m property revaluation into its accounts, total recognized gains would have been £7m. 42
statutory regulation 337–338

sterling 249–250, 255–257
sterling certificates of deposit (*see* certificates of deposit)
sterling index 250
stock. Used in the sense of government stocks. A stock unit, however, is the same as a share for practical purposes.
stock exchange (*see* London Stock Exchange, New York Stock Exchange)
Stock Exchange Council 344
Stock Exchange floor 97
Stock Exchange money brokers 212
stockbroker 35, 103, 107 *et seq*, 225
stockmarket (*see* stock exchange)
stockmarket launch (*see* new issue)
stockmarket reports 115
stocks (in balance sheet) 48
stop-go pattern 116
stop-loss. An instruction (probably given to a broker) that a security should be sold if its price falls below a certain value.
straights (bonds) 267, 273
striking price (in tender) 139, 210–211
strips, stripping. Strips are the securities that result from stripping a bond into its separate components of rights to the interest payments and rights to repayment of the principal. If a 20-year government bond in the UK were stripped, this would result in 40 coupon strips (each carrying the right to receive one of the half-yearly interest payments) and one principal strip (carrying the right

to repayment of the capital after 20 years). These strips could be sold separately and – since they themselves do not pay interest – would be sold at a discount. In effect, strips are a form of **zero-coupon bond**. The Bank of England is planning an official market in stripped gilt-edged stocks. 212–213

stub equity. The very high-geared residual ordinary share capital in a company which has been financially restructured with massive debt via some form of leveraged operation: a leveraged takeover or a leveraged buy-out.

subordinated loans. Loans which rank for interest and repayment after all the other borrowings of the company. Are issued by UK banks and others, and for some purposes are treated more as share capital than as borrowings. 223

subscription price 92, 150
subsidiary companies, subsidiaries 45
sub-underwriters 140
sugar (commodity) 294
supervisory systems 231, 337–348
support (for currency) 245–246
support (for share price) 163, 168
surplus (pension fund) 322
surplus over book values 94
surrender values (insurance policies) 321
surveyors and estate agents (*see* **chartered surveyors**)
swap (interest rate or currency) (*see also* **equity-for-debt swap**) 78, 225, 243, 259, 271–272

switching 194
syndicate (at Lloyd's) 296–298
syndicated (venture capital finance) 176
syndicated loans 224–225, 230, 264, 311
syndicates (of banks) 224–225, 264
systemic risk 220

take-out (for financier) 176
takeover 126, 159–173
takeover activity 159
Takeover Code 164–170
Takeover Panel 164–170, 344
taking position in shares 102
TALISMAN (*see* **settlement**)
tangible assets 82–84
tap stock 210
TAURUS (*see* **settlement**)
tax (*see also* **Capital Gains Tax, Corporation Tax, Income Tax**) 2, 37, 52–55, 202 *et seq*, 317–318
tax advice 319
tax avoidance, **evasion**. Tax avoidance normally covers the lawful methods of minimizing tax liability. Tax evasion describes the unlawful methods.
tax credit 53, 54–55
Tax Exempt Special Savings Account (TESSA) 336
tax haven. A country or area with low rates of tax where companies may register or individuals may hold their investments to minimize tax liabilities. The Bahamas, Cayman Islands and, up to a point, the Channel Islands are examples.
tax payable 49
tax shelter. A framework in which assets can be held to minimize tax liabilities. **Personal**

equity plans or **PEPs** provide a tax shelter for the investments held within them. 178–180
technical factors, analysis 120, 122–123, 196
technical correction 122
tender (Treasury bills) 238
tender offer 137, 139, 140, 210
tender panel 241
term insurance 320
term loan 46, 49
TESSA (*see* **Tax Exempt Special Savings Account**)
Third Market 102, 135
Third World debt 227
tick (in financial futures) 292
time value (of money) 18
time value (of option) 288
times earnings (*see also* **price-earnings ratio**) 67
tin 293
tip (a share) 40, 120, 351
tip sheets 353
tombstone advertisements 272–273
top slice (property income) 309
TOPIC (screen information system) 105–106
total assets less current liabilities 49
total return (*see* **overall return**)
touch (of share price spread) 114
trade bill 237
trade buyer 176
trade credit 48
trade creditors 48
trade investment 84
trade-weighted index (of a currency) 249–250
traded options (*see also* **LIFFE**) 33, 92, 98, 287–293
traders 274
trading floor 97
tranchettes (of gilt-edged stock) 210

transaction-based banking 12
treasury, treasurer. The treasury is the department in a company that manages the raising and investing of cash, foreign exchange transactions, hedging operations, etc. The treasurer is the person in charge. In a larger company the treasurer is probably subordinate to the finance director, who is more concerned with financing policy than day-to-day operations.
Treasury bills 235, 238, 243
Treasury stocks 199
trigger points (for disclosure, etc.) (*see also* **disclosure**) 165–166
triple-A-rated (credit rating of a borrower) (*see also* **credit rating**) 272
troughs 116
true and fair view 42, 343
turn (marketmaker's, jobber's) 102, 113
turnover (of gilt-edged stocks) 194
turnover (of shares, etc.) 98–99, 107, 110, 159
turnover (sales) 51

UITF (*see* **Urgent Issues Task Force**)
unauthorized property unit trust 328
unauthorized unit trust 328
unbundling. Euphemism for breaking up a company into its constituent businesses, which are probably sold individually. Sometimes not vastly different from **asset stripping**.
unconditional (of takeover offer) 167–168, 170

undated stocks (*see* **irredeemable**)
undercapitalized 103
undersubscribed (*see also* **Blue Arrow affair**) 140
undervalued 119
underwriters (of shares) 125
underwriting (insurance) 296, 298
underwriting (of share issue) 108, 140–141, 149, 150, 164
underwriting agent (Lloyd's) 298, 299
underwriting commitment 223
underwriting cycle (*see* **insurance cycle**)
underwriting fees 140, 150
underwriting profit 296
underwritten 149
underwritten cash value 164
unit-linked assurance 325–326, 329–330
unit-linked investment vehicles 325–331
unit trusts 32, 34, 325 *et seq*, 343
United States (takeover tactics) 170–171
unitization 311–312, 334
unitize (an investment trust) 334
unitized property 311–313
Unlisted Securities Market (**USM**) 100–101, 135

unrelieved ACT. The **advance corporation tax** (**ACT**) that companies pay to the Inland Revenue in respect of dividends is really a form of basic-rate income tax they deduct on behalf of the shareholder. It is called **advance corporation tax** because companies can offset the amount deducted against the corporation tax they are due to pay on their UK income. Companies with a high proportion of earnings from abroad may not pay enough UK corporation tax to be able to offset the whole of the ACT against it. The amount that cannot be offset is known as **unrelieved ACT**. Companies in this position are effectively being taxed twice on part of their income. (*See also* **foreign income dividend**).

unsecured loan stock 85, 216

upside potential. Scope for rising in value. 'The shares have upside potential' means they stand a good chance of rising. Opposite of **downside potential** (q.v.).

upward re-rating 119
upwards only (rent review clause in property lease) 315
Urgent Issues Task Force 188–189, 342

US GAAP. Generally accepted accounting principles in the United States. Some multi-national UK companies will produce abbreviated accounts prepared according to US principles in addition to their UK accounts. The main differences between the two probably arise in the treatment of goodwill. 95

USM (*see* **Unlisted Securities Market**)

valuations (of property) 38, 307–309
value of the pound 24, 25, 249, 254–257
variable rate (*see also* **floating rate**) 27, 61
variable rate notes (**VRNs**).

This term has come to describe a particular form of floating rate note where the interest rate will float in line with movements in LIBOR in the normal way, but also the margin over LIBOR paid on the notes will be reset at intervals.

vendor placing 146, 151–152, 154
venture capital 174–181
venture capital funds 175–177
venture capital trust 180
volatility (*see* **beta**)
volumes (share dealing) (*see* **turnover of shares**)
votes, voting structure 41, 161–162
voucher (tax) 53

Wall Street 125–126, 127 *et seq*
wallpaper 163
War Loan 197
warehousing (of shares) 167
warrant 92, 98, 149, 267
wasting asset. Asset with a finite life whose value erodes with the passage of time. An option is a wasting asset in the sense that it becomes valueless on its expiry date if it is not exercised. Commonly used of short leases in the property world. The buyer of a five-year lease on a building needs to **amortize** (depreciate) the cost of his investment by setting aside each year enough money to have written off the cost of the lease by the end of the fifth year.
wealth of individuals 318–319
weight of money 124
white knight 162
whizz kid. Most frequently used of financially hyper-active entrepreneur who attempts to build a financial empire by frequent takeovers on the Stock Exchange. May also be used of particularly bright sparks in their chosen line of investment or business management.
whole life assurance 320
wholesale funds, deposits 32, 220, 224, 233
wider share ownership (*see* **share ownership**)
winding up. The process of closing down a business and realizing its assets, after which the value of any assets will be distributed to those entitled. (*See also* **liquidation**.) 37, 89
window-dressing 44, 56
withholding tax. Tax deducted at source on interest, dividends, etc, making it harder to cheat the tax man. Investors generally hate it. 265
with-profits policy (life assurance) 321
working capital 77
working underwriter (Lloyd's) 298
write (an option) (*see also* **naked writer**) 287
write down, write off. Companies may need to write down the value of certain assets if these are no longer worth the figures at which they are shown in the books. A rag trade company might need to write down its stocks of mini-skirts if hemlines moved down and made them difficult to sell. Any company might need to write down its debtors if it is owed money by a customer who has gone bust and is unlikely to pay. Write-offs are more severe than

write-downs – the whole of the value of the asset is deducted. **Written-down value** is the value in the accounts after write-downs. 93

written-down (*see* **write down**)

xa (*see* **ex-all**)
xc 156
xd 70, 71, 204
xr 147–150

yankee bond 263
years' purchase (of property) 307
yield (*see also* **redemption yield**). To calculate the income yield on an investment you multiply the annual gross dividend or interest payment by 100 and divide by the market price. If the gross dividend on a share is 10p and the market price is 200p, the yield is 10 x 100/200, or 5 per cent. 14, 19–20, 24, 28, 66, 117 *et seq*, 138, 307–309, 315

yield curve (*see also* **negative yield curve**) 243

zero-coupon bonds (*see also* **strips**) 217, 267
zinc 293